Economic and Social History of Ancient Greece:
An Introduction

Economic and
Social History
of Ancient Greece:
AN INTRODUCTION

M.M. AUSTIN
and
P. VIDAL-NAQUET

Translated and revised by
M.M. AUSTIN

UNIVERSITY OF CALIFORNIA PRESS
Berkeley   Los Angeles

First English language edition 1977
Originally published in France as
Économies et sociétés en Grèce ancienne
by Librarie Armand Colin, Paris

First edition 1972
Second edition 1973

University of California Press
Berkeley and Los Angeles, California

First Paperback Printing 1980
ISBN 0-520-04267-0
LC 73-90665

Printed in the United States of America

1 2 3 4 5 6 7 8 9

Contents

List of Maps

Preface

This book is an English version of the book originally published in French under the title of *Économies et sociétés en Grèce ancienne* (Paris, Armand Colin, Collection U 2, 1972; 2nd edition, 1973). The opportunity has been taken to correct some errors, update bibliographical references, add a few passages to the selection of ancient sources in Part 2 (nos 41, 46, 99, 102, 131), and improve the material presentation in several respects. But otherwise this remains substantially the same book as the original French version.

The book is aimed in the first place at an undergraduate audience, though it is hoped that it will also be of interest to a wider, non-specialist readership interested in the history and civilization of Ancient Greece. It attempts to meet a need well-known to all those who have to teach Greek history in universities. Students, long dissatisfied with a purely political approach to Greek history, ask for more 'economic and social' history. One then has to answer – and this book is a very modest attempt at an answer – that neither the 'economic' nor the 'social' category had in the Greek city the same independent status they now enjoy. The book takes its starting-point in this ambiguity; it accepts the challenge, but rejects the formulation of the question. Anyone who has been asked to explain once and for all the role played by slaves in social conflicts in the Greek world will understand what we mean.

The book is divided in two parts, the first comprising a general introduction to the subject in several chapters, the second a selection of ancient sources[1]; all sources are reproduced in

---

1. The plan of the book was agreed in common, Michel Austin being more particularly responsible for the first part and Pierre Vidal-Naquet for the second; the authors take joint responsibility for the book as a whole. The translation of the ancient sources are original except for those passages listed in the Acknowledgments and the translations of Thucydides, which are by R. Crawley.

translation therefore they are fully accessible to the Greekless reader. The period covered is vast and the introductory chapters cannot aim at more than a very brief sketch, outlining the main problems. The sequence followed is partly chronological and partly thematic, but in both cases liberties have been taken, as for example in the chapter dealing with fifth-century Athens the subject of the metics has been followed down to the fourth century in order to bring out both resemblances and differences. The ancient sources in Part 2 have a double function: they serve partly to provide a direct illustration and justification for what is said in the corresponding chapter in Part 1 (though certain passages may correspond to more than one chapter, and detailed cross-references have been provided throughout), but partly also to provide a counterpoint, to introduce a qualification or a different point of view. Starting from the premiss that a source only 'speaks' if it is made to speak (though without necessarily having recourse to torture), each translated passage has been provided with an introduction, sometimes very brief when the introductory chapters or the related passages provide enough material to make them intelligible, sometimes much more detailed. The notes aim at recalling briefly some facts or definitions, or at providing supplements to the introduction to each passage and facilitating the commentary.

These passages represent, of course, only a selection, which may always be described as arbitrary. The reader, if he is a beginner, will anyhow understand quickly that written sources are only one element, and not always the most important, in the economic and social history of Greece. Nor are they always easily translatable. It is difficult to see, for example, how one could translate without a vast scholarly apparatus the 'tribute lists' recording the quota from the tribute paid to Athens by the cities under her domination[2]. The reader does not therefore have before him, even in summary form, a documentary *corpus* corresponding to all the relevant problems. On the other hand, a number of passages have been included in the selection which, according to the usual classification, do not provide evidence about *facts*, but about the way the Greeks apprehended them. To know how the Greeks thought about economic and social matters is surely as

---

2. B.D. Meritt, H.T. Wade-Gery, M.F. McGregor, *The Athenian Tribute Lists* I–IV (Cambridge–Princeton, 1939–53).

important as to know the levels of prices and wages in classical Athens.

Many friends and colleagues helped directly or indirectly in the writing of the original book and in the preparation of the English edition: J. Bollack, B. Bravo, S. Clavel, R.M. Cook, M.H. Crawford, J. Detienne, Y. Garlan, Ph. Gauthier, G. Hirzel, S.C. Humphreys, G.E. Rickman, J. Rougé, P. Schmitt, Alain and Annie Schnapp, P. Veyne. It is a pleasure to thank them here; but they are not responsible for any errors in this book. Our thanks also go to M.I. Finley, who more than any other present-day historian has renewed our understanding of the economic and social history of the Greek world, as will be apparent in many places in this book, and finally to P. Lévêque, who very kindly asked us to write this short chapter in *The Greek Adventure.*

No attempt has been made to systematize the transcription of Greek words and proper names; for a justification of this cavalier procedure the reader is referred to the Preface to T.E. Lawrence's *Seven Pillars of Wisdom.*

Acknowledgments

Acknowledgments are due to Oxford University Press for permission to reproduce E. Barker's translation of Aristotle's *Politics* (1946) in nos 2, 5, 14, 19, 34, 51A, 64, 114, 128, 129 and 132, W.D. Ross's translation of Aristotle's *Nicomachaean Ethics* (1925) in no 44, and F.M. Cornford's translation of Plato's *Republic* (1941) in nos 6A, 105, 112 and 131; to Loeb Classical Library (Harvard University Press: William Heinemann) for permission to reproduce H.G Evelyn-White's translation of Hesiod's *Works and Days* (new ed., 1936) in nos 10, 31 and 32, and on p. 59; to Verlag Walter de Gruyter for permission to reproduce R.F. Willett's translation of *The Law Code of Gortyn* (1967) in no 62; and finally to the Archaeological Institute of America for permission to reproduce the tables on pp. 277 and 279.

Abbreviations

AJA   *American Journal of Archaeology*
BSA   *Annual of the British School at Athens*
BCH   *Bulletin de Correspondance Hellénique*
Bull.   J. et L. Robert, 'Bulletin épigraphique' in *REG*; numbers refer to entries
CP   *Classical Philology*
CQ   *Classical Quarterly*
Dittenberger, *Sylloge³*   W. Dittenberger, *Sylloge Inscriptionum Graecarum*, 3rd ed., 1915-24
FGrHist   F. Jacoby, *Die Fragmente der Griechischen Historiker*
JHS   *Journal of Hellenic Studies*
Meiggs–Lewis   R. Meiggs and D.M. Lewis, *A Selection of Greek Historical Inscriptions* (Oxford, 1969)
NC   *Numismatic Chronicle*
REA   *Revue des Études Anciennes*
REG   *Revue des Études Grecques*
Studies in Ancient Society   M.I. Finley, ed., *Studies in Ancient Society* (1974)
TAPA   *Transactions and Proceedings of the American Philological Association*
Tod, GHI   M.N. Tod, *A Selection of Greek Historical Inscriptions* I (2nd ed., 1947), II (1948)
ZPE   *Zeitschrift für Papyrologie und Epigraphik*

Part 1
Introduction

I Concepts and General Problems

The controversy over the ancient Greek economy[1]
Political history is a time-honoured invention; it originated, of
course, with the Greeks. Economic history, on the other hand, is
a discovery of the nineteenth century. Now it would be wrong to
say that before this time economic questions in the history of
antiquity had failed to attract attention, since already in the
eighteenth century one finds studies of detail on such matters. In
1817 August Boeckh published his great work on the political
economy of the Athenians, *Die Staatshaushaltung der Athener*.
Yet all these works exercised no immediate influence on historians
of antiquity. Economic history remained for some time a separate
sphere, not yet integrated into general history. Thus one of the
greatest historians of Greece, George Grote, could write a
History of Greece (which appeared in London from 1846 to 1856)
in which economic questions, although they were not entirely
missing, occupied only a very limited space and were not subjected to any systematic enquiry. And yet Grote, an influential
businessman in the City, was in a good position to appreciate
their importance, even though he may only have apprehended
them through the distorting lens of English liberalism. But in the
long run the problem of how the new economic dimension was to
be integrated into the history of Greece[2] could not fail to arise.

The first general attempt came towards the end of the nineteenth century and is associated with the names of the great
German philologist-historians Eduard Meyer, K.J. Beloch and
Georg Busolt (especially Eduard Meyer)[3]. Some German
economists of the nineteenth century had constructed theories
which were designed to summarize in broad outline the economic
evolution of man through the ages, and for this purpose they

made use of the concept of stages of development through which the history of mankind was supposed to have progressed. Thus one of them, Karl Bücher, in his book *Die Entstehung der Volkswirtschaft* (The Origins of National Economy), which appeared first in 1893 and was subsequently reissued several times, identified three stages in economic evolution, 'closed household economy' (*geschlossene Hauswirtschaft*, a concept which he borrowed from a predecessor, Karl Rodbertus), 'city economy' (*Stadtwirtschaft*) and 'national economy' (*Volkswirtschaft*). In his mind these three stages corresponded roughly to the three great divisions of history: 'closed household economy' corresponded to antiquity, 'city economy' corresponded to the Middle Ages and 'national economy' corresponded to the modern world. Bücher's scheme, a mere abstraction characteristic of the great syntheses of the nineteenth century, could not stand up to scrutiny, least of all as far as antiquity was concerned. Ed. Meyer, and following him the other German historians, set out to destroy it and substitute a more 'realistic' view of the ancient Greek economy. Their avowed intention was to write a history of Greece which would be more 'modern' than those written till then, and from this point of view the economy was destined to find at last its due place in a history of ancient Greece. To be sure, the aim was an entirely reasonable one, but it led them straight to a different error. Just as their conception of the political history of Greece was distorted by the contemporary German pre-occupation with the problem of national unity, so too the picture they drew of Greek economic history was a more or less faithful replica of the economic development of modern Europe. The concepts and terminology of contemporary economic history were applied by them more or less literally to the Greek world. According to them, as early as the eighth century, the Greek world witnessed a considerable development of industry and commerce, production and exchanges of a capitalist kind expanded, and a monetary economy came into existence. Already then the old economic regime based on the land was doomed, the old landed aristocracies were replaced by moneyed aristocracies, and the landowners gave way to 'industrialists' and traders. The political history of Greece was then reinterpreted in the light of the alleged economic revolution and its presumed social consequences. Greek states were credited in their political behaviour with commercial considerations of a very modern kind. These historians had no scruples in drawing parallels, whether real or imaginary, with the history of modern Europe. 'In the history of Greece', wrote Ed. Meyer, 'the seventh and sixth centuries correspond to the fourteenth and fifteenth in the modern world, the fifth corresponds to the sixteenth[4].' One could not be more explicit. K. Bücher responded as best he could to the attack of the Greek historians; he had no trouble in pointing out numerous gaps and weaknesses in the theories of his opponents, who relied on a highly subjective use of ancient sources. But this did not corroborate his own interpretation of the ancient economy.

Clearly the discussion had been wrongly approached and so made a bad start. One may even say that it has never quite overcome this false start, all the more so as the prestige and authority of the German historians has often succeeded in imposing a view of the Greek economy which is surely untenable. And yet responsibilities were shared. The fundamental mistake made by both Bücher and Meyer as well as all their respective disciples consisted in the very terms in which the discussion was approached. The problem was forced (and has long continued to be forced) into the straitjacket of a simple alternative: was the Greek economy modern or primitive? Quite apart from value judgments implicit in such a formulation, which consciously or not, could affect one's point of view, both sides in the controversy started from the premiss that economic evolution was a unilinear process which in theory followed a regular curve (although in practice it need not be strictly continuous). In studying the Greek economy the task was therefore to determine what point on the curve it had reached and, according to the answer one gave, one described the Greek economy as having been modern, primitive, or as having reached only an intermediate stage. The fundamental question of deciding whether or not it was possible to study the Greek 'economy' in isolation and with the use of concepts created for the modern world was not even raised. Whereas the discussion ought to have centred first on concepts, the procedure was as if it was all only a question of facts: study economic facts and everything was solved. As the facts clearly invalidated the theory of Bücher, the 'modernists' were able to believe that the controversy was settled in their favour.

A fresh start was needed to emerge from the impasse, and to the great German sociologist Max Weber belongs the credit for the initiative which led to a better understanding of the position held by the 'economy' in Greek history[5]. From the outset Weber rejected the false alternative 'modernism or primitivism' to which historians had attempted to confine the discussion (and yet the alternative continued to be invoked subsequently)[6]. He approached the subject from the angle of institutions and laid stress on the particular characteristics of Greek history; his aim was to define the ancient Greek city as opposed to the medieval city. The Greek city was an aristocracy of warriors – or even of sailors – and a city of consumers, whereas the medieval city was a city of producers. A craftsman in fourteenth-century Florence, a city which exercised its sovereignty over the countryside (*contado*), was a citizen in so far as he belonged to one of the *arts*, and he exercised his share of sovereignty through the *art* of which he was a member. There was nothing comparable in Athens; ironmongers, potters and shopkeepers, even if they were citizens (which was not always the case), did not owe their citizenship to their craft but to the fact that they were born from a citizen and the daughter of a citizen, and were duly registered and recognized in their phratries and demes. Weber emphasized particularly the role of war in Greek history: Greek democracy, a political club of the citizens, would redistribute to its members the fruits of war – tribute, land and so forth. These ideas of Weber were taken up and further developed by Johannes Hasebroek in two works, *Staat und Handel im alten Griechenland*[7], and *Griechische Wirtschafts- und Gesellschaftsgeschichte bis zu den Perser-kriegen*[8], the former being the more important work from the theoretical point of view. Following the example of Weber, Hasebroek shifted the discussion away from the forms and range of economic activity to the links between the economy and the political life of the Greek city. According to him there could be no question of economic policy in the modern sense in the Greek cities (mercantile policy, competition for outlets, etc.), because there was no *national* commerce or industry in them as a result of the considerable role played by outsiders, whether free or unfree, in economic activity, and by definition these had no access to political power in the cities. The citizens reserved for themselves a monopoly of land ownership, and the other economic activities (commerce, manufacture, etc.) were to a great extent left to outsiders. In so far as Greek states showed any interest in economic problems, they sought only to secure imports of materials and commodities essential for the life of the city: citizens mattered only as consumers, not as producers[9]. Otherwise the state was concerned with its revenues, and these were catered for by means of taxes on economic activity or quite simply through war and foreign domination in its various forms.

One can see where the genuinely new and positive contribution of Weber and Hasebroek lies. What they did was to lift the discussion from the level of facts and economic forms in the abstract to that of the relationship between the economy and the institutions of the Greek city: there could be no valid study of the Greek economy outside the framework of the city.

One might imagine that the work of Weber and Hasebroek freed the discussion once and for all from the impasse which had been reached. Unfortunately this has not quite been the case. Hasebroek's works created a stir and gave fresh impetus to the controversy between 'modernists' and 'primitivists' (a controversy which now was, or ought to have been, superseded). Hasebroek was open to criticism through excessive schematism, some questionable assertions and gaps in his knowledge. But this did not mean that one could brush aside the essential terms of his and Weber's analysis, and yet this is what has often happened. Though there has been progress since Hasebroek in our detailed knowledge of the Greek economy, the fundamental problems have been frequently neglected, and no comprehensive theory has been put forward to replace Hasebroek's in a study of the ancient Greek economy. At times scholars even proceed as though the controversy had not even taken place and the position of Ed. Meyer and his disciples were still tenable[10].

One must however mention here the work of the Hungarian–American historian and anthropologist Karl Polanyi as occupying a special position, for although Polanyi was no specialist in the ancient Greek economy and did not attempt to put forward a theory designed to apply specifically to Greek history, his ideas mark an important step forward in the approach to the study of the economy in societies other than those of the modern world, and they can provide us with a useful starting point for a number of general considerations[11].

In his study of the position occupied by the economy in human societies Polanyi drew a very clear distinction between modern and other societies. In modern societies, the economy has 'freed' itself and become 'disembedded'. It has become a sphere of its own and can therefore be studied in isolation, with the help of concepts which have been created for it alone: the economy is a sphere which obeys its own laws. In other societies, by contrast, and in particular in 'primitive' and archaic societies, the economy is always more or less 'embedded' in society and all its institutions; it is not a separate sphere, experienced and organized as such by that particular society. It cannot therefore be studied in isolation; it has no fully independent existence and its functioning will constantly be under the influence of social factors of a non-economic kind which are alien to it. It follows that to study the place occupied by the economy in a society of this kind one cannot apply the concepts and terminology of modern economies, for these apply only to the world for which they have been created.

To replace modern economic concepts in the study of other societies Polanyi put forward four schemes by reference to which one might understand the circulation and distribution of goods in such societies: reciprocity, redistribution, exchanges by means of trade, and household economy. One need not attach absolute significance to these four schemes or try to apply them systematically to Greek history, though they may be able to shed light on particular aspects of it[12].

On the other hand, the distinction drawn by Polanyi between economies which are autonomous in relation to society and economies which are more or less embedded in society is a fundamental one. It brings out explicitly the underlying trend of the Weber–Hasebroek analysis, namely the impossibility of studying the Greek economy in isolation and without reference to the social and institutional framework of Greek history. One may therefore apply Polanyi's distinction to the Greek world to see how the Greek economy was embedded in society, and what consequences follow for the study of the subject.

The economy in Greece is embedded in society

One fact which must be noted at the outset is that the very concept of 'the economy' in the modern sense is untranslatable in Greek, because it simply did not exist. The Greek word *oikonomia* does not mean the same as our word 'economy', although the latter is of course derived from it. It means 'management of the household' (the *oikos*) in its broadest sense (domestic economy, one might say), and not only in its strictly economic sense. It can also mean 'management, administration, organisation' in a more general sense and be applied to different spheres; thus one may talk of the '*oikonomia* of the affairs of the city', and that is the origin of our expression 'political economy'. There are two extant treatises of the fourth century both entitled *Oikonomia*, one by Xenophon and the other in three separate books, perhaps the work of three different writers of the Aristotelian school. In the work by Xenophon the subject under discussion is the management of the family estate and the role of the head of the *oikos*. The strictly economic part is concerned with the running of the rural estate: agriculture is praised and sharply contrasted with other forms of economic activity – such as manufacture – which are said to be unworthy of a gentleman. One will find in Xenophon's work a discussion of agriculture and technical advice is provided, but one will also find a discussion of how the head of the *oikos* ought to treat his wife and slaves. In other words, Xenophon's work does not include a study of the different forms of economic activity in general, but only of agriculture, and under the heading of *Oikonomia* many non-economic functions are included, because they derive from the role of the head of the *oikos*: economic and non-economic functions are fused together in the same person without it being possible to distinguish between them [*see no* 4]. The same is true of Book I of the Aristotelian *Economics*, which in fact often echoes the work of Xenophon. Book III takes up in greater detail one of the themes sketched in Book I, that of the relations between husband and wife [*see no 1*]. Book II is a collection of fiscal expedients – one might even say stratagems – whereby rulers, generals and cities tried to extricate themselves from economic crises or sought to increase their revenues. The collection is preceded by a brief introduction in which the author distinguishes four types of 'economy' – royal economy, satrapal economy, political economy and private economy. He is not dealing with economy in the modern sense, but simply with budgeting. The author's approach is in any case extremely pedestrian: the principle common to all these forms of 'economy' is that 'expenditure must not exceed income'. In this spirit the author then goes on to collect those fiscal stratagems that seem most interesting to him and likely to be of future use [*see no 91*].

Since the economy in the modern sense never was for the Greeks an autonomous category, one should not expect to find any genuine economic thought or analysis in Greek writers (although there has sometimes been a temptation to do so)[13]. What has often been labelled economic analysis usually turns out to be common-sense observations on economic activity or even has nothing to do with economic analysis proper. This does not mean that the Greeks failed to grasp the importance of economic factors in history (this would be manifestly untrue), it means only that these factors were not experienced in their own right as strictly economic ones. They existed only in relation to other factors which seemed to the Greeks to have greater importance. For Greek historians there was no such thing as economic history, but only political history. Thus Thucydides in the opening chapters of his *History* outlined the stages in the evolution of the Greek world from its primitive origins up to his own time, and in this scheme economic factors play a large part:

> Without commerce, without freedom of communication either by land or sea, cultivating no more of their territory than the exigencies of life required, destitute of capital, never planting their land (for they could not tell when an invader might not come and take it all away, and when he did come they had no walls to stop him), thinking that the necessities of daily sustenance could be supplied at one place as well as another, they cared little for shifting their habitation, and consequently neither built large cities nor attained to any other form of greatness[14].

Yet subsequently Thucydides gives very little space to economic factors in the history of his own time. For him true history and its analysis exist only at a higher level, that of politics. As soon as one has got beyond the primitive stage of economic development, economic preoccupations cease to be decisive and can be relegated to the background. In other words, economic history comes into play only when political history is not yet possible. Thucydides' point of view is indicative of the place that the Greeks attributed to the economy in the scale of values. One may say that any economic analysis of Greek history will inevitably lead up to political analysis and merge with it.

For all his differences from Thucydides, Plato's reasoning is similar. It is necessity that brings about the development of the elementary city[15], but as the edifice is built up it appears that the fate of the economy is to be brought under control. The producers are radically separated from the warriors and the philosophers. Conversely, when Plato describes the decline of the city in Books VIII and IX of the *Republic*, one sees gold playing an ever more important and pernicious part [*see no 105*].

What one may henceforward refer to conventionally as the 'economy' was not for the Greeks a separate sphere. To use once more the terminology of Polanyi, the economy was embedded in society in its widest sense. 'Economic' matters were constantly under the influence of factors and considerations which nowadays we might describe as 'non-economic'. Consequently economic analysis will lead up not only to political analysis, but also to ethical analysis and the study of values in general.

'Non-economic' factors and economic activity

In mentioning in this way the 'values' which conditioned the Greeks' approach to questions which nowadays we describe as 'economic' it is not intended to pass judgment on their importance *a priori*. They are a result as much as a cause, but the study of these values and intellectual habits provides a convenient starting point.

Among the mental habits which influenced the economic behaviour of the Greeks there comes first the fundamental distinction one comes across frequently in the classical period between different occupations [*see nos 3, 4, 5, 12*]. Some were considered to be alone worthy of a gentleman, others inferior and hence fit only for the lower social classes, outsiders or slaves. In this hierarchy of occupations agriculture almost always held a place of its own at the top of the scale and was sharply distinguished from other economic activities. For most the ideal was represented by the landowner, free, independent and capable of providing for himself. The earliest literary sources, Homer and Hesiod, are already familiar with the conception of agriculture as one of the foundations of civilized life [*see no 30*], closely connected with sacrifice, cooking and family life[16].

At the bottom of the scale one finds the other forms of economic activity, trade and all the so-called 'banausic' occupations which implied manual work. These occupations were pronounced unworthy of a gentleman. In practice a man's social status might have exercised a decisive influence on his occupation; conversely one will often find that manufacture, trade, etc., were (at least to some extent) left in the hands of the lower classes or outsiders.

The artisan might, however, be called the hero of Greek history, but he is a secret hero. There is not a single one of the material creations of Greek civilization which does not bear his mark: the architect of the Parthenon was an artisan (and not an engineer) just as much as the sculptor of the Chryselephantine statue of Athena. The writings of Plato, who excluded artisans from the governing functions of the city, teem with metaphors from the crafts and tributes to the work of artisans. What is more, it has been shown that in Plato's cosmology the *demiourgos* who builds the world makes use of all the techniques of artisans known in Plato's time, with at the top the techniques of metallurgy[17]. Plato, like Xenophon, placed agriculture well above the crafts, and yet it is the inferior parts of 'creation' which are due to agricultural techniques, and the word which denotes the material world (*chora*) is the word used to denote the countryside and cultivated land. This said, it remains true of the whole of classical antiquity that while the work of the artisan was admired, he was neglected or down-graded as a person [*see no 11*]. And what is most important, there never was, except in the constructions of some theorists like the town-planner and philosopher Hippodamus of Miletus, any such thing as a category of artisans.

The word *demiourgos* itself had two different meanings in different parts of the Greek world: in Athens, for example, it was used for the artisans and these were generally men of humble status. In other states, on the other hand, in the Peloponnese and in central and north-western Greece [*see no 54*], it was applied to the chief magistrates, who were men of high social status [*see also no 28*][18]. In the classical city technical functions and political functions did not depend on each other; rather, they were two different spheres which did not overlap. In Athens citizens, metics and slaves were to be found doing the same kind of work: but only the citizen had access to political power. In the organization of the city's space there were, to be sure, quarters which corresponded to economic functions (quarters for the various crafts, a commercial harbour, etc.); but there were no quarters reserved for metics or slaves.

The ambiguous role of technical and economic activity in Greek thought can be illustrated by a number of facts from religion. Prometheus the hero was an ambivalent figure: through his inventions he was man's benefactor, but at the same time he was the opponent of Zeus. It has been said of Hermes that he was the representative of a social class, that of the traders, but in fact Hermes' function of protecting trade derived in the first instance from his role as mediator. Hephaistos, the god of technical functions, whose skill was highly praised, notably in Homer, was unlike the other gods a lame and misshaped being. Athena, by contrast, who among other functions was the goddess of feminine skills, escaped from this slur. One might imagine that the same value system did not apply to women as to men, but in any case Athena's role was a wider one: she represented a particular form of intelligence, prudent and practical intelligence (*metis*), which is displayed in particular in her connections with seafaring (construction and piloting of the ship), and there is no sign here of any negative judgment on these sides of her activity[19].

Besides the hierarchy of occupations, and indeed hardly to be distinguished from it, there existed a hierarchy of modes of acquisition: some were considered legitimate, others were susceptible of incurring moral reprobation, depending on the spirit in which they were resorted to. Here again ethical considerations intervened to counteract the development of strictly economic values. Trade in itself was not necessarily considered good or bad. It was admissible in so far as it aimed at ensuring self-sufficiency by providing those necessities for life which were missing, but no more. But if trade became an end in itself and sought nothing but the highest profit, it was then decried. One finds this point of view already in Homer; centuries later, at the end of the classical period, Aristotle expounds it clearly [*see nos 2, 26, 128, 129*]. Retail trade was worst of all, since it implied crookedness and deceit: by definition the retail trader sought to sell his merchandise at a price higher than its real value.

By contrast war and politics were perfectably respectable – or at least legitimate – modes of acquisition [*see nos 7, 8, 9*], and this holds good for every period of Greek history (with certain qualifications, of course)[20]. The victor in war enjoyed free disposal of the persons and chattels of the vanquished, and this fundamental right was never contested. In fact, war in antiquity remained one of the chief sources of supply for the slave trade. To be sure, war as a mode of acquisition worked only within limits. It is only rarely that wars between Greeks were aimed at the acquisition of territory (wars against non-Greeks were a different case, as will be seen in the 'colonial' Greek world); there were some exceptions, as for example Sparta in the early archaic age, or some Sicilian tyrants in the fifth and sixth centuries. Athens in the fifth century did not annex her conquests[21]; what is more, Athenian settlements abroad were normally garrisons, and imperial colonies like Amphipolis were generally established at the expense of non-Greeks. Even granted these limitations, it would be wrong to imagine that every war was undertaken in an acquisitive spirit. It would be even more dangerous to state that wars in Greece had 'economic causes'. The causes of wars were often to be found at a political level. But once war had been declared, no one ever challenged the legitimacy of acquisition through conquest. One may say that in ancient Greece one often reaches economics via war, but could hardly say that one reaches war via economics. For example, the conflicts between Greeks and Persians probably did not have 'economic causes'. On the Persian side there was the will for power and domination, on the Greek side the will to preserve political liberty. But subsequently these conflicts could easily assume economic aspects as well. The Athenian general Cimon, for instance, enriched himself and his fellow citizens on plunder from the territory of Persia. No one at the time would have thought of criticizing him for this, whereas had he turned to trade in order to build up his fortune, it would have been a different story[22].

Another series of important facts in the study of the economy in Greece concerns work[23]. The first point is that the unified concept of work as one of the great functions of man which falls into a multiplicity of different forms was unknown to the Greeks. Where we identify amidst many forms of human activity one single great function productive of social values, namely work, the Greeks only saw a multiplicity of different occupations (the status of which might vary considerably, as has been seen), and did not establish a single connecting link between all of them. They even at times opposed one type of occupation (agriculture) to others (manufacture, trade, etc.) [*see nos 4, 5*].

Another point is that work as such never acquired for the Greeks any positive value of its own. One may search in vain through Greek literature for traces of a genuine ideology of work. Of course, work was for most people an unavoidable necessity, but for all that it did not acquire any intrinsic value. Hesiod in the *Works and Days* never tires of preaching to his brother Perses the need for work in order to avoid penury [*see no 10*], but he does not rise from this to a positive evaluation of it[24]. In any case Hesiod takes for granted the existence of servile labour as a supplement to the work of free men.

Another distinction must be mentioned, and once more it is of a moral kind. Work in itself need not be considered either good or evil. What mattered as much or more were the conditions under which work was carried out. In the modern world a man's labour has become distinct from his person: it is a saleable commodity which he can sell to others without this implying, in theory, any subjection on his part. In the Greek world, by contrast, this distinction was unknown: to work for someone else meant to subject oneself to one's employer. And 'the condition of the free man is that he does not live for the benefit of another'[25]. The free man, if he had to work, wanted therefore to work for himself, not for someone else. One will see later the results of this way of thinking on the organization of manufactures in Athens (Chapter 5).

In sum, what we call the productive spirit was unknown to the Greeks, whereas it is characteristic of the modern world, though within limits[26]. One may note in this connection some limitations in the Greek conception of the division of labour. In many Greek writers there are ideas which may superficially recall the modern theory of the division of labour. But looking at these more closely one realizes that they have nothing to do with division of labour in the modern sense, i.e. they are concerned not with an increase in production, but with an improvement in the quality of the goods produced through greater specialization [*see no 6*].

Should one see in all these ideas nothing but the reflection of aristocratic prejudices and dreams of reactionary philosophers? To deny to these ideas any influence on Greek history, one would need to demonstrate the existence of a rival value system, formulated by the lower classes or for them, which rejected aristocratic values and substituted in their place the values of work and economic activity. In practice there are only few traces of such a value system: one might think of the role played in the fifth century, in Herodotus for example, by the theme of the 'first inventor', a culture hero, whether an individual or a group, who has liberated mankind from bondage thanks to a discovery which might be that of a technique[27]. And yet, even in this period which has often been compared to that of the modern 'Enlightenment', an invention once made did not appear susceptible of progress and development: as a whole the aristocratic values were not challenged.

What, finally, was the Greek definition of wealth and poverty[28]? For us wealth and poverty refer to two extremes which do not overlap: one is wealthy if one has more than is necessary to live an 'honourable' life, one is poor if one has less than this minimum. Consequently there are many between the extremes who are neither wealthy nor poor. The criterion is not the need for work in itself, but whether one has attained a certain standard of wealth: one may be wealthy and work, or one may be poor and idle. The Greek definition was quite different: the two categories did not correspond to two extremes, on the contrary they touched each other and could even overlap. The criterion was not a given standard of wealth but the need for work. A Greek was wealthy if he could live without having to work, poor if he did not have enough to live on without working. From this point of view the majority of people in Greece were 'poor' since they had to work. In addition, the Greeks drew a distinction between the poor man and the beggar who was completely destitute and was forced to live off the generosity of other people. Very often moral qualities were attached to notions of wealth and poverty: wealth was generally considered a 'blessing'[29] and a precondition for the development of human virtues, whereas poverty was a 'misfortune', which corrupted man and made him incapable of virtue [*see nos 18, 113*]. All this brings one back to what was said earlier on the absence of any positive evaluation of work: leisure and the absence of need for economic activity represented a very widespread ideal.

Admittedly, one must be careful not to generalize too much and suppose that these ideas applied with equal force to every period and every place in Greek history. There was first some evolution in time. Thus it has been pointed out that the unfavourable verdict against manual work which is well known in the classical period does not seem always to have been so strongly pronounced. It has been emphasized that in Homer the heroes do not shrink from manual work as such. The explanation for this apparent evolution in ideas lies once more, it would seem, in the conditions and spirit in which the work was carried out, and here again the criterion of self-sufficiency and personal freedom came into play. Odysseus could without shame set his hand to work, because in so doing he was trying to preserve his economic self-sufficiency. By contrast, an artisan in the classical city was in any case dependent on others; he could not be self-sufficient as the free peasant could, and was therefore in some way inferior to him.

A distinction should also be drawn between different Greek states. The same ideas did not exercise a comparable influence in states as different in their structure and mentality as Athens and Sparta. In Sparta the rejection of economic activity in any form whatever was complete as far as the *Homoioi* (the Peers), were concerned [*see no 56*]. That was an extreme case, and one may contrast with it a different climate of ideas in Athens and some degree of acceptance of technical skill, though one must still define clearly the limits within which this evolution took place (see Chapters 4 and 5).

But one must also avoid the opposite excess which consists in seeing in these ideas nothing but aristocratic prejudices or philosopher's utopias which had no real influence on Greek history. For one thing these ideas are found far too frequently for them to be devoid of any significance and, as has been seen, aristocratic values were by and large not seriously challenged. For another it is easy to establish frequent connections between the utopias of philosophers and historical reality. Both Plato and Aristotle, for example, would have debarred artisans from citizen rights in their ideal states, although they admitted that they were indispensable to the material existence of the state [*see no 5*]. That was precisely the situation in some Greek states. 'In Thebes', writes Aristotle, 'there was a law that no one who had not kept away from the *agora* for the last ten years might be admitted to office'[30] (that is to say who had traded there or practised a craft) [*see also no 4*]. Similar in spirit, though often obscure in its detail, is a fragmentary inscription from Cyrene dating from the late fourth century, in which a constitution is laid down for the city under the supervision of Ptolemy. The possession of full civic rights is restricted to those with a minimum property qualification of 20 minae, and various political disabilities are imposed on those practising certain trades; these include (lines 43–5) exclusion from all magistracies of men employed by the city as doctors, teachers, instructors of archery, horse riding and fencing, and heralds of the prytaneion, and (lines 48–50) exclusion from the office of *strategos* of anyone carrying on financial activities, or who had worked in the stone quarries or was a merchant or 'entered the palace of Ptolemy because he carried on a banausic trade[31] . . .' We are dealing here not with a philosopher's utopia but with historical reality. Nor are we dealing with some remote archaic period, for this is already beyond the classical world and at the start of the Hellenistic age.

Slavery in Greece [see nos 12, 14, 15]

So far no mention has been made of slavery in Greece except indirectly. But from what has been said above on negative judgments on manual work, on the absence of an ideology of work, on the ideal of leisure and the role of war in the life of the Greek states, it will be clear why servile labour should have appeared to the Greeks to be the unavoidable precondition of civilized life[32]. To account for the institution of slavery, one must, of course, also bring other factors into play, though here again it is difficult to draw a clear dividing line between causes and results. For one thing there was the relative stagnation of techniques which made it impossible to bring about an increase in production except through recourse to servile labour. This stagnation was in part linked with the absence of the notion of progress as we know it[33]. To be sure it would be wrong to say that the very notion of progress was unknown to the Greeks. The Greeks in the classical period were well aware of the fact that their civilization had started from modest origins and had gradually risen to a higher level (the opening chapters of Thucydides are an excellent illustration [see nos 7, 53, 55, 107]). In this evolution a positive contribution was ascribed to the development of certain basic techniques. It was thanks to his technical skill that man had been able to create civilization. But progress in the past did not automatically mean the possibility and need for progress in future. Once a certain level of civilization had been reached, technical progress lost its worth and genuine values were transposed to a different level. Some form of progress, both technical and economic, was the precondition for the existence of civilized states, but was not the purpose of their existence[34].

In addition, the acceptance of the inequality of mankind was a fundamental premiss of Greek history, and one that was never seriously challenged in practice[35]. What is more, Greek history even intensified inequalities by developing simultaneously the notion of the free citizen and that of the chattel slave who was bought on the market (even though one might subsequently bring up his children at home) and who (in theory, at least) had no rights at all. To our way of thinking there is a flagrant contradiction between the freedom of some and the servitude of others. But the Greek point of view was different: the freedom of some could not be imagined without the servitude of others and the two extremes were not thought of as contradictory, but as complementary and interdependent.

It is to be expected, therefore, that one should find servile labour in one form or another at every period of Greek history, and that no one should have seriously questioned the need for it. Already in Homer and Hesiod the existence of servile labour is a self-evident assumption, and it remained so throughout the history of antiquity. In the classical period, during the early fourth century, an invalid in Athens, pleading for the maintenance of the pension paid to him by the city, says to the jurors: 'I have a trade, but it is only of slight help to me; as it is, I have difficulty in carrying it out myself, and I am not yet able to procure someone to take it over from me.'[36] Elsewhere Xenophon writes in his *Memorabilia*: 'Those who can buy slaves so as to have companions in their work.'[37] Clearly, for the average Athenian in the classical period nothing seemed more natural than to wish to pass on to slaves part at least of one's work. Utopias here reflected historical reality. One example may suffice (quite apart from Plato and Aristotle [*see no 14*]). In the *Ecclesiazousai* of Aristophanes, the women seize power and a regime of common ownership of property is set up. When asked by Blepyros 'Who will cultivate the land?', Praxagora answers simply: 'The slaves' (line 651) [*see also no 13*].

Admittedly, towards the end of the fifth and the beginning of the fourth century there emerged tentatively a line of thought which denied any fundamental differences between Greeks and barbarians and asserted that slavery was nothing but a mere convention which could not be justified on a theoretical level. Aristotle in Book I of the *Politics* set out to refute this point of view and sought to demonstrate that on the contrary the antithesis between masters and slaves was a fact of nature, and that just as some were masters by nature others were born to be slaves. Aristotle's argument was anything but watertight; yet slavery continued to be accepted as before, even when it could not be logically justified.

Social history

From what has been said, it is clear that there can be no question of writing an economic history of Greece as one might do with the modern world, nor with the same concepts – and besides, there is the inadequacy of the available source material, on which more will be said below. But what of social history?

The problems one meets in the study of Greek social history are of the same kind as those which concern economic history, and to some extent they are connected. Just as there are dangers involved in trying to apply modern economic concepts, so too one must ask how far concepts developed for the study of social history can really be applied to ancient Greece. Just as there was a 'modernizing' period in the study of Greek economic history, so there was a 'modernizing' period (or rather, tendencies) in the study of Greek social history. Modern representations of social classes and class struggles were applied more or less literally to Greece, with the result that Greek social history was turned into a faithful replica of Europe after the industrial revolution[38]. The extreme point on this line was reached not by the German historians mentioned above (Ed. Meyer and others) but by R. von Pöhlmann in his *Geschichte der sozialen Frage und des Sozialismus in der antiken Welt*. Marxist theories on class struggles formed the starting point of the enquiry. Although the writer protested that it was not his intention to modernize the history of antiquity, it is clear that that was precisely the mistake he made (see the useful Appendix to the 3rd edition by Fr. Oertel). Pöhlmann based his reconstruction on a modernizing conception of the Greek economy, according to which it belonged to the modern capitalist type, with all the political and social consequences which followed. Since this conception was certainly false, Pöhlmann's interpretation of Greek social history lapsed with it. But should one therefore abandon modern concepts of social classes and class struggles in the study of Greek social history?

One preliminary point is that just as there was no autonomous 'economic' category for the Greeks, similarly there was no independent 'social' category. One may therefore expect *a priori* that Greek social history will merge into political history, just as is the case with economic history.

The question of the place occupied by class struggles in ancient society, and in particular the role played by slaves in these struggles is a serious one which needs to be approached with great caution. Admittedly, there is no definition of a 'social class' which would command general assent, but modern concepts and controversies revolve around three fundamental representations. The first is essentially empirical: a social class is a group of men who hold a more or less defined place in the social scale, e.g. the upper classes, middle classes, or lower classes. English-speaking writers have, as is well known, refined and elaborated these distinctions, multiplying subdivisions, much in the way that Sir Arthur Evans and his followers, after adopting a threefold classification of 'Minoan' finds into Early, Middle and Late Minoan, then subdivided each period into three (Early Minoan I, II, III, etc.), as though universal history automatically followed the ternary rhythm of a speech by Cicero. In addition, Marxism introduced two concepts which have played a fundamental role. A class is defined, on the one hand, by reference to the position it occupies in the relations of production: is it the class which produces, or does it enjoy the benefits of production without taking part in it directly? Here, in Marx's view, lay the opposition between the working class and the bourgeoisie. Marxism then also introduced a further concept, that of class consciousness: community of interests, development of a common vocabulary and programme, and the putting into practice of this programme in political and social action. These last two concepts (that of class in itself and class for itself) do not overlap. Marx was able to say without contradicting himself in a passage in *The Eighteenth Brumaire of Louis Bonaparte* (1852) that French peasants are a social class because 'their style of living, their interests, their culture' (one may add, their place in the relations of production) 'set them in opposition to the other classes of society', and also that because of their fragmentation, they had no more connection with each other than potatoes in a bag, and thus were not a class.

But what of the world of ancient Greece? Should one take literally the opening words of the *Communist Manifesto*: 'The history of all human society, past and present, has been the history of class-struggles. Freeman and slave, patrician and plebeian, baron and serf, guild-burgess and journeyman – in a word, oppressor and oppressed – stood in sharp opposition to each other.' In other words, there are two questions here: is class struggle characteristic of ancient Greece? Does the axis of this struggle go through the opposition between slave-owners and slaves? The answer is not easy. If one opens the greatest work of reflection on political, economic and social facts handed down to us by ancient Greece, namely Aristotle's *Politics*, one notices that from the beginning of his work the philosopher lays down as a fundamental principle the separation between the slave, who is defined as an 'instrument' – as is natural in a world of artisans – and the master: '. . . certain beings are destined from birth, some to obey, others to command'[39]. Aristotle calls the first 'slaves by nature'. But later, when considering the movement of Greek society, and in particular in Book V the phenomenon of *stasis* (internal disorders in the cities), he is constantly reasoning in terms of class struggles, with each of the rival groups aiming at governing by itself the whole of the city. Indeed one will find in the second part of this book that there is no lack of ancient sources which vividly express violent class feelings, on both sides of the struggle. But these two facts do not overlap and are far from coinciding with modern representations of class struggles. In particular one will search in vain for the place held by different groups in the relations of production as a criterion of ancient class struggles. There was of course nothing approaching what we call a 'working class', but most important it is not their place in production which separates social groups. An Athenian citizen, working with his hands on the same site or in the same workshop as a metic or a slave (whether his own or someone else's) was separated from his working companions by a social gulf. No common struggle brought them together (and no competition brought them into conflict – over wages and employment, for example). To be sure tasks that were thought inferior or physic-ally exhausting (and in the first place mining work) tended to be more or less exclusively in the hands of slaves, but this did not by any means imply the growth among slaves of a common con-sciousness. In Athens a miner, a stone-cutter, a policeman, and even in some cases what we might call a higher civil servant, could all be slaves, but they shared no other demand in common apart from freedom; they did not aim at replacing the governing group in society, still less did they aim at establishing a 'classless society' of the kind which the modern bourgeoisie imagined it would bring about when its struggles had brought it to power, or of the kind which is demanded by socialist ideology.

Slaves, or at least those one calls 'chattel-slaves', did not there-fore constitute a class, though this did not prevent them from being, as was understood by Aristotle, the 'instruments' without which the Greek city would simply have been inconceivable. Aristotle's formulation is well known: 'If every instrument could do its own work when ordered to, or through anticipation, like the legendary statues of Daedalus or the tripods of Hephaistus, which the poets say "enter the company of gods of their own movement"[40], if thus shuttles could weave and quills play the cithara themselves, then master craftsmen would have no need of assistants nor masters of slaves[41].' But the point is (and one generally forgets to mention this) that Aristotle is not opposing here only masters and slaves. It is true, however, that there is one group of 'slaves' which displays characteristics which brings it close to a modern social class: the Spartan Peers (*Homoioi*) were not themselves producers, but lived off the agricultural production of the Helots. These had common demands which were expressed in permanent revolt (see Chapter 4), but another factor of differentiation must be introduced. Since the conquests of the bourgeoisie modern social classes are characterized, if not by their mobility in practice, then at least by their legal permeability. A workman's son or a workman can in law become a bourgeois. With the exception of one special category on which there is no need to dwell here (that of the *mothakes* who were said to share in the education of the young Spartiates), the Helots could not legally become fully fledged Spartiates. One must therefore reject completely the conception often expressed according to which the struggle between masters and slaves was the manifestation of class struggle in antiquity, just as one must reject the parallel conception, born of the modern struggle for the abolition of colonial slavery[42], which sees in classical slavery the corrupting agent of Greek society. On the contrary it made that society possible by guaranteeing the freedom of the citizen[43].

Once one has eliminated the opposition between masters and slaves as a fundamental ingredient of class struggles in the Greek world, what then were the essential characteristics of these struggles? They are twofold, and inseparable. In the first place the antagonism was not to be found between groups holding different places in the relations of production but, roughly speaking, between the propertied and the non-propertied, with ownership of land as the main form of wealth. In practice the antagonism was for most of the time between a wealthy minority and a more or less impoverished majority, though it must be noted, as Aristotle pointed out, that the essential criterion was not that of numbers but that of wealth. The terminology used by the Greeks to designate these two opposed groups is remarkably rich [*see no 18*]: on one side one finds the *aristoi, esthloi, eugeneis, epieikeis, gennaioi, gnorimoi, kaloikagathoi, chrestoi, charientes, beltistoi*, etc., to designate the wealthy minority; on the other the *plethos, demos, ochlos, kakoi, deiloi, poneroi, cheirous*, etc., to designate their opponents[44]. There is no point in trying to find an exact shade of meaning for each one of these words; in practice they are synonymous and interchangeable. The colouring of these words, and therefore their origin, will not escape notice: the laudatory words are kept for the minority, and most of the words used for the majority are pejorative. It will also be noted how moral qualities are implicitly attributed to social classes: positive qualities are the privilege of the wealthy minority (cf. above on wealth and poverty).

The antagonism between the propertied minority and the non-propertied majority was fundamental in Greek class struggles; yet by itself it was not sufficient to set in motion conflict between organized groups. And here the second essential characteristic comes in: class struggles could be expressed between citizens only through their belonging to the state (or the possibility of belonging to it) and the possession of political power which this implied. There were wealthy and destitute men outside the citizen body, but no antagonism between them could take shape for the simple reason that they had no access to political power. This partly accounts for the lack of participation of slaves as a group, in cities such as Athens, in social and political conflicts between citizens. Conversely, it helps to explain the active role which groups like the Helots played in conflicts in Sparta, precisely because to some extent they were part of the state (or at least could claim to be).

From what has been said one would not expect that struggles between citizens revolved purely around specifically economic issues, and in fact political demands and economic demands often formed a single inseparable whole. The constitution of Greek states tended to reflect the social composition of the citizen body and the way in which wealth was distributed among its members [*see no 19*]. A political revolution therefore often meant simultaneously a social revolution. But without wishing to play down the political aspect of struggles between citizens one may still attempt to isolate the strictly economic factors involved. It should be emphasized that, in contrast to the modern world, economic demands were never concerned with working conditions and salaries, since, as has been seen, there was no working class and no labour market. Nor were there any protests on the part of the poor citizens against the competition which slave labour might have represented. Already in the archaic age the revolutionary slogans were cancellation of debts and redistribution of land. Positive economic demands always concerned either the redistribution for the benefit of the citizens of the surplus of the city's wealth [*see nos 20, 111, 115*], or, and especially, the redistribution of landed property, which was almost everywhere in the Greek world the exclusive preserve of the citizen body (see Chapter 5). Ownership of land was very often the foundation of the citizen's rights; but the relationship could be reversed, and membership of the citizen body become the justification for the claim to ownership of land, all the more so as it was agreed that among citizens (and not only in democracies) the notion of equality ought to operate to some extent (its interpretation in practice was obviously controversial) [*see no 114*]. There was therefore a certain logic behind the slogan of redistribution of land. The tension between citizens found its expression at the economic and social level in the tension between the great landowners and the small independent farmers. The great achievement of the classical period (the 'Greek miracle', one might say) was to have made possible the rise of the peasants within the city: the peasant became, at least in certain cities, a full citizen, a phenomenon unknown to history before the Greeks. When during the fourth century and for a variety of reasons (see Chapter 7) the ideal of the peasant-citizen began to lose ground both in reality and in ideology, the classical *polis* then started on its decline. It was also then that the slogan of redistribution of land reappeared in Greek history with increased violence.

The antagonism between the propertied and the non-propertied among the citizens was much the strongest and most important of the divisions which split the citizen body, but it was not the only one. As will be seen, Aristotle was quite conscious of this [*see no 14*], as were many other Greeks as well.

One of these divisions was that between men and women [*see nos 15, 16*][45]. The classical city of the Athenian type was, of course, a 'men's club' and was characterized by a twofold exclusion: on the one hand that of outsiders (and the slave is the extreme type of the outsider who is deprived of any rights), and on the other that of women. In this type of city it was inconceivable that slaves could aim at achieving political power: that was a hypothesis which even the fantasy of the comic poets was unable to conceive. As for feminine power, it was not a direct political threat, but belonged to the realm of utopia. How Aristophanes made use of this theme in *Lysistrata* and the *Ecclesiazousai* is well known. But the situation was different in archaic societies, of which Sparta is the best known representative. In those societies, just as political demands on the part of 'slaves' of the Helot type were a permanent reality of their history, so too one can see in legend and some traditions the possibility of feminine power emerging ('gynaecocracy', to use the Greek word). It is a phenomenon which Aristotle censures in the institutions of Sparta in a passage of the *Politics* where the danger of feminine power is placed on the same level as that of servile power[46].

Another division is that which existed between young and old[47]; this may represent the reworking of a distant past but it can still be seen at work right in the middle of the historical period [*see no 17*]. The Greek city, which is usually and rightly considered to be the typical institution of Greek history, was nevertheless of relatively recent origin in the history of the Greek people. The city had in a way been superimposed on more ancient institutions and groupings without obliterating these completely. Age classes are an illustration of this and are found in many parts of the Greek world [*see no 129*]. Sparta and the Cretan cities show them in their most developed form [*see no 57*]: age classes played a fundamental role in the organization of society. All Greek states, whether democratic or oligarchic, made use of the principle of seniority in the attribution of political power. Some specific cases are known in Greek history where one can see the antithesis between young and old within the city assuming the dimensions of a direct political conflict, and the city finding itself divided into two hostile groups.

The main sources

It has been stated above that for the Greeks there did not exist any autonomous economic and social categories. One cannot therefore expect to find any specialist literature on this subject among Greek writers. One may mention, however, as having special importance (apart from the historians) the writings of the political theorists of the fourth century, Plato and Aristotle, and especially the latter's *Politics*; the treatises on *Economics* mentioned above, which have some affinities with Hesiod's *Works and Days*, a didactic poem which gives valuable information on the life of a Bocotian peasant around 700 BC; the so-called *Ways and Means* of Xenophon, a pamphlet dating from about 355 BC in which the author suggests a number of remedies designed to rescue Athens from the financial difficulties in which she found herself, and which is a remarkable commentary on the economic mentality of a Greek city in the classical period; Attic comedy; the orators of the late fifth and fourth centuries; and others besides.

Besides literary texts there is the evidence of inscriptions (there are of course no documentary papyri before the Hellenistic period)[48]. Useful inscriptions of the archaic age are few, and it is only with the development of the radical democracy in Athens in the middle of the fifth century that the practice of publishing public documents more or less systematically (such as decrees, treaties, etc.) became general. The contribution of inscriptions to social and economic history is considerable. Here too, it is the whole of epigraphic evidence which is liable to provide information. One may mention especially texts on state finances (inventories, accounts of the treasuries of temples, accounts of state expenditure, the so-called 'tribute lists' of the fifth-century Athenian empire, legislation on certain economic questions, etc.); treaties with foreign states which included at times some economic clauses; the *Horoi* (stone pillars) found on estates in Attica in the fourth century; many inscriptions relating to metics and slaves; and so forth.

Finally, there is the contribution of archaeology. There is no point in listing here what archaeology has added and may still add to our knowledge of social and economic history; it is enough to refer to a number of recent works[49]. Archaeology may reveal all sorts of facts otherwise unknown: for example, it may tell us something on trade and relations between Greek states, or between Greeks and non-Greeks. It can also confirm, correct and amplify what was already known through literary sources (as for example the activity of the Greeks in Egypt in the archaic period)[50]. In general, whatever is unearthed through excavation is liable to fit into a social and economic framework. Among the types of objects which are more specially useful for economic history one must mention coin hoards[51] and especially vases, though one must be wary of drawing too far-reaching conclusions from the evidence of pottery finds alone, a temptation historians have often succumbed to[52].

When all these different types of sources, literary, epigraphic, and archaeological are put together, the evidence for Greek social and economic history may seem abundant. And yet one must never lose sight of the limitations of our knowledge. One of the major gaps in the study of Greek economic history is the lack of reliable statistical data, and the consequent impossibility of any detailed statistical approach to the subject. Thus we do not know for sure the exact population figures for Athens in the classical period, let alone other Greek states, and what can be put forward on this subject must remain more or less plausible guesses. In general the classical period is much better known than the centuries which preceded it. The quality and amount of the evidence vary also from region to region. As for Greek history in general, Athens takes the lion's share in most of the extant sources. It would be foolish to deny the gaps and risks of imbalance which any enquiry into Greek history must face.

Notes

1   The following pages give only a very brief summary of the controversy; for a detailed account, with bibliography, see Ed. Will, 'Trois quarts de siècle de recherches sur l'économie grecque antique', *Annales* 9 (1954), pp. 7–22; see more briefly Harry W. Pearson, 'The Secular Debate on Economic Primitivism', in *Trade and Market in the Early Empires*, ed. by Karl Polanyi, Conrad M. Arensberg and Harry W. Pearson (Glencoe, 1957), pp. 3–11. Add the surveys by M.I. Finley and Ed. Will on the classical and archaic periods respectively in *Second International Conference of Economic History, Aix-en-Provence 1962* I (Paris and The Hague, 1965), pp. 11–35 and 41–96, and P. Vidal-Naquet, 'Économie et société dans la Grèce ancienne: l'oeuvre de Moses I. Finley', *Archives européenes de sociologie* 6 (1965), pp. 111–48. Ed. Will includes a section on Greek social and economic history in his regular bulletin on Greek history in the *Revue historique*

(1965, 1967, 1971 and 1974 so far). On every aspect of the subject M.I. Finley, *The Ancient Economy* (London and Berkeley, 1973) is essential (on this work, cf. A. Momigliano, *Rivista Storica Italiana* LXXXVII, 1 (March 1975), pp. 167–70). See also S.C. Humphreys, 'Economy and Society in Classical Athens', *Annali della Scuola normale superiore di Pisa* 39 (1970), pp. 1–26, and 'The Work of Louis Gernet', *History and Theory* 10 (1971), pp. 172–96. On the contribution of Italian scholars see E. Lepore, 'Economia antica e storiografia moderna', in *Ricerche storiche ed economiche in memoria di Corrado Barbagallo* I (Naples, 1970), pp. 3–33.

2 The question arose, of course, for the whole of antiquity, but in fact it was chiefly over prehellenistic Greek history that the controversy developed.

3 It is noteworthy that the controversy remained for a long time essentially a German one and with few exceptions was hardly echoed abroad.

4 Ed. Meyer, *Kleine Schriften* I (Halle, 2nd ed., 1924), pp. 118–19.

5 The contribution of Max Weber is not brought out by Ed. Will, art. cit. above, which may surprise as J. Hasebroek appealed explicitly to the example of Max Weber. Weber's key works here are *Wirtschaft und Gesellschaft* II (Tübingen, 4th ed., 1956), pp. 735–822; *Typologie der Städte: die nicht legitime Herrschaft* (English translation by D. Martindale and G. Neuwirth, *The City* (New York, 1966)); and 'Agrarverhältnisse im Altertum', in *Gesammelte Aufsätze zur Sozial- und Wirtschaftsgeschichte* (Tübingen, 1924), pp. 1–288. Max Weber's *Agrarverhältnisse* is now available in translation: *The Agrarian Sociology of Ancient Civilizations*, trans. R.I. Frank (London, 1976). Weber's characterization of the ancient city was not completely novel; it had, for instance, been strikingly anticipated by Karl Marx, who followed the lead of B.G. Niebuhr on Roman history, but this was in the *Formen* which were only published in 1939; see the English translation with an introduction by E. Hobsbawm, *Pre-capitalist Economic Formations* (London, 1964). On Karl Marx and Greek history see further n 38 below.

6 See for example how Fr. Oertel summarizes the controversy in his Appendix to R. von Pöhlmann, *Geschichte der sozialen Frage und des Sozialismus in der alten Welt* II (Munich, 3rd ed., 1925), pp. 516–18.

7 Tübingen, 1928; English translation, *Trade and Politics in Ancient Greece* (London, 1933).

8 Tübingen, 1931.

9 Hasebroek's point of view had already been anticipated in France by L. Gernet in his study 'L'approvisionnement d'Athènes en blé aux Ve et IVe siècles', in G. Bloch, *Mélanges d'histoire ancienne* (Paris, 1909), pp. 269–391. Gernet was actually the only scholar in France to review Hasebroek favourably in *Annales* 5 (1955), pp. 561–6.

10 An example of a book which seems to bypass the whole controversy is A. French, *The Growth of the Athenian Economy* (London, 1964); the very title is revealing (see M.I. Finley, in *The Economic Journal* 75 (1965), pp. 849–51).

11 See especially *Primitive, Archaic and Modern Economics: Essays of Karl Polanyi*, ed. George Dalton (Garden City, N.Y. 1968) and the critical discussion with full bibliography by S.C. Humphreys, 'History, Economics, and Anthropology: the Work of Karl Polanyi', *History and Theory* 8 (1964), pp. 165–212; also Yvon Garlan, 'L'oeuvre de Polanyi: la place de l'économie dans les sociétés anciennes', *La Pensée* no 171 (October 1973), pp. 118–27; L. Valensi, 'Anthropologie économique et Histoire: l'oeuvre de Karl Polanyi', *Annales* 29, 6 (Nov.–Dec. 1974), pp. 1311–19; the same issue of *Annales* contains extensive discussions of the notion of reciprocity. For a wide-ranging discussion of the place of the market economy in many societies, including the ancient Near East and the Greek world, see Maxime Rodinson, Preface (in French) to P. Chalmeta Gendron, *El 'señor del zoco' en España* (Madrid), 1973), pp. xv–lxix.

12 On the meaning of these terms see especially the article by S.C. Humphreys; she has attempted to apply them to the Greek world in a brief sketch of its economic history, op. cit., pp. 207–12. Another concept one owes to Polanyi is that of the 'port of trade', a specifically economic zone through which exchanges between two societies of different economic type might be organized; on this concept see further Chapter 3.

13 See M.I. Finley, 'Aristotle and Economic Analysis', *Past and Present* 47 (May 1970), pp. 3–25 (= *Studies in Ancient Society*, pp. 26–52).

14 I, 2, 2.

15 *Republic* II, 369 b–c.

16 See P. Vidal-Naquet, 'Valeurs religieuses et mythiques de la terre et du sacrifice dans l'Odyssée', first in *Annales* 25 (1970), pp. 1278–97, and now in *Problèmes de la terre en Grèce ancienne*, ed. M.I. Finley (Paris and The Hague, 1973), pp. 269–92; the volume is essential reading for every aspect of the land in the Greek world.

17 Luc Brisson, *Le même et l'autre dans la structure ontologique du Timée de Platon* (Paris, 1974); cf. too P. de Fidio, *Parola del Passato* 26 (1971), pp. 233–63.

18 See K. Murakawa, 'Demiurgos', *Historia* 6 (1957), pp. 385–415; cf. too P. de Fidio, op. cit.; on artisans in ancient society see A. Burford, *Craftsmen in Greek and Roman Society* (London, 1972); on mythical aspects see F. Frontisi-Ducroux, *Dédale. Mythologie de l'artisan en Grèce ancienne* (Paris, 1975); on iconography see J. Ziomecki, *Les représentations d'artisans sur les vases attiques* (Wroclaw, 1975).

19 On Hephaistos see M. Delcourt, *Héphaistos ou la légende du magicien* (Paris, 1957); on Hermes see provisionally L. Demoule-Lyotard, *Annales* 26 (1971), pp. 705–22; on Athena the technician see M. Détienne, 'Le navire d'Athéna', *Revue de l'histoire des religions*, 1970, pp. 133–77.

20 See A. Aymard, 'Le partage des profits de la guerre dans les traités d'alliance antiques', *Études d'histoire ancienne* (Paris, 1967), pp. 499–512; *Problèmes de la guerre en Grèce ancienne*, ed. J.P. Vernant (Paris and The Hague, 1968); Vernant's preface, 'La guerre des cités', is also available in *Mythe et société en Grèce ancienne* (Paris, 1974), pp. 31–56; P. Ducrey, *Le traitement des prisonniers de guerre dans la Grèce ancienne* (Paris, 1968); W.K. Pritchett, *The Greek State at War*, Parts I and II (Berkeley and Los Angeles, 1971 and 1974); Yvon Garlan, *War in the Ancient World: A Social History* (London, 1975). On the causes of war in Greece see also G.E.M. de Ste Croix, *The Origins of the Peloponnesian War* (London, 1972), pp. 218–20.

21 It may be relevant in this context that the Athenian 'empire' should occasionally have been referred to, even in official documents, as the *hyperoria*, what is 'beyond the frontiers', thus *Syll.*³ 54; Ps.-Xenophon, *Constitution of the Athenians* I, 19; Xenophon, *Symposium* IV, 31 and *Memorabilia* II, 8, 1.

22 Cf. Plutarch, *Cimon* IX, 3–6; XIII, 5–7.

23 The essential studies are those of A. Aymard, 'L'idée de

travail dans la Grèce archaique', *Journal de Psychologie* 41 (1948), pp. 29–45; id., 'Hiérarchie du travail et autarcie individuelle dans la Grèce archaique', *Études d'histoire ancienne* (Paris, 1967), pp. 316–33; and of J.P. Vernant, *Mythe et pensée chez les Grecs* (Paris, 3rd ed., 1969), pp. 184–247.

24 The professional pride of the artisan should not be confused with an ideology of work.

25 Aristotle, *Rhetoric* I, 9, 1367 a 32 (for the translation, cf. G.E.M. de Ste Croix, *Arethusa* 8, 1 (Spring 1975), n 25, p. 39).

26 See Th. Veblen's classic *Theory of the Leisure Class.*

27 See A. Kleingünther, *Protos Heuretes. Untersuchungen zur Geschichte einer Fragestellung, Philologus Supplementband* XXVI, 1 (1933).

28 On what follows see J. Hemelrijk, *Penia en Ploutos* (Diss. Utrecht, 1925), in Dutch with a summary in German.

29 Greek literature does not always link happiness and wealth, although in Pindar gold shines on the kings he celebrates [*see no 52*], but the just and suffering man of the Bible is unknown to it; on this cf. G.E.M. de Ste Croix, 'Early Christian Attitudes to Property and Slavery', *Studies in Church History* 12 (1975), pp. 1–38, esp. 9–15 on the contrast between Graeco-Roman and biblical ideas on wealth and poverty.

30 *Politics* III, 1278 a 25; cf. 1321 a 29.

31 *Supplementum Epigraphicum Graecum* IX, 1 (on the date cf. *REG* 85 (1972), pp. xiii–xiv). B. Bravo has suggested to us that the exclusions are directed against those practising trades in the service of someone, rather than against the trades in themselves, the employer being the city in the first case and Ptolemy in the second if the reference to 'anyone who worked in the stone quarries or was a merchant (*phortegos*)' is indeed to past service with Ptolemy, as B. Bravo suggests.

32 On slavery see the articles collected with a bibliographical essay by M.I. Finley in *Slavery and Classical Antiquity* (Cambridge, 2nd ed., 1968), especially Finley's article 'Was Greek Civilization based on Slave Labour?', pp. 53–72; N. Brockmeyer, *Bibliographie zur antiken Sklaverei*, preface by J. Vogt (Bochum, 1971); J. Vogt, *Ancient Slavery and the Ideal of Man* (Blackwell, 1974); the 'Centre de recherches d'histoire ancienne' of Besançon organizes annual conferences (since 1970) on slavery in the ancient world, the first three of which have so far been published (Paris, 1972, 1973 and 1974).

33 See M.I. Finley, 'Technical Innovation and Economic Progress in the Ancient World', *The Economic History Review* 18 (1965), pp. 29–45; H.W. Pleket, 'Technology and Society in the Graeco-Roman World', *Acta Historiae Neerlandica* 2 (1967), pp. 1–25. On the idea of progress in antiquity see J. de Romilly, 'Thucydide et l'idée de progrès', *Annali della Scuola normale superiore di Pisa* XXXV (1966), pp. 143–91; L. Edelstein, *The Idea of Progress in Classical Antiquity* (Baltimore, 1968) (somewhat partisan); E.R. Dodds, *The Ancient Concept of Progress and Other Essays in Greek Literature and Belief* (Oxford, 1972), pp. 1–25.

34 See M.I. Finley, 'Metals in the Ancient World', *Journal of the Royal Society of Arts*, no 5170, vol. CXVIII (September 1970), pp. 597–607.

35 See H.C. Baldry, *The Unity of Mankind in Greek Thought* (Cambridge, 1965).

36 Lysias XXIV, 6.

37 II, 3, 3.

38 On what follows see J.P. Vernant, 'Remarques sur la lutte de classes dans la Grèce ancienne', *Eirene* 4 (1965), pp. 5–19 (= *Mythe et société en Grèce ancienne* (Paris, 1974), pp. 11–29); P. Vidal-Naquet, 'Les esclaves grecs étaient-ils une classe?', *Raison présente* 6 (1968), pp. 103–12. For a different approach, with a critique of the view outlined here, see G.E.M. de Ste Croix, 'Karl Marx and the History of Classical Antiquity', pp. 7–41 of the collective issue of *Arethusa* (8, 1, Spring 1975) entitled *Marxism and the Classics*, which contains also a bibliography (by Robert A. Padgug) on Marxism and Antiquity (pp. 199–225); a fuller statement of de Ste Croix's views will be given in his *The Class Struggle in the Ancient Greek World* (London, 1977 – forthcoming). Central to de Ste Croix's conception of class and class struggle is the emphasis (following Marx) on the 'fact of exploitation', while less importance is attached by him to class consciousness and overt struggles.

39 *Politics* I, 1254 a 22.

40 *Iliad* XVIII, 376.

41 *Politics* I, 1253 b 33–1254 a 1.

42 The first edition of the monumental *Histoire de l'esclavage dans l'antiquité* appeared in 1847, a year before the decree which abolished the slavery of the Blacks in the American

South, and was the work of the abolitionist Henri Wallon.

43 On all these questions and notably on the possible application to the Greek world of the Roman (and subsequently medieval and classical) concept of *orders* see further the collective volume *Recherches sur les structures sociales dans l'antiquité classique* (Paris, 1970); M.I. Finley, *The Ancient Economy* (1973), Ch. III.

44 For a collection of evidence see G. Busolt, *Griechische Staatskunde* I (Munich, 3rd ed., 1920), pp. 210–19; cf. G.E.M. de Ste Croix, in *Historia* 3 (1954–55), pp. 21–30; R.A. Neil, *The Knights of Aristophanes* (London, 1909), pp. 202–9 ('Political use of moral terms').

45 See P. Vidal-Naquet, 'Esclavage et gynécocratie dans la tradition, le mythe, l'utopie', in *Recherches sur les structures sociales dans l'Antiquité classique* (Paris, 1970), pp. 63–80 (English translation forthcoming in *Myth, Tragedy and Society*, ed. R.L. Gordon); cf. Simon G. Pembroke, 'Women in Charge: the Function of Alternatives in Early Greek Tradition and the Ancient Idea of the Matriarchy', *Journal of the Warburg and Courtauld Institutes* XXX (1967), pp. 1–35; on the antithesis between men and women in religion and rites see briefly L. Gernet and A. Boulanger, *Le génie grec dans la religion* (Paris, new ed., 1970), pp. 51–3. See now the collective issue of *Arethusa* VI, 1 (1973), *Women in Antiquity* with a bibliography by Sarah B. Pomeroy, pp. 125–57, and her book *Goddesses, Whores, Wives and Slaves: Women in Classical Antiquity* (London, 1976).

46 *Politics* II, 1269 b 7–1270 a 31.

47 See H. Jeanmaire, *Couroi et Courètes* (Paris and Lille, 1939) and especially P. Roussel, 'Étude sur le principe d'ancienneté dans le monde hellénique', *Mémoires de l'Institut National de France*, Académie des Inscriptions et Belles-Lettres 43 (1951), pp. 123–227. On some particular aspects cf. P. Vidal-Naquet, 'The Black Hunter and the Origins of the Athenian Ephebeia', *Proceedings of the Cambridge Philological Society* 194 (1968), pp. 49–64 (to be re-issued in a modified form in *Myth, Tragedy and Society*, ed. R.L. Gordon (Cambridge, forthcoming)), and 'Les jeunes. Le cru, l'enfant grec, et le cuit', in the collective volume *Faire de l'histoire*, III (Paris, 1974), pp. 137–68; N. Loraux, 'HBH et ANΔREIA: deux versions de la mort du combattant Athénien', *Ancient Society* 6 (1975), pp. 1–31. The

most recent general study is A. Brelich, *Paides e Parth-oi* (Rome, 1969).

48 See the selection by H.W. Pleket, *Epigraphica vol. 1: Texts on the Economic History of the Greek World* (Leyden, 1964). A good illustration of the use of inscriptions in one particular field, that of building activity, is the book by A.M. Burford, *The Greek Temple Builders at Epidauros. A Social and Economic Study of Building in the Asklepian Sanctuary, during the Fourth and Early Third Centuries B.C.* (Liverpool, 1969). The entire scholarly output on Greek inscriptions is mentioned and analysed by J. and L. Robert in their annual 'Bulletin épigraphique' in *REG* since 1938, now reprinted separately (till 1973); a full index of the 'Bulletin' is in course of publication.

49 See for example P. Courbin, ed., *Études archéologiques* (Paris, 1963), notably the chapters by Ed. Will, G. le Rider, G. Vallet and F. Villard; on coinage see especially C.M. Kraay and Max Hirmer, *Greek Coins* (London, 1966); C.M. Kraay, *Greek Coins and History* (London, 1969); C.M. Kraay, *Archaic and Classical Greek Coins* (London, 1976); on the problems in the use of archaeological evidence for the history of Greek trade, see the cautionary remarks of Ed. Will in *Atti del XII convegno di studi sulla Magna Grecia* (Naples, 1975), pp. 21–67. For new possibilities on the use of archaeological evidence see S.C. Humphreys, 'Archaeology and the Economic and Social History of Classical Greece', *Parola del Passato* 114 (1967), pp. 374–400.

50 See M.M. Austin, *Greece and Egypt in the Archaic Age* (Cambridge, 1970).

51 M. Thompson, O. Mørkholm, C.M. Kraay, *An Inventory of Greek Coin Hoards* (New York, 1973).

52 See R.M. Cook, 'Die Bedeutung der bemalten Keramik für den griechischen Handel', *Jahrbuch des deutschen archäologischen Instituts* 74 (1959), pp. 114–23; and briefly in *Greek Painted Pottery* (London, 2nd ed., 1972), pp. 270–4, 275–6; G. Vallet and F. Villard, n 49 above, and 'Céramique et histoire grecque', *Revue Historique* 225 (1961), pp. 295–318.

2   The Homeric World

The Mycenaean world

The history of the Greeks in antiquity went through two quite distinct phases: the best known and most important is the history of the cities, which begins roughly in the eighth century with the end of the 'Dark Age' and the beginning of the archaic period. Yet chronologically it is, so to speak, only the second history of Greece: it was preceded by another quite different history, that of Mycenaean Greece in the Bronze Age, a history not of cities, but of kingdoms, which although small scale were centralized and bureaucratic in character, and to some extent imitated the contemporary civilizations of the Near East. They are partly known to us through the archaeological discoveries begun last century by Heinrich Schliemann, which have been carried on subsequently, and which have brought to light the great palaces of Mycenae, Tiryns, Pylos and other sites, and partly through the decipherment in 1952 by Michael Ventris of the tablets in syllabic writing, known as Linear B, from Cnossos, Mycenae and Pylos (and now Thebes as well). The decipherment revealed in detail the working of the great centralized palaces which subjected all economic activity to accounting of a remarkably minute kind. The Mycenaean world collapsed during the twelfth century, at the time when the entire eastern Mediterranean was going through a period of profound upheaval. With the passing of the Mycenaean world the type of social structure which it had represented disappeared once and for all from Greek history, and so did all the institutions and cultural elements which were linked with it. Greek history in the classical period was not to be the history of accounting and bureaucratic palaces, but became the history of cities. The break which occurred at the end of the Bronze Age was therefore the most profound in Greek history[1].

36

The Homeric poems as historical sources

The history of the Mycenaean world lies outside the scope of this book, yet it has to be mentioned briefly. The first historical documents to have come down to us after the fall of the Mycenaean world, and the first literary works of Greek history are the Homeric poems, the *Iliad* and the *Odyssey*. Ostensibly these poems look back to events which took place in the Mycenaean world during the Bronze Age. The question of deciding what historical period the evidence of 'Homer' can be referred to, and to what extent he can be used as a historical source, has been the subject of a long debate which is still far from settled, but in which one cannot avoid taking sides. In other words, what do the Homeric poems represent as historical sources[2]?

According to some, and they are the majority, the Homeric poems give simply a more or less faithful picture of the vanished Mycenaean world, and Homer would then have to be listed side by side with the archaeological discoveries and Linear B as a major source for the history of Greece in the Bronze Age. Although this view is a widespread one, it is surely untenable. It is true that the Homeric poems seek to portray this lost world. It has often been pointed out that they contain a number of Mycenaean elements which disappeared with the fall of the palaces, but which Homer remembered (place names, objects, customs, etc.). And yet all told this is very little in comparison with all that had been forgotten between the Mycenaean world and Homer in the way of institutions and cultural elements. There are also in Homer a number of anachronisms which do not fit into the framework of the Mycenaean world but belong in fact to a later period. The decipherment of Linear B has brought out even more clearly the difference between the Mycenaean world and Homeric society: there is a gulf between the Mycenaean palaces with their meticulous bureaucracy and the palaces of the Homeric kings, infinitely less complex in their organization, and in which writing, an essential element in the Mycenaean world, is completely missing. Between the Mycenaean world and Homer a whole type of society disappeared once and for all, and Greeks of later generations had no inkling of its existence[3].

Should one then consider the Homeric poems to reflect primarily the time in which they were composed, that is to say (according to the chronology most widely accepted at the moment) the eighth century, with the *Iliad* coming at the beginning of the century or slightly earlier, and the *Odyssey* in the second half? This point of view is less widespread than the previous one, but it has been defended. Admittedly, one may identify elements which quite probably belong to the world in which the poet lived. Thus it has been possible to point to the links between the *Odyssey* and the beginnings of colonization in the west in the second half of the eighth century [*see no 30*]. Yet on the other hand one could hardly see in the Homeric poems a literal description of the world in which the poet lived. One must always reckon with the archaizing tendencies of the poet, who is looking back towards a lost world he is trying to recall. He is aware that deep changes have taken place at a relatively recent date, and he avoids alluding to them. Thus he says almost nothing of the Dorians, who settled in Greece after the fall of the Mycenaean palaces (only one allusion), nor of the Greek migration to Asia Minor during the Dark Age. He was seeking to recall a lost society, but there were no available landmarks to guide him. What he described was in all likelihood neither the Mycenaean world, nor his own time, but a world chronologically in between the two, namely the Greek world of the Dark Age in the tenth and ninth centuries, after the fall of the Mycenaean palaces but before the development of the *polis* in the eighth century which ushered in a completely new period of Greek history[4].

Yet one cannot start from a literal equation of the Homeric world with the Greek world of the Dark Age. To describe Homeric society is not the same thing as to describe the historical Greek society of the tenth–ninth centuries. One must make allowances for anachronisms in both directions. Schematically one may say that three historical levels coexist in Homer: the Mycenaean world the poet is seeking to recall; the Dark Age; and the poet's own time. It may often not be easy to distinguish clearly what belongs to one rather than to the other.

These problems are in any case far from exhausting the historical interest of Homer's work (including the aspects with which we are concerned here). This vast poetic discourse can and must be approached as a discourse the laws of which merit study. Oppositions then appear which will be found subsequently right through Greek civilization. Thus when it is seen that Homer draws a fundamental antithesis between men, who eat bread, cultivate the soil, raise cattle and offer sacrifices, and who in the *Odyssey* are found at Pylos, Sparta and Ithaca, and all the nonhumans, whether man-eating monsters, sirens or goddesses, whom Odysseus meets in his travels, that antithesis transcends the question of deciding whether Nestor's Pylos is identical with what the Cincinnati archaeologists found at Epano-Engliano. That should not prevent the historian from being watchful. Thus the story of the Cyclops in Book IX of the *Odyssey* describes at the same time both savages in the mythical sense – 'barbarian' stock-breeders such as the Greeks may have come across – and a land about which a realistic invitation to colonization is made [*see no 30*].

Be that as it may, and to return to more concrete problems, one notes that Homer is aware of the fact that the vanished Mycenaean world was richer and more powerful than the one he was living in. He recreates this world as he imagines it to have been, and for this purpose he deliberately exaggerates the wealth of his kings. One cannot take literally the description of the Homeric palaces with their vast treasures and their many slaves: the precision of the numerical data is purely illusory and should not mislead. One will vainly search through the archaeology of the tenth–ninth centuries for the traces of dwellings such as the great house of Odysseus on Ithaca. The picture of the Greek world of the time that has been revealed by archaeology is far less impressive: material culture undergoes a considerable impoverishment – many sites are abandoned, and relations with the outside world virtually interrupted. It is only gradually that the Greek world recovered and began to consolidate after the disturbances which marked the end of the Mycenaean period[5].

Furthermore the Homeric world is far too uniform: there is seemingly no awareness of the diversity between different parts of the Greek world at the time. It is difficult to believe that such was the situation in reality. At almost every period of its history the Greek world was characterized by inequality of development between different regions. But for the period which is roughly that of Homeric society, the means of control are lacking, and the picture of the Homeric world must of necessity remain somewhat abstract.

Finally one must emphasize the differences between the *Iliad* and the *Odyssey*[6]: strictly speaking there is no such thing as a 'Homeric society', there is the society of the *Iliad* and that of the *Odyssey*. There is first of all a difference of age: the *Iliad* reflects a world that is more archaic and less open than the *Odyssey*.

Then there is the difference of subject: the *Iliad* depicts a society at war in which a warrior aristocracy plays the leading role, thanks to its military supremacy, and in which the role of the lower classes is accordingly more shadowy, since 'they count for nothing in war and in council' [*see no 21*][7]. By contrast the *Odyssey* gives a much more detailed picture of society and of what we call the economy. In particular the *Odyssey* devotes much more space to individuals: humble folk, whose role in the *Iliad* is limited, appear much more frequently and the poet shows greater interest in their fate. It is difficult to attempt a picture of the society of the *Iliad*. What follows applies in the first instance to the *Odyssey*, and differences with the *Iliad* will be noted whenever possible.

Characteristics of the Homeric world

The central institution in the Homeric world is, or at least appears to be, the aristocratic *oikos*. The great heroes hold the front of the scene and usually act on their own behalf, as though the community did not exist. The role of the *polis* and of the community is an ambiguous one, and indeed the whole position of the *polis*, and the temptation to analyse the Homeric world more difficult to assess as one is inevitably influenced by one's knowledge of later Greek history and the subsequent emergence of the *polis*, and the temptation to analyse the Homeric world solely in relation to future Greek history is strong.

It is true that one finds cities in Homer in the sense of urban settlements, with a centre where people meet together (the *agora*). What is more, these cities are the only type of settlement known to the poet: there is no mention in Homer of villages which must have existed then in many parts of the Greek world just as they existed later. But these Homeric cities are not *poleis* in the later, classical sense – independent and sovereign political associations. The words *demos, polis, politai*, which later came to be used for these notions, are indeed found in Homer, but their content is much less full than it subsequently became. But one has occasional glimpses, for example in the scene at the *agora* of Ithaca in Book II of the *Odyssey*, of a certain community consciousness, at times in latent conflict with the aspirations of the heroes: there is therefore some tension between the Homeric city and the aristocratic *oikos*[8].

What is an *oikos*? The word is sometimes rendered 'family'[9]. But this is too narrow a translation and could be misleading. An *oikos*, even in its purely human aspect, is much more than a family in the present sense of the word (that is to say, the group of parents and children as a minimum, the nuclear family). Our concept of the 'family' in that sense cannot be translated into Greek. In its purely human aspect, it is true, the *oikos* has at its centre a more or less extended family group. But it includes also all those people, whether free or slave, who depend directly on the head of the *oikos* – all those servants who are assigned to the many tasks required by the economic life of the *oikos*. Of course, the larger and more powerful the *oikos*, the greater will be the number of dependents. In other words the *oikos* in its purely human sense is not an institution based solely on kinship.

But the notion of *oikos* covers much more than just a human group. The *oikos* includes the possessions of every kind which in practice are inseparable from the human group since they ensure its material existence. Consequently, land, buildings, livestock, reserves of all kind, equipment and so forth, are all part of the *oikos*. The *oikos* is an economic as well as a human unit, and it is managed by the head of the *oikos*, who in the Homeric world is a great war leader like Menelaus or Odysseus. From the economic point of view the ideal of the *oikos* is self-sufficiency (this ideal will enjoy a long history in the Greek world): as far as possible the *oikos* must be able to produce within itself all that it needs for its existence. There are strictly speaking no exchanges inside the *oikos*: the entire production is gathered into the hands of the head of the *oikos* who then shares it out as he wishes. The *oikos* is therefore at once a unit of production and consumption, and most of its material needs are catered for without contacts with the outside world and apart from any commercial exchanges.

What was the basis of the material wealth of an aristocratic *oikos*? In the first instance, land: the noble warriors were land-owners to start with. Already in Homer one finds the conception of agriculture as the foundation of civilization[10] [*see no 30*]. Land is used in every form, for agriculture, the cultivation of shrubs (vines, olive trees, fruit trees), the cultivation of vegetables, though in practice pastoral economy predominated (or at least, that is the impression given)[11]. The wealth of the great landowners was reckoned particularly in terms of the number of head of cattle, especially oxen, they had on their estates [*see no 24*].

Apart from landed wealth, herds and flocks (and also slaves, who can be reckoned among the chattels of the *oikos*), there was the accumulated 'treasure', kept in a special room in the centre of the manor. In it were stored food reserves, such as grain, jars of wine or oil, and also precious materials, metals both common and precious, in the shape of ingots or as weapons, tripods and cauldrons [*see no 23*]. It was not merely for strictly utilitarian purposes that one had to have as large a treasure as possible (although this motivation did exist, cf. below), but also out of prestige considerations. The power of a wealthy warrior was assessed among other things by reference to the size of his treasury and the splendour of the presents he was able to make to men of the same social standing as himself who were his guests.

As mentioned the economic ideal of the *oikos* was self-sufficiency. In practice it was not always possible to maintain this strictly, and one had to reckon with the insatiable appetite for wealth of the nobles. Among the essential commodities which the *oikos* was unable to provide were notably metals and slaves: it was thus impossible to be entirely without relations with the outside world. The way the heroes went about providing these vital necessities is revealing of the mentality and values of the Homeric world.

The first means of acquisition was simply war, and in Homer, and especially of course in the *Iliad*, war is shown in a more forthright and brutal light than subsequently in Greek history. Raids organized with a view to plunder are commonplace in Homer, and Homeric heroes are used to boasting about their exploits [*see no 25*]. Odysseus at the palace of Alkinoos begins his narrative of his travels from Troy with the following words: 'From Ilion the wind drove me along and brought me to Ismaros, in the land of the Ciconians. There I sacked the city and put the men to death. We captured from the city their wives and much treasure, and divided it all among us, in such a way that no one went away deprived of his fair share through me[12].' The booty taken from the enemy would then be shared out among those participating in the expedition, the leader being entitled to a special share[13].

War, however, could not be the only means of acquisition. To obtain metals and precious objects it was generally necessary to resort to exchanges, and war in any case had its dangers: one might be facing a stronger opponent and aggression would then recoil on the aggressor. In fact, although violence plays a great role in the Homeric poems, they are also familiar with a whole code of relations with the outside world, at least in the *Odyssey*, and by means of it exchanges could be organized without at the same time infringing aristocratic values. In the *Odyssey* (but not in the *Iliad*) one finds many examples of a technique of exchanges, that of gift and counter-gift, which is well known in many 'primitive' societies[14]. In the Homeric world, as in many archaic societies, there are no disinterested gifts: one does not give simply in order to please, but because one anticipates in the long run a gift or a service in exchange. The principle is so completely taken for granted in the Homeric world that it is never discussed: it is a practice which the poet takes as self-evident. A gift creates the obligation of a counter-gift. Thus the heroes are seen entertaining their guests and eagerly offering them 'presents' (weapons, metals, precious objects, etc.) and they inevitably expect a return in kind or compensating services [*see no 26*]. By means of this institution exchanges could be organized and gaps in self-sufficiency filled. The strictly non-commercial character of these exchanges must be emphasized; all notions of profit were systematically excluded. On the contrary the notion which operated was that of equivalence: gifts on both sides must balance each other, and there was no question of making the slightest profit on the transaction. Exchanges of this kind could thus fit acceptably into the framework of aristocratic values. Hence one will see Homeric heroes undertaking themselves long journeys to obtain by means of exchanges what was lacking in the *oikos*. But what position did commerce itself hold in the Homeric world?

Commerce existed, to some extent [*see no 30*], more in the *Odyssey* than in the *Iliad*, but was far from being very developed. There are no fairs in Homer and the *agora* of cities has no economic function, but is only a meeting place. Homer has no technical term to denote the trader; traders are for him only vague *prekteres* (that is to say, agents)[15]. The word *emporos* which later referred to the maritime trader *par excellence* still only means 'passenger' (on a ship). The only genuine specialized traders were foreigners, in particular the Phoenicians (that is to say, for the Greeks, all Levantines generally). They do not appear very much in the *Iliad*[16], but are much more conspicuous in the *Odyssey*. One sees them bringing precious objects such as works of art, trinkets and slaves. At times they can easily turn into pirates and sell their passengers into slavery. Their reputation is unfailingly bad; one welcomes their goods but one does not trust them. They did not help towards a positive evaluation of trade[17]. The place occupied by commerce in the Homeric scale of values is clear. The most explicit illustration is provided by the Phaeacians [*see no 27*]. The Phaeacians were maritime people *par excellence*; personal names among them were even derived from the sea and navigation[18]. Their naval skill was extraordinary and belonged at times to the realm of magic. But did this mean that the Phaeacians were maritime traders? In fact they had no relations with the outside world and showed nothing but distrust towards foreigners. They did not live from maritime trade, but from the land. Although a maritime people they rejected commerce, and it was precisely in Phaeacia that Odysseus suffered the supreme insult of being accused of being a trader, mindful of his wares and his profit, an insult which he could only wipe off by demonstrating in the most convincing fashion his physical prowess, and thereby his status as a hero[19].

The lower classes in Homer

Homer is primarily interested in the heroes; he therefore gives us only inadequate information concerning the lower classes. In the *Iliad* they do not count for much. The *Odyssey* shows more interest in them, not only as a group, but also as individuals (the difference in subject of course plays a part). But the margin of uncertainty remains wide: the hierarchy of the lower classes is therefore very controversial.

According to one widespread point of view, the essential criterion for determining a man's status in the Homeric world was not the possession or lack of personal freedom, but one's position in relation to the *oikos*. A man's status is not defined in the abstract but by reference to his belonging or not belonging to a group, and in the Homeric world the basic unit was the aristocratic *oikos*. Hence, it has been suggested, the lowest grade was not the position of the slave, but that of the *thete*, a free man but with no resources or property of his own, who was therefore obliged to earn a living by selling his services to someone else; he thus placed himself under someone else's dependency without for all that being sure of being paid the agreed salary. Achilles in the Underworld says he would prefer to be a *thete* on earth, working for the service of a poor man, than to rule over all the dead in the land of Hades [*see no 29*]. The life of such a *thete* was a precarious one: he was unattached and did not belong to the aristocratic *oikos* as did a slave, who from this point of view was in a more fortunate position than him.

Besides, it is clear that the status of a slave could vary a great deal in reality. There was no distinction between free man and slave in the type of work they performed (even the heroes are capable of taking part in work: as seen earlier, the negative judgment against work as such was not as pronounced then as later)[20]. Within the *oikos* the status of a slave could vary: among the slaves who belonged to the *oikos* of Odysseus, both men and women, one may distinguish two groups. Besides the ordinary slaves who only carried out the instructions given to them, there was a group of privileged slaves who enjoyed the confidence and esteem of their masters and took part in the management of the *oikos*. Eumaeus had received from Odysseus a plot of land and a wife, and in addition he had bought a slave. He had not been manumitted (the notion of manumission is unknown to Homer), but it was much the same thing. The status of Eumaeus might appear to be higher than that of some free men[21].

And yet it does not seem that one ought to deny all significance to the antithesis between free man and slave. For a start the *thete* mentioned by Achilles need not have been a typical case; the status of the *thete* might have varied in practice and need not have represented a well-defined lower limit in the social scale. Similarly with Eumaeus: his was an exceptional case, and the fate of the slave in the *Odyssey* was generally a less enviable one. In any case even Eumaeus, privileged as he was, did not become wholly free, but remained attached to the *oikos* of Odysseus. Several passages lead one to believe that the antithesis between free man and slave was already strongly felt: for a free man there is no worse misfortune than slavery, for 'Zeus takes away half a man's worth when the day of slavery comes upon him'[22].

There is little information on the other members of society. One has glimpses of the existence of independent shepherds, but one knows very little about their lot. There is no trace of dependent peasants, such as are to be found in the archaic period, but of course this does not necessarily mean that they did not exist in Homeric times. Artisans are also to be found. One special group seems to be that of the *demiourgoi*. These were not specifically artisans, since prophets, doctors, bards and heralds belonged to this group [see no 28]. Theirs were all somewhat specialized activities which did not fit into the framework of the *oikos*: the *demiourgoi*, then, were travelling specialists who offered their services to the community (that is the meaning of the word) and their skill conferred on them a somewhat special status.

Such, in broadest outline, is the society of the *Odyssey*. T¹⁴ distance which separates this world from that of the classical *polis* is obviously great, and there is no need to dwell on the point. One should rather emphasize the continuities and resemblances between this world, or rather its ethics and value system, and that of the following centuries.

The next literary source on Greek history, Hesiod, provides information about an aspect of Greek society which Homer more or less completely neglected – the life of small peasants. Hesiod parts company with Homer on a fundamental point, his complete rejection of violence and war. But, granted the difference in scale, his ideal of independence is not funamentally different from that of the Homeric *oikos*, and the spirit of gift and counter-gift is not unknown to him [see no 31]. The Homeric conception of commerce is remarkably close to the considerations of Aristotle several centuries later: commerce is mean in so far as it seeks profit, and is essentially the business of foreigners; the only admissible exchanges are those of a non-commercial kind which aim at achieving self-sufficiency [see no 2]. The ambition of Homeric heroes is to acquire through their exploits immortal fame: this same ideal will be found expressed by Pericles in his speeches in Thucydides, but transposed to the civic level and in the context of the struggles between the Greek cities.

Finally, there is an episode in the *Odyssey* to which one must draw attention, as it seems to anticipate the future, namely the utopia of the Phaeacians, the first utopia in Greek literature [see no 27]. The real world of the *Odyssey*, the world of Ithaca, is not a world of specialists. The women in the palace of Odysseus have learnt every skill; the only specialists among them are some women grinding the millstone, and one of them bewails her fate[23]. Besides, Ithaca, although an island, still remains a world of land-owners. In Phaeacia, by contrast, the women share diverse functions among themselves, and what is more this specialization of functions is linked with the naval skill of the Phaeacians. One can identify in this Utopia traits which look forward to classical

Athens centuries ahead, and this suggests of course that the Athenian model was not a complete innovation, which is something that Thucydides understood very well when he projected the model back into the past in the opening chapters of his history (the so-called *Archaeology*) [*see no 43*]. And yet it remains true that the Phaeacians who appear to us to be pointing to the future are not the heroes of the *Odyssey*. At the very moment when the first maritime and colonial ventures were taking place, Homer was telling of a world based on the land.

Notes

1 For a recent survey see M.I. Finley, *Early Greece: the Bronze and Archaic Ages* (London, 1970). J.T. Hooker, *Mycenaean Greece* (London, 1977).

2 See P. Vidal-Naquet, 'Homère et le monde mycénien, à propos d'un livre récent et d'une polémique ancienne', *Annales* 18 (1963), pp. 703–19; see also notes 3 and 4.

3 For one particular example, see M.I. Finley, 'Homer and Mycenae: Property and Tenure', *Historia* 6 (1957), pp. 153–69, reprinted in *The Language and Background of Homer*, ed. G.S. Kirk (Cambridge, 1964), pp. 191–217. For a review of the whole question, see M.I. Finley, 'Schliemann's Troy – One Hundred Years After', *Proceedings of the British Academy* LX (1974).

4 That is the position adopted by M.I. Finley, *The World of Odysseus* (revised ed., Penguin 1967; a new edition is in preparation). See also the French edition (Paris, 1969) with a bibliographical appendix by P. Vidal-Naquet. Finley defends his position in 'The World of Odysseus Revisited', *Proceedings of the Classical Association* LXXI (1974), pp. 13–31; *contra*, for a very sceptical view, see A.M. Snodgrass, 'An Historical Homeric Society?', *JHS* 94 (1974), pp. 114–25.

5 On the archaeology of the Dark Ages see V.A. Desborough, *Greece in the Dark Ages* (London, 1972), historically much less critical than A. Snodgrass, *The Dark Age of Greece: an Archaeological Survey of the 11th to the 8th Centuries B.C.* (Edinburgh, 1971), which is fundamental. On both cf. Annie Schnapp, 'Les "siècles obscurs" de la Grèce', *Annales* 29, 6 (Nov.–Dec. 1974), pp. 1465–74.

6 On this and on all that follows see Alfonso Mele, *Società e lavoro nei poemi omerici* (Naples, 1968).

7 *Iliad* II, 202.

8 See for example W. Hoffman, 'Die Polis bei Homer', *Festschrift für Bruno Snell* (Munich, 1956), pp. 153–65, reprinted in *Zur Griechischen Staatskunde*, ed. F. Gschnitzer (Darmstadt, 1969), pp. 123–38; P.A.L. Greenhalgh, 'Patriotism in the Homeric World', *Historia* 21 (1972), pp. 528–37 (who does not, however, refer to Hoffman).

9 Thus frequently W.K. Lacey, *The Family in Classical Greece* (London, 1968).

10 See P. Vidal-Naquet, 'Valeurs religieuses et mythiques de la terre et du sacrifice dans l'Odyssée', cited Chapter 1, n 16.

11 Homeric data on the land are collected by W. Richter, *Die Landwirtschaft in homerischen Zeitalter* (Gottingen, 1968), where they are unfortunately mixed with Mycenaean data.

12 *Odyssey* IX, 39–42.

13 Cf. *Iliad* I, 165–8; XIV, 365–8.

14 The role of this institution in 'primitive' societies was first seen by M. Mauss, 'Essai sur le don, forme primitive de l'échange', *Année sociologique*, 1923–4, pp. 30–186, reprinted in *Sociologie et anthropologie* (Paris, 1950). On the antecedents of this idea, cf. Marshall Sahlins, 'Philosophie politique de l'"Essai sur le Don"', *L'Homme*, Revue française d'anthropologie vol. VIII, Cahier 4 (1968), pp. 5–17; for its application to Homer see M.I. Finley, *The World of Odysseus*, pp. 73–7.

15 *Odyssey* VIII, 162. See however Chapter 3, n 11 for a more technical interpretation of this passage.

16 VI, 289–91; XXIII, 740–5.

17 *Odyssey* XIV, 287, 309; XV, 415–84; on the historicity of Homer's Phoenicians see J.D. Muhly, 'Homer and the Phoenicians', *Berytus* 19 (1970), pp. 19–64.

18 *Odyssey* VIII, 111–19.

19 *Odyssey* VIII, 145–93 (cf. n 15 above).

20 See for example *Odyssey* XXIII, 189–201.

21 *Odyssey* XIV, 5–28; 61–7; 449–52. See generally J.A. Lencman, *Die Sklaverei im mykenischen und homerischen Griechenland*, translated from the Russian (Wiesbaden, 1966).

22 *Odyssey* XVII, 322–3; cf. the fears expressed by Hector over Andromache, *Iliad* VI, 450–63.

23 *Odyssey* XX, 105–19.

3 The Archaic Period (Eighth–Sixth Centuries)

The development of the 'polis'

The archaic period is perhaps the most important period in Greek history. The civilization of classical Greece may be more striking and better known, and hence attract greater attention, yet it cannot be conceived without the period which preceded it. In every field the archaic period introduced fundamental innovations.

As far as institutions are concerned the major novelty was the development of the *polis*, which was to become the essential framework in which Greek civilization flourished for several centuries, until the Hellenistic period.

The birth of the *polis* is obscure. In fact it is difficult to try to establish an absolute beginning: the *polis* represents an 'ideal type', and all depends on what criteria one adopts. Furthermore the *polis* did not develop everywhere in the Greek world (see further Chapter 4), nor according to the same rhythm. Besides, contemporary evidence is scanty and not very explicit. The ill-defined role of the *polis* in Homer was seen earlier. According to Hesiod's *Works and Days* it would appear that in Boeotia around 700 BC the unification of city and countryside, a fundamental characteristic of the classical city, at least, had not yet taken place: for Hesiod in his village of Ascra the city of Thespiae is a distant and hostile world where rule 'the bribe-devouring kings' [*see no* 32]. The really explicit literary sources do not go further back than the second half of the seventh century[1]. Archaeology is not always of great help: urbanization does not automatically imply the development of the *polis* and, besides, urbanization proper seems to have been a fairly slow process apart from Asia Minor (cf. the excavations at Old Smyrna) and subsequently in the colonies. The most secure proof of the beginnings of the *polis* is provided by the so-called 'colonizing movement' which began towards the middle of the eighth century. More will be said later on the causes and character of colonization, but the important points here are first, that this was no haphazard drifting of populations but in each case a movement organized (to some extent) by the individual mother cities, and second that the settlements established in Sicily, south Italy, and elsewhere, were, with the exception of a few *emporia* (see below), *poleis* right from the start, which often reproduced the institutions of their mother cities, a clear proof of the existence of the *polis* from the start of the colonizing movement.

The causes of the development of the *polis* are not well known. It is customary to invoke geographical factors and to say that the physical fragmentation of Greece led to its political fragmentation. Now it is true that the developed *polis* in the classical period often fits into a physical setting characteristic of Greece. In a 'typical' *polis*, the urban settlement is established at the foot of an acropolis which serves as a place of refuge for the inhabitants. Near the urban settlement one finds the civic land, which belongs to individuals (though this would not apply to Sparta, cf. Chapter 4) and is made up of one or several fertile plains. Beyond the cultivated land one rises rapidly into the hills; one reaches the wild countryside, which belongs to the community and not to individuals, and is suitable only for pasturing [*see no 78*], or this might also be a wooded zone where woodcutters work. The urban settlement is generally located near the sea, but only rarely directly on the sea; when the city has a harbour (whether a military or a commercial one) it is often distinct from the urban settlement (the case of Athens and Peiraieus is particularly clear).

And yet the geographical explanation really proves very little. For one thing, the *polis* made only a rather belated appearance in Greek history, and the geographical factor ought to have operated earlier. For another, the distribution of *poleis* does not always correspond to geographical fragmentation. One finds few if any cities in the western parts of Greece, where more might have been expected. Attica, although fairly fragmented, constituted only one city, whereas Boeotia despite greater geographical unity was split up among several. One finds several cities in small islands like Ceos [*see no 86*] or Amorgos, but only one in the large islands of Chios and Samos. Clearly geography cannot explain everything.

It has been pointed out that there is a connection between the distribution of *poleis* in eastern and central Greece, in the islands of the Aegean and in Asia Minor, and that of the principal known Mycenaean sites. In other words some of the earliest cities grew up around former Mycenaean citadels which served as places of refuge (that is the old meaning of the word *polis*, a meaning which survived, for example, in official texts in Athens where as late as the beginning of the fourth century the word *polis* is found to designate the Acropolis). And yet one must not expect more from archaeology than it is able to provide: continuity of settlement by itself proves nothing, as for example at Salamis in Cyprus, where continuity can be traced from Mycenaean times, but which was in the classical period a highly dubious *polis*. It would seem however that the recent Swiss excavations at Eretria in Euboea reveal the transformation of a funerary monument of the eighth century centred on the tomb of a warrior into a collective place of worship in the following century². If the tomb of a warrior or a king has become the sanctuary of a hero, one may say that the transition from 'Homeric times' to the period of the archaic city has been made, but the point is that it has already been made as soon as one can observe it.

As a matter of fact the process of the emergence of the *polis* eludes us entirely and it could hardly be otherwise. Discussions on this subject serve only to show how impossible it is for us to adopt a criterion which fits simultaneously the *polis* in the early archaic period, in the classical period, or even the Hellenistic and Roman period. Any search for 'origins' is in fact a forecast of the future. Any argument can be made to stand on its head. It has just been noted that in Hesiod the peasant only feels bound to Thespiae by the hatred he feels against the judges who are despoiling him, but it might be objected that this dependence is itself a link which shows that a collective source of authority has been established. It is hard to avoid reading the past in the light of the future.

Are the two cities, the warlike and the peaceful, described by Homer in Book XVIII of the *Iliad*, with warriors on one side and judges on the other, genuine *poleis* in the classical sense? They were so without question for a fifth-century Athenian. One should add that only the end of the process is in fact known to us through the written sources. The most ancient document attesting the existence of formulae of collective decision such as 'It has been resolved by the *polis*' and of such a typically civic institution as the ban on reappointment to a magistracy within a lapse of ten years, is a Cretan inscription from Dreros, dating from the second half of the seventh century, and roughly contemporary with Draco in Athens[3]. There can be no doubt that at that time the *polis* as a collective singular or as a plural (the Athenians, the Spartiates), in other words as an organized society, has been existing for some appreciable lapse of time, but there again one is compelled to predict the past in relation to the future. One must therefore simply register the fact that the *polis* now exists and that it is the body of the citizens (a word which is also defined partly in relation to the future), a body which is sometimes more restricted, and sometimes wider, which is henceforward the ruling element. This body faces the material realities of the age and seeks to transform them.

The main achievements of the archaic age in this field may be briefly noted. First, from the seventh century onwards, there was the codification of the laws, often through the action of a legislator, a figure whose function was at once secular and public in character. The norms which governed society were defined and removed from the arbitrary interpretation of powerful men, and justice became a matter of public concern. In the terminology of Louis Gernet, one moved from the stage of *prédroit* to that of *droit*[4]. In general, the social and economic position of the citizens improved (cf. below). One main characteristic of the development of community consciousness, whether merely a sign of this evolution or a cause of it, was the so-called 'hoplite reform' which took place in the course of the seventh century: the citizen-soldier fighting in a group became the military reflection of the city [*see no 34*][5].

Concurrently with the notion of citizen there developed gradually the antithetical notions which were to be clear-cut in the classical period, first that of the non-citizen, who was outside the political community, secondly and especially that of the slave, the complete outsider, deprived of liberty and who in theory had no rights at all. The notion of citizen, in other words, was at once an inclusive and an exclusive one. The connection between the development of these two extreme and opposed notions, that of the free citizen and that of the slave, is more than a theoretical one. The archaic age witnessed simultaneously *both* the development of the notion of community and the rise of the citizens within the city, *and* the development of chattel-slavery on a substantial scale[6]. To be sure, servile labour in one form or another was not a novelty in itself in the archaic age: Homer already mentions slavery. Besides, the Greeks had been acquainted with other more archaic forms of subjection than chattel-slavery, in particular helotage, a point we shall revert to later. But the institution of chattel-slavery, and the way in which it spread, were a new development of the archaic age, and one which cannot be dissociated from the growth of the city. The Greeks themselves were aware of the fact. Thus Herodotus, when writing about events which took place in 'prehistoric' times, says: 'At that time the Athenians like the other Greeks did not have any slaves' [*see no 15*], though for the Greeks the 'beginnings' of chattel-slavery were placed before history, whereas helotage (at Sparta and elsewhere) was always thought of as having a definite origin in historical times[7]. There once existed a whole body of writing on the 'invention' of chattel-slavery from which Athenaeus collected a large number of quotations [*see nos 50, 51*]. It is interesting to see that the people of Chios were reputed to have been the first to turn to the purchase of foreign slaves, as it is precisely from Chios that comes one of the earliest pieces of evidence showing an evolution towards democracy[8]. The two processes are linked: one clear instance will be seen below in connection with Solon's reforms in Athens.

The troubles of the archaic age

These transformations in Greek history did not take place without much upheaval. In fact the archaic age was full of crises, and one must try to elucidate their causes and see what solutions were provided.

One theory which originated last century and which is due to German historians (Ed. Meyer and others) sought to relate many of the tensions of the archaic age to its social and economic development. According to this theory, an economic revolution took place from the eighth century onwards, and production, manufacture, and commerce developed on a large scale. According to some (e.g. Ed. Meyer), colonization was the consequence of this process and consisted in part in the search for new outlets for the surplus production of the Greek cities. According to others (e.g. Beloch), colonization did at least stimulate the evolution. In one way or another, analogies were drawn beween the development of Europe and that of archaic Greece. The social consequence of the economic revolution was said to be the formation of a new class of wealthy industrialists and traders who then went on to demand equality of political rights with the old landed aristocracy. One sign of the development of production and exchanges was alleged to be the invention of coinage, an invention which was also supposed to have benefited the wealthy and aggravated the difficulties of small peasants by making it easier for them to fall into debt. The tyrants of the seventh–sixth centuries were often portrayed as the champions of the new social classes, which thanks to them obtained political equality with the old aristocracy.

This theory has enjoyed great popularity, and has occasionally led to extreme exaggerations[9]. Nowadays it is certainly on the wane, but it continues to exercise its influence, and traces of it can be found almost everywhere. How much of it can be preserved?

There is no doubt, of course, that the archaic age witnessed a substantial development of manufacture and commerce, nor that colonization may have at least stimulated the process, and there are many signs of this. In Boeotia around 700 BC Hesiod still knows only of the seasonal trade of the farmer who disposes elsewhere of his agricultural surplus[10]. But already in the seventh century maritime commerce becomes an activity in its own right, even if it had not been earlier: the word *emporos* in the sense of 'maritime trader' appears, whereas in Homer it did not as yet have a technical meaning[11]. The trading vessel becomes differentiated from the warship. Instances will be seen below of Greek settlements abroad of a purely economic kind and of the development of trade with non-Greek countries and peoples. As for the development of manufacture there is tangible archaeological proof of the flourishing of the pottery workshops in the seventh and sixth centuries, in particular in Corinth, Asia Minor and Athens. But it must be said that it is the only Greek manufacture of any importance of which one can form a reasonably accurate picture and that one should not generalize from pottery alone and treat it as a reliable index of economic activity as a whole (although this has been done time and again). Nevertheless there is no doubt that there grew up in the archaic age an urban *demos* based on manufacture. In general there are many signs of rising prosperity in the Greek world. Archaeological finds are richer and more varied than in the previous period. Architecture develops (civic buildings, temples, etc.), and offerings in sanctuaries bear witness to a new prosperity and exchanges with foreign countries (there are many objects imported from the East), and the taste for luxury goods spreads among the upper classes. It is likely that the development of manufacture and commerce contributed to this in some way. Cases are known in the archaic age of successful traders who made a fortune; to be sure, these may represent exceptional cases, but at least it was becoming possible to live from things other than the land [*see no 40*]. Besides, the development of commerce must have made some indirect contribution to the prosperity of the cities by enabling them to raise revenues by means of taxes on economic activity: such was the case with Corinth which was outstandingly well placed to control the traffic by land between the Peloponnese and central Greece and by sea between the Saronic gulf and the gulf of Corinth (as early as the seventh century, a towpath – the *diolkos* – was built across the isthmus of Corinth). The oligarchy of the Bacchiads which preceded the tyranny of the Cypselids did not fail to exploit its position [*see nos 42, 43*]. All this, then, seems to be well established, but much less certain are the presumed consequences of the evolution in the social and political fields.

One must note first the silence or imprecision of the available sources: whether contemporary or of later date they give no sign of the rise of a new social class based economically on commerce and industry. It is true that Theognis complains of the coming to power of the 'wicked' *nouveaux riches* who set themselves at the head of the city at the expense of the power of the 'good men' (the aristocracy) [*see no 33*]; but he does not tell us anything concrete about the economic basis of this transformation[12]. The aristocracies of the archaic period, including that of the Bacchiads, were, as far as is known, essentially landed aristocracies. It is significant that when, in 594, the Athenian Solon decided to introduce census groups for the attribution of political power, the only criterion of wealth which he recognized was that of agricultural produce, and hence of landed wealth. The sources are usually not very explicit about the social and economic background of the conflicts of the time. To give but one example, there were political disturbances in Asia Minor (notably Ionia) in the course of the sixth century, which often resulted in the seizure of power by tyrants. Were these disturbances connected with the economic development of Ionia? That has been assumed[13], but in fact the sources are by no means explicit and it is difficult to catch glimpses of the social and economic background of the history of Ionia in the sixth century. One must be careful not to extrapolate where precise evidence is lacking. Wherever the sources are somewhat more explicit, it would appear that in so far as the conflicts had an economic aspect the problems were in one way or another related to the land: we shall see a specific case in connection with Athens later on.

The origins of coinage

We may digress here on the subject of coinage: substantial progress has recently been made in the study and interpretation of its origins. First, there is a wide measure of agreement among many numismatists that the chronology of the earliest issues (produced in Asia Minor) should be brought down to the second half of the seventh century. As a result the chronology of the other coinages of the archaic age would have to be adjusted downwards[14]. But that is not the most significant point. Recent studies have renewed the conception historians had of the reasons for the invention and spread of coinage and have shifted the emphasis to the non-economic aspects of the process[15]. It used to be believed that coinage had from the very beginning the economic function of serving as a standard of value in order to facilitate exchange. It seemed quite natural to suppose that the invention of coinage was intended to serve that purpose, and that it therefore provided decisive proof of the development of exchanges in the archaic period and of the beginnings of a monetary economy.

And yet the problem is a more complex one: it does not appear that coinage necessarily had from the beginning the same significance and function that it subsequently had. First of all it has been pointed out that Aristotle, who is familiar with the purely economic explanation of the invention of coinage, seems also to have preserved if not the memory then at least the concept of an ethical explanation of the role of coinage [see nos 2, 44]. The invention and spread of coinage would have to be placed in the framework of the development of social relations and the definition of values, a fundamental tendency of the archaic age, when laws were codified and published in order to remove them from arbitrary interpretation. The life of the civic community could not be conceived without the existence and enforcement of norms known to all, and the invention of coinage would fit into this context. Indeed, there are signs of the continued 'ethical' function of coinage in the classical period.

In addition, the study of Greek coin hoards of the sixth and fifth centuries has led to important conclusions. The absence of small denominations in the coinage of many cities implies that the invention of coinage did not aim initially at facilitating local trade. Furthermore large denominations do not seem to have circulated very widely outside their area of issue (as for example the Sicilian coinages); circulation of goods and circulation of coinages do not by any means overlap systematically[16], and long-distance trade need not have been one of the factors in the creation of coinage. There are two exceptions to this rule: Athens and the cities on the coast of Thrace and Macedon. Their coinages are found widely exported abroad, notably in the Levant and in Egypt. But it is clear that they were exported strictly for their metallic value as silver, and not as money proper. Both areas had silver mines available and were in a position to produce sufficient metallic currency for it to be exported in large quantities. It is also certain that these coinages were exported by people other than the Athenians or the Greeks of the coast of Thrace; they do not therefore prove by themselves the existence of a direct commercial link between their place of origin and the place they were found[17].

What then is the significance of the invention and spread of coinage? Various considerations have been put forward (besides the general phenomenon of the normalization of social life), such as the development of the fiscal role of the state (fines, taxes), the financing of mercenary armies (subsequently there will often be a link between the issuing of coinage and the financing of mercenaries). One must emphasize especially the development of civic consciousness: in the history of the Greek cities coinage was always first and foremost a civic emblem. To strike coins with the badge of the city was to proclaim one's political independence[18]. When Athens in the fifth century tried (but without complete success) to ban the silver coinages of her allies and impose her own, the significance of this step was probably in the first instance political: the idea was to demonstrate in this way the power of

Athens [*see no 101*]. The rapid spread of coinage during the sixth century, which was to begin with a purely Greek phenomenon (although the very first coins were struck in Lydia), is thus to be linked with the phenomenon of the development of the cities and of civic consciousness. Once more it can be seen that it is impossible to reach 'economics' in a pure form.

Agrarian aspects of the crisis
It seems that the economic causes of the crises of the archaic period – when it is possible to catch a glimpse of them – were connected directly or indirectly with the land, and the demands of an economic kind which were heard then, as later in Greek history, centred around the land.

Many parts of the Greek world seem to have suffered from the eighth century onwards from overpopulation, attested to indirectly by the considerable increase in the size and numbers of settlements revealed by archaeology. This overpopulation was certainly more relative than absolute, and was in itself indicative of a decline in the mortality rate. The difficulties presented by this were aggravated by the inadequate use of the soil, an unequal distribution of the land (one does not know how it was 'originally' made) and the practice of dividing estates among heirs, a practice which is already attested in Homer and Hesiod (the starting point of the *Works and Days* is the partition which was made between Hesiod and his brother Perses at their father's death). Such partitions disadvantaged small landowners who could not divide up their land endlessly without being reduced to poverty[19]. In particular there was the greed of the wealthy and powerful landlords, who were in power everywhere and were only too prepared to enlarge their estates and increase the size of their dependent labour force. There are two contemporary sources on this tension between the great and the small landowners, namely Hesiod for Boeotia around 700 BC and Solon for Athens at the beginning of the sixth century. But one must not make them both say the same thing: they deal with two different places and a century or more separates them.

Hesiod complains about the greed of the 'kings' (that is to say the aristocracy) of Thespiae, whom he describes as 'bribe-devouring' kings who give 'crooked sentences' and violate justice through the lure of gain [*see no 32*]. The world described by this peasant-poet, who uses the language of Homer, and codifies agricultural labour as well as divine genealogies, is the world of the 'race of iron', condemned to work, a harsh, complex and contradictory world, in which it is difficult to sort out what is a description of reality from what is a norm put forward for the benefit of landowners with small or medium-sized holdings. The poet is not addressing himself to a poor audience when he says for example:

> Set your slaves to winnow Demeter's holy grain, when strong Orion first appears, on a smooth threshing floor in an airy place. Then measure it and store it in jars. And so soon as you have safely stored all your stuff indoors, I bid you put your labourer out of doors and look for a servant girl with no children – for a servant with a child to nurse is troublesome. And look after a dog with jagged teeth, without grudging him his food . . . Bring in fodder and litter so as to have enough for your oxen and mules. After that, let your men rest their knees and unyoke your pair of oxen[20].

Hesiod can give to his brother the following double and contradictory piece of advice:

> You should have only one son, to feed his father's house, for so wealth will increase in the home; but if you leave a second son you should die old. Yet Zeus can easily give great wealth to a greater number. More hands means more work and more increase[21].

Profit therefore does exist, and human activity is possible. Admittedly Hesiod is not the prophet of social revolution that he has been claimed to be, as has also (and with as little justification) his contemporary the prophet Amos, but against the 'bribe-devouring kings' he raises the demand (which one might call a social one) of the justice of Zeus. One might describe him as the witness of the rise of the hoplites without whom the cities cannot face their enemies, and who almost everywhere begin to play the leading role in them from the early seventh century onwards[22].

The evidence of Solon, a century later, is completely different [*see no 36*]. It is not however by any means clear, even when we have his own words – or rather the citations from his poems which have been preserved. Solon's time is that of the beginnings of a civil war in which he is the arbiter. Zeus and the gods are still the supreme authorities to whom Hesiod appealed, but in a way which the lapse of time causes to appear dramatic they have become integrated in the institutions of the city. What is the issue at the heart of this civil war, a culmination of which we do not know the beginnings[23]? It is usually assumed that the essential problem was that of debt: the mass of the Athenians had in one way or another placed itself in debt with the wealthy and had been reduced to the status of *hectemoroi*, that is to say 'sixth-parters' who were compelled to pay to their creditors one-sixth of their produce (these are none-monetary loans, similar to those already mentioned by Hesiod). In case of default they might be sold as slaves, which happened in many cases: up to the time of Solon loans were made on the security of persons.

And yet it is likely that the situation was in reality more complex. It is probably incorrect to assimilate all the indebted Athenians to the hectemors. These constituted perhaps a separate group, the origins of which are lost in time. They were the people who were liable to be sold in slavery in case of default. On the other hand there was a mass of Athenians who were debt-bondsmen: the debt, rather than default, may well have been the cause of their bondage. Parallels drawn from other societies allow this inference: small peasants placed themselves under the dependence of great landlords to protect their livelihood, and the latter sought in this way to increase the size of their labour force. On both sides the debt (or the loan, according to the point of view) would have been only a means in the transaction, and not an end in itself.

The evidence of Solon does not of course explain why what had been tolerated for a long time suddenly ceased to be, nor does it reveal anything about the forms taken by the struggle of the classes. More will be said later about the reforms: an extraordinary cascade of legislation, affecting every aspect of communal life, from party walls to weights and measures, and – a fact of capital social importance – this legislation was written and public.

The case of Athens is the only one known in any detail in the archaic period. But it is certain that similar problems must have arisen elsewhere in the Greek world; there are some indirect indications of this, notably for Ionia.

The different solutions to the crisis: colonization

One of the most important characteristics of the archaic age was what is conventionally, though misleadingly, referred to as the 'colonizing movement', which started towards the middle of the eighth century and went on to about the end of the sixth, and scattered Greek cities in Sicily, south Italy, along the south coast of France and the east coast of Spain, in Cyrenaica, along the coast of Thrace, and on the shores of the Helles-pont and the Black Sea. The colonizing movement was clearly linked to the problems which affected the Greek world at this period.

Colonization has often been discussed according to this simple alternative: did it represent a search for new land or was it motivated by trade? The formulation is not a satisfactory one. For one thing, one needs to define what one means by 'trade', which can mean either the search for markets (export trade), or the quest for vital necessities (import trade), or transit trade. For another, the two alternatives are not necessarily mutually ex-clusive. In fact to explain the vast movement which led the Greeks to spread out around the Mediterranean and the Black Sea, one must introduce several different factors and distinguish between different types of settlements[24].

There is first the essential distinction between the typical 'colony', the *apoikia*, which was founded from the outset to become an independent city (although more or less close rela-tions, depending on circumstances and periods, would subse-quently be maintained with the mother city)[25], and the strictly commercial settlement, the *emporion*, of which several cases are known in the archaic period.

The typical colonies, and by far the most numerous, were essentially agrarian settlements, as is now generally accepted, and as a whole series of indications leads one to suppose. The Greeks in the classical period took it for granted that the effect of colonization was to act as a safety valve against overpopulation[26]. Admittedly, the stories of the foundation of particular colonies are generally not very revealing, but occasionally they give hints that the search for new land abroad was the main purpose of the undertaking, with an element of compulsion entering into the despatching of colonists by the mother cities [*see no 45*]. In some colonies the first settlers were called the *gamoroi*, that is to say 'those who shared the land' (at Syracuse, for instance). The sites

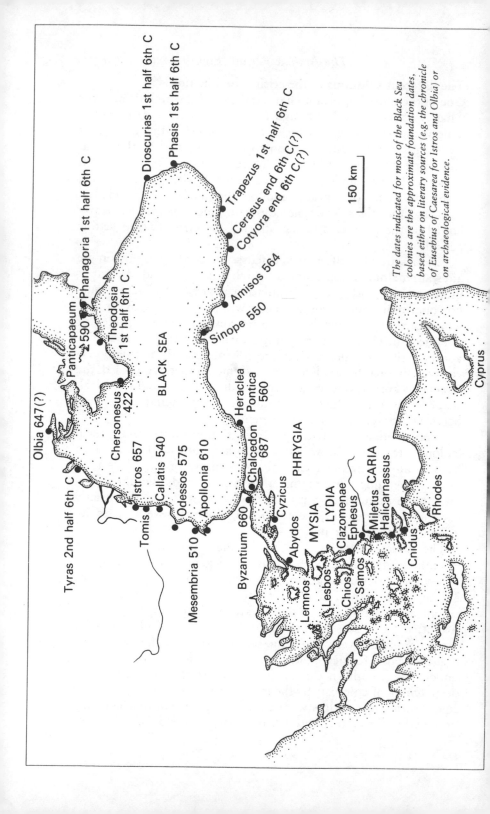

Olbia 647(?)

Tyras 2nd half 6th C

Tomis

Istros 657

Callatis 540

Odessos 575

Mesembria 510

Apollonia 610

Chersonesus 422

Panticapaeum
↙590

Theodosia 1st half 6th C

Phanagoria 1st half 6th C

Dioscurias 1st half 6th C

Phasis 1st half 6th C

Trapezus 1st half 6th C

Cerasus end 6th C(?)

Cotyora end 6th C(?)

Amisos 564

Sinope 550

BLACK SEA

Heraclea
Pontica
560

PHRYGIA

Chalcedon
687

Byzantium 660

Cyzicus

Abydos

MYSIA

Lemnos

Lesbos

Chios

Samos

Clazomenae

Ephesus

LYDIA

Miletus CARIA

Halicarnassus

Cnidus

Rhodes

Cyprus

150 km

*The dates indicated for most of the Black Sea
colonies are the approximate foundation dates,
based either on literary sources (e.g. the chronicle
of Eusebius of Caesarea for Istros and Olbia) or
on archaeological evidence.*

of many colonies were obviously chosen because of the fertility of the neighbouring territory: so, for example, the colonies in Sicily and south Italy where Metapontum adopted as its symbol on coins a perfectly explicit ear of corn. The search for new land, then, was the principal cause of archaic colonization. Little is known of the system of land tenure which was instituted in the new colonies, and it is likely that conditions varied from one colony to another[27]. It is not known how far allotments of land were meant to be egalitarian nor how far plots once divided up were considered to be inalienable. In any case, whatever the original state of affairs, inequalities frequently developed subsequently. One source of tension could arise from the inequality between the first settlers or their descendants and later comers (for example in Cyrene [*see no 45*]). But it seems also that the possibility of a fresh arrival of settlers might be catered for and that virgin land would be set aside with them in mind. Some colonies struck deep roots and sought to enlarge their territory at the expense of the natives (Syracuse, Gela); others, by contrast, quickly reached the limit of their expansion (Tarentum, Megara Hyblaea). But in any case agricultural settlements controlled a much wider territory than the strictly commercial settlements.

Such were the typical colonies: autonomous agricultural communities founded under the aegis of a mother city which provided the *oikistes* (the founder) and presumably also provided ships, technicians, etc. to found the new colony. Colonization bears witness to the magnitude of the population crisis which affected a large part of the Greek world. Many cities participated in it directly to a greater or lesser extent. Other cities took part indirectly, for it is well attested that even when a foundation was made under the aegis of a particular city, it happened quite often that men from other cities joined in the undertaking. This must probably be how some cities managed to collect an impressive number of colonies which they could hardly have founded on their own (thus, notably, the many Milesian foundations around the Black Sea).

Among these typical settlements there is a further distinction to be added, the distinction between those that were strictly self-sufficient and depended for their livelihood only on the cultivation of their territory by the settlers themselves, and those which relied partly or wholly on a 'barbarian' labour force, consisting

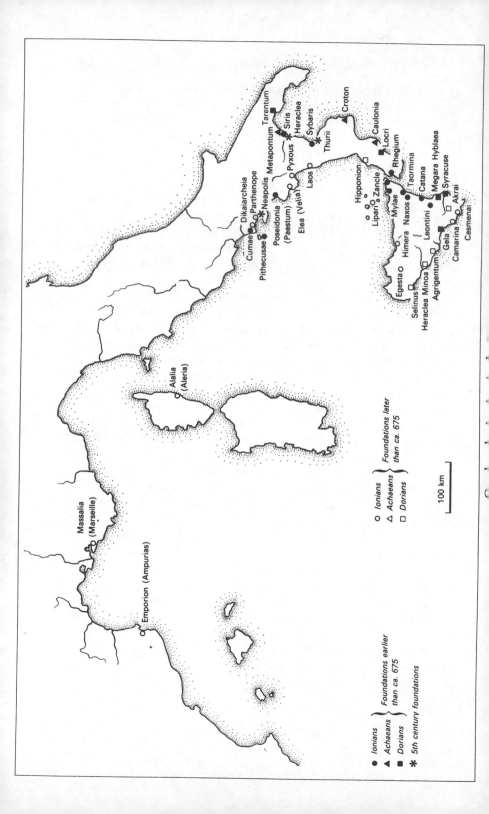

Ionians ●   Ionians ○ } Foundations later
Achaeans ▲   Achaeans △ } than ca. 675
Dorians ■   Dorians □ }
          ✳ 5th century foundations

} Foundations earlier
} than ca. 675

100 km

Emporion (Ampurias)

Massalia (Marseille)

Alalia (Aleria)

Cumae
Dikaiarcheia
Pithecusae
Parthenope
Neapolis
Poseidonia (Paestum)
Elea (Velia)
Laos
Pyxous
Metapontum
Tarentum
Siris
Heraclea
Sybaris
Thurii
Croton
Caulonia
Locri
Hipponion
Rhegium
Zancle
Lipari
Mylae
Taormina
Naxos
Catana
Leontini
Megara Hyblaea
Syracuse
Akrai
Casmenai
Camarina
Gela
Himera
Agrigentum
Heraclea Minoa
Selinus
Egesta

of native populations enslaved by the Greeks at their arrival and compelled by them to cultivate the land.

This form of subjection of native peoples represents a fairly archaic institution, quite different from classical chattel-slavery, and which existed in certain parts of the Greek world already before the start of colonization[28]. In this category must be placed the *Helots* of Sparta, the *Klarotai* of Crete, the *Woikiatai* of eastern Locris, and the *Penestai* of Thessaly: more will be said about these in the following chapter. There may have been more elsewhere. One major gap in our knowledge concerns the situation in the Greek settlements of Asia Minor, the foundation of which goes back to the Dark Age and which do not belong to the same movement as the colonization of the eighth century and after. It has been assumed that in some cities the Greeks had reduced the natives to the status of dependents (as for example at Miletus where the *Gergithes* might be just one such group). But there is no definite evidence for this period, and it would seem doubtful that the same was true everywhere: the people of Chios, at any rate, would hardly have resorted to the large-scale purchase of barbarian slaves to cultivate their land if they had had a class of dependent natives at home.

The evidence on those colonies which made use of the labour of natives reduced to the condition of dependents is inadequate. The certain, or fairly certain, cases occur at Syracuse (the *Killyrioi*) and probably also in other cities of Sicily and south Italy; occasionally it is possible to interpret certain archaeological data along these lines (as the disappearance of native necropoleis coinciding with the arrival of Greek settlers and the enslavement of the natives)[29]. They are also found in the east, at Byzantium (the *Bithynians*), at Heraclea Pontica (the *Mariandynians*); it even appears possible that the subjection of native peoples was more or less the rule in all the Greek colonies around the Black Sea[30].

Such were the typical agricultural foundations of the archaic period; but the search for new land was not the only aim of the maritime enterprises of the Greeks at this time. There can be no doubt that the search for certain indispensable commodities (metals to start with) led the Greeks to come and settle abroad to trade with barbarian peoples; it was seen earlier how Homeric heroes did not disdain to travel themselves to carry out certain essential exchanges. It even seems probable that these commercial settlements may in some cases have preceded the start of the colonizing movement proper towards the middle of the eighth century. One example has been brought to light by archaeology, namely the half-Greek and half-Levantine settlement at the mouth of the river Orontes in northern Syria at a place called Al Mina (the Greek name is not known for sure). Greek presence there goes back perhaps to the end of the ninth century. It has proved possible to identify with a high degree of probability the Greeks who traded there from their pottery. Up to the end of the eighth century they were mostly Euboeans from Chalcis and Eretria, who had probably come in search of metals (and Euboea enjoyed some reputation for metalwork). It is also the Euboeans who a little later founded the first colonies in the west at Ischia and Cumae. It is possible that there too trade in metals with the Etruscans was one of the aims of these settlements, though this time they were not solely commercial settlements, for they lived off the territory they occupied and constituted autonomous civic communities, whereas Al Mina does not appear to have been a genuine *polis*, but only a meeting place for Greeks and non-Greeks for the purpose of exchanges.

The best-known commercial settlement in this period is Naukratis in the Nile Delta in Egypt [*see no 48*]. The settlement was quite different from a typical colony[31]. Naukratis had not been 'founded' as, for example, Syracuse was by Corinth. She owed her existence to the private initiative of a number of traders who had for the most part come from Asia Minor and the neighbouring islands, and also from Aegina. The beginnings of Naukratis date from around the end of the seventh century. The traders obtained from the Pharaoh the right to build sanctuaries to their gods. Besides this trading community there was another Greek settlement, apparently of a non-commercial kind, though very little is known of it. Was this other settlement a *polis*? The problem is an obscure one. What matters is that even if there was in Naukratis a *polis* as early as the archaic age, it first developed only after the arrival of the traders, who were the initial cause of the growth of Naukratis, and secondly the traders had no part in it. In other words the economic settlement was not a civic settlement; the same might apply to Al Mina, as well as to other settlements of the same kind.

Naukratis is the best-known example at this period of what Polanyi called the 'port of trade', a purely economic settlement

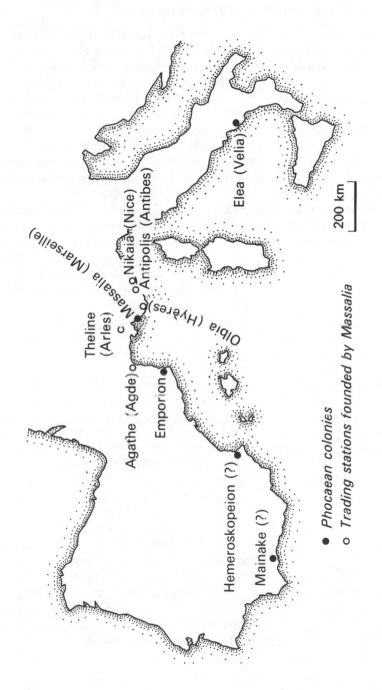

● *Phocaean colonies*

○ *Trading stations founded by Massalia*

Theline (Arles)

Agathe (Agde)

Massalia (Marseille)

Olbia (Hyères)

Antipolis (Antibes)

Nikaia (Nice)

Emporion

Hemeroskopeion (?)

Mainake (?)

Elea (Velia)

200 km

Emporion was probably founded by Phocaea then taken over by Massalia. (For a critical survey of Phocaean colonization see J.P. Morel, BCH, 99, 2 (1975), pp. 853–96.)

3   The Phocaean foundations in the West

through which exchanges between two societies of different economic types could be organized and controlled[32]. What is known of Naukratis is instructive: the Greek settlement depended on the Pharaoh who exercised a strict watch over it. All the trade between Egypt and the Greek world was channelled and therefore controlled through this port. In Naukratis the Greek quarter was clearly separated from the Egyptian one, and mixed marriages between Greeks and Egyptians were expressly forbidden (whereas the Greek and Carian mercenaries who were permanently settled in Egypt had the right of intermarriage with Egyptian women).

Should one go further and suppose that some cities (along the lines opened up by the activity of Chalcis and Eretria) had a commercial and maritime activity in which large-scale trade was as completely civic in character as for example warfare? The evidence of Herodotus, on the Phocaeans, whose colonies, it has been noted, whether direct foundations by themselves (Massilia, Velia) or indirect (Emporion in Catalonia founded by Massilia [*see no 47*]), did not seek to conquer a wide strip of territory, is striking and coherent. The Phocaeans, he writes[33], were the first long-distance navigators, and their journeys were not made with the round vessels which are typical of commerce, but with warships propelled by 50 oarsmen (penteconters). Their friendship with the Iberian king of Tartessos (near Cadiz) brought them so much silver that they built with it a wall which protected the whole of their city, and which may have been the only one of its kind in Ionia. Alone among the Greeks of Asia Minor they answered the Persian invasion with a collective refusal to stay on the spot[34]. The men of Chios refused to yield to them some small islands for fear that they might turn them into an *emporion* from which they would be excluded[35]. During the revolt of Ionia in 498, it was their admiral Dionysios who tried to impose on the Ionians the rudiments of the naval skill which Athens was to practise later. This same Dionysios, still refusing to yield, subsequently went on to practise a rather special form of commerce known as piracy, but was careful not to attack any Greek ship[36]. The case of Phocaea is therefore a remarkable one, in which traders and warriors followed the same civic model, but it is a case that one should be careful not to generalize[37].

The imports of corn

One important economic novelty of the archaic period was the development of an import trade in corn towards the Greek world. This trade seems to have begun towards the end of the seventh century. There is no decisive proof of this, but the surest indication is in fact the establishment of the port of Naukratis in Egypt at about this time. Egypt was subsequently one of the principal granaries of the ancient world, and it is legitimate to suppose that Naukratis was intended right from the start to promote the grain trade with Egypt (at least to some extent). It is also at the same time that the Greek colonization on the northern shore of the Black Sea started, and that region also supplied in the classical period grain to certain Greek cities of the Aegean, notably Athens, though whether this was true of the archaic period as well has been doubted [*see nos 80, 81*]. In both cases, the activity in Egypt and the activity in the Black Sea, the largest share in the initial enterprise was undertaken by Greeks of Asia Minor (see the list of cities which participated in the trade of Naukratis [*see no 48*]).

This may not be a coincidence: it may be that this move corresponds to the pressure which these cities of Asia Minor came under at that time, notably on the part of the Lydian kingdom. The imports of grain would then have constituted originally a means of facing these pressures and freeing oneself from total dependence on one's own territory[38]. But once the example had been given it was to be followed by others. It is possible that the Greek cities of Sicily exported corn to the Greek world already in the archaic age, but there is no direct proof of this. During the sixth century Athens began to show interest in the problem of the import of foodstuffs. Solon placed a ban on the export of all Athenian agricultural produce from Attica with the exception of olive oil. Though there may not be any proof of Athenian activity in Egypt at this period, the Athenians sought on the other hand to secure the control of the straits leading to the Black Sea, perhaps already in Solon's time, and in any case certainly under the tyranny of Peisistratus (cf. the Athenian settlements at Sigeum and in the Thracian Chersonese). One is still a long way from the policy of large-scale food imports known in the classical period, but this is at least the prelude to it.

Redistribution of land and improvement in the status of the peasants

Colonial emigration was one of the available solutions to deal with the problem of the relative overpopulation of Greece. But what happened to all those who stayed at home or were unable to leave?

The answer varies from place to place, or at least those places for which some evidence is available. And yet the general tendency of the period is clear; with the development of the *polis*, community consciousness comes into full play. The development of the notion of citizen implied the development of new aspirations and new demands. Mention was made earlier of the role of legislators and the codification of the laws. During the seventh century tyrants also made their appearance in Greek history. The causes of tyranny vary from place to place, but most often tyranny was anti-aristocratic in character [*see no 39*]. Its function was to put an end to the quarrels of the aristocracy, to check its greed and ostentation, and to promote the rise in the *polis* of the lower classes on which tyrants based their support. It was during the seventh century that the characteristic slogan of Greek history – redistribution of land – made its appearance. It is attested in Sparta at the time of Tyrtaeus, in Megara, in Athens at the time of Solon; it must have been heard elsewhere too. Some tyrants must have carried out a redistribution of land (for example the Cypselids in Corinth)³⁹; Solon connects redistribution of land with tyrannical violence [*see no 36*]. In addition the tyrants contributed to the development of civic consciousness, through the building of temples, civic monuments, the promotion of religious festivals and popular cults such as that of Dionysus, the creation of a currency. This is all the more remarkable as the tyrants were more or less always in some sense in a marginal position in relation to the city. Their power was a *de facto* one, which could not be expressed in an acceptable way in the institutions of the city: tyrants existed in a sense apart from the *polis*. But at the same time their power and success depended on the promotion of the interests of the community.

The only example of an agrarian crisis of the archaic period for which any detail is available comes from Athens [*see no 36*]. The main elements of the crisis were seen above, namely the existence of a category of 'hectemors' who could be sold into slavery, the debt-bondage to which many Athenians were subject, and the excesses of the aristocracy. Solon's solution reflects the development of community consciousness: the fact is that the existence of hectemors and debt-bondage had long seemed acceptable. In addition, it was not slavery as such that Solon was opposed to [*see no 51B*], but only the reduction to slavery of Athenians, and especially of Athenians in Athens. Solon's reform was strictly a matter between Athenians and did not affect the foreigners in Athens, whether slaves or others. Solon's solution was a drastic one: he abolished once and for all the status of hectemor, he brought back (so far as was possible) the Athenians who had been sold in slavery abroad, he cancelled existing debts and for the future banned slavery for debt. Henceforward there were no longer any Athenian subjects in Athens. Solon, however, was careful not to redistribute the land, as many Athenians from the lower classes were urging him: redistribution of land was for him a tyrannical measure. Peisistratus has often been credited with the redistribution of land which Solon had refused to carry out. Yet this does not seem very likely: the silence of the sources seems decisive, and the tradition on the tyranny in Athens is fairly abundant. It is doubtful whether a large-scale redistribution of land, had it taken place, would not have left any traces in the tradition. How then should one explain the importance of small- and medium-sized holdings which was the pattern in the classical period? Here one must resort to conjecture. What may have happened was that the liberation by Solon of the hectemors and the debt-bondsmen automatically brought about their transformation into small free landowners: it was not quite the redistribution of land asked for by many, but it was a considerable step forward. What then happened to the other Athenians who had been disappointed in their hopes? Some quite probably turned towards manufacture (and it is a fact that the pottery production of Athens expanded on a large scale under the tyranny, though once more one should not generalize from the evidence of pottery alone, nor should one assume without explicit evidence that the tyrants deliberately fostered the process). Others may have found employment in the building projects of the tyrants. Others probably took part in Athenian settlements abroad, at Sigeum, in the Thracian Chersonese, at Chalcis in 506 where the Athenians sent 4,000 settlers on estates confiscated from the Hippobotai, the aristocracy of 'knights' of Chalcis, during a war against that city.

The significance of Solon's reforms must be underlined. They proclaimed that henceforward no Athenian would ever again be a slave in Athens: there would no longer be any internal subjects. Athens became in the classical period the city in which the citizen saw his power and his rights develop further than anywhere else; but it was at the same time the city in which chattel-slavery achieved its greatest extent. There is more to it than mere coincidence: it is in fact the clearest case for which it is possible to establish a connection between the two processes: on the one hand the development of the notion of the free citizen and the elimination of internal subjects, on the other the development of a new form of servitude, that of chattel-slaves imported from abroad. But from the archaic to the classical periods, there does remain one common denominator all the same – the need for subjects.

Notes

1 Cf. V. Ehrenberg, 'When Did the *Polis* Rise?', *JHS* 57 (1937), pp. 147–59; id., 'An Early Source of *Polis*-Constitution', *CQ* 37 (1943), pp. 14–18, both reprinted in *Polis und Imperium* (Zurich, 1965), pp. 83–97 and 98–104.
2 See Cl. Bérard, *Eretria* III (Bern, 1970), though cf. Cl. Rolley, *Revue Archéologique* fasc. 2, 1974, pp. 307–11. [See now *Cahiers du Centre Jean Bérard*, II, Naples, 1975.]
3 Meiggs–Lewis no 2.
4 L. Gernet, 'Droit et prédroit en Grèce ancienne', *Année sociologique* 1951, pp. 21–119, reprinted in *Anthropologie de la Grèce antique* (Paris, 1968), pp. 175–260.
5 On the 'hoplite reform' see A.M. Snodgrass, 'The Hoplite Reform and History', *JHS* 85 (1965), pp. 110–22; M. Détienne, 'La phalange: problèmes et controverses', in *Problèmes de la guerre en Grèce ancienne* ed. J.P. Vernant (Paris and The Hague, 1968), pp. 119–42; P.A.L. Greenhalgh, *Early Greek Warfare* (Cambridge, 1973).
6 M.I. Finley, *Historia* 8 (1959), p. 164.
7 See P. Vidal-Naquet, 'Réflexions sur l'historiographie grecque de l'esclavage', *Actes du Colloque 1971 sur l'esclavage* (Paris, 1973), pp. 25–44.

8 Meiggs-Lewis no 8. This evolution towards democracy does not however appear to have been pursued subsequently.

9 This applies, for example, to P.N. Ure, *The Origin of Tyranny* (Cambridge, 1921).

10 *Works and Days*, 618–94.

11 The question of the personnel of archaic trade is, however, an obscure one and there is little concrete evidence to go on. A valuable new hypothesis has been put forward by B. Bravo, *Dialogues d'histoire ancienne* I (1974), pp. 51–4 (to be elaborated in a forthcoming study in *Dialogues d'histoire ancienne* III), according to which in the archaic age in the absence of the metic system and of the technique of maritime loans known to us in Athens in the late fifth and fourth centuries (see Chapters 5 and 7) trade may often have been conducted on behalf of wealthy landowners by men who were in one way or another their dependents. B. Bravo interprets the *prekteres* of *Odyssey* VIII, 162 as being traders of this kind, and conjectures a similar relationship of dependence between Achillodoros and Anaxagores in the lead letter from Berezan [*see no 41*].

12 S.I. Oost, 'The Megara of Theagenes and Theognis', *CP* 68 (1973), pp. 186–96, is, like others, speculative.

13 Notably by C. Roebuck, *Ionian Trade and Colonization* (1959), p. 137; *TAPA* 92 (1961), p. 506.

14 See notably E.S.G. Robinson, 'The Coins from the Ephesian Artemision reconsidered', *JHS* 71 (1951), pp. 156–67; id., 'The Date of the Earliest Coins', *NC* 1956, pp. 1–8; W.L. Brown, 'Pheidon's Alleged Aeginetan Coinage', *NC* 1950, pp. 177–204. A reappraisal of the chronology is announced by M. Price and N. Waggoner, *Archaic Greek Coinage* (London, 1976); C.M. Kraay, *Archaic and Classical Greek Coins* (London, 1976). See now Ph. Grierson, *The Origins of Money* (London, 1977).

15 See Ed. Will, 'De l'aspect éthique des origines grecques de la monnaie', *Revue historique* 212 (1954), pp. 209–31; id., 'Réflexions et hypothèses sur les origines de la monnaie', *Revue de numismatique* 17 (1955), pp. 5–23; id., 'Fonctions de la monnaie dans les cités grecques de l'époque classique', in the collective volume *Numismatique antique, problèmes et methodes* (Nancy and Louvain, 1975), pp. 233–46; R.M. Cook, 'Speculations on the Origin of Coinage', *Historia* 7

(1958), pp. 257–62; C.M. Kraay, 'Hoards, Small Change and the Origins of Coinage', *JHS* 84 (1964), pp. 76–91; cf. P. Vidal-Naquet, in *Annales* 23 (1968), pp. 206–8.

16 For one good illustration over a long period of time see E. Schönert-Geiss, 'Die Wirtschafts- und Handelsbeziehungen zwischen Griechenland and der nordlichen Schwarzmeerküste im Spiegel der Münzfunde (6.-l.Jh.v.u.Z.)', *Klio* 53 (1971), pp. 105–17.

17 Cf. M.M. Austin, *Greece and Egypt in the Archaic Age* (Cambridge, 1970), pp. 37–40, with bibliography.

18 For one particular example in the second half of the sixth century (the creation of a Boeotian coinage following the formation of the Boeotian league), see J. Ducat, *BCH* 97 (1973), pp. 71–2.

19 One may mention by the way a modern theory on land tenure in the early archaic age. According to some historians land remained for a long time under a system of joint-ownership by the family in the wider sense; according to others there had even existed a system of collective ownership by the members of the same village or tribe [*see no 49*]. Individual ownership by the head of the *oikos* then only developed gradually and sometimes in conflict with the earlier forms of ownership. But the sources on which these theories are based are scanty and unreliable. Already in Homer the system of land-tenure one sees is one of individual ownership and the head of the *oikos* disposes of his land as he pleases (on this cf. M.I. Finley, art. cit. chap 2, n 3). On the whole controversy see the bibliographical references in A.M. Babacos, *Actes d'aliénation en commun et autres phénomènes apparentés d'après le droit de la Thessalie antique* (Thessalonica, 1966), pp. 32–9, esp. pp. 32–3.

20 *Works and Days*, 598–608 (transl. H.G. Evelyn-White).

21 *Works and Days*, 376–80 (transl. H.G. Evelyn-White).

22 On Hesiod see the contrasted views of Ed. Will, 'Aux origines du régime foncier grec: Homère, Hésiode, et l'arrière-plan mycénien', *REA* 59 (1957), pp. 5–50 (pp. 12–24 on Hesiod), and Ernest Will, 'Hésiode: crise agraire? ou recul de l'aristocratie?', *REG* 78 (1965), pp. 542–56.

23 On what follows see M.I. Finley, 'La servitude pour dettes',

Revue historique de droit français et étranger, 1965, pp.
159–84, esp. pp. 168–71. On Solon see the lucid survey by Ed.
Will cited chap 1, no 1 (pp. 78ff.) together with his bibliographical surveys in Revue historique and V. Ehrenberg, From
Solon to Socrates (London, 2nd ed. 1973), ch. 2. On the
general problem of legislation on debt see D. Asheri, Leggi
greche sul problema dei debiti (Pisa, 1969).

24 Modern literature on the subject of Greek colonization is
considerable in bulk. For a lucid synthesis see Cl. Mossé, La
colonisation dans l'antiquité (Paris, 1970), and for a good
summary of the archaeological evidence see J. Boardman, The
Greeks Overseas (Harmondsworth, 2nd ed. 1973). On the
western colonies see E. Lepore, 'Osservazioni sul rapporto tra
fatti economici e fatti di colonizzazione in Occidente',
Dialoghi di Archeologia fasc. 1–2, 1969, pp. 175–212, and the
regular annual congresses on Magna Graecia since 1961, esp.
I–III and VII. For recent literature see further Ed. Will, Revue
historique 238 (1967), pp. 442–8; 509 (1974), pp. 153–7. On
the question of land see M.I. Finley, 'The alienability of land
in Ancient Greece: a point of view', Eirene 7 (1968), pp. 25–32,
reprinted in The Use and Abuse of History (London, 1975),
pp. 153–60; D. Asheri's critique (Parola del Passato 157
(1974), pp. 232–6) is inconclusive.

25 A.J. Graham, Colony and Mother City in Ancient Greece
(Manchester, 1964).

26 For example Plato, Laws V, 740 b–e.

27 Archaeological evidence on land distribution in Greek colonies
is as yet scanty but is now attracting greater attention; most of
the available material, however, dates from the classical period
or later. Thus a division of the land into lots is known in the
Crimea, each lot having a homestead farm on it (whereas such
isolated farms appear to be rare in Greek history otherwise),
though it dates from the fourth century or later; see J. Pečirka
and M. Dufková, 'Excavations of Farms and Farmhouses in
the Chora of Chersonesus in the Crimea', Eirene 8 (1970), pp.
123–74; J. Pečirka, 'Country Estates of the Polis of Chersonesus in the Crimea', Studi in memoria di Corrado Barbagallo I (Naples, 1970), pp. 459–77; id., 'Homestead Farms in
Classical and Hellenistic Hellas', in Problèmes de la terre en

Grèce ancienne, ed. M.I. Finley (Paris and The Hague, 1973), pp. 113–47. A similar division has been identified in the territory of Metapontum in south Italy, though its character, extent and the question whether it can be dated as far back as the archaic age, let alone the very foundation of the city, are unclear and disputed; see D. Adamesteanu, 'Le suddivisioni di terre nel Metapontino', ibid., pp. 49–61, and the cautionary comments of E. Lepore and R. Martin, ibid., pp. 45–7 and 100–7.

28 See D. Lotze, *Metaxu eleutheron kai doulon* (Berlin, 1959); M.I. Finley, 'The Servile Statuses of Ancient Greece', *Revue internationale des droits de l'Antiquité*, 3rd series, 7 (1960), pp. 165–89; id., 'Between Slavery and Freedom', *Comparative Studies in Society and History* 6 (1954), pp. 233–49.

29 It is interesting to note the difference between the Chalcidian colonies in Sicily and some of the Dorian ones (Syracuse, Gela) in their relations with the natives: the former established peaceful intercourse with them, while the latter's dealings with them were based on force; see M.I. Finley, *Ancient Sicily* (London, 1968), pp. 18–22; E. Sjöqvist, *Sicily and the Greeks: Studies in the Interrelationship between the Indigenous Populations and the Greek Colonists* (Ann Arbor, 1973).

30 See D.M. Pippidi, *I Greci nel basso Danubio* (Milan, 1970), pp. 185–7; id., 'Le problème de la main-d'oeuvre agricole dans les colonies grecques de la Mer Noire', in *Problèmes de la terre en Grèce ancienne*, ed. M.I. Finley (Paris and The Hague, 1973), pp. 63–82. This, however, might not apply in the case of Olbia where, according to archaeological research, the native Scythian population was purely nomadic and only became agricultural in part and later in time, under Greek influence; see A. Wasowicz, *Olbia pontique et son territoire* (Paris, 1975), pp. 29–39.

31 On what follows see M.M. Austin, *Greece and Egypt*, op. cit., pp. 22–33.

32 See S.C. Humphreys, in *History and Theory* 8 (1969), pp. 191–6; Maxime Rodinson, op. cit., Chapter 1, n 11.

33 I, 163.

34 I, 164–5.

35 VI, 11.

36 VI, 17.

37 See G. Vallet and F. Villard, 'Les Phocéens et la fondation de Hyélè', *Parola del Passato* 108–10 (1966), pp. 166–90; E. Lepore, 'Strutture della colonizzazione focea in Occidente', ibid., 130–3 (1970), pp. 19–54; see now the important survey by J.P. Morel, *BCH*, 99, 2 (1975), pp. 853–96.

38 Thus C. Roebuck, *Ionian Trade and Colonization* (1959).

39 Cf. Ed. Will, *Korinthiaka* (Paris, 1955), pp. 477–81.

4 The Archaic States and Sparta

Typology of Greek states

Mention was made earlier of the inequality in development which characterized the Greek world even in the classical period. It is appropriate at this stage to draw up a brief typology of different Greek states, classified according to the degree of development they had reached. The 'degree of development' in question should not be assessed solely in relation to the evolution of constitutional forms (how close a given state was to, or how far from, democracy of the Athenian type, which one may justifiably consider to be at once the logical conclusion of the internal political evolution of the Greek city and also a kind of extraordinary exception). It should also be assessed in relation to the whole of social and economic life, and when mention will be made later of Greek states which were more or less 'archaic' or 'modern' in character, these epithets will reflect the overall judgment which many Greeks of the classical period, and notably Thucydides, passed on them. In what follows we are dealing of course with 'ideal types' which serve only as a means of reference and do not lay claim to anything more than classificatory convenience. As with all Greek institutions, a great deal of variety is to be found, owing to the existence of intermediate types in the principal categories.

The first distinction which must be made is that between *ethnos* (people, tribe) and *polis* (city) which is best rendered as 'state without an urban centre' and 'state with an urban centre'[1]. Athens was here a perfectly typical *polis* state: her territory (the *chora*) included the whole of Attica (only a few frontier regions like *Oropia* were at times not included in the civic territory), but the city of Athens (the *asty*) was its political centre. In an *ethnos* state, by contrast, there might even be no urban centre at all. The

78

population lived scattered about in villages over a more or less wide area. The political links which bound them together might be of a very loose kind; the 'state' existed only in a very diffuse sense. One factor which was often decisive in their lack of centralization was their geographical extension, which made it difficult for them to be transformed into genuine *poleis* with a single urban centre. The *ethnos* type of state represents a much less developed stage than the *polis* and chronologically it precedes it. It is in fact exactly in those regions where the *polis* developed little if at all that the *ethnos* was to be found, that is to say in the north-western parts of Greece, which had not been penetrated by Mycenaean civilization [*see nos 7, 53, 54*]. The unity of the original tribal groupings was able to preserve itself in different degrees for a considerable time. Among these *ethnos*-type states may be reckoned the Macedonians, the Thessalians, the Phocians, the Locrians, the Aetolians, the Acarnanians, the Achaeans and the Arcadians. It should be noted straightaway that here and there development beyond the most 'primitive' stage began to take place: within the same 'ethnic' group *poleis* might begin to grow up, become more or less independent from the *ethnos* and pursue an autonomous political life. Such was the case, for example, with the cities of Tegea and Mantineia in Arcadia or with the tiny cities of Chaleion and Oiantheia in Locris. There might even be tension between the unitary *ethnos* and the separatist *poleis*, as happened in Thessaly in the classical period. One special case where one can see the original unity of the *ethnos* more or less eliminated by the development in its midst of *poleis* is that of Boeotia: in the classical period the Boeotians were divided into several autonomous *poleis*. There was admittedly a Boeotian federal state, but when one looks at it more closely one realizes that it was in fact most of the time nothing but a Theban empire in disguise. The unity of the Boeotians was only an artificial one, imposed from above by the most powerful city. Here the *ethnos* had given way to *poleis*, whereas elsewhere the evolution had not gone so far.

If one looks at a map one sees that these *ethnos*-type states occupied an appreciable part of the Greek peninsula; and yet their importance in Greek history down to the fourth century was a limited one. With the exception of the Locrians and Achaeans, these states took no part in the great colonizing movement of the Archaic age, and their contribution to Greek history and civilization in the classical period was meagre. For a fifth-century Greek these were parts of the Greek world that were still backward, in which archaic forms of life had been preserved, and in which social and economic development was at a primitive stage. The political theorists of the fourth century ignored them more or less completely in their search for an ideal state: it had to be a *polis* to begin with. And yet it is during the fourth century that some of these *ethnos*-type states, which had hitherto played only a limited part in Greek history, began to take over politically from the principal *poleis*, which by this time had exhausted themselves; in the following century they were even to play a leading role. This applies notably (in the third century) to the Aetolians and Achaeans, who eventually developed federal states, and especially to Macedon, a rather special case because of the survival there from the earliest times of a hereditary monarchy, which was then built up and 'modernized' in the fourth century, chiefly by Philip II. Because of its restricted importance in the classical period, and in spite of its geographical extension, no more need be said about the *ethnos* type of state[2].

Another distinction which may be made is that between the classical city (of which Athens is the obvious prototype) and those states which did not undergo an equally developed evolution in certain essential fields. This distinction, it must be noted, only partly overlaps with the preceding one. The 'modern' state is always a *polis*; the 'archaic' state, on the other hand, might be either a *polis* (as in the case of the Cretan cities) or an *ethnos* (as in the case of the Thessalians and Locrians; on the special case of Sparta, an untypical *polis*, see below). The essential criterion which distinguishes modern states from the more archaic types is the degree of clarity with which the notions of citizen and free man as opposed to slave were defined. It was said earlier that the evolution of these notions and their progressive differentiation was one of the essential innovations of the archaic period in the institutional field. The evolution reached its logical conclusion in classical Athens where the antithesis between citizens and outsiders, and free men and slaves, was complete: the notions were clear cut and intermediate categories were eliminated. On one side were the citizens, who all enjoyed the same legal status (with a few exceptions), on the other the outsiders, who were divided into free men (the metics) and slaves, and these had no share in the decisions of the political community, though the metics had some share in the military functions of the city[3]. But not every Greek city reached this stage: in archaic states the notions of citizen and free man were less precise, the categories less clear cut and the existence of intermediate stages between the categories helped to blur the outlines even further. Whether these were *poleis* (the Cretan cities) or *ethne* (the Locrians and Thessalians) they were essentially rural communities, which lived more or less apart from the outside world and the main lines of communication, or were even deliberately xenophobic like Sparta. Foreigners from the outside world only played a limited role in them, whereas they were one of the most characteristic elements of states of the Athenian type. Their place was held by internal subjects, over whom ruled an aristocracy of warriors which had reduced them to subjection in one way or another.

Sparta will be taken as an illustration of these archaic societies, because she was the most famous representative of them and far more information is available in her case[4]. But although Sparta resembled the other archaic societies in many ways, as will be seen, she differed from them in others and should not be taken as altogether typical. The description which follows applies to Sparta at the end of the sixth century and during the whole of the fifth. Nothing will be said, beyond a few allusions, about the more or less insoluble problem of the origins of classical Sparta, which is one of the most obscure and controversial questions of all Greek history[5]. Fourth-century Sparta will also be left aside for the time being, for it is clear that after the Peloponnesian War, and to a great extent because of the war and its consequences, Sparta underwent profound internal changes which were to put her on the road to decline.

The principal categories in Sparta

The population of Sparta (or more accurately the population living in all the territory which belonged to or depended on Sparta) was divided into three principal categories: the Spartiate citizens with full rights (the *Homoioi*, that is to say the 'Peers', who were all equivalent, and each *Homoios* was in theory as good as another); the Perioikoi, who formed communities of free men but which were subjected to Sparta; and the Helots, a people who in the historical period were subject to and belonged to the Spartan state. These three categories do not bear any resemblance

to the three legal categories in Athens (citizens, metics, slaves),
despite superficial similarities, as will be seen below. Besides, and
contrary to the situation in Athens, there was in Sparta a whole
proliferation of intermediate categories which tended to blur the
clarity of the distinctions between the principal ones. The
° differences between Sparta and the Athenian type of state will be
seen below.

The Homoioi (Peers)

At the top of the scale were the Spartiates proper, 'citizens' with
full rights, who were at all times a small privileged minority in the
midst of the rest of the population which outnumbered them by
a very wide margin. Few accurate figures are available for the
population of Sparta. The highest known number of Spartiates
is 5,000 at the battle of Plataea in 479[6], and this figure kept on
diminishing subsequently. A century later, at the time of the
battle of Leuctra, there were only about 1,000 Spartiates with full
rights left (on the causes of this evolution, which was fatal to
Sparta, see briefly Chapter 7)[7].

The Spartiates represent the most extreme example in Greek
history of the rejection of economic activity [*see nos 37, 56*]. It
was strictly forbidden for them to engage in economic activity of
any kind; they depended for their economic needs on the other
categories, the Perioikoi and especially the Helots. The Spartiates
were masters of the land: they kept for themselves the best land,
at first in Laconia, then in Messenia as well after the subjection
of the Messenians (towards the end of the eighth century), but
they did not cultivate it themselves. For this they relied on the
labour of the Helots, who were bound to the land and compelled
to pay a quota of their produce to their masters. Manufacturing
activity was similarly in the hands of the Helots and especially,
one must presume, of the Perioikoi. Freed from all economic
preoccupations, the Spartiates devoted themselves exclusively to
military training: they were a hereditary group of professional
warriors. Their whole life was organized by the state with this
one end in mind – to turn them into soldiers used to obeying their
leaders and elders and drilled to fight as a group. The Spartiates
were the finest exponents of the hoplite style of warfare. Everything was deliberately sacrificed, or even repressed, to make way
for this one requirement. The Spartan system represents in fact a
reaction against the tradition of the *oikos*; as part of this reaction

all family values were repressed and crushed. Family life was deliberately reduced to a minimum. At the age of seven the young Spartiate was taken away from his family and his education was taken in charge by the state (the Spartan *agoge*). From then on he lived and exercised with the young men of his age, who were put in a whole series of age groups to which technical names were attached. The idea was to channel the loyalty of the Spartiate towards his comrades and to instil in him obedience towards his elders. At the age of 20, once his education was completed, the young Spartiate entered the category of the grown-up men[8]. He then had to get married, but the marriage ceremony was a cheerless and furtive affair, and did not mark the beginning of a normal family life as in the rest of Greece. Up to the age of 30, the Spartiate continued to live with his comrades, and only paid rare and infrequent visits to his wife. Even after his 30th year he continued to take his meals in common with his comrades (the *syssitia*); possession of full civic rights depended on ability to contribute to the *syssitia* and regularity of attendance [*see no 57*]. In this way family life was devalued from start to finish: its only aim was to produce vigorous citizens who would become fine soldiers. To achieve this restricted purpose the Spartans even occasionally disregarded the principle of monogamy observed everywhere else in Greece: it is attested that in certain circumstances one might 'lend' one's wife to someone else (genuine bigamy, on the other hand, was extremely rare)[9].

Among the Spartiates equality was the ideal, and this ideal was expressed in the very name they gave themselves, the Peers. They exercised together, shared the same life and the same table, and fought side by side. But in fact there was always a certain gap between the ideal and reality; the gap never ceased to widen and became in the end one of the essential causes of the decline of Sparta.

The first derogation from the egalitarian ideal was the existence of the double kingship, an institution of unknown origins and one which has no parallel in the rest of the Greek world. There is an occasional tendency to underestimate the importance of the kings in Sparta; and yet a large part of the history of Sparta can be written around the personality of its kings (or at least of one of the two kings at a time). It is enough to look at the ancient sources to see the prestige enjoyed by the double monarchy in Sparta[10]. There were thus two men among the Peers who were automatically privileged, and who owed their privileges solely to birth and not to any personal merits. Besides, it is clear that within the body of the Peers there existed a *de facto* aristocracy, which surpassed in wealth and influence the other less fortunate Peers. This aristocracy may well have existed from the very origins of classical Sparta. What is more, the general evolution tended to reinforce these social differences and encourage the concentration of wealth (especially landed property) among an ever more restricted number of people. As has been said, membership of the category of the Peers depended on the ability to make regular contributions to the *syssitia*: if one failed to meet this obligation one fell apparently into a lower category, that of the *Hypomeiones* or 'Inferiors', which implied the loss of full civic rights [*see no 61 and n 3*]. There may also have been other, 'non-economic', ways of becoming an 'Inferior'. Generally speaking the competitive spirit which animated the Peers and informed the whole of their life encouraged the formation of élites, and hence implied at the same time the existence of a less successful majority[11]. Among the Peers one hears of the existence of privileged groups, such as the body of the 300 *Koroi*, known also as the *Hippeis* (but who were not cavalry), who were chosen among the youngest warriors and formed a guard of honour for the kings [*see no 61 n 15*]. Such too were the *Kryptoi*, a chosen band of young men sent by the ephors (magistrates) singly and without weapons (apart from a dagger) in the countryside in order to kill Helots[12]. In this way élites grew up among the Peers. At the other end of the scale were all those who had 'failed' in one way or another [*see no 60*]. Apart from the 'Inferiors', there were the *Tresantes*, that is to say 'those who had trembled' in war and who were consequently penalized and lost some of their civic rights. Equality among the Spartiates was therefore never more than an impossible ideal and reality moved further and further away from it.

The Perioikoi

About these there is comparatively little information. They formed small independent communities, in Laconia in particular, but also in Messenia (about a hundred altogether); these communities enjoyed some degree of local autonomy, but were entirely subordinate to the government of Sparta for war and the whole field of foreign policy. In the classical period they spoke the Doric dialect, but that does not tell us anything about their origins, a subject which is in fact very obscure and largely speculative.

One noteworthy fact which illustrates the difference between archaic states and modern ones of the Athenian type is that the Perioikoi, although they had no share in the decisions of the government of Sparta, were nevertheless in some way part of the state. They were more than mere allies or subjects of Sparta. The official designation of what we call the Spartan state was not 'the Spartiates', as might be expected on the analogy of, say, the Athenian state ('the Athenians'), but 'the Lacedaimonians', a word which expressly included all the Perioikoi, who were in a sense second-rank 'citizens'. But at the same time as they shared in the Spartan state, the Perioikoi were also 'citizens', each of his own small community. One can see how in Sparta the notion of citizen is much more diffuse than in Athens.

Furthermore, the small communities of the Perioikoi were homogeneous and owned their land, and here again they are in sharp contrast to the metics in Athens, whose origins were very mixed and who were debarred from the right of owning land, a privilege which was restricted to citizens (see Chapter 5). They did not pay regular contributions to the Spartiates (unlike the Helots), but the kings of Sparta each held a *temenos* (a special estate) which was taken from among the lands of the Perioikoi and was cultivated by them. They were regularly recruited into the Spartan army in substantial numbers (nothing is known in detail of their training, nor indeed of the military training of such Helots as were conscripted for military service, cf. below). Up to the Persian wars they served in separate contingents; later on, during the Peloponnesian War, they are found mixed with the contingents of Spartiates. The change may have been introduced after the catastrophic earthquake of 465, which inflicted heavy manpower losses on Sparta; the intention probably was to conceal the numerical weakness of the Spartiates. But although they served in the army, the Perioikoi were not bound by the aristocratic values of the Spartan warriors. They could therefore engage in all those economic activities which the Spartiates rejected. They cultivated their lands and carried on manufacture; they must have been responsible, for example, for providing the state with weapons. It is probably to them too that one must attribute the so-called 'Laconian' pottery of the archaic period[13]. Although deprived of political power, the Perioikoi all the same enjoyed a fairly enviable position: the Spartan system and the geography of the Peloponnese guaranteed them security such as few Greek states enjoyed for so long. It is therefore exceptional to detect among them signs of disaffection towards the Spartiates [*see no 61*]. In general they were one of the essential elements in the stability of Sparta.

The Helots

The Greeks of the classical period often referred to the Helots as 'slaves', even in official texts: thus in the text of the alliance between Sparta and Athens which followed the peace of Nicias in 421 it was specified that 'if the servile class' (the *douleia*) 'revolted, the Athenians would come to the help of the Lacedaimonians with all their strength to the best of their ability[14].' But one should not be misled: between the slaves of the Athenian type, who were chattel slaves imported from abroad and bought on the market, and groups of the Helot type, there was a fundamental difference. They represent two quite different types of subjection, which have a distinct history and origins: slavery of the Athenian type was a more modern institution and Helotage a more archaic one, with the former eventually establishing itself in the classical period as the 'normal' type in Greek history. In fact some Greeks were well aware of this. From the fourth century, onwards, historians and theorists began to discuss slavery and its 'origins' and sought to introduce distinctions between different categories of slaves. A Hellenistic writer, whose formulation is reproduced by the lexicographer Pollux, defines groups of the Helot type as having a status 'between freedom and slavery'. That may not be a very precise definition, but it reveals at least the lack of clarity in the notions of freedom and slavery in these archaic societies[15].

What characterizes Helot-type groups by contrast with slaves of the Athenian type is first of all their homogeneity: they were all native peoples (whether Greek or non-Greek), who spoke the same language, and who are commonly held to have been reduced to the status of dependents through conquest, at the time of the arrival of those who later were to become their masters and form a warrior aristocracy [*see nos 50, 58, 63*]. They all had collective names, the meaning of which is not always clear[16]: the *Helots* in Sparta, who were interpreted as the 'captives' or the people of Helos in Laconia, the *Penestai* in Thessaly, the *Klarotai* in Crete (those who were bound to the plot of land – the *klaros*), also in Crete the *Mnoitai* (those who had been dominated?), the *Gymnetai* in Argos (the naked, that is to say those who were unarmed), the *Woikiatai* in Locris (the people of the *oikos*), the *Killyrioi* in Syracuse, and finally the *Mariandynoi* at Heraclea Pontica.

By contrast slaves of the Athenian type were of very mixed origins and could not be called by a collective name: they had no identity, whereas groups of the Helot type to some extent had one. Being homogeneous peoples these groups could reproduce themselves: one did not buy Helots at the slave market, whereas slaves in Athens were generally imported and purchased like any other commodity. These differences between the two types of subjects explain the difference in behaviour between the two groups and their relative importance to the states in which they lived.

In Athens it was rare to recruit slaves for military service: the known cases are few and always occurred in emergency situations. Besides, when one had recourse to use slaves for warfare, one began by liberating them. In Sparta, by contrast, it was regular (at least from the time of the Peloponnesian War onwards) to use Helots in warfare. In this case, if they were freed (which did not follow automatically) it was sometimes (though not always) after their period of service, and subsequently they continued to be liable to military service [*see nos 59, 60*]. (Nothing is known in detail of the process of selection of Helots for military service nor of their training; what is noteworthy is that Helots used in war were consistently loyal[17].) In theory, the Helots were not part of the state: the designation 'the Lacedaimonians' included the Spartiates and the Perioikoi, but excluded the Helots. Yet the Helots might claim to have a share in the Lacedaimonian state, whereas it was inconceivable that slaves in Athens should demand citizenship there or indeed anywhere. Because of their homogeneity the Helots enjoyed the possibility of common action denied to slaves of the Athenian type. The Helots freed by the state (they could not be manumitted by individuals, unlike the slaves in Athens who mostly belonged to individuals) became *Neodamodeis*, that is to say 'new members of the damos'; they were thus in a (to us mysterious) sense 'citizens' of Sparta without being on the same footing as the Peers.

The pattern of Helot revolts further underscores the differences between the two types of subjects. In spite of the high number of slaves in Athens there were no genuine slave revolts in Athens in the classical period (see Chapter 5). It is noteworthy that in the treaty of alliance between Sparta and Athens in 421 there was no reciprocal clause committing Sparta to help Athens in the event of a slave revolt there – the possibility was never expected to arise. The situation was quite different in Sparta; Helot revolts were a permanent factor in her history [*see nos 50, 58, 59, 61*]. As a matter of fact it would be more correct to speak of revolts of the Helots of Messenia rather than Helot revolts in general, for here one must distinguish between two groups, the Helots of Laconia and those of Messenia. The latter were only conquered at a relatively late date (about the middle of the eighth century), and they subsequently preserved a clear memory of their original identity, which the Helots of Laconia seem to have lost, and it is chiefly from Messenia that all the great Helot revolts originate: in the seventh century in the time of Tyrtaeus, from 464 to 460 after the great earthquake which endangered the very existence of Sparta[18], and finally in 370–369 after the defeat of Leuctra when Messenia seceded from Sparta and established herself as an independent state, recognized as such by the other Greeks, as had happened already in the case of Messenians who escaped at other periods (as for example the Messenians settled at Naupactus by the Athenians in 459 [*see no 53*]). The demand for secession and 'Messenian power', then, was the other course of action open to the Messenian Helots, apart from integration in the Spartan state. It was quite inconceivable that such a thing should happen in Athens: the numerous slaves who escaped in the final years of the Peloponnesian War [*see no 74*] could never have constituted an independent state (see Chapter 5).

The case of the Helot revolts in Sparta is the best known of its kind, but it would seem that it is typical of these groups[19]. One may say that every time one can see servile groups taking a direct part in political conflicts, these are groups of the Helot type. Thus the Killyrioi in Syracuse rose with the *demos* against the oligarchy of the Geomoroi[20], and the Penestai of Thessaly often rose against their masters[21]. The Klarotai of Crete, on the other hand, did not stir. In Aristotle's view that was an oddity which demanded explanation, and Aristotle[22] attributed this to the fact that since all the Cretan cities had Klarotai and were often at war with each other, they avoided stirring up the Klarotai of their opponents for fear that the attempt might recoil on them. In other words, this was the exception that proved the rule. But it is interesting to note that the only *Doulopolis* (slave city) mentioned in the Greek world should be precisely in Crete: it is only in these archaic cities that a slave city was even conceivable. Another characteristic of the Spartan Helots is also found elsewhere: the use in war of Penestai (in Thessaly) and Mariandynians (at Heraclea Pontica) is attested.

Mention was made above of marriages in Sparta. It is worth saying a little more about unions other than those strictly between Spartiates, for these give a further illustration of the difference between archaic and modern-type Greek societies. In Athens, after the law of Pericles of 451–450, only marriages between Athenians were legally recognized and to be an Athenian citizen one had to be descended from both citizen parents. Previously it was enough if the father was an Athenian citizen. Unions between Athenians and slaves had no legal validity. The situation was different in archaic societies. The Law Code of Gortyn caters for the possibility of marriages between different categories of people [*see no 62*]. In Sparta unions between Peers and Helots could result in children who had, or at least'might lay claim to, citizenship of sorts. Mention was made earlier (Chapter 1) of the possibility of 'feminine power' in Sparta and in archaic societies via unions between Spartiate women and Helots, with the children from such unions laying claim (according to certain traditions) to political power. One special group in Sparta was that of the *Mothakes*: its exact composition is not known and the sources are unclear. It included either slaves born at home (from a Spartiate father and a Helot mother), or Helots who shared the education of the young Spartiates and who received their freedom from the state (without for all that being admitted to the group of the *Homoioi*, or even being part of the Lacedaimonians)[23].

One famous episode in the history of Sparta sums up very well the difference between the two types of society, namely the conspiracy of Kinadon in 397 [*see no 61*]. What was remarkable in this episode was the participation in the plot against the Peers of all the lower categories in the state. In Athens a plot of this kind, grouping together metics and slaves against the citizens, was quite simply inconceivable, because, among other reasons, metics and slaves were excluded from the state, whereas in Sparta everyone, from the Peers to the Helots, through all the intermediate categories, had some share in the state in different degrees. The ethnic homogeneity of the different categories made possible the existence of a common consciousness and unity of action which would have been impossible to achieve in Athens.

The originality of Sparta

Such are in briefest outline the main characteristics of Spartan society. Sparta has been taken as an illustration of these archaic societies, and there are indeed many similarities between them and Sparta, which have been pointed out above. But on the other hand there are certain peculiarities of Sparta which made her a state unique in Greek history. One may pass rapidly over certain characteristics, such as the fact that Sparta controlled an expanse of territory much larger and of far better quality than other Greek states, which enabled her to achieve gradually (except in time of war) the ideal of self-sufficiency, and consequently to reduce to a minimum contacts with the outside world. In fact it would seem from the evidence of archaeology that imports to Sparta ceased completely in the course of the sixth century. One may also pass over an institutional oddity like the double kingship, which has no parallel in the rest of the Greek world. One may also note the unusual fact that Sparta, although she was considered a *polis* by the other Greek states, and although her history belongs to the history of the *polis* in general, was untypical in comparison with other *poleis* in that she had no proper urban centre: not only were there no fortifications (only the men were to defend the city), but there was not even a fortified acropolis, such as were known in many civic centres. Instead, the Spartiates lived scattered about in five villages [*see no 55*].

Taken in isolation there are few elements in Spartan society which cannot be paralleled in the rest of the Greek world: all the ritual and archaic traits of Sparta – the existence of age groups and the survival (or rather readaptation) of many 'rites of passage' like the Krypteia, though they may have been more pronounced in Sparta – are also to be found everywhere in the Greek world (and not only in archaic societies).

At the root of the great originality of Sparta, providing the starting point for the 'Spartan mirage', a mirage which has had a long history from antiquity to the present day[24], is the way in which all the different elements were combined together towards a single end, and the way in which the state deliberately organized the education of the Peers to instil in them its own ideal of military excellence and obedience. It is the only historical example of a Greek state deliberately attributing to itself the role of educator of its members, because it believed that its survival required their subordination to a single purpose. Sparta, although a military state, was not strictly a militaristic one, and did not pursue victory in war over foreigners and conquest by force as ends in themselves. These motives did once exist at an earlier stage in the history of Sparta. Then came the decisive change, after the second Messenian war, in the time of Tyrtaeus. Sparta became an introverted state which aimed at nothing but its own preservation.

Notes

1 Thus V. Ehrenberg, *The Greek State* (London, 2nd ed., 1969), p. 22.
2 Though not concerned specifically with the *ethnos*-type state, J.A.O. Larsen, *Greek Federal States* (Oxford, 1967) is a mine of information on the subject.
3 Cf. Ed. Will, *Revue historique* 509 (1974), p. 158, n 2 (on the French edition of this book).
4 For important general analyses of Spartan society see notably M.I. Finley, 'Sparta' in *Problèmes de la guerre en Grèce ancienne*, ed. J.P. Vernant (Paris and The Hague, 1968), pp. 143–60, reprinted in *The Use and Abuse of History* (London, 1975), pp. 161–77; G.E.M. de Ste Croix, *The Origins of the Peloponnesian War* (London, 1972), ch. IV; P. Vidal-Naquet, 'Les jeunes. Le cru, l'enfant grec et le cuit', in the collective volume *Faire de l'histoire* (Paris, 1974), III, pp. 137–68, esp. pp. 156–62. For a projected Marxist analysis of Sparta see Paul Cartledge, 'Towards the Spartan Revolution', *Arethusa* 8, 1 (Spring 1975), pp. 59–84.
5 For a lucid introduction to the main problems, with bibliography, see Cl. Mossé, 'Sparte archaique', *Parola del Passato* 148–9 (1973), pp. 7–20 and V. Ehrenberg, *From Solon to Socrates* (London, 2nd ed., 1973), ch. 2.
6 Herodotus IX, 28.

7 On the problem of Spartan *oliganthropia* (shortage of men) see most recently de Ste Croix, *Origins of the Peloponnesian War*, op. cit., pp. 331–2.

8 On the Spartan blurring of the transition from youth to manhood see P. Vidal-Naquet, op. cit. in n 4 above, pp. 158–9.

9 Xenophon, *Constitution of the Lacedaimonians* I, 3–9; Plutarch, *Lycurgus* XIV–XV.

10 See for example Herodotus VI, 56–9.

11 See especially Plutarch, *Agesilaus* V: 'The Spartan lawgiver seems to have introduced the spirit of ambition and contention into the constitution as an incentive to excellence (*arete*), desiring that good citizens (*agathoi*) should always be at variance and in conflict with each other, and he believed that submissiveness which weakly yields without contradiction, which knows no effort and no trouble, does not deserve the name of concord.'

12 It has been possible to identify in the Krypteia a very ancient 'rite of passage' for which primitive African societies provide striking parallels; at Sparta this rite was then readapted to a policing function. See H. Jeanmaire, 'La cryptie lacédémonienne', *REG* 26 (1913), pp. 121–50; id., *Couroi et Courètes* (Paris and Lille, 1939), pp. 540–69; cf. P. Vidal-Naquet, *Proceedings of the Cambridge Philological Society* 194 (1968), pp. 55–6; A. Brelich, *Paides e Parthenoi* (Rome, 1969), pp. 155–7.

13 There is, however, very little positive evidence on the economic activity of the Perioikoi, cf. R.T. Ridley, *Mnemosyne* XXVII (1974), pp. 281–92 (not very rigorous).

14 Thucydides V, 23, 3.

15 See the bibliography mentioned in Chapter 3, n 7 and n 28, and Pollux III, 83; see also J. Ducat, 'Le mépris des Hilotes', *Annales* 29, 6 (Nov.–Dec. 1974), pp. 1451–64.

16 The etymologies given by Greek sources have no value.

17 See Y. Garlan, 'Les esclaves grecs en temps de guerre', in *Actes du Colloque d'histoire sociale 1970* (Paris, 1972), pp. 29–62; some additions in *Actes du Colloque 1972 sur l'esclavage* (Paris, 1974), pp. 15–28.

18 According to a tradition mentioned by Plato (*Laws* III, 692 d, 698 e), there was another revolt of Messenia at the time of the battle of Marathon in 490.

19 See Cl. Mossé, 'Le rôle des esclaves dans les troubles politiques

du monde grec à la fin de l'époque classique', *Cahiers d'histoire*
6 (1961), pp. 353–60; Y. Garlan, n 17 above.

20 Herodotus VII, 155.

21 Cf. Xenophon, *Hellenica* II, 3, 36; Aristotle, *Politics* II, 1269
a 36–7, 1269 b 5–7.

22 *Politics* II, 1269 a 39–1269 b 3.

23 There may not be a contradiction between these two definitions.

24 See F. Ollier, *Le mirage spartiate*, 2 vols (Paris, 1933 and 1943);
E. Rawson, *The Spartan Tradition in European Thought*
(Oxford, 1969); E.N. Tigerstedt, *The Legend of Sparta in
Classical Antiquity* I (Stockholm, 1965).

5 Classical Athens[1]

Characteristics of the Athenian type of state

The essential characteristics of the Athenian type of state were defined above in antithesis to archaic states of which Sparta is (unfortunately) the best known but very untypical example. Briefly, they included the complete elimination of internal subjects (after Solon there were no more slaves of Athenian origin in Athens), and the placing on the same level of political and legal equality of all the citizens. Despite the fact that certain magistracies were reserved to citizens of the first census group, there were not different degrees of participation in the state as was the case in Sparta: in Athens one was a citizen and had a share in the state or one was not and consequently remained an outsider as far as the political community was concerned, whether a free man (a foreigner (*xenos*) or a metic) or a slave. One may leave aside certain groups of disqualified citizens, such as those ostracized or under a sentence of *atimia*[2]: these were clearly special cases which did not invalidate the general rule, and which cannot properly be compared with the 'Inferiors' and other similar groups in Sparta. In Athens the distinction between the various legal categories was clear cut: the distinction between free man and slave as that between citizen and non-citizen was sharply drawn, and intermediate categories were eliminated. Concurrently with the disappearance of internal subjects the role of outsiders developed (both free men and slaves): the two processes were linked.

Furthermore, at the same time as the inequalities in status of the Athenians were removed and the progression towards democracy was pursued, the body of the Athenians became an entirely exclusive one closed to outsiders. Until the law of Pericles in 451–450, to become a citizen it was enough to have a citizen father: there are several famous examples of members of the Athenian aristocracy who had a non-Athenian, or even a non-Greek, mother (Cleisthenes, Themistocles, Cimon). These 'international' unions between aristocratic families are characteristic of the archaic age (one well-known example mentioned by Herodotus³ is the marriage of Agariste, daughter of Cleisthenes, tyrant of Sicyon, with the Athenian Megacles, a marriage from which Cleisthenes the legislator was born). Then came the law of Pericles in 451–450 which coincided with the completion of the democracy: henceforward only children born from two citizen parents were to be Athenian citizens⁴. To be sure, Pericles' law was not enforced in its full rigour: the Euboeans received the right of *epigamia* (the right to contract legally valid unions with Athenians) before 413, and during the Peloponnesian War the law fell into disuse. But the principle it implied was felt to be fundamental: one of the measures of the democracy when it was restored in 403 was to reaffirm the law of Pericles in the same terms as previously.

The grant of Athenian citizenship to outsiders was always therefore in principle a privilege, conferred sometimes on individuals, more rarely on groups. There are, however, examples: the survivors of the siege of Plataea in 427 (with some restrictions); the metics who had fought at the battle of Arginusae in 406; in 405 the people of Samos received *isopoliteia* (equality of political rights with the Athenians) for their loyalty to Athens. The behaviour of the restored democracy in 403 was significant: one might have expected to see Athens dispense citizenship generously, partly to reward the metics who had fought on the side of the democrats, and partly to build up again the citizen body which had been severely depleted after the Peloponnesian War and the civil war of 404–403. A proposal to this effect was made by the democratic leader Thrasybulus: it was not followed up, and it would seem that citizenship was granted only to a small number of metics (a little over a hundred?), and only with some delay, in 401–400. The citizen body thus remained as exclusive as before [*see no 70*]⁵.

The population living in Athens and Attica fell into three legal categories: citizens, metics and slaves.

The citizens
The only genuine economic distinction which separated citizens

from non-citizens (whether free or slave) – but it was a fundamental one – concerned the ownership of land. The right to
acquire, own and alienate an estate in Attica was the exclusive
privilege of the citizen. This link between the citizen and the
cultivated land was very strongly marked, as for example in the
oath sworn by Athenian ephebes when becoming hoplites, an
archaic or archaizing oath which is known to us notably from a
fourth-century inscription[6]. After calling to witness the deities of
plant growth, the young Athenians invoked 'the frontiers of the
fatherland, the fields of corn and barley, the vineyards, the olive
trees and the fig trees'. Although a non-citizen might occasionally
be granted this right (*enktesis ges kai oikias*) it was always a
special privilege, an exception, never the rule [*see no 72*][7]. No one
in Athens ever went so far as to propose the complete abolition
of the restriction on the right to own land. Xenophon, for
example, in his pamphlet on the *Ways and Means* in the 350s,
suggested that the state of the city's finances might be improved
by encouraging metics to come and settle in Athens in as large
numbers as possible to carry on their activities there. With this
aim in mind he proposed a number of improvements in the legal
status which they enjoyed, including the right to acquire a house
in town, but he was careful not to propose granting them *en bloc*
the right of *enktesis* without restriction [*see no 122*]. Subversive
as his proposal may have been, it thus took into account the
antithesis between city and countryside which manifested itself
in the fourth century (see Chapter 7). Xenophon did not mind
letting metics own a fraction of the city's land, but he never
dreamed of allowing them to acquire agricultural land in Attica.
There was nothing exceptional here about the case of Athens: on
the contrary, it reflected a very widespread Greek notion, namely
that ownership of land was the privilege of the citizen. Every
Greek community in the classical period was in the first instance
a community of landowners, even though fortunes not in land
might subsequently develop side by side with landed ones.

This link between the land and the citizen had in practice
several consequences. For one thing it was an accepted notion in
many Greek cities that the possession of civic rights must depend
in some way on the ownership of land; examples were seen
earlier of cities which restricted the possession of full civic rights
to landowners (Thebes, Cyrene). Athens diverged from other
Greek states in that citizens without landed property were

eventually admitted to full participation (or nearly) in political rights. The evolution took place in stages. Tenure of the archonship, for example, was until the time of Solon a privilege of the aristocracy. After Solon it was open to men of the first census group (or possibly of the first two groups). The third census group was admitted to it shortly before 457 or 456. The fourth group, that of the thetes, was never admitted in theory; in practice the law ceased to be enforced.

On the other hand the link between the land and the citizen could work in the other direction: the citizen wanted to be a landowner, and his status as a citizen served as a basis for his claim to the ownership of land. Since the ownership of land was the only field in which there was a genuine economic distinction between citizens and non-citizens, it was around land that most of the economic demands of citizens were to revolve: this we have already seen for the archaic age, and shall see again for the fourth century. Even when the idea was not pushed to its furthest limit, namely the demand for a complete redistribution of land, it encouraged the citizen to be (or to remain) a landowner if he was able to, because of the special prestige that was attached to land. This can be observed in Athens: after the restoration of the democracy in 403 a proposal was made by a certain Phormisios to limit civic rights to those who owned land in some form. The proposal was defeated. We are told that, had it been accepted, some 5,000 Athenians would have lost their civic rights. The figure has been much discussed. If one accepts it, it means that at the end of the fifth century, and taking into account Athenian losses during the Peloponnesian War, only about a quarter of the citizens did not own any land [*see no 66, cf. nos 65, 76*]. And yet Athens was at the time the city in the Greek world where manufacture and commerce had reached their greatest development: in other cities it is likely that the proportion of citizens with a share in landed property was higher still.

The intellectual and social élite of Athens was always to a great extent composed of landowners, at least until the Peloponnesian War, when a new evolution set in. Till this date the governing aristocracy was, without known exception, made up of the great landowners of Attica. The fact is clearly exemplified in the two great rival statesmen Cimon and Pericles, although the use they made of their fortune was quite different, since Cimon lived on his estates in Attica which he left open for his fellow demesmen to enjoy, while Pericles lived in the city and left the running of his family estate to a manager who paid him a regular rent out of which Pericles met his daily expenses[8]. It was only at the beginning of the Peloponnesian War that a change set in, and one saw some *nouveaux riches*, whose fortune was not based on landed property, presume to lead the people as Pericles and his predecessors had done. This evolution aroused many a hostile echo in sources which stigmatize the ambitions of these vulgar 'demagogues' and show a generally anti-democratic bias: but one must determine exactly the significance of the change[9]. These 'demagogues' were not paupers; their coming to power did not signify a radical change in Athenian policy, whether internally or externally, and in their function they did not differ fundamentally from their aristocratic predecessors who were 'demagogues' just as much as they. The real change consisted in the development of fortunes not in land, an evolution which was to carry on in the fourth century (see Chapter 7).

A few words may be said here on a subject which has been at the centre of a long controversy, namely the question of the inalienability of land[10]. It has been maintained that land remained inalienable in Attica right down to the Peloponnesian War, and that the restriction then disappeared because of the upheaval caused by the war [*see no 65*]. When put in such extreme terms the theory is unacceptable. It is quite simply incredible that land in Attica should have remained literally inalienable for centuries, or even from the very first settlement of Greeks in Attica (and as is well known the Athenians boasted of being autochthonous, unlike many other Greeks). In fact a number of exceptions to the alleged rule of inalienability are known. It would also be astonishing that such a great upheaval as is alleged to have taken place during the Peloponnesian War should not have left any explicit traces in the sources. That the Peloponnesian War did affect the conditions of land tenure in Attica is certain, and besides it is obviously true that in the fourth century land was alienable; the fact is, however, that for the fourth century the sources are much fuller than before (notably the orators). Yet it is not enough to say merely that the land was alienable: alienation does not necessarily mean commercialization and it will be seen that in the fourth century, although land did indeed change hands, it did not for all that become a commercial asset (see Chapter 7). One cannot in fact talk of alienation in the abstract: one must define different forms and different conditions in which alienation might or might not take place, and take into account the institutional, social and economic framework of the society in question.

The metics

The metics were free men, both Greek and non-Greek, domiciled in Athens or in Attica, some in a more or less permanent way, others for a more limited period of time[11]. Most of the information about their legal status dates from the fourth century or later still, and one cannot always be certain that the same rules were applied in the fifth century. It seems that beyond a certain period of stay (the exact length of which is not known but which may have been one month [*cf. no 54*]), a foreigner (*xenos*) in transit in Athens had to register as a metic, otherwise he could be sold into slavery. In other words, the process of becoming a metic was an automatic one (this view has admittedly been challenged). Metics were subjected to a number of different obligations: they had to pay the *metoikion* (the tax on the metics), which may not have been very high (12 drachmae a year for grown-up men, 6 drachmae for adult women if they lived on their own), but which symbolized the inferiority of their status as compared with citizens. Citizens did not pay taxes on their persons, only on their property, and that not on a regular basis (see Chapter 6). Here again failure to comply led to being sold into slavery. Besides, metics had perhaps to pay certain taxes on foreigners (the *xenika*), such as the tax to have the right to trade in the *agora* [*see no 12*]. But it could happen that one granted to a metic the privilege of *isoteleia* (equality of taxation) which put him on the same level as citizens for all financial obligations and meant that he did not have to pay the *metoikion*. Metics also each had to find a *prostates* (a patron), an Athenian citizen who would undertake to represent them at law [*see no 64*]. The exact role of the *prostates* is not well known; it may have become less conspicuous in the course of the fourth century, and already in the fifth century it was possible for foreigners to go to law without the help of a *prostates*. All the same the penalty for a metic who neglected this obligation was once more to be sold into slavery. Metics also had to register as being domiciled in one of the demes of Attica (the majority lived in Athens and especially in Peiraieus, the main centre of economic activity in Attica), but they were not members of the demes in the same way as citizens. The distinction is clearly drawn in inscriptions. The names of citizens are followed by the demotic, those of metics only by the words 'domiciled in the following deme' (those of slaves are not followed by anything at all, except at times the name of their master) [*see no 73*]. Finally the metics were subjected according to their wealth to the same financial obligations as citizens (liturgies, war taxes – see Chapter 6). They served in the land army in separate contingents, but generally did not take part in campaigns far from Attica; they could also serve in the navy as rowers [*see no 68*].

These obligations may not have been particularly burdensome, but all the same the status of metic suffered from a number of obvious limitations as compared with that of citizen. A metic had no political rights; he could not take part in the assembly or sit in the council, nor be appointed to any magistracy [*see no 64*]. There was no automatic process of naturalization, no right of *epigamia* with citizens, and consequently no hope for a metic (except in the case of a special grant) of obtaining the status of citizen. Although a metic was protected by law, his legal personality was inferior to that of the citizen: the murder of a metic was assimilated to involuntary homicide and treated as such. From the economic point of view a metic suffered from one major restriction – the impossibility of acquiring land and houses in Attica, except as a special privilege. Hence he was unable to borrow or lend money on the security of land [*cf. no 91A*]. The economic consequences of this restriction can easily be imagined: being debarred from the right to own land, metics automatically turned to all forms of economic activity other than agriculture, such as manufacture, commerce, banking business, etc. The world of money thus developed side by side with the world of land, and these two worlds coexisted on two different levels without ever fusing into one (see Chapter 7).

It is difficult to attempt a genuine history of the Athenian metics before the end of the fifth century: it is only then and especially for the fourth century that adequate sources are available. Little is known about the origins of the status of metic and the development of the group. When one reaches the second half of the fifth century the system is already fully developed. No exact figures are available for this period (the only overall figure known dates from the end of the fourth century: the census of Demetrius of Phalerum is reported to have produced a total of 21,000 citizens and 10,000 metics, but this was past the period of the greatest success of the metic system). One may, however, be certain that they were numerous in the fifth century, more so probably than in the fourth.

How does one account for the presence of all these foreigners in Athens? – and also, it should be added, in many other Greek cities, for although the metic system enjoyed great success in Athens, the only city where it is relatively well known in the classical period, it was not peculiar to it and is attested in many other Greek cities. The answer, whether given by philosophers, statesmen or just ordinary citizens, is not in doubt: the city needed the metics, because of all the economic services they provided (manufacture, trade), because of the revenues they brought to the city without costing anything, and because of their use in the army and navy [*see nos 74, 122, 127, 128, 129*]. This point of view remained a constant one throughout the classical period. Philosophers admitted the need for the presence of outsiders in the city to cater for its economic life, even though they were in principle wary of the harmful influences which might result from contacts with the outside world. When Xenophon around 355 BC wanted to suggest ways of increasing the revenues of Athens, he proposed that metics should be offered extra privileges: merely by coming to Athens metics would automatically increase the wealth of the city and of individuals. The point needs underscoring: the presence of metics was not merely tolerated but actively encouraged by the city (and as will be seen below citizens did not consider metics to be rivals in economic activity). The metics were indispensable to the economic life of the city and yet they were not really part of the city, since they were excluded from all political rights. Theory and practice converged at this point: the *polis* of the citizens could not exist without the presence of outsiders[12].

The slaves

Slaves in theory had no rights at all: they were the property of their master and he might dispose of them freely as he liked. In practice slaves in Athens enjoyed some protection from the law: one could not maltreat a slave or put him to death with impunity (the murder of a slave, as that of a metic, was assimilated to involuntary homicide). But the slave had no legal personality: with the possible exception of some privileged groups (like certain public slaves – the *demosioi* – and the *choris oikountes*[13] – the slaves 'living apart' who paid a rent to their masters but who otherwise were more or less independent), slaves could not in general go to law on their own behalf, but were entirely dependent on their masters (there was however a slight evolution in the fourth century connected with the development of commercial law: see Chapter 7). A slave's evidence in court was usually only accepted under torture.

On the functions performed by slaves in Athens one can lay down as a general rule that there were hardly any specifically servile activities, and that slaves did much the same things as free men in Athens. One must of course set aside some obvious restrictions. Slaves had no political rights; although they were occasionally recruited in the navy, it was always an emergency measure; slaves in Athens, unlike Helots in Sparta, did not normally take part in war. With these exceptions, slaves were to be found in more or less every branch of Athenian activity, and doing the same work as free men: agriculture, commerce, manufacture, domestic work, etc. There were also public slaves assigned to various state functions, such as clerks, secretaries, prison officials; one special group was that of the 300 Scythian archers who served as a police force. Mining alone tended to be considered an activity more suited to slaves, because of the particularly harsh conditions involved, and although free men were to be found working in the mines there is no doubt that servile labour predominated heavily [*see nos 76, 79, 96*]. But generally speaking there was little distinction in practice between the type of work performed (servile work as opposed to the work of free men). The real distinction lay in the conditions under which work was performed. A free man worked (or wanted to work) for himself, whereas the majority of slaves worked for someone else (with the exception of those few privileged slaves who enjoyed a certain *de facto* independence). The organization of manufactures illustrates clearly this way of thinking: as a general rule all larger establishments employed servile labour, and not free men (the highest known figure for classical Athens is about 120 slaves employed in the arms factory of the metics Lysias and Polemarchus in Peiraieus, in the final years of the Peloponnesian War [*see no 69*]). The free artisan wanted to work for himself in order to remain independent; establishments employing solely free men were always small family concerns. The same pattern may be observed in mining enterprises: free prospectors worked on their own, whereas groups of men working for someone else were made up solely of slaves.

The legal categories do not correspond to social classes

Such were the three legal categories in to which the population domiciled in Athens and Attica was classified. They were clearly defined: any movement, whether in an upward or a downward direction, went directly from one category to the next without going through intermediate stages. An Athenian whose citizenship was challenged and pronounced invalid fell into the category of metics. A metic who failed to meet his obligations was sold into slavery. Conversely a manumitted slave had a status similar to that of a metic (he did not become a citizen as was the case in Rome), and the highest privilege to which a metic might aspire was that of obtaining Athenian citizenship (which was always an exception). But although the categories were clear cut from a legal point of view, they must not be pictured as three well-defined social classes, for many reasons[14].

Of these three legal categories, the citizen body was by far the most homogeneous. From an ethnic point of view citizens were more or less a unity: the great majority of Athenians were indigenous, and there were among them only very few foreigners who had been granted Athenian citizenship. This ethnic homogeneity can only have been reinforced by the citizenship law of Pericles. But from a social point of view the Athenians did not constitute a single social class. There were among them considerable differences in wealth, with at the top of the scale a small very wealthy minority, at the bottom the poor Athenians who owned little or no land (the thetes), although it is impossible to draw a very clear line between rich and poor (in our sense of the word). This antagonism remained latent most of the time in Athens, except in the final years of the Peloponnesian War, and classical Athens experienced a degree of social peace which many Greek cities might have envied her, and which was one of the main factors in her great stability. The democracy did not rest on the poorest citizens, as the enemies of democracy kept on repeating. It also enjoyed a wide measure of support among the wealthier classes, who as a matter of fact provided Athens with the majority of her political leaders during her history.

There was no similar homogeneity among the other two

categories. Metics were of very mixed origins. There was here an evolution from the fifth to the fourth centuries. In the fifth century, metics in Athens were generally Greeks, and tended to prefer to settle in Athens in a more or less permanent way; on the social plane these metics could achieve a high degree of assimilation with the Athenian community [*see nos 67, 68, 69*]. In the fourth century, by contrast, metics tended in increasing numbers to be 'barbarians' from many different countries – Thrace, Lydia, Caria, Phoenicia, Egypt, etc. More and more these metics did not integrate in the Athenian community. Even when they settled in Athens, they preserved their original identity (for example they brought their own cults with them); but quite often these barbarian metics did not settle once and for all in Athens [*see nos 71, 72, 122*]. Thus the category of metics showed the greatest diversity in its ethnic composition. Besides, there were always considerable differences of wealth among metics. Some, like the brothers Lysias and Polemarchus, with their arms factory employing some 120 slaves, belonged to the wealthiest members of Athenian society, others were as poor as the poorest of the Athenians.

What did citizens think of the metics? To be sure, traces of hostility against them are found in certain writers [*see no 74*]; it is generally a question of sources with an anti-democratic and xenophobic bias which complain of the freedom granted to foreigners and slaves in Athens (as compared with Sparta, for example). In the fourth century, speeches delivered in the law courts occasionally make appeals to the xenophobia of the jurors in trials against metics [*see no 84*][15]. Granted this, no one questioned the need for metics; even the 'Old Oligarch' admitted it. Besides, it is clear that there could be a fairly high degree of social assimilation, at both ends of the scale, at least in the case of the metics of Greek origin in the fifth century. The metic Cephalus and his sons Lysias and Polemarchus belonged to the social and intellectual élite of Athens. As the 'Old Oligarch' reveals, there could also be some assimilation with the lower classes: in Athens, he complains, one could not distinguish a poor citizen, a metic and a slave. The traces of hostility against metics that one occasionally comes across have at their root xenophobic feelings or social prejudices; what is never at issue is economic rivalry of any kind between citizens and metics. The Athenians did not by any means have the feeling that metics might rival them in this field. Xenophon, in his pamphlet *Ways and Means*, does not even seem to raise this possibility when he argues that more metics must be persuaded to come to Athens in order to improve the finances of the city (whereas he does at least raise the question in the case of slaves, cf. below). In their attitude towards the democracy one does not see the metics forming a separate, let alone antagonist, group against the citizens, with a programme and demands of their own. Although some metics were compromised in the mutilation of the Hermae in 415 [*see no 75*], it is clear that a large number of them did not by any means wish to overthrow the democracy and bring about a political revolution. During the civil war of 404–403, many metics fought on the side of the democrats of Peiraieus against the Thirty Tyrants [*see no 70*]. Some metics, such as Lysias, completely assimilated in Athenian society, certainly hoped for Athenian citizenship [*see no 69*]. But it does not appear that metics as a group ever made this demand: for barbarian metics who were not integrated in Athenian society, citizenship would have been quite meaningless. The majority of metics simply accepted the existing state of affairs which enabled them to prosper in peace and enjoy the benefits of the power and wealth of Athens.

A number of similar remarks may be made about the slaves in Athens. There was no unity in their origins: to be sure, Phrygians (especially in the mines) and Thracians were numerous, to such an extent that *Manes* (a Phrygian name) and *Thratta* (the Thracian) were, in the language of the comic poets, immediately understood as referring to slaves[16], but no people specialized in providing Athens with slaves [*see no 75*]. Anybody might become a slave through the risks of war, piracy, etc. Among slaves in Athens, some were Greek, but in fact barbarian slaves predominated, especially in the fourth century, as with metics [*see no 131*]. Again, as with metics, there were great differences in social status among slaves in Athens. Some enjoyed an almost privileged position, like the public slaves or the slaves 'living apart', who were in practice more or less free and whose position did not differ much from that of small free artisans. Domestic slaves might hope to be manumitted sooner or later. On the other hand the fate of slaves working in the Laurion mines in harsh conditions was a grim one, and no hope of freedom lay before them. Given all these differences in the position and origin of slaves in Athens it will be readily understood why Athens in spite of the numbers of slaves it owned – which must have been high[17] – never experienced any slave revolts (that is, of course, organized revolts), unlike Sparta and other archaic societies where Helot revolts were a permanent reality. Athenian slaves had neither unity, nor any class consciousness, nor any common programme of action. All they could demand was simply their freedom, and even that on a purely individual basis. Since access to political power was unthinkable for them, the only form of action to which they could resort was simply running away when a favourable opportunity arose: thus the occupation of Deceleia in Attica by the Peloponnesians and their allies from 413 onwards caused many flights of slaves [*see no 76*].

Athenian slaves did not therefore constitute a social class, and no more than the metics were they considered by the citizens to be rivals in economic activity. It has often been said that the competition of slave labour had aggravated the position of the poorer citizens and had fostered tension between them and the slaves. Had this been the case there would certainly have been echoes of this rivalry in the sources, but in fact there are none. At most Xenophon in his pamphlet *Ways and Means* raises the possibility of a competition between servile labour, which in his scheme was to be used in the mines by the city, and private prospectors. But the case he envisages is a very special one, and the antagonism he mentions is that between the city and inviduals, rather than between slaves and free men. It is emphatically not a case of general competition between free labour and servile labour, and in any case Xenophon refutes the objection after raising it[18]. It would not seem, then, that poor citizens saw in slaves possible rivals; on the contrary, they regarded them as 'working companions'[19]. The slaves were there to supplement and if possible replace the work of free men: between these groups there could not be any real economic competition. Inscriptions on temple buildings illustrate very well the absence of economic competition between the different legal categories: one can see there citizens, metics and slaves working together on the same site, doing the same kind of work and being paid the same salary [*see no 73*].

The economic effectiveness of the Athenian type of state
The social and economic differences between states that had a 'modern' outlook and states that had an 'archaic' one are

obviously considerable. But how far did 'modern' states seek and succeed in bringing about a higher degree of economic effectiveness than their rivals?

It is plain that in Athens one found a different attitude towards everything concerning economic activity than was the case in Sparta. A number of aristocratic value judgments against work were deliberately combatted. There was in Athens a law attributed to Solon (whether rightly or wrongly does not matter, since the law certainly existed in the classical period) directed against idleness, which instructed citizens to teach their sons a trade [*see no 37*]. Another law forbade someone to reproach anyone else with his poverty or the trade he exercised [*see no 12*]. To practice a manual craft did not disqualify citizens from enjoying their full political rights, and in the assembly were to be found many citizens who were artisans, shopkeepers, workers and traders[20]; elsewhere, as in Thebes and even more in Sparta, this would have seemed out of place. In Athens a citizen did not have to be a landowner, and although in practice the majority of Athenians did in fact own land in some form, an innovation of principle had been made. In general one may note in fifth-century Athenian literature an evolution in ideas: traditional value judgments on wealth and poverty and the moral qualities which were supposed to be connected with them are occasionally questioned[21]. In Aeschylus' *Prometheus Vinctus* there is no trace of any hostile judgment against technical skill. What is more, in fifth-century Athens technical skill was not merely accepted but to some extent honoured: for the Athenians as for their opponents Athens was the city of *techne* par excellence. All these new attitudes exercised some influence on the economic evolution of the city: Athens was in the fifth century (and remained in the fourth) the most developed Greek city from the economic point of view, and the real commercial centre of the whole of the eastern Mediterranean. To account for this expansion, one must no doubt bring into play factors other than the evolution of ideas (in particular the political supremacy of the Athenian empire in the fifth century), but the freer atmosphere of Athens must undoubtedly have made its contribution too.

But was the evolution a radical one? It seems not, and it appears to have remained circumscribed within certain limits[22]. One may first point out that the legislation encouraging work and economic activity would not have been necessary if hostile attitudes had not existed. In fact there are various indications which lead one to believe that such sentiments continued to be voiced freely in spite of the laws: one recalls the sarcasms of the comic poets of the second half of the fifth century against the vulgar 'demagogues', who according to them were guilty of practising such vile trades as tanner (Cleon), lamp-maker (Hyperbolus) or lyre-maker (Cleophon). Some speeches in the law courts in the fourth century reflect this same attitude, in that the speaker does not hesitate to stigmatize his opponent publicly by reproaching him with his poverty or the trade he practised [*see nos 12, 113*].

As for the law against idleness, it was not directed against idleness as such, but only against the idleness of poor men who did nothing to earn a living and turned instead to begging: the idleness of the well-to-do who did not have to work to gain a living remained enviable and worthy of respect. As for the positive estimate of *techne*, it did not in fact extend equally to all aspects of technical skill: the *techne* praised by the Corinthians[23] and Athenians in Thucydides is military (or more exactly naval) and political in character [*see no 79*]. The great teachers of *techne*, the sophists, restricted themselves in practice to certain *technai*, in particular rhetoric and politics. What interested them primarily was the art of working on other men, and not on matter. *Techne* mattered to them only in so far as it was a means towards self-sufficiency (thus Hippias of Elis). The *techne* of artisans did not achieve for them the status of genuine knowledge, and the sophists neglected it. In the classical period one cannot trace any revolution in techniques such as might have accompanied the birth of new attitudes. Paradoxical as it may appear, it even seems that artisans may have lost some of their prestige as compared with the archaic period: manufacture became separated from magic, but lost in the process some of its value and was demoted to the level of a routine. At the same time the conditions in which manufacturing activity was carried out evolved to its disadvantage: urbanization brought with it a certain division of labour, but from the psychological point of view this division reinforced the dependence of the worker on others, and only the farmer preserved his personal autonomy almost completely.

Athens' contribution in the field of economic activity remained therefore more limited than might have been expected, and was essentially a negative one. It consisted chiefly in combatting some of the hostile value judgments against economic activity, and that without complete success. In Athens, practising a manual craft did not prevent a citizen from enjoying full political rights, but that was all; one was a citizen because one was descended from Athenian parents, but not, it must be repeated, because one was an artisan. There were no guilds grouping together all the members of the same profession, as was to be the case in medieval cities. Athens did not seek to create a new system of values, among which economic activity might have held a position of honour, and to substitute it for aristocratic values. The true values of Athens had nothing to do with technical skills or economic activity, but were to be found elsewhere. This can be seen in Pericles' funeral speech in Thucydides, a genuine manifesto of the values of democratic Athens in the fifth century[24]. Values were political ones: Pericles expressed himself in terms of power and glory, and not of profit or production. Here one finds again the old aristocratic values, but extended this time to a whole people, in the context of the political rivalry between the Greek cities.

Notes

1   This chapter deals mainly with fifth-century Athens. It has, however, been necessary to use fourth-century evidence also, though whenever there is a definite evolution from the fifth to the fourth centuries this has been pointed out. Some characteristics which are peculiar to the fourth century will be mentioned in Chapter 7.

2   *Atimia* was a penalty which deprived a citizen of his political rights.

3   VI, 126–31; cf. L. Gernet, 'Mariages de tyrans', in *Anthropologie de la Grèce antique* (Paris, 1968), pp. 344–59; J.P. Vernant, 'Le mariage', in *Mythe et société en Grèce ancienne* (Paris, 1974), pp. 57–81.

4   On Pericles' law and its effects see recently S.C. Humphreys, 'The Nothoi of Kynosarges', *JHS* 94 (1974), pp. 88–95.

5   See generally Ph. Gauthier, ' "Générosité" romaine et "avarice" grecque: sur l'octroi du droit de cité', *Mélanges d'histoire*

ancienne offerts à William Seston (Paris, 1974), pp. 207–15.
6 See L. Robert, *Études épigraphiques et philologiques* (Paris, 1938), pp. 297–307, and add *Bull.* 1972, 149.
7 J. Pečirka, *The Formula for the Grant of Enktesis in Attic Inscriptions* (Prague, 1966).
8 Plutarch, *Cimon* X; *Pericles* XVI.
9 See M.I. Finley, 'Athenian Demagogues', *Past and Present* 21 (1962), pp. 3–24 (=*Studies in Ancient Society* (London, 1974), pp. 1–25); W.R. Connor, *The New Politicians of Fifth-Century Athens* (Princeton, 1973).
10 See M.I. Finley, 'The Alienability of Land in Ancient Greece: a Point of View', *Eirene* 7 (1968), pp. 25–32, reprinted in *The Use and Abuse of History* (London, 1975), pp. 153–60. The thesis that land in Attica had remained inalienable down to the Peloponnesian War was defended by J.V.A. Fine, 'Horoi. Studies in Mortgage, Real Security and Land Tenure in Ancient Athens', *Hesperia* Supplement IX (1951).
11 On metics M. Clerc, *Les Métèques athéniens* (Paris, 1893), though dated, is still valuable; the best account now is in Ph. Gauthier, *Symbola. Les étrangers et la justice dans les cités grecques* (Nancy, 1972). There is a forthcoming study by D. Whitehead (to be published as *Supplement* IV of the *Proceedings of the Cambridge Philological Society*).
12 See J. Pečirka, 'A Note on Aristotle's Conception of Citizenship and the Role of Foreigners in 4th C. Athens', *Eirene* 6 (1967), pp. 23–6.
13 See however E. Perotti, *Actes du Colloque 1972 sur l'esclavage* (Paris, 1974), pp. 47–56.
14 On what follows see the articles by Vernant and Vidal-Naquet mentioned in Chapter 1, n 38; for a different view of slaves as a class cf. G.E.M. de Ste Croix, ibid.
15 See R. Seager, *Historia* 15 (1966), pp. 178–82.
16 See generally O. Masson, 'Les noms des esclaves dans la Grèce antique', *Actes du Colloque 1971 sur l'esclavage* (Paris, 1973), pp. 9–23.
17 No reliable figures are available, for there did not exist any register of slaves; figures given in ancient sources are occasionally fantastic, and the estimates of modern scholars vary considerably.
18 *Ways and Means* IV, 32 and 39.
19 Xenophon, *Memorabilia* II, 3, 3.

20 Xenophon, *Memorabilia* III, 7, 6.
21 J. Hemelrijk, *Penia en Ploutos* (Diss. Utrecht, 1925), pp. 147–8.
22 On what follows see the studies by Aymard and Vernant mentioned in Chapter 1, n 23, and P. Vidal-Naquet, in *Archives européenes de sociologie* 6 (1965), pp. 144–8.
23 I, 70–1.
24 II, 35–46.

6 The Greek Cities and Economic Problems

The economic behaviour of Greek states

To what extent were Greek states conscious of economic problems, and to what extent did economic considerations influence their behaviour? The answers given by many historians to these questions were for a long time dominated – and sometimes still are – by the modernizing conception of the ancient Greek economy established by some German historians of the nineteenth century, notably Ed. Meyer, K.J. Beloch and G. Busolt (see Chapter 1). Since they did not see any fundamental difference between the ancient Greek economy and the economy of the modern world, they were quite naturally led to suppose that the economic behaviour of Greek cities may have been influenced, or even dictated, by economic considerations similar to those which influence modern states. One then discovered in Greek history the existence of factors more or less unsuspected before, but for which ancient sources provided no concrete evidence. For example, the 'colonizing movement' of the archaic period was alleged to have been prompted by the aim of seeking new outlets for the 'industrial production' of the mother cities which was showing a surplus. Historians talked freely of aristocracies of 'great ship-owners' or of 'great slave-owning entrepreneurs', who were supposed to have been in control of the policy of many Greek cities already at an early date[1]. Many conflicts, even at a very remote period, were explained in terms of commercial rivalries, such as the 'Lelantine War' in Euboea, which was supposed to have witnessed the clash of two rival leagues which between them grouped together the main 'commercial powers' of the age. The underlying cause of the Peloponnesian War was not the political rivalry between Athens and Sparta and the fear aroused in Sparta by the growth of Athenian power, as Thucydides believed. The real cause was the 'commercial rivalry' between Athens and Megara on the one hand (the Megarian decree, which was wrongly held to have excluded Megarian goods from the Athenian market, as well as from her 'empire', and of which Thucydides was alleged to have misunderstood or even distorted the real significance), and between Athens and Corinth on the other hand (sparked off by the intervention of Athens in the 'commercial sphere' of Corinth via the alliance with Corcyra). This explanation of the Peloponnesian War has enjoyed great success in one form or another; traces of it may still be found today[2].

And yet it is clear that just as the modernizing conception of the Greek economy must be abandoned, so too one cannot attribute to Greek cities an economic mentality which in all probability they never had. One must start from the fact, mentioned earlier, that the 'economy' never was for the Greeks an autonomous category. In the life of the Greek cities in the classical period it was subsumed under politics. As a result, in so far as economic factors may have affected their behaviour, they were not experienced as such but were subordinated to political considerations.

Policy of imports and not exports

It is to Max Weber that one owes one of the fundamental generalizations on the economic behaviour of Greek cities; his views were subsequently worked up in detail by J. Hasebroek (see Chapter 1). When one says that Greek cities had an economic policy, what one means in practice is usually that they had an import policy which aimed at ensuring the supplying of the city and the citizens with a number of goods essential for their livelihood, but not an export policy aimed at disposing on favourable terms or even imposing abroad 'national' produce in competition with rival cities. If a Greek city took into account the economic interests of its members, it was solely as consumers and not as producers. One cannot therefore talk of any 'commercial policy' on the part of Greek cities except in a deliberately very restricted sense: what they practised was solely an import not an export policy.

With the Greek cities there simply cannot be any question of industry or commerce being 'national' in character, least of all in

Athens where economic development had reached a fairly high level (see the previous chapter). The fact is that strictly speaking there could not be any national industry or commerce because of the considerable role played in the whole of economic activity by outsiders (notably metics), both in manufacture and in all trading activity, whether import or export trade, and whether long range or short range. There is really no such thing as 'Athenian industry' or 'Athenian trade' (concepts which, in fact, cannot be translated into Greek). How then could Athens have sought to protect or encourage what were only abstractions, and abstractions created by modern historians at that[3]?

Another factor which prevented the development of modern-style economic policies in Greek cities was the fragmentation of economic activity. Not only was economic activity shared out among citizens and non-citizens, but it generally remained small scale in its organization. Large-scale enterprises with a wide range of action were usually not to be found; a great deal was produced and consumed locally. It is rare to find a regular link between producers and exporters. In any case the precariousness of living conditions (insecurity on land and sea, etc.) did not encourage the development of a more advanced organization of economic life.

The organization of the pottery industry in Athens, about which a certain amount is known or can be inferred, may be adduced to illustrate all these points. First, it was not strictly speaking a national industry, for non-Athenians were found among the potters and painters in Athens. Besides, pottery workshops remained always small scale and only employed a small number of workmen, and that in spite of the fact that Athens in the classical period supplied fine painted vases to most of the Greek world as well as to some non-Greek peoples. Furthermore it is only rarely that a permanent link between a potter and a foreign market can be traced. Some types of vases appear to have been made with some particular foreign customers in mind; but usually vases were exported almost anywhere according to demand and circumstances. Another characteristic fact is that the export of vases from Athens never seems to have been solely in the hands of Athenian traders. Many Attic vases of the late sixth and early fifth centuries appear, from graffiti they bear, to have been exported abroad by traders from Ionia: in other words the potters in Athens did not organize themselves the export of their own vases[4]. Another point is that among the many names of potters and painters of Athens known to us from inscriptions on vases, none is found in any classical literary source. The world of the artisans (the potters in this case) remained a separate world, neglected by the historical tradition whose interests lay in another direction.

The import trades

Among the different import trades, the grain trade occupies a very special position. The beginnings of the import of corn towards the Greek world from Egypt, the Black Sea and Sicily in the archaic age were seen earlier (see Chapter 3). In the classical period this trade developed on a substantial scale in many Greek cities, and especially in Athens where the considerable growth of the city in the fifth century increased Athens' dependence on imports of foreign corn[5].

In the fifth century there is as yet little information on the workings of this trade in Athens. However, one can catch glimpses of the important place that food supplies might hold in Athenian foreign policy. The concern to control directly or indirectly the sources of the supply of corn was a recurring factor in her policy. Immediately after the Persian Wars, the Athenians made a fresh attempt to control the straits leading to the Black Sea. On several occasions they sought also to remove Cyprus from Persian domination, though without success; apart from her strategic location and her mineral resources (notably her copper mines) the island was rich in corn. Later, around the middle of the century, they intervened to give support to Egypt in revolt against the Persian Empire: had Egypt been liberated and brought into the Athenian alliance she would have been of considerable importance to her for her corn supply. The interest shown by the Athenians in Sicily, perhaps from as early as the middle of the fifth century, may also be explained in part by the hope of laying hands on its resources in corn[6]. Euboea, Lemnos, Imbros and Skyros were more or less closely controlled by Athens, often by means of settlements of Athenians on the spot: here again, as well as lying on the route to the Black Sea, these were islands rich in corn. During the Peloponnesian War the Athenians even instituted a special guard on the Hellespont to protect the corn ships coming from the Black Sea[7].

But it is only for the fourth century that one has more specific evidence about the means used by the Athenians to safeguard their supplies and the relations they maintained with certain states or rulers who controlled important supplies of corn. There was in Athens a whole body of legislation on the grain trade; one cannot be certain that it already existed in the fifth century, and it is possible that it did not. In the fifth century Athens was at the height of her power and in a position to intervene directly to safeguard her interests, whereas in the fourth century she was obliged to have recourse to indirect means, such as legislation.

A law which probably dates from the middle of the fourth century forbade anyone domiciled in Athens or Attica (whether a citizen or a metic) to lend money on a ship importing corn to any place other than Athens [*see no 82*] (on this technique of maritime loans see Chapter 7). Another law of earlier date also forbade anyone domiciled in Athens or Attica to transport corn to any harbour except Peiraieus, and two-thirds of his cargo had to be disposed of in Athens. Besides, the corn retailers (the *sitopolai*, who were metics) were not allowed to purchase from importers more than 50 measures of corn at a time, in an attempt to prevent fraudulent speculation [*see no 84*]. Among magistrates appointed to supervise the functioning of economic activity, the *sitophylakes* had the task of supervising the grain trade and the inspectors of the commercial port (the *epimeletai emporiou*) had to enforce the rules on the sale of corn imported to Athens [*see no 89*]. It is also known that in Athens the assembly of the people had to include regularly on its agenda the question of the corn supply as well as the defence of the city's territory: both problems were on the same level[8].

The grain trade is the only trade which Athenian law sought to regulate in this way: it is clear that the only concern of the city here was to ensure the regularity of imports and protect the interests of the citizen-consumers. It is particularly noteworthy that the city never apparently worried about the citizens who were themselves corn producers in Attica and the possible effects on them of large-scale imports of foreign corn.

But internal legislation was not enough by itself. In the fourth century Athens was less well placed to enforce her political supremacy, and had to seek to conciliate in different ways the good will of the traders who imported corn (see Chapter 7). She also had to resort to diplomacy to seek to conciliate foreign states or rulers who controlled the essential sources of supply of corn. It is likely, for example, that the relations between Athens and Evagoras of Cyprus in the early fourth century were partly dictated by economic considerations; a ruler friendly to Athens and in control of the whole island would have been of considerable help for Athens' supplies in the difficult years after the Peloponnesian War. But it was with the Greek rulers of the Crimean Bosporus that relations were particularly close and durable [*see nos 80, 81*]. According to Demosthenes, Attica imported every year 800,000 medimni of corn, half of which came from the Black Sea. In return for various privileges and honours attested by literary and epigraphic sources, the rulers of the Bosporus granted to the Athenians particularly favourable export terms.

The other commodities for which Athens sought to control, directly or indirectly, the sources of supply were what one may refer to as strategic materials [*see no 85*]. Under that heading one can include anything which might be of importance in the manufacture of weapons, and especially in the construction and equipping of the war fleets on which the power of Athens rested. It is one of the paradoxes of the history of Athens that, although she was primarily a naval power, she did not have in Attica adequate resources for her navy. These included, in particular, construction timber, but also metals, linen for sails, pitch and vermilion for the painting of the hulls [*see no 86*]. The means used by Athens to secure these commodities varied at different times. Sometimes Athens simply relied on her military and political supremacy, at other times she had to resort to diplomacy. Already in the time of Peisistratus the Athenians showed interest in the coast of Thrace and Macedon, probably for all the economic assets they had (timber and metals). Subsequently, and up to the time of Philip of Macedon, they continuously sought to establish their influence in the region, through the foundation of colonies under Athenian control (as for example the foundation of Amphipolis on the Strymon in 437–436 after several unsuccessful attempts in previous decades [*see also no 99*]), through military intervention, or by means of understandings with the kings of Macedon who held a monopoly of the export of timber from Macedon. As revealed, for example, by an Athenian decree in honour of the Macedonian king Archelaus[9], or the text of an alliance between another Macedonian king (Amyntas) and the Chalcidian federation in Thrace[10], economic considerations were often explicitly involved in such diplomatic relations.

The special character of the economic preoccupations of Greek cities must be underscored; strictly speaking they were not concerned with economic problems as such but with political ones. As far as the Athenian assembly was concerned the question of the corn supply was a political concern, of the same kind as the security of the territory. When the Athenians voted honours to a trader who had imported corn in a period of shortage or to a foreign ruler who had facilitated the export of the resources of his kingdom on terms favourable to them, they expressed themselves in exactly the same language they would have used for services of any kind done to the community of citizens. For them these were civic benefactions done to the people of Athens, and not just strictly economic services.

The fiscal policy of Greek cities

Greek cities, then, only had a commercial policy as far as imports were concerned, and among imports only those which were essential for the existence of the city. Everything else did not interest the city directly: this means that a very large part of economic activity took place without any intervention on the part of the city, or at least intervention of a kind designed to encourage or restrict the working of economic life.

For the rest, the overriding preoccupation of the city was simply to secure its revenues, and here again the limits of this policy are apparent. The fiscal policy of Greek cities was generally speaking of a very rudimentary kind, both in its objectives and in its methods. The cities were not acquainted with the notion of the budget which draws up a regular balance sheet of public expenditure and revenue and tries to make long-range economic forecasts. Greek cities tended to live from hand to mouth. The case of Athens in the years before the outbreak of the Peloponnesian War is a special one: besides the large-scale accumulation of reserves [*see no 87*], the Athenians created at the instigation of Pericles a special money reserve, which was intended to cater for a major conflict with Sparta and her allies, which could be foreseen years ahead. By contrast Sparta and her allies, although they too were expecting the possibility of a conflict, had not built up any cash reserves before the start of hostilities and were caught unprepared when the war broke out. Hence they had to resort to fiscal expedients such as begging for contributions from their allies and friends in the Greek world on an individual basis [*see no 88*].

What is striking in the fiscal practices of Greek cities is the crudeness of the devices they often resorted to. It could happen in extreme cases that the city assumed a right of intervention in the affairs of its members with the sole purpose of bringing in revenues willy-nilly. The second book of the *Economics* of Ps.-Aristotle contains a whole collection of such fiscal stratagems which cities or rulers (both Greek and non-Greek) resorted to [*see no 91*]. It must, however, be emphasized that the majority of examples collected by the author date from the fourth century, a period of crisis in the Greek world (see Chapter 7), and that examples from before this period concern especially tyrants whose economic behaviour was not strictly comparable to that of republican cities.

The way in which Greek cities disposed of any surpluses of revenue is characteristic of their economic mentality: instead of seeking to invest them profitably, they tended to spend them largely on non-economic enterprises – prestige projects in which pride and civic patriotism were allowed to express themselves freely with naive self-satisfaction, such as the construction of public monuments, both religious and secular. The fifth-century Athenian constructions spring immediately to mind [*see nos 55, 90*]; they are the most famous, but are far from being unique in the Greek world. In the sixth and fifth centuries the Greek cities of Sicily spent their wealth in the construction of monuments which yield nothing in magnificence to those of Athens[11].

Another way for Greek cities to spend the surplus of their revenues was the (more or less direct) redistribution of the wealth of the city among the citizens [*see nos 20, 111, 115*]. It was an old idea, widely accepted among the Greeks, that the wealth of the city belonged to all the citizens (and not just the poorer ones)[12]; a citizen might go so far as to expect to be maintained at the expense of the city. Xenophon in *Ways and Means* declared quite frankly that the aim of his economic projects was to make it possible for the citizens to live at the city's expense.[13] In practice these conditions were rarely realized, and in the majority of cases, even in democratic Athens at the height of her power, the citizens had to a great extent to provide for themselves. But all the same one expected contributions on the part of the city in one form or another, such as periodic distributions of money or corn,[14] the sharing out of sacrificial meat at the time of the great religious festivals, payments by the city for the tenure of all magistracies in democratic Athens and elsewhere[15], payments for attendance at the assembly in fourth-century Athens, subsidies enabling citizens to attend the great religious festivals [*see nos 111, 115*] (these were to increase in importance in the fourth century; see Chapter 7).

There is a strong temptation to describe all such distributions and subventions as emanating from the abstract 'state', but the temptation must be firmly resisted. The 'state' did not exist as an abstraction for the citizens[16]. It was not the 'state' which distributed money to Athenians who wished to attend performances at the theatre during the festivals of Dionysus, in the same way as Social Security pays out sickness benefits; what happened was that the Athenians redistributed among themselves part of the revenues of the community. There was not even any difference in principle between distributing money and building ships, even though in practice conflicts might arise between opposite decisions and the policies they implied.

The Greek cities and their revenues: mines

For Greek cities which had important mines on their territory or in their sphere of control (and this was always the exception: generally speaking the essential sources of metal, both precious and common, were to be found outside the Greek world[17]), there was a source of revenue which could not be allowed to remain in the form of private property. The general tendency for Greek cities was therefore to monopolize the ownership of mines in order to ensure their revenues [*see nos 20, 94*]. There is little information on the exact modes of exploitation of the mines, which must have varied according to time and place. The best-known case is that of the Laurion mines in Attica from which Athens derived the largest part of the silver which she used for striking her abundant silver coinage in the classical period and which was one of the key elements in her prosperity [*see nos 95, 96*]. Little is known of the exploitation of these mines in the fifth century. In the fourth century, by contrast, more detailed information is available, though it is fragmentary: a few allusions in the orators, Xenophon's *Ways and Means*, and the lists of the mining leases from 367–366 to 307–306 or a little later. The city kept for itself the ownership of the mines, but instead of exploiting them directly for her own benefit leased them out to individuals (who were all apparently citizens) for periods and sums which varied according to the type of mine that was being worked (the details are often uncertain). Although some leaseholders worked their mines themselves, slave labour was generally resorted to. In periods of most intensive working there may have been several tens of thousands of slaves active at Laurion, among them many slaves of Thracian and Paphlagonian origin who came from mining regions. It would appear from the inscriptions that the leaseholders were more or less always Athenian citizens. Among the known names one finds many men who played an important role in the political and social life of Athens in the fourth century. If lucky, a leaseholder might make a fortune; but there was always an element of risk in enterprises of this kind, and the exploitation of the mines varied in intensity according to political and economic conditions[18].

Taxation

Taxation remained of course the main source of revenue for the majority of Greek cities. The use they made of it is revealing not only of their economic mentality but of the whole system of values on which the Greek city was built.

Direct and regular taxes on the property of citizens and especially their persons were usually avoided; they were felt to be degrading. Tyrants resorted to them occasionally, but cities with republican-type constitutions abolished them as far as possible. By contrast there was no hesitation in taxing non-citizens. Thus metics in Athens had to pay regularly a special tax, the *metoikion*, which was admittedly moderate, but which symbolized their inferior status as compared with citizens (see Chapter 5).

But if regular taxes on citizens and their property were felt to be unacceptable, the city had all the same to make use of the wealth of its members. Here a convenient way round was available, in that it was an accepted principle in Greek cities that the wealthier citizens had a moral obligation to spend their wealth for the public good [*see no 97*]. This obligation, although unwritten, was strongly felt and consequently impossible to avoid altogether. It was by appealing to public spirit and devotion to the interests of the community that the city could use for its own ends the wealth of its richer members. In Athens citizens (and also metics) were obliged, according to their wealth, to undertake *liturgies* (literally, services for the community[19]), such as the trierarchy, in which the state supplied triremes, while the trierarchs had to provide for their upkeep and commanding, or the choregia, in which the choregoi had to recruit, train and pay a chorus for the great dramatic competitions. In the fourth century there were more than a hundred regular civil and religious liturgies, not counting the military liturgies the frequency of which might vary[20]. In spite of the frequently high expenses incurred in the discharge of liturgies, they were not thought of as strictly economic services, but as civic services with honorific connotations. Thus it happened frequently that a wealthy citizen or metic undertook more liturgies than was strictly necessary, and made a point of discharging his functions with the greatest possible lavishness, to demonstrate in this way his devotion to the community. In the law courts defendants never failed to try to influence the verdict of the jurors by pointing to all the services they had performed by means of their liturgies.

Indirect taxes, by contrast, were frequently resorted to by Greek cities and were one of their main sources of revenue [*see no 92*]. What was characteristic here was the almost complete absence of any discrimination between citizens and non-citizens in the raising of these taxes (one exception was the tax paid by foreigners to trade in the *agora* at Athens; it is not known whether metics were affected or not by this tax [*see no 12*]). The city taxed economic activity in its various forms in different ways, without ever wondering whether it was thereby harming the interests of citizens or not. For instance, in 413 at a time of financial stringency caused by the Peloponnesian War, the Athenians thought of increasing their revenues by abolishing the annual tribute they exacted from their allies in the Delian League and replacing it by a 5 per cent tax on all the trade transiting in the harbours of the Athenian empire[21]; later on, between 390 and 387, they sought to reimpose this same tax on their former allies. This tax fell indiscriminately on the Athenians, their allies and everybody else, Greek or non-Greek, who traded in the Athenian sphere of influence. Generally speaking it would appear that before the Hellenistic period taxes on economic activity only served a purely fiscal purpose of raising revenue. The idea of erecting customs barriers to protect the 'national' industry or trade does not even seem to have occurred to anyone. One may once more verify in this way how the economic interests of citizens, as far as the city was concerned, never were interests of citizen producers, but only of citizen consumers.

The exploitation of economic activity for fiscal purposes originated, as has been seen, in the archaic period (see Chapter 3). In the classical period Athens pursued these techniques with even greater success in that the growth of Athenian power after the Persian Wars made Peiraieus not only the most important military port in the eastern Mediterranean, but also its greatest economic centre. The power and prosperity of Athens attracted traders there from almost everywhere in search of a market where everything might be bought and sold. Athenian sources of the classical period never fail to emphasize the variety and abundance of all the foreign goods that were to be found in Athens [*see no 83*]. Even after the disaster in the Peloponnesian War, Peiraieus did not lose its role as a great economic centre; it was partly this which helped Athens to get over the worst moments of the financial crisis after the Peloponnesian War. The main tax at Peiraieus was the tax of one-fiftieth (2 per cent) raised on all goods, both exports and imports, and whatever their country of origin [*see no 93*]. Other taxes were raised on goods sold in the *agora* in Athens, on foreigners who traded there, on sales by the city of goods which belonged to it (through confiscation, for example), through fines in the law courts, etc [*see nos 75, 98*].

The control of economic activity

The raising of these various indirect taxes was generally carried out by private contractors. The farming of the taxes was auctioned by the city (as in the case of the tax of one-fiftieth at Peiraieus [*see no 93*]). But there also existed a number of magistracies which dealt with economic activity in general, as for example in Athens in the fourth century the inspectors of the market (*agoranomoi*), the inspectors of measures (*metronomoi*), the commissioners of the corn trade (*sitophylakes*) and the inspectors of the commercial harbour (*epimeletai emporiou*) [*see no 89*]. These magistracies performed different functions. Some supervised the corn supply, as seen above (the *sitophylakes* and the *epimeletai emporiou*), others dealt with the policing of markets more generally; no specifically economic preoccupation was involved here, but only a concern to supervise and keep law and order. It is probably to this same concern for law and order that one must attribute the practice, widely attested from Thucydides onwards, of establishing special temporary markets outside cities when foreign armies happened to be passing by and asked to be allowed to supply themselves[22]. Occasionally in some oligarchic states the wish to supervise economic activity was prompted by deeper motives and it was economic activity as such that was to be kept under control. In Thessaly, for example, the different functions of the *agora* (which was originally a meeting place for the community before it became an economic centre) were deliberately separated: there was a 'free' *agora* which was reserved for civic and political activity, and from which all economic functions were deliberately excluded [*see no 129*]. The latter were concentrated in a special *agora*, the commercial one. These same principles are found again in the philosophers: Aristotle adopted for his own purposes the distinction between the 'free' and the commercial *agora*, and Plato in the *Laws* laid down that foreign traders should be received only outside the city and that one should have only the minimum of relations with them [*see nos 127, 129*]. Here one meets once more old prejudices, directed partly against economic activity as such and partly against the outside world and all the risks of harmful foreign influences that it involved.

The Greek cities and coinage

A few words may be said here about the monetary policy of Greek cities. The origins of coined money in archaic Greece were seen above: whatever 'economic' motives were involved it is likely that other 'non-economic' ones were also present. In the classical period, the use of coinage became more and more widespread, and in Athens in the fourth century all values were eventually expressed in monetary terms. However, coinage always preserved some aspects which one could hardly describe as strictly economic[23]; the possession of an autonomous coinage was a symbol of political independence, and the right to strike coinage was of course an exclusive privilege of the city. When Athens in the fifth century sought to impose on the members of her empire the use of her own weights, measures and silver coins, this was probably a political move in the first instance, rather than any sort of 'economic' or 'commercial imperialism' as has often been said [*see no 101*]. Usually, however, most Greek cities did not seek to impose their coinage abroad and were in any case not in a position to do so (even Athens had only limited success in her attempt, it seems). The popularity and circulation of coins was therefore conditioned by factors which were outside the control of any particular city. On the other hand, they did naturally impose the use of their own coins within their own territory, though not necessarily to the exclusion of other coinages, and could at times take direct steps to enforce this, as has been shown again by a recently discovered Athenian law on coinage of 375–374 [*see no 102*]. Another law on coinage from Olbia in the fourth century laid down among other rules the obligation of using solely coins from Olbia in all transactions inside the city; here again the motives were probably civic pride rather than any strictly economic calculations [*see no 103*]. What is more, the law of Olbia prescribed a fixed rate of exchange for coins of the city only against Cyzicene staters. Everything else, including the import and export of all coinages, whether foreign or local, and the rates of exchange, was left to the initiative of individuals.

'Imperialism' and tribute

Apart from the various fiscal practices there remained another possible source of revenue for Greek cities: this was simply the exploitation for economic purposes by the more powerful cities of their political and military superiority. In the Greek world, what nowadays we would call 'imperialism' was the natural concomitant of factors that have been mentioned earlier on, namely negative value judgments of work and economic activity, the acceptance in one form or another of war as a means of acquisition, the notion that ideally the citizen ought to live off the resources of the city. All these elements contributed to the acceptance of domination over foreigners as a permanent fact in relations between Greek cities. Nothing seemed more natural than to seek to throw back on foreigners a burden which citizens preferred not to have to carry themselves.

At first sight one might be tempted to see in this way of thinking a contradiction with the much-proclaimed ideal of freedom and autonomy: how, one wonders, could a Greek reconcile the desire for freedom on the part of a city with domination exercised at the expense of other cities? But in fact there was no necessary contradiction for the Greeks. If one asks the question, How did the Greeks define the freedom of a city?, the answer given right through Greek literature is explicit: the freedom of a city consisted not only in freedom from any foreign domination, but also in the possibility of imposing on others one's own domination [*see no 132, cf. too no 18*]. Just as with the antithesis between free and slave, the two extremes were not felt to be incompatible, but were complementary and interdependent: full freedom could not be conceived without domination over others[24].

Consequently the most powerful cities sought to impose their domination on others. Sometimes it was only a political and military supremacy in which the leading city did not automatically seek to derive economic advantages from its supremacy. Such was the case with the so-called 'Peloponnesian League' which was dominated by Sparta and which arose in the second half of the sixth century. It was mainly a permanent military alliance aimed at preserving the balance of power in the Peloponnese and ensuring Sparta's own security, especially vis-à-vis the Helots, and the member states did not pay any tribute to Sparta or any contributions to the treasury of the league. One special form which certain dominations could assume was that of a mother city over her colonies; such was the case with the 'colonial empire' established by the tyrants of Corinth in the early sixth century. The links established between Corinth and her colonies were still in existence in the classical period. Such was also the case with the domination established by Sinope over her colonies on the south coast of the Black Sea: the colonies of Sinope had to pay tribute to their mother city [*see no 100*].

But the most important domination (*arkhe*) of Greek history in the classical period was of course that of Athens. The 'Delian League' founded in 478–477 and which included many cities of the Aegean, gradually became an Athenian empire, and the process was complete by the time of the 30 years' peace of 446–445 which formalized the division of the Greek world into two power blocks, the one dominated by Sparta and the other by Athens. The empire lasted until the capitulation of Athens in 404 at the end of the Peloponnesian War[25].

A tradition which goes back to the fourth century, and which is reproduced in Plutarch, credits Athenian statesmen in the first generation of the history of the League with having been opposed to the growth of Athenian 'imperialism' at the expense of the allies. Cimon, in particular, is alleged to have sought to defend the interests of the allies, and it is said that it was only the statesmen of the following generation, and especially the so-called demagogues who came after Pericles, who showed themselves harsh towards their subjects. It seems, however, that this is an artificial point of view. There is no echo of any divergence of opinions among the Athenian leaders on the subject of the league (and personal rivalries as well as conflicts over internal and foreign policy were not lacking at this period). Cimon himself was for a while in charge of operations against Thasos which was in revolt from Athens in 465–463. The clash involved strictly Athenian interests and could hardly be justified from a league point of view[26]. It was only in the 440s, after the death of Cimon and after the end of hostilities between Athens and the Persian Empire in about 449 that the question of the tribute of the allies was raised by Thucydides son of Melesias in the course of his struggle against Pericles [see no 90]. One must anyhow define clearly the limits of his programme: Thucydides was not really the champion of the allies as he has often been made out to be; what he was attacking was solely the use made by Athens of the tribute of the allies to finance the construction of her public buildings, and he did not advocate the dissolution of the league even after the end of hostilities against Persia. In any case a majority of Athenians took the side of Pericles; Thucydides was ostracized in 443, and for many years Pericles had no direct rival at the head of the Athenian state. It would seem in fact that for most of the history of the empire the majority of Athenians, both rich and poor, took the existence of the empire completely for granted. The deepest motivation may well have been a psychological one – the will for power – but all the 'economic' advantages that flowed from it, such as tribute, cleruchies and other settlements [see no 99], economic exploitation by the city or by individuals[27], control of foreign sources of corn and metals and other commodities [see no 85], and so forth, were generally taken for granted [see no 98]. Even the defeat of Athens in the Peloponnesian War did not apparently bring about an immediate reversal in men's attitudes. In the first decades of the fourth century the Athenians sought to reconstruct their fifth-century empire in one way or another, pretending even at first that it had never ceased to exist, despite the outcome of the Peloponnesian War. It was only gradually in the course of the fourth century that doubts began to be raised against 'imperialism' as such, or at least imperialism practised at the expense of other Greeks, because of the deep changes provoked by the crisis in the Greek world.

Notes

1 For one example see the misapplication of Marxist categories by G. Thomson, *Studies in Ancient Greek Society* II: *the First Philosophers* (London, 2nd ed., 1961), esp. ch. IX; even the Pythagoreans at Croton are turned into members of 'the new class of rich industrialists and traders' (p. 252).

2 The theory of the commercial origins of the Peloponnesian War has been disposed of once and for all by G.E.M. de Ste Croix, *The Origins of the Peloponnesian War* (London, 1972), a book which, among other things, is an important contribution to the theme of 'trade and politics' in the Greek world.

3 On the absence of merchant navies in the Greek cities and the consequences this had see de Ste Croix, op. cit., pp. 393–6 (though cf. Xenophon, *Ways and Means* III, 14 [*see no 122*], a passage not mentioned by de Ste Croix). On imports to, and exports from, Athens, see the collection of evidence by E. Erxleben, *Klio* 57, 2 (1975), pp. 365–98.

4 See the works by Cook mentioned in Chapter 1, n 52; T.B.L. Webster, *Potter and Patron in Classical Athens* (London, 1972) (speculative); A.W. Johnston, 'Trademarks on Greek Vases', *Greece and Rome* XXI (1974), pp. 138–52.

5 See L. Gernet, 'L'approvisionnement d'Athènes en blé aux Ve et IVe siècles', in G. Bloch, *Mélanges d'histoire ancienne* (Paris, 1909), pp. 269–391; F.M. Heichelheim, in *Real-Encyclopaedie*, Supp. VI (1935), cols 833–44; G.E.M. de Ste Croix, *The Origins of the Peloponnesian War*, op. cit., pp. 46–9, 314.

6 Cf. Thucydides III, 86, 4.

7 Cf. Meiggs–Lewis no 65, lines 34–41 with the commentary.

8 Aristotle, *Constitution of Athens* XLIII, 4.

9 Meiggs–Lewis no 91.

10 Tod, *GHI* II, no 111.

11 Cf. Diodorus XIII, 81–4 (Acragas).

12 See K. Latte, 'Kollektivbesitz und Staatschatz in Griechenland', *Kleine Schriften* (Munich, 1968), pp. 294–312.

13 IV, 33.

14 One example in 445–444: Philochorus, *FGrHist* 328 F 119; Plutarch, *Pericles* XXXVII, 4.

15 See G.E.M. de Ste Croix, 'Political Pay outside Athens', *CQ* 25 (1975), pp. 48–52; on the range of meanings of *misthos* see Ed. Will in *Hommages à Claire Préaux* (Brussels, 1975), pp. 426–38.

16 What did exist, however, was the abstract name of Athens as an object of reverence, as evidenced, for example, by the funeral orations of the classical period; a dissertation on this subject by N. Loraux (*Athènes imaginaire*) will be completed shortly. See provisionally N. Loraux, *REA* LXXV (1973), pp. 13–42; *Antiquité Classique* XLIII (1974), pp. 172–211.

17 On the whole question of metals for coinage see Ed. Will, 'Les sources des métaux monnayés dans le monde grec', in *Numismatique Antique, Problèmes et Méthodes* (Nancy-Louvain, 1975), pp. 97–102.

18 See R.J. Hopper, 'The Attic Silver Mines in the Fourth Century B.C.', *BSA* 48 (1953), pp. 200–54; id., 'The Laurion Mines: a Reconsideration', ibid., 63 (1968), pp. 293–326.

19 See N. Lewis, '*Leitourgia* and Related Terms', *Greek, Roman and Byzantine Studies* III (1960), pp. 175–84; VI (1965), pp. 226–30.

20 See J.K. Davies, 'Demosthenes on Liturgies: a Note', *JHS* 87 (1967), pp. 33–40.

21 Thucydides VII, 28, 4.

22 See for example Thucydides VI, 44, 2–3; Xenophon, *Anabasis* V, 5, 14–19; see further R. Martin, *Recherches sur l'agora grecque* (Paris, 1951), pp. 285–7; G.E.M. de Ste Croix, *The Origins of the Peloponnesian War*, op. cit., pp. 399–400.

23 See Ed. Will, 'Fonctions de la monnaie dans les cités grecques de l'époque classique', in *Numismatique antique . . .* (op. cit. in n 17 above), pp. 233–46.

24 See J.A.O. Larsen, 'Freedom and its Obstacles in Ancient Greece', *CP* 57 (1962), pp. 230–4.

25 See now for all aspects R. Meiggs, *The Athenian Empire* (Oxford, 1972).

26 Cf. Thucydides I, 100, 2.

27 For one particular instance of exploitation by individuals see Ph. Gauthier, 'A propos des clérouquies athéniennes du Ve siècle', in *Problèmes de la terre en Grèce ancienne*, ed. M.I. Finley (Paris and The Hague, 1973), pp. 163–78.

7 The Time of Crises

The Peloponnesian War and Greek history
The Peloponnesian War marks a decisive turning point in the
history of Greece, whether one considers it from its political,
social or economic aspects. It ushered in the beginning of the
decline of the city as it had existed in the fifth century. Many of
the characteristic features of the fourth century made their
appearance with the Peloponnesian War and were in part caused
by it, or at least were chronologically linked with it, such as the
transformation of military techniques, social and political conflicts and their consequences, and innovations in the economic
life of Athens; some even preceded it.

It should be made clear at the outset, however, that the fourth
century should not be regarded as a period of unqualified 'crisis'
for the Greek world. One could hardly talk of a general crisis of
Greek civilization in view of all the cultural achievements of the
fourth century, nor of a general economic crisis. If one looks
beyond what had been the main centres of the Greek world in the
fifth century, notably Athens and Sparta, then it is clear that the
Greek world as a whole was going through a period of growth
which in retrospect may be viewed as the prelude to the expansion
of the Hellenistic age. This is made clear by the multiplication of
tombs and archaeological finds in many parts of the Greek world
(Magna Graecia, Thrace, the Black Sea). The 'crisis' was rather
a crisis of the *polis* and its institutions as they had existed till then.

The history of the Greek city might be described as the history
of an impossible ideal which was almost never achieved completely and never for any great length of time. The city aimed at
ensuring the livelihood of its members. For this it presupposed
concord among the citizens (and the absence of too glaring

economic inequalities), economic self-sufficiency and political and military independence. Between the ideal and the reality there always was, even in the classical period, a certain gap. Internal balance was often broken by social and political conflicts, economic self-sufficiency was difficult to achieve fully, especially for larger cities, and notably in the case of the supply of corn and metals, and political autonomy was regularly threatened, not only by foreign powers (such as Persia or Macedon), but also by other Greek cities with ambitions of hegemony such as Athens in the fifth century. In the fourth century the gap between ideal and reality kept on widening; the *polis* gradually lost its military and political effectiveness and was increasingly under the shadow of monarchies, a process which started in the fourth century and was to be characteristic of the Hellenistic world. For all that, the *polis* as such did not disappear and the battle of Chaironeia in 338 did not mark its 'end'.

War in the fourth century
The first characteristic of the fourth century was the prevalence of war. The state of war became more or less permanent: from 431 to 338, for almost a century, the Greek world experienced almost without interruption a state of large-scale war, not to mention purely local conflicts. The causes of this are many. In the first place there was the failure of attempts at imperial hegemony, which had succeeded in the fifth century in the case of Athens, but which in the fourth century resulted in a series of more or less unsuccessful attempts which exhausted the Greek cities without producing any clear result.

In 404 Athens capitulated to Sparta and had to dissolve her empire, but all the same she tried to reconstitute it from the very beginning of the fourth century. Although checked by the King's Peace (387–386), she soon resumed the attempt and this culminated in the formation of a new maritime league in 378. The venture had some initial success, but although the new league was only finally dissolved in 338, it declined rapidly and never reached the level of the fifth-century empire.

Sparta, succeeding Athens in 404 as ruler of much of the Aegean Greek world, declined much more abruptly. The ancient sources in fact date her decline from the acquisition of an empire which was the direct cause of it [*see nos 104, 105, 106*]. The Spartan system, too rigid and introverted, was unable to adapt to

4 Greece in 431

The date of 431 has no relevance as far as the underlined names are concerned.

50 km

○ democratic constitution

● oligarchy

▲ constitution unknown

Larissa: city with rural dependants (of the Helot type)

AETOLIA: ethnos type states

the needs of governing an empire which spread out well beyond the limits of the Peloponnese. With the victory of 404 the whole Spartan system was put to the test. The wealth drawn by a minority from the empire contributed to the aggravation of existing social inequalities and encouraged the concentration of landed property among an ever-decreasing number of citizens with full rights. Since the Peers formed the core of the Spartan army, the military power of Sparta declined at the same time. Contemporary sources also speak of a general decline in Spartan traditions, an explanation which may be somewhat too moralizing, but one which from being a consequence then became a cause. Soon after its foundation, the empire of Sparta began to totter; it was re-established for a while thanks to the alliance with Persia (the King's Peace), but it soon began to tremble again, and at the battle of Leuctra in 371 it was finally overthrown. Henceforward Sparta was only a second-rank city, limited in her authority to the Peloponnese over which she never managed to re-establish her former domination.

Sparta was succeeded by her rival Thebes, who had just destroyed her power. For about a decade Thebes attempted to play the role of Sparta on land and for a brief period that of Athens at sea. This new attempt at hegemony was no more successful than the previous ones: at the battle of Mantineia in 362 the death of the Theban general Epaminondas deprived Thebes of the fruits of victory and brought an end to her ascendancy. The historian Xenophon commented on the battle in the following disillusioned terms:

These events had the opposite result of what men expected. For since nearly the whole of Greece had been assembled and drawn up on opposite sides, there was no one who doubted that, if a battle took place, the victors would rule and the vanquished would be subjects. But the deity so arranged things that both sides set up a trophy as though they had won the battle, and neither side prevented the other from doing so, and both sides asked to have their dead back under truce as though they had lost the battle. Both sides claimed to have won the battle, but neither side was wealthier in territory, cities or power than before the battle had taken place, and the uncertainty and confusion in Greece was greater after the battle than it had been before[1].

Soon a new power, Macedon, was to appear in the north: the political horizon of the fourth century was widening, the former powers found themselves challenged more and more, a process which was to carry on into the following period. Within 20 years, Philip of Macedon was to become master of the Greek world and plan the conquest of Asia which his son Alexander realized after him. The hegemony exercised by individual cities over greater or smaller parts of the Greek world was at an end, and gave way to the hegemony of the great monarchies which were to dominate the Hellenistic period.

The development of military techniques

Another characteristic of the fourth century, which was partly connected with the previous one, but which was also caused by other factors, was the growing specialization in warfare and the development of new military techniques [*see nos 107, 108B*]. Up to the end of the fifth century, war in the world of the Greek cities was in general not the business of specialists. It was simply one of the functions of the citizen to be a soldier. The case of Sparta, where the citizens with full rights formed a specialist military élite, was an exceptional one; in any case the Spartiates did not have an absolute monopoly of the military function, since Perioikoi and Helots also took part in war. The techniques of fighting on land were essentially fixed since the seventh century and hardly varied for a long time: the heavily armed formation of hoplite infantry predominated, cavalry and light-armed troops had only limited importance, and there was no genuine siegecraft. The hoplite style of fighting reflected the economic, social and political conditions of Greek cities, and around it grew up a system of values which helped to perpetuate it. Naval warfare, by contrast, evolved more rapidly, thanks to the example of Athens in the fifth century, whose sailors achieved a level of technical skill previously unknown [*see no 79*]. But Athens in the fourth century did not succeed in reconstructing her former naval supremacy fully; in fact it was on land that most of the major conflicts of the fourth century were decided, and it was in the techniques of land warfare that the major innovations rapidly appeared[2].

Already in the Peloponnesian War the role of light-armed infantry, which had hitherto been neglected, made its appearance.

It went on developing in the fourth century, and formations of professional 'peltasts' (soldiers equipped with a small round shield, the *pelte*) played an effective role in land warfare (cf. the defeat of a battalion of Lacedaimonian hoplites at Lechaeum in 390 by the peltasts of the Athenian general Iphicrates)[3]. Techniques of siegecraft made a noted appearance, first in Sicily with the tyranny of the Elder Dionysius (cf. the capture of Motye in 398)[4]. Later on, Philip of Macedon and especially Alexander were to improve on these techniques. A technical body of writing on the art of war made its appearance (cf. the writings of Xenophon and of Aeneas Tacticus [*see no 110*]).

The history of the *strategoi* in Athens gives a good illustration of the evolution towards greater specialization in warfare. During most of the fifth century, an Athenian *strategos* was not necessarily a military specialist, although his main function was to command the Athenian army and navy. The office of *strategos* was simply the one held by all those in Athens who wished to play an important political role in the state (until at least the death of Pericles): Pericles himself, who was *strategos* year after year from 443 to 429, was hardly a great general. Hoplite warfare could do almost completely without specialized military leaders (by contrast naval warfare, as developed by the Athenians at the same period, consciously depended on specialized technical skill). From the time of the Peloponnesian War one finds the beginnings of a greater specialization of functions: the 'demagogues' in Athens formulated the policy of the state, while its execution was entrusted to others. The *strategoi* became more frequently military specialists. In the course of the fourth century the separation became complete: the orators who directed the affairs of state (such as Demosthenes) no longer were *strategoi* and the *strategoi* (such as Iphicrates and others) were solely professional captains[4a].

Of particular seriousness for the history of the Greek city was the considerable development of mercenary service in the fourth century [*see no 108*]. The phenomenon had many interlocking causes: social unrest and the impoverishment of the masses, which left them with no other means of livelihood than to sell their physical strength to any willing employer, a process which was itself linked with the state of near-permanent war which devastated the countryside and hit small peasants hard; political disturbances and internal revolutions which caused many exiles; the absence of the natural outlet of colonization which could have acted as a safety valve as in the archaic period, when mercenary service, although it did exist [*see no 35*], does not seem to have reached the scale it did in the fourth century; the development of military monarchies which created a demand for professional soldiers; a demand in the Middle East (the Persian Empire and Egypt, which had revolted from it) for soldiers and Greek captains whose superiority was evident; and finally the specialization in war which encouraged the development of the profession of mercenary. To be sure, mercenary service was not an innovation in the fourth century[5]. Some, such as the Arcadians, had been mercenaries regularly for a long time. But the phenomenon reached alarming proportions as early as the end of the fifth century (cf. the so-called 'Ten Thousand' in the service of the Persian prince Cyrus in 401–400) and became increasingly serious during the fourth century. Greek mercenaries then could be reckoned in tens of thousands. In this way many peoples who had been only partially affected by the civilization of the *polis* made their entry onto the stage of Greek history. The *polis* still remained an effective model, as is shown by foundations such as those of Messene and Megalopolis in 369 and 368, the latter the capital of the federal state of the Arcadians. But for thousands of men from the poorer regions of Greece, mercenary service was the only form of social promotion before the conquests of Alexander turned them into citizens of the new cities in Asia or cleruchs (military settlers) in Egypt. For thousands of men, too, the army was itself a city, sometimes the only one they knew [*see no 130*].

These mercenaries were to be found almost everywhere, in the Greek cities, in the military monarchies of Sicily, among the Carthaginians, both in the service of the Great King and in that of satraps or provinces in revolt (Cyrus, Evagoras of Cyprus, Egypt). To be sure, citizen armies did not by any means disappear all of a sudden as a result. Aeneas Tacticus, for example, still presupposes the existence of citizen armies [*see no 110*]. But in the long run the consequences for the Greek cities were fatal, since they gradually lost control of warfare. Mercenaries and their captains were foreigners as far as the city was concerned: they did not owe any loyalty to their employers, and furthermore they were very expensive to maintain [*see no 108B*]. They were a luxury which Greek cities could not easily afford on a regular basis. The case of the Phocians who in 356–346 recruited a large army of mercenaries was altogether exceptional: they had laid hands on the treasures of the sanctuary at Delphi. Usually only powerful monarchs, whether Greek or non-Greek, had the necessary resources to make effective use of mercenaries on a large scale.

Confronted by these new developments in the military field, contemporaries reacted in different ways. As far as Isocrates was concerned, the problem was essentially a social one. One needed to settle all the footloose mercenaries on land conquered from the Persian Empire, and the main difficulties of the Greek world would be resolved [*see no 108*]. With Demosthenes, the transformation in military techniques intensified even further the regrets he felt for a past he refused to believe had gone beyond recall [*see no 107*]. After the battle of Chaironeia (338) an archaizing reaction took place in Athens: the military service of the young Athenians (the ephebes), which they performed between the ages of 18 and 20, an institution which probably existed before and which must have been extremely ancient (originally a 'rite of passage' which marked the transition from adolescence to maturity), but which in the classical period served as preparation for hoplite fighting, was now reorganized under the supervision of the city[6]. The philosophers admitted the importance of the evolution of military techniques, but they hesitated to draw all the conclusions from it. Aristotle, after conceding the importance of a certain degree of specialization in war, still held on to the notion of an army of citizens[7]. Plato, after admitting in the *Republic* the new aspects of war in the fourth century and postulating the necessity of a specialized army in his ideal city[8], reverted in the *Laws* to the idea of the citizen-soldier[9]. The trend of Greek history was soon to demonstrate the failure of this notion, and thereby the military failure of the city itself.

Social conflicts and the impoverishment of the masses

One of the main characteristics of the fourth century, and one of the main causes of the problems which affected the Greek cities, was the spread of social conflicts (*staseis*) between rich and poor. Just like mercenary service, of which it was a major cause, *stasis* made a brutal reappearance during the Peloponnesian War. The opposition between Sparta and Athens was in part the opposition between democracy and oligarchy and the two social classes on which they were each based[10]. During the fourth century the gulf between rich and poor kept on widening. Egalitarian aspirations implicit in the notion of citizen aggravated tensions, and social inequalities were all the more keenly felt as a result. Furthermore the principle of equality was in itself ambiguous and liable to be controversial in its interpretation [*see no 114*]. In many cities revolutions, exiles and confiscations of property succeeded each other without ever leading to a clear decision. The slogan of redistribution of land was often heard. The defeat of Sparta at Leuctra in 371 was the signal for a series of democratic revolutions in the Peloponnese accompanied by massacres and exile of the rich [*see no 109*]. In Sicily it was only the tyranny of the Elder Dionysius which put an end to a situation of chronic *stasis* [*see nos 117, 118*], and immediately after the fall of the Younger Dionysius *stasis* made its reappearance. The situation became steadily worse in much of the Greek world. The League of Corinth formed in 338 under the aegis of Philip of Macedon had among its objectives that of trying to put an end to all forms of subversion and internal disturbances in Greek cities. It was the first time that a treaty among Greeks had a clause of this kind written into it. The pamphlet of Aeneas Tacticus *On Siegecraft* (*Poliorcetica*) reflects the same fear of internal subversion [*see no 110*]. The philosophers and political thinkers of the fourth century were all preoccupied with the problem of *stasis* and of internal concord among the members of the same city, which was essential for the life of the community. Aristotle devoted a whole book to it (Book V) [*see no 114*]. Plato, in Books VIII and IX of the *Republic*, drew a striking picture of the decline of a state, a picture which is in part abstract and theoretical, but which also reflects many aspects of fourth-century Greece. In this picture economic factors play a decisive role, but an entirely negative one. Gold, which is absent from the ideal city, spreads gradually through the city and overwhelms it, and the desire for gain leads to the internal destruction of a state, by dividing the community into rival groups of rich and poor [*see no 112*][11].

Admittedly the crisis was not equally serious everywhere. Despite her internal stresses, her failures abroad and the loss of Messenia after the battle of Leuctra, Sparta did not experience a social revolution until the Hellenistic period. The conspiracy of Kinadon in 397 was a failure and the attempt was not subsequently renewed [*see no 61*]. Athens, in particular, escaped from the worst of the troubles of civil war. Admittedly, the Peloponnesian War caused extensive damage: heavy losses in manpower, and the loss of the various revenues derived from the empire [*see no 76*]. The strategy of Pericles, which yielded the territory of Attica to the enemy [*see no 65*], and which gathered the rural population behind the Long Walls during the periods of invasion, was, as has been shown[12], the logical consequence of a policy initiated by Pericles of fortifying the urban area, and also the consequence of the effective primacy – whatever the principles may have been – of the city over the countryside. It resulted in extremely serious social consequences.

There is much contemporary evidence on the impoverishment of the Athenians at this time. One can detect signs of tension between rich and poor, and this tension was reinforced by the fact that each group had recently taken opposing sides in internal politics: many members of the wealthier classes had at first sided with the Thirty. In spite of the amnesty of 403, which was by and large respected, tensions were not completely eliminated. The worst losses incurred in the Peloponnesian War were however made good, but Athens never quite managed to recover her former prosperity. Although really precise evidence is lacking, it seems that there was a certain move from the countryside to the city, which may reflect an impoverishment of the peasant class, though it may be too much to speak of a concentration of landed wealth in a few hands[13]. There would also seem to have been an increase in the number of citizens of the lowest property group, the thetes, who had little or no land. Finally, it seems that in the fourth century the poorer citizens depended more on the different forms of payments by the city (the *misthoi*), and especially the Theoric Fund (the fund for the dramatic festivals), which in practice provided assistance to the poorest citizens [*see nos 111, 115*].

Here again, the Peloponnesian War must have marked a turning point. What means, indeed, were available to poorer citizens who had lost their land and had come to settle in the city? If they did not simply become expatriates and turn to mercenary service, they often disliked the idea of turning towards economic activity of some kind, because of the tenacious survival in the fourth century of 'anti-banausic' attitudes. The alternative therefore was to have recourse to the city's generosity. The impoverishment of the citizens of the lower classes had as its counterpart the wealth of a minority, which displayed itself with a lavishness that struck contemporaries [*see no 116*][14].

One may mention in this connection a modern theory on the impoverishment of the masses in the fourth century. According to the Russian historian M. Rostovtzeff, one of the main causes of the impoverishment of Greece in the fourth century was a relative decline of Greek industries, a decline caused by the economic emancipation of many parts of the non-Greek world, which until then had been among the best customers of the Greek cities. This emancipation reflected an awakening of national consciousness among these various peoples, and is alleged to have led to the decline of many Greek industries.[15] Although this theory has often been accepted, it has its weak points. For one thing the evidence is almost exclusively archaeological and therefore only concerns objects that are indestructible, and especially pottery. Yet pottery is not an infallible index of the general level of economic activity of the producing city. What is more, most of the evidence concerns 'Athenian' industries (especially pottery), and it would be all the more dangerous to seek to generalize from the sole case of Athens to the whole of the Greek world that it was precisely in Athens that the social crisis seems to have been least acute in the Greek world. It is likely that there was a certain impoverishment of the lower classes in Athens, but Athens in the fourth century did not experience social conflicts such as did other Greek cities. There are no traces at the time of the slogan of redistribution of land and cancellation of debts such as were heard elsewhere. The restoration of democracy in 403 was not the prelude to a class victory, and this provoked the astonishment and admiration of Aristotle:

The Athenians seem, both in private and in public, to have adopted the most admirable and public-spirited attitude to their recent disasters. For not only did they cancel all the accusations bearing on the past, but they repaid to the Lacedaimonians out of the public funds the money which the Thirty had borrowed for the war, although the convention required each side, the men of the city and the men of Peiraieus, to pay back its debts separately, because they believed this act to be the first step towards unity. But in other cities the people when victorious not only does not contribute out of its own pocket but even carries through a redistribution of land[16].

The progress of monarchy and monarchical ideology

Another characteristic of the fourth century was the massive return of tyranny in many Greek cities, after a virtual absence from Greek history during the fifth century (except in Sicily, where tyrants maintained themselves until the 460s). The reappearance of tyranny had many reasons behind it, which varied according to places and circumstances. In general one of the main causes was the development of the antagonism between rich and poor; tyrants came to power exploiting a social and political imbalance within the state. Changes in the technique of warfare also played a role. Tyrants were often military leaders, and this gave to tyranny in the fourth century a more strictly military aspect than in the archaic period (cf. Dionysius of Syracuse, Jason of Pherae). Occasionally an outside threat contributed another element; tyrants were then military leaders who defended their cities against foreign threats (as for example the Elder Dionysius against the Carthaginians in Sicily).

By far the most famous tyranny of the fourth century, or even of the whole of Greek history, was that of the Elder Dionysius in Sicily. Dionysius came to power in Syracuse in 406–405 and remained there till his death in 366; his rule marked in fact the end of the Greek city in Sicily. He brought the larger part of Sicily under his control (with the exception of the western part of the island which remained a Carthaginian preserve), and extended his power to the south of Italy. His empire was a territorial one, which anticipated in some ways that of the Hellenistic monarchies. Dionysius was not tyrant of Syracuse in the same way as Peisistratus had been tyrant of Athens. Syracuse was for him a capital and a fortress, from which he governed his empire, and to which he transplanted the population of enemy cities he destroyed. Dionysius had the official title of 'archon of Sicily', a new title which reflected his territorial ambitions. At his death his son the Younger Dionysius succeeded him without difficulty. Subsequently, it is true, the tyranny collapsed through internal dissensions in the tyrant's house. But in spite of the attempt of the Corinthian Timoleon, who from 344 till his death in *c.* 336 sought to free Sicily from her tyrants and to re-establish the autonomy of the Greek cities and their prosperity by means of a programme of colonization, the Greek city in Sicily had long had its day [*see no 119*]. Twenty years later, tyranny returned to Syracuse in the person of Agathocles, who began his career as a tyrant to end it as a Hellenistic monarch who was recognized as such by the other rulers of the time.

In Sicily, in other words, the city had failed earlier, even before the Peloponnesian War, and more completely than in the rest of the Greek world. Syracuse only experienced a brief 'democratic interlude' of some 60 years between the tyranny of the Deinomenids in 466 and the beginning of the tyranny of the Elder Dionysius, an interlude which was frequently a very disturbed one and which is in striking contrast to the stability of Athens, her great democratic rival in the east [*see nos 117, 118*]. Why the difference? The reasons in fact are far from obvious. It is customary to invoke the 'Carthaginian threat': the Greek cities of Sicily, incapable of resisting Carthage by their own means, had to turn to strong men to ensure their defence. This factor is a real one, but the problem is more complex. Carthage is far from having been a systematically aggressive state, and in between several conflicts with the Greeks there were long periods of peace. Besides, most of the time the Greeks were the aggressors. Though the Carthaginian threat played a definite role (as in 406–405 when Dionysius seized power), one must also bring other factors into play, and especially the social instability which characterizes the whole history of the Greeks in Sicily. From beginning to end one comes across the problem of social inequality, without being able to account fully for it, though it was undoubtedly aggravated by the characteristic brutality of the Sicilian tyrants who already in the fifth century did not hesitate to destroy Greek cities and to transplant their population and who also made use of mercenaries on a scale unknown in eastern Greece, incorporating them by force into the citizen body. The stability of the city presupposed the stability of the social body. The Greek cities in Sicily experienced it to an even lesser degree than those of the east, and Timoleon's attempt at restoration came too late to reverse the course of events. Timoleon himself, the enemy of the tyrants, resembled them in many ways, not least in his need to base his power on armies of mercenaries.

In the fourth century, monarchy progressed in actual fact, both in the old Greek cities and in fringe areas (cf. the rulers of Salamis in Cyprus, of the Crimean Bosporus [*cf. no 81*], the kings of Macedon); monarchical ideology also developed. Although all the political thinkers and philosophers of the fourth century staunchly defended or took for granted the superiority of the city as the only acceptable framework of civilized life, they none the less made increasingly great allowances for the reality of monarchy. In 380 Isocrates still envisaged bringing the Greek world together under the aegis of a city, Sparta or Athens. But subsequently he turned more and more to the strong men of the times, and in the end to none other than Philip of Macedon [*see no 108*]. In the writings of all the political thinkers of the fourth century one may detect monarchic tendencies, and these reflect the evolution of the times. Effective power passed more and more from the old cities to individual rulers, Greek and non-Greek, who had the financial means available to secure the military power which was eluding the cities. By losing control over warfare the cities also lost the initiative in the political field.

Internal aspects of the decline of the city in Athens
Athens, as has been seen, experienced the crisis much less severely than other Greek cities. All the same one can trace there many signs of the evolution that was taking place. In the fifth century politics took precedence over everything else and the life of the citizen was to some extent taken up by the city. In the fourth century politics gradually ceased to play such a dominating role; they were no longer automatically everybody's concern. Just as warfare tended to become the business of specialists, so too politics became increasingly the concern of professional orators like Demosthenes. The social élite was no longer coterminous with the political élite. Politics and the affairs of state gave way little by little to private affairs. The change of tone is manifest in comedy; politics were eventually completely excluded from it.

The typical characters are now the cook, the soldier, the courtesan and the parasite. Besides the citizen, there was now the private man. Family and private values, which are less apparent to us in the fifth century because of the triumph of the democratic city, now become more visible. This fact is manifest in art, notably in funerary art, which was a more direct expression of everyday life than monumental art. Family feelings are expressed there in a lively way (in fact already in the last third of the fifth century on white-ground funerary lekythoi). Philosophers and doctors took far greater interest than in the past in the feeding and education of children in their early years. The frameworks of social life were no longer just those of the city. Within the city itself there began to spring up private associations (of a social and religious character), but the interesting fact is that although the development of these associations, which was to be pursued on a larger scale in the Hellenistic period, was a sign of the loss of ground of the city, the way in which they were organized was none the less copied from the institutions of the democratic city[17]. In spite of its decline, the city continued to exercise its influence.

The reactions to the crisis

In the face of the obvious failure of traditional-style attempts at hegemony by the Greek cities (Sparta, Athens, Thebes) and the state of virtually permanent but fruitless war, there developed a movement towards peace. In 380 Isocrates in his *Panegyricus* was still seeking to defend the empire of Athens in the fifth century. But in his pamphlet *On the Peace* of 356 he condemned the methods of the past and sought to persuade the Athenians to base their supremacy on peaceful means. Xenophon in his pamphlet *Ways and Means* at the same time echoed these ideas and sought to convince his readers that peace was more beneficial to states than war – for a Greek a novel point of view which was by no means self-evident. Plato condemned war among Greeks and assimilated it to civil war [*see no 131*]. Aristotle too criticized the old forms of domination, in particular that of Sparta after the Peloponnesian War.

In the field of institutions one may also observe a new evolution in the fourth century. The idea of a common peace between Greeks developed; the common peace guaranteed autonomy to all Greek states (of mainland Greece and the Aegean), whether they had been involved in warfare or not, and without any time limit. From all these points of view, it represented a remarkable step forward as compared with former diplomatic practice[18]. Formerly treaties were only on a bilateral basis between two warring states and were designed to put an end to the state of war (as for example the treaties between Sparta and Athens in 446–445 and in 421). Besides, these treaties were almost always concluded for a limited period of time (30 years in 446–445, 50 years in 421): it has been said that until the fourth century peace was only considered an interruption of war. And finally, treaties before the fourth century did not recognize that autonomy was the normal state of all Greek cities without distinction.

All the same, the evolution in ideas and institutions could not reverse the course of events. The state of war was the one which predominated, and attempts at dominating other Greeks, although they did not lead to any lasting results, remained very much alive. The common peace may have been admirable in theory, but in practice it was no more than a slogan: the first common peace, from which all subsequent ones were derived, was the King's Peace of 387–386, which gave up the Greeks of Asia Minor to the authority of the Great King, and the clause on the autonomy of the Greek cities which was written into it served as a pretext for Sparta to break up all rival coalitions in the Greek world (the renascent empire of Athens, the Boeotian league dominated by Thebes, later the Chalcidian league in Thrace), without for all that dissolving her own Peloponnesian League. Sparta, the guarantor of the King's Peace, clearly did not care very much for the principle of autonomy in itself.

The age also witnessed a certain realization of the importance of social and economic problems, and this new preoccupation can be observed both at the institutional and at the ideological level. In the fourth century, many Greek cities suffered from social and economic troubles: in Book II of the *Economics* of Ps.-Aristotle there are many illustrations of the expedients which cities and rulers frequently had recourse to so as to try to remedy them [*see no 91*]. In Athens, magistracies with purely financial duties acquired an importance which they did not have during the period of prosperity in the fifth century; statesmen were often experts in financial matters, as for instance Callistratus of Aphidna in the 370s and 360s, Eubulus in the 350s and 340s, and Lycurgus in the 330s and 320s. The literature of the age also reflected this new awareness. It is visible already in the last comedies of Aristophanes, where from the broadly political themes of the Peloponnesian War one passes to social preoccupations: the *Plutus* of 388 deals with the theme of wealth and poverty. The first writings which deal more or less directly with economic problems date from the fourth century: there is Xenophon's *Economics* and especially *Ways and Means*, and the three books of the *Economics* of Ps.-Aristotle. But these were only the timid beginnings of independent economic thought, and they were never really followed up subsequently.

Innovations in the economic life of Athens
The fourth century was not solely a time of crisis and decline of the old institutions, it witnessed also some genuine innovations in the economic field, at least as far as Athens was concerned. To be sure, Athens is the only city for which adequate evidence is available (the private orations collected under the name of Demosthenes are a particularly valuable source for the economic life of Athens at this period). None the less it is likely that the innovations in economic life in the fourth century were to be found only in Athens, which remained at this period the most important centre of economic activity in the Aegean world, despite the loss of her political supremacy. In Athens one may observe a certain development of what Aristotle called '*chrematistike*' and which he contrasted with the art of acquisition which is limited to what is strictly necessary and is thereby legitimate: *chrematistike* by contrast was unnatural, it was the appetite for unlimited wealth, which he notes as a characteristic of the age, without however saying that it was altogether new at the time [*see no 2*].

One notes first from the second half of the fourth century an evolution in commercial law, which replaced the old *symbolai* (judicial treaties) which used to be concluded bilaterally between two states in order to resolve disputes between citizens of the two states concerned. Athenian commercial law of the second half of the fourth century shows a number of new characteristics which seem peculiar to Athens[19]. First, the legal personality of slaves, hitherto not well defined or inexistent in law up to that time, began to emerge. Slaves were allowed to give evidence like free men (whereas torture had up till then been the rule), they could enter into contracts on their own behalf and be personally prosecuted. There was a similar evolution with non-citizens: foreigners were placed on the same level as citizens, commercial law did not specify anything in connection with their nationality, they could go to law on an equal footing with Athenian citizens, they appeared before the same magistrates and did not need a *prostates* (patron) to represent them. Commercial law attributed greater importance to the written act, whereas previously only witness were taken into account. Finally, commercial lawsuits enjoyed an expeditious jurisdiction, for they had to be decided within the month. The idea was to favour traders by allowing them to sail away rapidly without wasting time[20].

Another innovation in economic life was the development of maritime loans, commonly known as bottomry loans [*see no 121*][21]. Because of the lack of liquid capital, maritime traders usually had to borrow money for their business journeys. There arose a type of loan which was quite distinct from loans on the security of land (cf. below for the latter). The sums borrowed rarely exceeded 2,000 drachmae, the loans were concluded for the duration of the trip only (a few months at most), and were registered in a written act. The risks of the journey fell on the creditor, and the borrower offered as security his ship, his cargo, or both at once. Interest rates were extremely high but could vary considerably; the risks involved were great (because of the insecurity of the seas due to piracy, wars and storms), but the profits for the creditor might be considerable.

There was also in the fourth century a certain development in banking activity[22]. Some of the Athenian bankers of the time are known through the private orations [*see nos 120, 124*]. The most famous among them, Pasion, who died in 370, had at first been a slave before gaining his freedom, and eventually Athenian citizenship. Pasion owned a workshop which made shields and a bank, and at his death left to his son Apollodorus landed property to the value of 20 talents, scattered among three demes in Attica. He left his wife a dowry of 2 talents, a house worth 200 minae, gold, clothes and jewellery.

The development of fortunes other than in land was also characteristic of the fourth century. The evolution had started at the beginning of the Peloponnesian War, and corresponded to the rise to power of the 'demagogues' after the death of Pericles – men such as Cleon, Hyperbolus and others. Their wealth consisted generally in a workshop staffed by slaves. The trend carried on in the fourth century, and several cases are known of wealthy Athenian citizens whose fortunes depended partly or wholly on such workshops and not on landed property [*see no 120*].

All these signs of innovations in economic life must however be interpreted with caution. It has sometimes been said, on the evidence of these, that in the fourth century the Greek economy was becoming 'modern' in character[23]. The old value judgements against economic activity were on the wane, overcome by the rise of new and strictly economic values. A new economic rationalism brought about the division of labour and the specialization of production. The *homo politicus* of the fifth century was going to be replaced by the *homo oeconomicus*[24]. But what of the situation in reality? Without wishing to deny the novelty of certain aspects of the economic life of Athens in the fourth century, one must determine their precise limits.

As far as commercial law is concerned, it has been pointed out that its development coincides with the decline of Athenian power at about this time, and this decline aggravated the problem of the food supply of Athens, primarily in corn. The development of legislation favouring traders was aimed in the last resort at encouraging them to import corn to Athens. Athens, less well placed now than before to impose her power, had to secure the goodwill of the foreign traders on whom she depended for her survival [*see no 122*]. The judicial protection guaranteed by Athens extended solely to enterprises which had their starting or finishing point in Athens, and not to the whole of Athenian commercial activity in general.

As for the banks, here again the evolution had its limits: the very word 'bank' which one inevitably uses can be misleading. There is a vast difference between a modern bank and an Athenian one. A modern bank is primarily a credit institution which aims at encouraging economic activity. Athenian banks, by contrast, worked on a small scale: they were primarily money-changing establishments and pawn-brokers. Much of the moneyed wealth which existed never came into their hands but remained most of the time hoarded away and not put to productive uses. The sums which were entrusted to them were not invested in economic enterprises; it does not appear that the banks invested their clients' money in maritime loans. Those bankers who were metics (and many of them were) could not give loans on the security of land, since metics were debarred from the ownership of land. Athenian banks were not credit institutions designed to encourage productive investments. In other words, the essential characteristic of a modern bank was missing in classical Greece.

Besides the development of maritime commercial loans one must mention the institution of loans on the security of landed property, an institution which is known to us partly through the private orations of the fourth century, and partly through a series of inscriptions of the fourth and third centuries; these were plain inscribed stones (*Horoi*) placed in full view on the lands, houses or workshops which were pledged as security to publicize the existence of the debt [*see nos 123, 124*] (these stones, it must be said incidentally, having nothing to do with the *horoi* of the time of Solon [*see no 36*] and consequently are not evidence for a possible crisis affecting small peasants; the estates involved are all large ones and belonged to the wealthier classes). These loans are quite different in character from the loans on maritime trade[25]. Apart from differences in form (the loans were often concluded orally before witnesses, without any written act – hence the use of inscribed stones, the sole means available of publicizing the debt), these loans were quite different in kind. Often they did not bear any interest at all, or the interest rate was much lower than that for maritime loans (from 10 per cent to 18 per cent approximately); the element of risk was obviously much smaller. There was in particular one essential difference: they were loans for what one might call prestige purposes. The loans were always aimed at enabling their recipients to discharge political functions (liturgies, for example), or served purposes of a social kind (the providing of dowries to daughters, or of security for fathers-in-law). The loans were not used for the improvement of property or economic enterprises of any kind. They were never concerned with productive investments, and what is remarkable is that the sums involved were often larger than those invested in maritime commerce, the only form of genuinely productive investment known at the time. Between the two types of loan there was thus the difference of two separate worlds and two different value systems. The world of land remained dissociated from that of money. Although land did indeed change hands frequently in the fourth century, it did not for all that become a genuine marketable commodity exploited for its economic possibilities. A whole system of archaic values remained linked to it, values of a non-economic kind, far removed from the spirit of Aristotle's *chrematistike*.

As far as fortunes not in land are concerned, it is noteworthy that the *nouveaux riches* in Athens in the fourth century tended to take over the aristocratic values of the social élite once they had reached the top. Pasion, after making his fortune and becoming a citizen, eagerly acquired estates which conferred on him the social respectability reserved to landowners. His son Apollodorus could be mistaken for a member of the aristocracy of Athens as far as his behaviour and ideas were concerned. Demosthenes, who had inherited from his father a fortune not in land, was in his ideas a man of the fifth century. Right in the middle of the fourth century, and in spite of the evolution in economic life, the old values remained very much alive. Negative judgments against economic activity were to be heard frequently (as indeed in Demosthenes himself) [*see nos 12, 113*]. The poorer citizens preferred the *misthoi* paid by the city to economic activity; their right to the *misthoi* symbolized for them their status as citizens. Generally speaking, commercial and industrial enterprises of the time remained relatively small scale. The different workshops owned sometimes by a single individual remained separate and were not fused into a single large company.

The abandonment of the ideal of the peasant-citizen

The real novelty of the fourth century does not therefore lie in any economic revolution which might have had at its roots a deep change in ideas and values. Paradoxically, it may be said to lie in a return to archaic models which had been superseded at an earlier stage of Greek history. One of the major achievements of the classical period was the development of the ideal of the peasant-citizen. In contrast to peasants in the civilizations of the Near East, and in contrast also to groups of the Helot type in Sparta and elsewhere in the Greek world and the colonies, the peasants in the classical city strengthened their economic and political position and became citizens with full rights. Thus the antithesis between city and countryside was eliminated. In the fourth century the ideal corresponded less and less to reality, because of the weakening of the peasant class in much of the Greek world. What is more, although the ideal continued to be expressed, it was henceforward subjected to an implicit critique. The antithesis between city and countryside reappeared, even in Athens. In Aristophanes' *Clouds* (423) the type of the country boor (the *agroikos*) as opposed to the town-dweller (the *asteios*) appeared in the person of Strepsiades. The type was taken up in New Comedy (there existed several comedies entitled the *Agroikos*), and it was included by Theophrastus among his *Characters* [*see no 125*]. Plato in the *Laws* sought to counteract the antithesis between city and countryside by simply suppressing it altogether: the citizens were to have land both in the centre and in the fringe areas [*see no 126*].

To meet the social crisis which affected the Greek world and which had as one of its manifest signs the development of mercenary service, a solution was put forward by the political thinkers and subsequently applied in practice. Although 'imperialism' met with increasingly strong criticism in the fourth century, criticism was not directed against 'imperialism' as such, but only against 'imperialism' when practised at the expense of other Greeks. Domination aimed at barbarians, and especially the Persian Empire and the peoples of Asia, was by contrast perfectly legitimate. A convenient solution to the social problems of Greece was at hand, which had already been sketched at the end of the fifth century: the Greeks should conquer part of Asia and settle there, exploiting the labour of the enslaved barbarian peoples. Thus the problems from which the Greek world suffered would be solved. As early as the end of the fifth century Xenophon had thought of founding a colony of mercenaries on the south coast of the Black Sea [*see no 130*]. The idea of a national war against Persia was launched at about the same time by Gorgias of Leontinoi. Isocrates combined these two ideas together, a war against Persia to be followed by the colonization of the land conquered by the Greeks, and this programme occupied a large part of his career as pamphleteer, from the *Panegyricus* of 380 till his death in 338 [*see no 108*]. In the *Politics* (Book I) Aristotle sought to provide a theoretical justification of slavery. The Greek people was made to rule, the peoples of Asia were made to obey; barbarians were therefore natural slaves [*see no 132*]. In his ideal city, the land belonging to the citizens should not be cultivated by them, but by slaves, of mixed origins if possible or at least a barbarian people reduced by force[26].

That is exactly what the work of Alexander was going to achieve. Alexander inherited from his father Philip the project of a conquest of Asia, which Jason of Pherae had already toyed with in the 370s. In the Hellenistic world conquered by Alexander, the Greek cities founded in Asia might bear a superficial resemblance to the classical city; but in fact they were often far removed from it, for the bulk of the labour was frequently provided by the enslaved peoples of the East.

Notes

1   *Hellenica* VII, 5, 26–7.
2   See J.K. Anderson, *Military Theory and Practice in the Age of*

Xenophon (Berkeley and Los Angeles, 1970); J.G.P. Best, *Thracian Peltasts and their Influence on Greek Warfare* (Groningen, 1969); Y. Garlan, *War in the Ancient World: a Social History* (London, 1975); id., *Recherches de Poliorcétique grecque* (Paris, 1974); Ed. Will, 'Le territoire, la ville et la poliorcétique grecque', *Revue historique* 514 (April–June 1975), pp. 297–318 (review of Garlan); F.E. Winter, *Greek Fortifications* (Toronto, 1969); W.K. Pritchett, *The Greek State at War*, Parts I and II (Berkeley and Los Angeles, 1971 and 1974).

3 Xenophon, *Hellenica* IV, 5, 12–17.

4 Diodorus XIV, 47–53.

4a See W.K. Pritchett, *The Greek State at War*, Part II (Berkeley and Los Angeles, 1974), pp. 59–132.

5 See H.W. Parke, *Greek Mercenary Soldiers* (1933); A. Aymard, 'Mercenariat et histoire grecque', *Études d'histoire ancienne* (1967), pp. 487–98; J. Roy, 'The Mercenaries of Cyrus', *Historia* 16 (1967), pp. 287–323; on the use of Greek mercenaries in the Persian empire note also R. Lane Fox, *Alexander the Great* (1973), pp. 157–60.

6 See Ch. Pélékidis, *Histoire de l'ephébie attique* (Paris, 1962); P. Vidal-Naquet, 'The Black Hunter and the Origins of the Athenian Ephebeia', and 'Les jeunes. Le cru, l'enfant grec, et le cuit', both mentioned in Chapter 1, n 47; O.W. Reinmuth, *The Ephebic Inscriptions of the Fourth Century* (Leyden, 1971).

7 *Politics* VII, 1328 b 5–24; 1329 a 2–18.

8 *Republic* II, 374 a ff.

9 *Laws* VIII, 829 1–835 d.

10 See especially G.E.M. de Ste Croix, *The Origins of the Peloponnesian War*, op. cit., pp. 34–44, with bibliography.

11 A study of social conflicts in fourth-century and Hellenistic Greece is announced by A. Fuks, 'Patterns and Types of Social-Economic Revolution in Greece from the Fourth to the Second Century B.C.', *Ancient Society* V (1974), pp. 51–81.

12 Y. Garlan, *Recherches de poliorcétique grecque* (Paris, 1974).

13 That is one of the theses of the book by Cl. Mossé, *La Fin de la démocratie athénienne* (Paris, 1962); since then the author has qualified her position, cf. 'Le statut des paysans en Attique au IVe siècle', in *Problèmes de la terre en Grèce ancienne*, ed. M.I. Finley (Paris and The Hague, 1973), pp. 179–86; 'La vie

économique d'Athènes au IVe siècle: crise ou renouveau?',
Praelectiones Patavinae (Rome, 1974), pp. 135–44, and the
latest statement of her views in Ed. Will, Cl. Mossé and P.
Goukowsky, *Le Monde grec et l'Orient* II (Paris, 1975), pp.
103–32. See also G. Audring, 'Grenzen der Konzentration von
Grundeigentum in Attika während des 4.Jh.v.u.Z.', *Klio* 56, 2
(1974), pp. 445–56; V.N. Andreyev, 'Some Aspects of Agrarian
Conditions in Attica in the Fifth to Third Centuries B.C.',
Eirene 12 (1974), pp. 5–46.

14 On the economy and society of Athens at this period see the
previous note and S.C. Humphreys, 'Economy and Society in
Classical Athens', *Annali della Scuola Normale Superiore di
Pisa* 39 (1970), pp. 1–26; J. Pečirka, 'The Crisis of the Athenian
Polis in the Fourth Century B.C.', *Eirene*, 9 (1976), pp. 5–29.
On imports to, and exports from, Athens, see the collection of
evidence by E. Erxleben, *Klio* 57, 2 (1975), pp. 365–98.

15 M. Rostovtzeff, *Social and Economic History of the Hellenistic
World* I (Oxford, 1941), pp. 104–25; Cl. Mossé, *La Fin de la
démocratie athénienne*, op. cit., pp. 125–31; but see S.C.
Humphreys, in *Parola del Passato* 114 (1967), pp. 388–9.

16 *Constitution of Athens* XL, 3.

17 See Fr. Poland, *Das Griechische Vereinswesen* (Leipzig, 1909);
W.S. Ferguson, 'The Attic Orgeones', *Harvard Theological
Review* 37 (1944), pp. 61–140.

18 See T.T.B. Ryder, *Koine Eirene* (Oxford, 1965), though cf.
P. Vidal-Naquet, *REG* 80 (1967), pp. 713–14.

19 See L. Gernet, 'Sur les actions commerciales en droit athénien', *Droit et société dans la Grèce ancienne* (Paris, 2nd ed.,
1964), pp. 173–200, and on slaves ibid., pp. 155–64. See also
E.E. Cohen, *Ancient Athenian Maritime Courts* (Princeton,
1973), who challenges (pp. 9–59) the usual interpretation of
dikai emmenoi as 'suits which had to be tried within a month'
(cf. next note and p. 367, n 13), though see Ph. Gautier, *REG*
87 (1974), pp. 424–5; on the legal status of slaves see generally
A.R.W. Harrison, *The Law of Athens* I (Oxford, 1968),
pp. 163–80.

20 There is evidence at Thasos near the end of the fourth century
of a category of suits which had to be tried within a month;
see F. Salviat in *BCH* 72 (1958), pp. 209–12. On the development of the written act see Cl. Préaux, 'De la Grèce classique
à l'Egypte hellénistique. Note sur les contrats à clause exécu-

toire', *Chronique d'Egypte* 65 (1958), pp. 102–12.

21 See G.E.M. de Ste Croix, 'Ancient Greek and Roman Maritime Loans', in *Debits, Credits, Finance and Profits. Essays in Honour of W.T. Baxter*, ed. Harold Edey and B.S. Yamey (London, 1974), pp. 41–59. A group of inscribed lead plaques from Corcyra, recording loans between individuals and dating from *c.* 500 BC, have been interpreted as early examples of bottomry loans (P. Calligas, *BSA* 66 (1971), pp. 79–94, at pp. 85–6), though there is nothing in the inscriptions to prove this.

22 See R. Bogaert, *Banques et banquiers dans les cités grecques* (Leyden, 1968), and cf. S.C. Humphreys, *JHS* 90 (1970), pp. 452–4. id., *Epigraphica* III: *Texts on Bankers, Banking and Credit in the Greek World* (Leiden, 1976).

23 M. Rostovtzeff, *Social and Economic History of the Hellenistic World* I (Oxford, 1941), pp. 100–1, but Rostovtzeff clearly emphasized the survival of the *homo politicus* in the old Greek world in the Hellenistic age (II, pp. 1119–22), and even to some extent in the new monarchies in Asia, though there the *homo oeconomicus* and *technicus* were more clearly in evidence (II, pp. 1074–7, cf. too I, pp. 411–12).

24 For an example of this formulation see L. Edelstein, *The Idea of Progress in Classical Antiquity* (Baltimore, 1967), pp. 81–3.

25 See M.I. Finley, *Studies in Land and Credit in Ancient Athens* (Rutgers, 1952), p. 27 and *passim*; id., 'Land, Debt, and the Man of Property in Classical Athens', *Political Science Quarterly* 68 (1953), pp. 249–68.

26 *Politics* VII, 1330 a 25–34.

Part 2
Ancient Sources

I Concepts and General Problems

1 Extracts from a treatise on 'Economics'
One would hesitate to begin this selection with two passages from
the *Economics*, which have come down to us among the works of
Aristotle, for this work, which is certainly later than the death of
Alexander, oversteps the chronological limits fixed in this book,
but for the fact that its very title has caused an ambiguity which
still persists. In connection with the second part of the work, M.
Rostovtzeff[1] had no hesitation in saying that one had there 'one of
the most interesting products of Greek speculative thought combined with practical sagacity', and that it gave a faithful picture
of a world where the two major forms of economy, that of the
city and the individual on the one hand, that of the empire of the
Great King and his satraps on the other, were in the process of
merging to give birth to the Hellenistic world. In fact the work is
a much more modest one, and is concerned not with economics
proper but with management. What is the status of 'economics'[2]
– that is to say the housewife's shopping-basket – in relation to
politics? That is the question asked by the disciple of Aristotle in
the first part of the work. As for the prologue to the second part
it does not distinguish between different economic spaces, but
between several levels of budgetary decision in an empire like
that of the Great King or his successor Alexander the Great.

A Between 'economics' and politics there is not only the same
difference that exists between the household (*oikia*) and the
state (*polis*) (for these are the objects of these two disciplines),
but there is also the further difference that politics is a matter
for several rulers whereas 'economics' concerns one only. Now
some of the arts (*technai*) can be divided between manufacture

and utilization: the lyre-player or flute-player is not himself the manufacturer of these instruments. But politics has as its object both the constitution of the city from the beginning and its proper running once it is established. It is therefore clear that 'economics' is concerned both with the foundation of a household (*oikos*)³ and with its proper management.

Now a city is an aggregate of houses, lands and possessions sufficient to make possible the good life. It is clear from the fact that if this end cannot be attained, the community itself is dissolved. Further it is with this end in mind (the good life) that men associate together; and the object for which any particular thing exists and has come into being, is in fact the very essence of that thing. It is therefore clear that 'economics' precedes politics in origin. Its function is also prior: a household is part of a city.

[ARISTOTLE], *Oeconomica* I, 1–2

B   Whoever proposes to manage properly a household must be familiar with the places where he will be active, and must be naturally gifted and deliberately industrious and upright. Should any of these characteristics be missing, he is liable to be unsuccessful in many of the enterprises he undertakes.

One may summarily distinguish between four types of 'economy'⁴ (it will be found that all others may be reduced to these): there is that of the Great King, that of the satrap, that of the city, and that of the private individual. Of these the most extensive and also the simplest is that of the Great King, [. . .]⁵, the most diverse and also the easiest that of the city, the most limited and most varied that of the private person. It is inevitable that they should share many common characteristics, but we must first examine the distinctive features of each. Let us consider the royal economy first. It is universal in its scope, but has four forms which are concerned with the currency, with exports, with imports, with expenditure. To take each in turn: as regards the currency there is the question when and how to strike it, whether at a high or a low value; as regards exports and imports, after receiving the contributions from the satraps, what to dispose of and when; as regards expenditure, what must be cut and when, and whether expenses are to be paid for in currency or in goods of an equivalent value.

Secondly, the economy of the satrap. It has six forms of revenue (from agriculture, from particular products of the land, from bulk trade, from taxes, from cattle and from all other sources). Of these, the first and most important is that from agriculture (which some call tax on land produce (*ekphorion*), others tithe). Then there is that from particular products of the land, gold in one place, silver in another, copper elsewhere or whatever is produced in the locality. Thirdly the revenues from ports of trade. Fourthly revenues from taxes on land and on markets. Fifthly, revenues from cattle, called tax on animal produce (*epikarpia*) or tithe. Sixthly, taxes on persons, called poll tax (*epikephalaion*) or tax on craftsmen (*cheironaxion*).

Thirdly, the economy of the city. Its most important source of revenue is from the particular products of the land, then also from ports of trade and transit dues, and also from regular taxes.

Fourthly and lastly, the economy of the private individual. This one is not uniform, as it must not aim at a single goal. It is the most limited of all, since income and expenditure are on a small scale. The most important revenue here comes from agriculture, then that from other kinds of property[6], thirdly that from money. Besides, there is a principle common to all forms of 'economy', which must not be treated lightly, particularly as regards the economy of the private person, and that is that expenditure must not exceed income.

[ARISTOTLE], *Oeconomica* II, 1, 1–6

1 *The Social and Economic History of the Hellenistic World* I (Oxford, 1941), pp. 74–5.
2 The word has been kept in the translation to bring out the ambiguity. In the following passage *oikonomia* will be translated 'household management'.
3 This word refers at once to the family, the house and the chattels.
4 On the meaning of the word *oikonomia*, cf. Chapter 1, pp. 8–9.
5 There is a probable lacuna in the Greek text.
6 The Greek text is corrupt here; this translates one of the possible corrections.

2   Aristotle: household management ('oikonomia') and the art of acquisition ('chrematistike')

Greek thought, which created so many sciences, did not invent political economy[1], that is to say the science which considers men as producers and consumers of wealth. Nothing allows one to gauge better the epistemological obstacle the Greeks came up against[2] than the very passage in Aristotle which comes closest to what we call economic analysis[3]. The question does not arise at the level of gathering facts: fourth-century Athens could provide these in plentiful supply, and Aristotle did not fail to collect them. One could say that there is an obvious obstacle and a more hidden one. By definition Greek science has as its object what is finite, and the infinite is very precisely what cannot be an object of science. Now the 'art of acquisition' (*chrematistike*)[4] in the second sense which Aristotle gives to this word, is concerned precisely with the infinite, and therefore belongs to non-science. But this scientific finiteness is itself connected with a social and technical finiteness (without any priority being postulated here). The space of the house, the very place of 'the economy', is finite, centred as it is on the hearth; similarly the city with its restricted number of citizens and its territory enclosed on itself (Greek social practice in fact assimilated the distant parts of the frontier zone to the savage world); and finally the work of the artisan is finite, for the artisan does not make things in a series and does not manufacture objects but a particular object: a vase, a statue, a column. The trader exists, but he comes from outside, and if the city experiences the novel consequences of his action, political thought tries to close the gap and keep the 'art of acquisition' within the limits of the city.

> It follows that one form of acquisition is naturally a part of the art of household management (*oikonomia*)[5]. It is a form of acquisition which the manager of a household must either find ready to hand, or himself provide and arrange because it ensures a supply of objects, necessary for life and useful to the association (*koinonia*)[6] of the *polis* or the household, which are capable of being stored. These are the objects which may be regarded as constituting true wealth; and the amount of property which suffices for a good life is not unlimited, nor of the nature described by Solon in the verse,
>
> 'There is no bound to wealth stands fixed for men'[7].

There *is* a bound fixed, as is also the case in the means required by the other arts (*technai*)[8]. All the instruments needed by all the arts are limited, both in number and size, by the requirements of the art they serve; and wealth may be defined as a number of instruments used in a household or state. It is thus clear that there is a natural art of acquisition which has to be practised by managers of households and statesmen; and the reason for its existence is also clear.

But there is a second form of the general art of getting property, which is particularly called, and which it is just to call, 'the art of acquisition' (*chrematistike*). It is the characteristics of this second form which lead to the opinion that there is no limit to wealth and property. There are many who hold this second form of the art of getting property to be identical with the other form previously mentioned[9], because it has affinities with it. In fact it is not identical, and yet it is not far removed[10]. The other form previously mentioned is natural: this second form is not natural, but is rather the product of a certain sort of experience and skill (*techne*)[11].

We may start our discussion of this form from the following point of view.

All articles of property have two possible uses. Both of these uses belong to the article as such[12], but they do not belong to it in the same manner, or to the same extent. The one use is proper and peculiar to the article concerned; the other is not. We may take a shoe as an example. It can be used both for wearing and for exchange. Both of these are uses of the shoe as such. Even the man who exchanges a shoe, in return for money or food, with a person who needs the article, is using the shoe as a shoe[13]; but since the shoe has not been made for the purpose of being exchanged, the use he is making of it is not its proper and peculiar use. The same is true of all other articles of property. Exchange is possible in regard to them all: it arises from the natural facts of the case, and is due to some men having more, and others less, than suffices for their needs. We can thus see that retail trade is not naturally a part of the art of acquisition[14]. If that were the case, it would only be necessary to practise exchange to the extent that sufficed for the needs of both parties. In the first form of association[15], which is the household (*oikia*), it is obvious that there is no purpose to be served by the art of exchange. Such a purpose only emerged when the scope of association had already been extended. The members of the household had shared all things in common: the members of the village, separated from one another, had at their disposal a number of different things, which they had to exchange with one another, as need arose, by way of barter – much as many uncivilized tribes still do to this day. On this basis things which are useful are exchanged themselves, and directly, for similar useful things, but the transaction does not go any further; wine, for instance, is given, or taken, in return for wheat, and other similar commodities are similarly bartered for one another. When used in this way, the art of exchange is not contrary to nature, nor in any way a form of the art of acquisition (*chrematistike*). Exchange simply served to satisfy the natural requirements of sufficiency (*autarkeia*). None the less it was from exchange, as thus practised, that the art of acquisition (*chrematistike*) developed, in the sort of way we might reasonably expect[16]. The supply of men's needs came to depend on more foreign sources as men began to import for themselves what they lacked, and to export what they had in superabundance; and in this way the use of a money currency was inevitably instituted[17]. The reason for this institution of a currency was that all the naturally necessary commodities were not easily portable; and men therefore agreed[18], for the purpose of their exchanges, to give and receive some commodity which itself belonged to the category of useful things[19] and possessed the advantage of being easily handled for the purpose of getting the necessities of life. Such commodities were iron, silver and other similar metals. At first their value was simply determined by their size and weight; but finally a stamp was imposed on the metal which, serving as a definite indication of the quantity, would save men the trouble of determining the value on each occasion[20].

When, in this way, a currency had once been instituted, there next arose, from the necessary process of exchange, the other form of the art of acquisition (*chrematistike*), which consists in retail trade (*kapelikon*)[21]. At first, we may allow, it was perhaps practised in a simple way: but in process of time, and as the result of experience, it was practised with a more studied technique (*technikoteron*), which sought to discover the sources from which, and the methods by which, the greatest profit could be made. The result has been the emergence of the view that the art of acquisition (*chrematistike*) is specially concerned with currency, and that its function consists in an ability to discover the sources from which a fund of money can be derived. In support of this view it is urged that the art is one which produces wealth and money; indeed those who hold the view often assume that wealth is simply a fund of currency, on the ground that the art of acquisition (*chrematistike*) and retail trade (*kapelike*) are concerned with currency. In opposition to this view there is another which is sometimes held. On this view currency is regarded as a sham and entirely a convention (*nomos*). Naturally and inherently (the supporters of the view argue) a currency is a nonentity; for if those who use a currency give it up in favour of another, that currency is worthless[22], and useless for any of the necessary purposes of life. A man rich in currency will often be at a loss to procure the necessities of subsistence; and surely it is absurd that a thing should be counted as wealth which a man may possess in abundance and yet none the less die of starvation – like Midas in the fable, when everything set before him was turned at once into gold through the granting of his own avaricious prayer.

Basing themselves on these arguments, those who hold this latter view try to find a different conception of wealth and a different conception of the art of acquisition. They are right in making the attempt. The (natural) art of acquisition and natural wealth *are* different. The (natural) form of the art of acquisition is connected with the management of the household (*oikonomike*); but the other form is a matter only of retail trade (*kapelike*), and it is concerned only with getting a fund of money, and that only by the method of conducting the exchange of commodities[23]. This latter form may be held to turn on the power of currency; for currency is the starting point, as it is also the goal, of exchange[24]. It is a further point of difference that the wealth produced by this latter form of the art of acquisition is unlimited [. . .].

The acquisition of wealth by the art of household management (as contrasted with the art of acquisition in its retail form) has a limit; and the object of that art is not an unlimited amount of wealth. It would thus appear, if we look at the matter in this light, that all wealth must have a limit. In actual experience, however, we see the opposite happening; and all who are engaged in acquisition increase their fund of currency without any limit or pause. The cause of this contradiction lies in the close connection between the two different modes of acquisition. They overlap because they are both handling the same objects and acting in the same field of acquisition; but they move along different lines – the object of the one being simply accumulation, and that of the other something quite different.

ARISTOTLE, *Politics* I, 1256 b 26–1257 b 39
(trans. E. Barker)

1   The paradox is worth underscoring: the word 'political economy', which etymologically and, as has been seen, according to the usage of the Aristotelian school, means 'domestic administration on the scale, and in the service, of the city', corresponds far better to the form of economic thought known to the Greeks than our own economic science.

2   The question of the social obstacle, that is to say in particular the division of classical society between masters and slaves, is left aside here; cf. above pp. 18–19.

3   See the previously mentioned article by M.I. Finley, 'Aristotle and Economic Analysis', *Past and Present* 47 (1970), pp. 3–25 (= *Studies in Ancient Society*, pp. 26–52).

4   The word comes from *chrema*, a thing one needs, in the plural, chattels, property, wealth, money. *Chrematistike* is the art of acquisition in general, and more particularly the art of making money.

5   Aristotle has just shown that all the arts, including hunting and war, presuppose the existence of a branch of acquisition.

6   *Koinonia* is a key word in Greek political thought. The economy is literally unthinkable outside a *community* which is distinct from the *inhabitants* (cf. no 64).

7   Solon, fr. 1, 71 Diehl (= fr. 13, 71 West); in fact Solon is explaining that profit is followed by the punishment of Zeus.

8   The single word *techne* denotes in Greek on the one hand the art of (say) getting rich, hunting or earning money, and on the other the trade of (say) baker, sculptor or smith. It cannot therefore be translated by any single word. It must be understood that anything which makes use of instruments (including living instruments like slaves) belongs to *techne*.

9 That which is limited by the natural needs of the family and of the city.

10 It is remarks such as these that show Aristotle's greatness: logical and ethical separation do not in his view exclude certain forms of affinity, the existence of which is manifested in daily life.

11 Another example of the complexity of the word *techne*, used here by Aristotle not in relation to the object with which the trade or profession is concerned, but to the form of activity itself.

12 Use and exchange (though not any form of exchange) conform to the nature of the objects made.

13 This remains within the limits of 'household management'.

14 In its second sense, unlimited gain. Aristotle shows later on that retail trade (*kapelike*), in so far as the concept of profit is attached to it, does lie at the roots of the 'art of acquisition'.

15 First in the logical rather than the historical sense of the word (cf. Plato, *Republic* II, 369 d ff.), and yet one is tempted to say that all modern theories on 'primitive communism' are derived from this passage.

16 This is the turning point in the passage, since Aristotle is now going to show that, according to reason if not to nature, it is from exchange, through the mediation of currency, that the 'art of acquisition' is derived. It is this passage which made Marx say that Aristotle had been on the verge of discovering exchange value – but only on the verge.

17 This whole paragraph on currency must be compared with the passage from the *Nicomachean Ethics* translated below (no 44) and the discussion of this passage in the previously mentioned article by Ed. Will, 'De l'aspect ethique des origines grecques de la monnaie', *Revue historique* 212 (1954), pp. 209–31.

18 A crucial stage in the argument: currency does not belong to nature but to the social compact, and therefore to the *polis*.

19 Aristotle thus defines currency simultaneously as a token and as a commodity, a definition which would not have suited shell currencies nor even ancient bronze coins.

20 Ancient coins rarely bear indications of quantity, but the seal of the city guarantees the value of the ingot of a given size.

21 This now deals with retail trade in so far as it is based not on exchange but on profit, profit of an immediate kind, since it

does not run the risks of maritime trade.

22 Aristotle's remark acquires its full value only in connection with purely token currencies such as those mentioned in no 44 below. Currencies such as these are obviously not the commodity described in the previous paragraph.

23 The trader who sells for two drachmae in the afternoon what he bought for one drachma in the morning is not creating anything, but he is creating money through the exchange, and that is a kind of intellectual scandal.

24 Currency is the object exchanged as well as the object of exchange. What is unlimited in the art of acquisition is precisely what ought to ensure its limitation, namely currency as a means and as an end.

3 Prestige of warfare and contempt for the trades among Barbarians and Greeks

The testimony of Herodotus starts, as is often the case with him, from a comparison with the barbarian world. In his eyes Egypt is at once the reverse and the source of Greek civilization[1], and yet as far as the contempt for trades is concerned, it does not lead to any cleavage between Greeks and Egyptians, or between Greeks and barbarians. This testimony is all the more striking as Herodotus is far from being an oligarch, since he belongs to the intellectual stream of the democrats favourable to Athens. The scale he draws is also interesting: the Spartan warriors are the most contemptuous of artisans, the traders of Corinth least so, but this scale is all within the same framework of values.

> (The Egyptian warriors) are forbidden to pursue any trade (*techne*), and devote themselves entirely to warlike exercises, the son following the father's calling. Whether the Greeks borrowed from the Egyptians this custom, among others, I cannot say for certain. I note that the Thracians, the Scythians, the Persians, the Lydians, and almost all other Barbarians, hold their fellow citizens who practise trades, and their children, in less repute than the rest, while they esteem as noble those who keep aloof from handicrafts, and especially honour such as are given wholly to war. Be that as it may, the Greeks have learnt this custom, especially the Lacedaimonians, while it is the Corinthians who despise artisans least.
>
> Herodotus II, 166–7

1 See for example II, 35 and II, 43.

4 Xenophon's Socrates and his attitude to artisans, farmers and warriors[1]

Compared with the previous passage the following extracts from the *Oeconomicus* (in its Latin rendering), a Socratic dialogue published by Xenophon in the first quarter of the fourth century, introduces a twofold variant. Xenophon, a professional soldier, sees war as a profession, which it had indeed become in the fourth century, and following a line of thought which was quite traditional he seeks to link it to the practice of agriculture. The latter, which traditionally was not thought of as a trade, thereby enters this category, and indeed the *Oeconomicus* suggests a few cautious improvements in Greek agricultural methods. Xenophon's citizen must therefore be a technician of war and a technician of agriculture, two 'trades' which are supposed to allow him adequate leisure.

> A   Socrates, why must you show me all the different trades? said Critobulus. It is not easy to get workmen skilled in all of them, nor is it easy to become expert at them oneself. But those trades which are reputed to be the noblest and which it would be most fitting for me to practise, show me what these are and who practises them, and do your best to help and instruct me.
>
> Well said, Critobulus, he answered. For the trades known as the trades of artisans (*banausikai*) are decried and with good reason held in low esteem in the cities. They disfigure the body of those who practise and pursue them, by compelling them to remain seated and in the shade, and some even cause you to spend the whole day sitting by the fire. When the bodies get softened in this way the souls lose a great deal of their strength. And especially, artisans' trades leave one very little time for friends and for the city, and the result is that men like these seem very inadequate in their relations with friends and when it comes to defending the city. Hence in some cities, especially those which have a military reputation, no citizen may pursue an artisan's trade.
>
> But, Socrates, what trade do you advise me to follow?
>
> Must we be ashamed, said Socrates, of imitating the Persian king? It is said that among the noblest and most necessary

obligations he reckons agriculture and the art of war, and he vigorously practises both of them.

Xenophon, Oeconomicus IV, 1–4

B   Well then, said Socrates, 'economics' appeared to us to be a branch of knowledge, and this branch of knowledge appeared to be the one which enable men to secure an increase in their household (*oikos*); the household seemed to be the sum total of one's possessions, and we defined as 'possessions' whatever each person found useful for his life; finally we discovered that all things which could be made to serve a purpose were useful. It did not seem to us possible to learn all the existing trades, and we agreed with the practice of cities in rejecting the trades known as artisans' trades (*banausikai*) on the grounds that they seem to disfigure the bodies and weaken the souls. The clearest proof of the matter we said to be this: if enemies were to invade the land, one should divide the farmers and the artisans into two groups and ask them whether they decided to defend the land or whether they would give up the land and man the ramparts[2]. We believed that in these circumstances those who live on the land would vote to defend it, while craftsmen would refuse to fight and, according to their training, prefer to sit without incurring toil or danger. We then reached the following verdict: for a gentleman (*kalos kagathos*) there is no work or science better than agriculture, and it is from it that men procure the necessities of life.

Xenophon, Oeconomicus VI, 4–8

1   Socrates is in conversation with the wealthy Athenian Critobulus.
2   The first strategy was the traditional one, the second was adopted by Pericles in 431 and presupposed destroying the balance between the city and the countryside. On both see Y. Garlan, *Recherches de poliorcétique grecque* (Paris, 1974).

5   Aristotle and the trades

There are further variants in the following two passages from Aristotle's *Politics*. The slave is distinguished from the free man by his trade (cf. also no 14); agriculture must therefore be removed from those activities allowed to citizens.

A In some states the artisans (*demiourgoi*) were once upon a time excluded from office, in the days before the institution of the extreme form of democracy. The occupations pursued by men who are subjected to rule of the sort just mentioned need never be studied by the good man, or by the statesman, or by the good citizen – except occasionally and in order to satisfy some personal need, in which case the distinction between master and servant would disappear.

ARISTOTLE, *Politics* III, 1277 b 1–7
(trans. E. Barker)

B Upon these principles it clearly follows that a state with an ideal constitution – a state which has for its members men who are absolutely just, and not men who are merely just in relation to some particular standard – cannot have its citizens living the life of mechanics or shopkeepers, which is ignoble and inimical to goodness. Nor can it have them engaged in farming: leisure is a necessity, both for growth in goodness and for the pursuit of political activity.

ARISTOTLE, *Politics* VII, 1328 b 37–1329 a 2
(trans. E. Barker)

6 Division of labour or division of trades

It has often been said that the philosophers of Antiquity foreshadowed the principle of the division of social labour, as outlined by Adam Smith in a famous passage of *The Wealth of Nations*. But in reality, as is shown by the nearly contemporary passages (about 375) in Plato and Xenophon, the stress is placed not on labour but on the trades, not on the possibility of increasing production but on that of improving quality[1].

A Plato relates how one passes from a 'primitive', but healthy, state to a modern one, that is to say one contemporary with the Athens of his day.

Socrates The community I have described seems to me the ideal one, in sound health as it were: but if you want to see one suffering from inflammation, there is nothing to hinder us. So some people, it seems, will not be satisfied to live in this simple way; they must have couches and tables and furniture of all sorts; and delicacies too, perfumes, unguents, courtesans, sweetmeats, all in plentiful variety. And besides, we must not limit ourselves now to those bare necessaries of house and clothes and shoes; we shall have to set going the arts of embroidery and painting, and collect rich materials, like gold and ivory.

Yes, he said[2].

Then we must once more enlarge our community. The healthy one will not be big enough now; it must be swollen up with a whole multitude of callings not ministering to any bare necessity: hunters and fishermen, for instance; artists in sculpture, painting, and music; poets with their attendant train of professional reciters, actors, dancers, producers; and makers of all sorts of household gear, including everything for women's adornment. And we shall want more servants: children's nurses and attendants, ladies' maids, barbers, cooks and confectioners. And then swineherds – there was no need for them in our original state, but we shall want them now; and a great quantity of sheep and cattle too, if people are going to live on meat.

Of course.

And with this manner of life physicians will be in much greater request.

No doubt.

PLATO, *Republic* II, 372 e–373 d
(trans. F.M. Cornford)

B   Xenophon describes the division of trades in the (imaginary) palace of his hero Cyrus.

Just as other trades (*technai*) are carried to a high degree of excellence in large cities[3], similarly at the court of the Great King the food which is prepared is particularly excellent. In small cities the same workmen make couches, doors, ploughs, tables, and often the same person actually builds the house, and is thankful if he finds enough employers to make a living. It is therefore impossible for a man who practises many crafts to do everything well. But in large cities because of the great demand for each particular trade, a single trade is enough to provide a living, sometimes even only a fraction of a trade. Thus one man will make shoes for men, another shoes for women, and there are even places where one man makes a living by stitching shoes together, another by cutting them, another by cutting only uppers, another by merely assembling all the pieces. The result is that a person who devotes himself to a very restricted kind of work has got to do it as well as possible[4].

Exactly the same thing happens with food. Where the same man makes up couches, lays the table, kneads bread, and prepares different dishes at different times, it is inevitable, I imagine, that things should go as best they can, according to each person's capacity. But where there is enough work for one person to boil meat and another to roast it, or for one to boil fish, another to roast it and yet another to make bread, and not all kinds of bread, but the kind for which he is famous, it is inevitable, I think, that food prepared in this way should be particularly excellent.

XENOPHON, Cyropaedia VIII, 2, 5–6

1   Cf. M.I. Finley, art. cit., in *Past and Present* 47 (May 1970), pp. 3–5 (=*Studies in Ancient Society*, pp. 26–7).
2   Adeimantus, Plato's brother, in conversation with Socrates.
3   As opposed to small ones.
4   The aim is therefore to improve production and not to increase it, as in Adam Smith's pin factory.

7   War in former times

Whenever Thucydides reasons about the past of Greece, which is also the present of the barbarians and even the present of the Greek peoples of the north west (cf. no 53), he quite naturally makes war the main mode of acquisition, though not any kind of war but specifically piracy.

For in early times the Greeks and barbarians of the coast and islands, as communication by sea became more common, were tempted to turn pirates, under the conduct of their most powerful men; the motives being to serve their own cupidity and to support the needy. They would fall upon a town unprotected by walls, and consisting of a mere collection of villages[1], and would plunder it; indeed, this came to be the main source of their livelihood, no disgrace being yet attached to such an achievement, but even some glory. An illustration of this is furnished by the honour with which some of the inhabitants of the continent still regard a successful marauder,

and by the question we find the old poets everywhere repre-
senting the people as asking of travellers arriving by sea – 'Are
they pirates?'[2] – as if those who asked the question would have
(were) no idea of disclaiming the imputation, or their interrogators of
reproaching them for it. The same rapine also prevailed by
land. And even at the present day many parts of Greece still
follow the old fashion – the Ozolian Locrians for instance, the
Aetolians, the Acarnanians, and that region of the continent;
and the custom of carrying arms is still kept up among these
continentals, from the old piratical habits. The whole of
Greece used once to carry arms, their dwellings being unprotected and their communication with each other unsafe; indeed, to wear arms was as much a part of everyday life with
them as with the barbarians. And the fact that the people in
these parts of Greece are still living in the old way points to a
time when the same mode of life was once equally common
to all.

THUCYDIDES I, 5–6, 2
(trans. R. Crawley)

1 Cf. nos 53, 55.
2 An allusion to the episode of Odysseus among the Cyclopes,
  Odyssey IX, 254ff.

8 Convention on the sharing of booty and on commerce between the Cretan cities of Cnossos and Tylissos (*c.* 450)

War in the previous passage was carried out without any conventions, and was so to speak war in a savage state. Here by
contrast is an example of a convention on the sharing of booty
between two Cretan cities acting under the patronage of Argos[1].
The convention draws a careful distinction between what is taken
by land, what is taken by sea (Tylissos was a maritime city), what
the cities are to keep and what goes to Delphi[2]. The two cities
conclude further a pact on free trading.

> [The Tylissian may] pillage [?][3] the territory of the A[charn-
> aeans] (?)[4] with the exception of [those parts] which belong to
> the city [of the Cnossians]. Whatever we both take together
> [from the enemy], the Tylissian shall have [a share] of one-
> third of all that is taken [by] land, and one-half of all that is
> taken [by] sea. The Cnossians shall have a tithe of whatever

we take jointly[5]. And of the spoils our two cities shall send jointly the finest to the sanctuary of Pytho[6]. The rest of our two cities shall dedicate jointly to [Ares at Cnoss]os. There shall be [freedom to export] from Cnossos to Tylissos and from Tyli[ssos to Cnossos]. But if (a Tylissian) exports goods beyond[7], he shall pay the same dues as the Cnossians. Goods from Tylissos shall be exported [freely].

Fragments of an inscription found at
Argos. MEIGGS–LEWIS no 42,
B 2–14

1 There are, however, two conflicting interpretations of this inscription and of the status of Tylissos: according to one view, the text is a treaty between Argos and Cnossos, and Tylissos only exists as a dependency of Argos; according to the other, Cnossos and Tylissos are concluding a treaty on a basis of equality as sovereign states; see the commentary of Meiggs and Lewis.

2 See A. Aymard, 'Le partage des profits de la guerre dans les traités d'alliance antiques', in *Études d'histoire ancienne* (Paris, 1967), pp. 499–512.

3 The Greek verb conveys simultaneously the legal notion of 'reprisals', that is to say the seizure of property belonging to a foreigner whose state has injured the citizens of a country which exercises this right, and also the very practical notion of pillage; this clause, however, is conjectural and based mainly on restoration. B. Bravo would interpret it quite differently as referring to rules for the cutting of wood, and would give a different meaning to the verb here translated as 'to pillage'. On the right of reprisals see generally B. Bravo, *Recherches sur le droit de représailles en Grèce ancienne* (forthcoming).

4 Possibly the modern village of Archanes, south of Cnossos.

5 This tithe indicates the superiority of Cnossos over Tylissos.

6 At Delphi; this probably refers to the finest weapons.

7 One must probably understand: if a Tylissian exports outside Cnossos and Tylissos goods from Cnossos.

9 The profits of war: the Athenians and the capture of Hykkara (summer 415)

This brief passage in Thucydides is interesting in two ways: the Athenians sack a Sicanian city and reduce its population to slavery[1] for purely financial reasons, but an agreement on the sharing of booty is implicit in the operation, since the territory of the captured city is handed over to the Egestaeans[2].

> Coasting along Sicily, with the shore on their left, on the side towards the Tyrrhenian Gulf, they touched at Himera, the only Greek city in that part of the island, and being refused admission resumed their voyage. On their way they took Hykkara, a petty Sicanian seaport, nevertheless at war with Egesta[3], and making slaves of the inhabitants gave up the town to the Egestaeans, some of whose cavalry had joined them; after which the army proceeded through the territory of the Sicels until it reached Catana, while the fleet sailed around the island with the slaves on board. Meanwhile Nicias sailed straight along the coast and went to Egesta and, after transacting his other business and receiving the 30 talents[4], rejoined the forces. They now sold their slaves for the sum of 120 talents.

THUCYDIDES VI, 62, 2–4
(trans. R. Crawley)

1 The rules and customs of war did not prohibit this kind of behaviour, even when the captured city was a Greek one.
2 Two interpretations of this have been given; according to E. Bikerman, *Mélanges F. de Visscher* III (Brussels, 1950), p. 119, n 79, Egesta being a Sicilian city had on the spot a kind of legal supremacy. A. Aymard (art. cit., p. 502) thinks on the other hand that there was only a *de facto* agreement without any previous convention.
3 Egesta (or Segesta), an 'Elymian' city but deeply hellenized.
4 A sum given by Egesta to the Athenians as price for their intervention.

10   Hesiod and the need for work

Work, or more exactly agricultural work[1], is for Hesiod the unfortunate lot of man in the age of iron, our own age which is separated from the age of gold when 'wheat-bearing earth' produced herself an ample and generous harvest[2]. Work does not have as its aim creation, still less development, but simply food production.

But do you at any rate, always remembering my charge, work, high-born Perses[3], that hunger may hate you, and venerable Demeter richly crowned may love you and fill your barn with food; for hunger is altogether a meet comrade for the sluggard. Both gods and men are angry with a man who lives idle, for in nature he is like the stingless drones who waste the labour of the bees, eating without working; but let it be your care to order your work properly, that in the right season your barns may be full of victual. Through work men grow rich in flocks and substance, and working they are much loved by the immortals[4]. Work is no disgrace: it is idleness which is a disgrace. But if you work, the idle will soon envy you as you grow rich, for worth[5] and renown attend on wealth. And whatever be your lot, work is best for you[6], if you turn your misguided mind away from other men's property to your work and attend to your livelihood as I bid you.

HESIOD, *Works and Days*, 298–316
(trans. H.G. Evelyn-White)

1 The work of the artisan is thought of as radically distinct from agricultural activity. Hesiod says to his brother: *'Pass by the smithy and its crowded lounge in winter time when the cold keeps men from field work; for then an industrious man can greatly prosper his house'* (*Works and Days*, 493–5, trans. H.G. Evelyn-White).
2 Ibid., 117–18.
3 Hesiod's brother; 'high-born' is ironical.
4 On the religious connotations of work in Hesiod, cf. M. Detienne, *Crise agraire et attitude religieuse chez Hésiode* (Brussels, 1963).
5 In Greek *arete*, a word taken over from heroic vocabulary.
6 A maxim addressed to all those who are unlucky not to be aristocrats.

11   **The distinction between the artisan and his work**
When Plutarch, writing in the second century AD, explains that one can admire the Zeus of Pheidias without admiring Pheidias himself, he is not reasoning in the same way as the modern critic who argued one day that great works ought to be anonymous, which would enable one to distinguish between Mr X, the author

of the *Soulier de Satin* and M. Paul Claudel, ambassador of France. Plutarch is in fact reproducing a very old tradition (see, for example, no 113). Thucydides mentions the chryselephantine statue of Athena (no 87), but does not say a word about its maker. A sculptor is an artisan, who may be paid for every piece of work done (no 73) and not on a *per diem* basis, but still is an artisan. The tradition on the history of art, which begins in the fourth century, seems to be very largely independent of the historical tradition proper, which is centred on the city.

We take pleasure in perfumes and purple garments, but we regard dyers and perfumers as men unworthy to be free and as mean artisans. Antisthenes[1] was therefore quite right in saying, when he was told that Ismenias[2] was an excellent flute-player, 'He is good for nothing, for he would not otherwise be such a good flute-player.' Similarly Philip, when his son[3] was playing the cithara at a banquet with much charm and skill, asked him: 'Are you not ashamed to play so well?' The point of this is that it is enough for a king to listen in his leisure time to others playing the cithara and he does sufficient honour to the Muses if he attends as a spectator competitions which involve others [. . .] No young man of good birth having seen the Zeus of Pisa[4] or the Hera of Argos desired to become Pheidias or Polycleitus, nor Anacreon, Philemon or Archilochus for having been delighted with their poems. A work may delight us with its charm, but there is no need to regard its creator with admiration.

PLUTARCH, *Pericles* I, 4 – II, 1

1 A philosopher and disciple of Socrates.
2 A Theban statesman.
3 Philip of Macedon talking to the future Alexander the Great.
4 The cult statue of Zeus at Olympia (on the territory of the former city of Pisa), one of Pheidias' major works.

12   Can one sell ribbons, be an Athenian woman and remain respectable?

The Athenian Euxitheos threatened in a law suit (*c.* 346) by a certain Euboulides with loosing his citizen rights, under suspicion of being born from foreign parents, defends in court with some embarrassment the respectability of the trades practised by his mother[1].

I shall now proceed to speak of my mother (for they have also made her a reproach against me), and I shall call witnesses in support of my statements. And, men of Athens, the reproaches which Euboulides has heaped upon us are not only contrary to the decree which regulates the market place, but also contrary to the laws which declare that whoever reproaches either a male or a female citizen with the trade he or she carries on in the market is liable to be punished for evil-speaking. We confess that we sell ribbons and do not live in the way we would wish. And if you regard this, Euboulides, as a proof that we are not Athenians, I will show you that it is just the reverse, and that it is not lawful for any foreigner to do business in the market[2]. [. . .] It is therefore your duty, men of Athens, to defend the laws and to hold, not that traders are foreigners, but that pettifoggers are scoundrels. And let me tell you, Euboulides, there is another law concerning idleness[3], to which you who denounce traders like us are liable. But such is our plight, that our opponent may make slanderous accusations unconnected with the case and do everything possible to prevent my obtaining justice, while you will perhaps rebuke me if I tell you what kind of trade this man carries on as he goes about the city - and with good reason too, for what need is there to tell you what you already know? But just consider. It seems to me that our trading in the market is the strongest proof of the falsity of this man's accusations against us. For when he says my mother was a seller of ribbons and notorious to all, there ought surely to have been witnesses to vouch for the fact from their own knowledge and not just from hearsay. If she was a foreigner, they should have inspected the records of the tolls in the *agora* to show whether she had paid the tax on foreigners and where she came from. If she was a slave, the person who bought her, or the person who sold her, should have come to give evidence of it; or, in default of them, someone else might have proved that she had been a slave or that she had been manumitted. Euboulides however has proved none of these things; he has only been abusive, and abusive (I think) in the highest possible degree. [. . .] He has also said this of my mother, that she was a wet-

nurse. It was at the time of the city's misfortunes, when everybody was badly off[4]. We do not deny that this happened. How
and why she became a wet-nurse, I will tell you plainly. And
do not let it prejudice you against us, men of Athens; for you
will find many citizen women who are serving as wet-nurses;
I will mention them to you by name, if you wish. Of course,
if we had been rich, we would not be selling ribbons, nor
would we have been in any kind of need. But what has this to
do with my family origins? Nothing at all, in my view.

DEMOSTHENES, *Against Euboulides*, 30–6

1 The fact that it is a woman who is working is obviously an
   aggravating circumstance.
2 In fact foreigners only had to pay a special tax, as is shown by
   the same speech further on.
3 A not very well-known law (cf. Lysias, fr. 11; Herodotus II,
   177; Plutarch, *Solon* XVII) which may have condemned those
   who squandered their inheritance.
4 The end of the Peloponnesian War.

13 Work and slavery

Aristophanes' utopia here becomes critical. In the *Women at the
Assembly*, the Athenian women having taken control of the city
anticipate naturally that the communist regime they are setting
up will be facilitated by servile labour to the exclusion of all
others (651–653). The scene in the *Ploutos* (from the name of the
god of wealth) in which *Penia* (Poverty) and Chremylos confront
each other, is already more complex. To purchase slaves, one
must also work. Athens presupposes both work and slavery.

What would happen if everybody was given wealth? Dialogue
between Poverty and an old Athenian (388).

Poverty If Ploutos were to recover his sight and to share
himself out equally, nobody would ever practise a trade
(*techne*) or a skill (*sophia*); once both of these had disappeared
from among you, who would want to be a smith, a shipwright,
stitch, make wheels, shoes, bricks, keep a laundry, be a tanner?
Who would want 'To break the soil with his ploughshare and
reap the fruits of Demeter'[1], if you were able to live in idleness
and not to worry about all these things?

Chremylos Rubbish! All these tasks you have just mentioned our servants will labour at for us.

Poverty And where will you get servants?

Chremylos We shall purchase them for silver, of course.

Poverty But first who will be the seller, when he too has silver?

Chremylos Some trader avid for profit, from Thessaly, the land of the insatiable slave-traders.

Poverty But first of all there won't be any slave-traders for a start, according to your own argument. Of course! For who, once he has become wealthy, would want to risk his life doing this job? You will wear your life out much more painfully than you do now, being forced to plough and dig and do all painful tasks.

ARISTOPHANES, Ploutos, 510–26

1 Tragic style.

14 Women, children, artisans, slaves: the different types of social authority

It was the genius of Aristotle to conceptualize everyday life in his time. Even when, as in the following passage, he starts from abstract theoretical premisses (in this case the division, platonic in origin, of the soul between a ruling and a ruled element), he reverts at the end of his reasoning to concrete reality, in this case the social groups which Greek society excluded or cast away on the fringes: women, children and slaves and, within limits which the philosopher seeks to define, artisans.

The soul has naturally two elements, a ruling and a ruled; and each has its different goodness, one belonging to the rational and ruling element, and the other to the irrational and ruled. What is true of the soul is evidently also true of the other cases; and we may thus conclude that it is a general law that there should be naturally ruling elements and elements naturally ruled. The rule of the free man over the slave is one kind of rule; that of the male over the female another; that of the grown man over the child another still. It is true that all these persons possess in common the different parts of the soul; but they possess them in different ways. The slave is entirely without the faculty of deliberation; the female indeed possesses it, but in a form which remains inconclusive[1]; and if children[2] also possess it, it is only in an immature form.

What is true (in this case) must similarly be held to be true of their possessing moral goodness: they must all share in it, but not in the same way – each sharing only to the extent required for the discharge of his or her function. The ruler, accordingly, must possess moral goodness in its full and perfect form, because his function, regarded absolutely and in its full nature, demands a master artificer, and reason is such a master artificer; but all other persons need only possess moral goodness to the extent required of them. [. . .]

We must therefore hold that what the poet Sophocles said of women

> A modest silence is a woman's crown[3]

contains a general truth – but a truth which does not apply to men. A child, again, is immature, and his goodness is therefore obviously not a matter of relation to his present self, but of his relation to the end and to the guiding authority[4]. Similarly too, the goodness of the slave is a matter of his relation to his master.

We laid it down[5], in treating of slaves, that they were useful for the necessary purposes of life. It is clear, on that basis, that they need but little goodness; only so much, in fact, as will prevent them from falling short of their duties through intemperance or cowardice. If this be true, the question may be raised whether artisans too ought not to have goodness, seeing that they often fall short of their duties through intemperance. But does not the case of the artisan differ greatly from that of the slave? The slave is a partner in his master's life: the artisan is less closely attached to a master. The extent of the goodness incumbent on him is proportionate to the extent of the servitude to which he is subject[6]; the mechanical type of artisan is subject only to what may be called a limited servitude. Again, the slave belongs to the class of those who are naturally what they are; but no shoemaker, or any other artisan, belongs to that class[7].

It is therefore clear that the master of a household must produce in the slave the sort of goodness we have been discussing, and he must do so not as a manager giving instructions about particular duties[8]. This is the reason why we may disagree with those who are in favour of withholding reason from slaves, and who argue that only command should be employed[9]. Admonition ought to be applied to slaves even more than it is to children.

This may serve as a sufficient discussion of these topics. There remain for discussion a number of questions – the relation of husband and wife, and that of parent and child; the nature of the goodness proper to each partner in these relations; the character of the mutual association of the partners, with its qualities and defects and the methods of attaining those qualities and escaping from those defects. All these are questions which must be treated later in the discourses which deal with forms of government[10]. Every household is part of a *polis*. The society of husband and wife, and that of parents and children, are parts of the household. The goodness of every part must be considered with reference to the goodness of the whole. We must therefore consider the government (of the whole *polis*) before we proceed to deal with the training of children and women – at any rate if we hold that the goodness of children and women makes any difference to the goodness of the *polis*. And it must make a difference. Women are a half of the free population: children grow up to be partners in the government of the state.[11]

ARISTOTLE, *Politics* I, 1260 a 4–1260 b 20
(trans. E. Barker)

1 The Greek text means exactly that a woman is capable of deliberation but cannot give the force of law to her deliberations.
2 This refers to children proper, but in Greek society the major problems arose of course during the transition from childhood to manhood.
3 Sophocles, *Ajax*, 293.
4 The adult is the 'end' of the child, just as the master is the end of the slave.
5 In the preceding passage of the *Politics*.
6 Aristotle is here considering the artisan only in so far as he is – because of the dependence which links him to the person who orders his work – a partial slave.

7 One is a slave by nature, but one is not a shoemaker or a tailor by nature.

8 What distinguishes the master is his status as a free man and not his competence as a manager.

9 This is aimed at Plato, cf. *Laws* VI, 777 e. The slave participates in reason but only in so far as he is capable of grasping the reasons of his master.

10 There is nothing in the preserved works of Aristotle which strictly speaking deals with this problem, but it is touched on in the *Economics* which have come down to us under his name.

11 The distinctions between men and women, and adults and children, are relevant for the author of the *Politics* only within the body of free citizens. Aristotle specifies elsewhere: 'A woman also can be good and so can be a slave, yet perhaps woman is a somewhat inferior being whereas a slave is completely ordinary' (*Poetics*, 1454 a 20). In the barbarian world of the 'slaves by nature', 'the female and the slave hold the same rank: the reason for this is that they do not have a class of natural rulers, and the conjugal partnership which is formed among them is just that of a male slave and a female slave' (*Politics* I, 1252 b 5).

15   Before slaves: women

The Athenians were well aware of the fact that women and slaves, without being on the same level, constituted two inferior categories of the population. In the mythical accounts they invented concerning the emergence of slavery, it is not the work of men which preceded the work of slaves but that of women[1]. Here are two examples of such accounts, one from Herodotus and the other from a comic poet contemporary with Aristophanes.

A   *The women of Athens and the Pelasgians*[2]

The Pelasgians had been driven out of Attica by the Athenians, whether justly or unjustly I cannot say, since I can only report what is said about this, which is as follows. Hecataeus[3], son of Hegesander, says in his *History* that it was unjustly. According to him, the Athenians had given to the Pelasgians a tract of land at the foot of Hymettus as payment for the wall with which the Pelasgians had surrounded the Acropolis[4]. This land was barren and worth little at the time; but the Pelasgians brought it into good condition, whereupon the Athenians became jealous and desired to recover it. And so, without any better excuse, they drove out the Pelasgians. But the Athenians maintain that they were justified in what they did. According to them, the Pelasgians, once settled at the foot of Hymettus, used it as a base to insult them in the following way. The daughters and children[5] of the Athenians used to fetch water at the fountain called 'the Nine Springs'[6]; for at that time neither they nor the other Greeks had any household slaves (*oiketai*); whenever they came, they were treated with rudeness and insolence by the Pelasgians. Nor was this enough; but in the end they laid a plot, and were caught red-handed. The Athenians showed how much better men they were than the Pelasgians; for whereas they might justly have killed them all, having caught them in the act of plotting, they refused to do so and only required that they should leave the country. The Pelasgians thereupon left Attica and settled in Lemnos and other places. Such are the accounts respectively of Hecataeus and the Athenians.

HERODOTUS VI, 137

B *In those days . . .*
In those days no one had any slaves, no Manes or Sekis[7], but the women had to do themselves all the housework. What is more, they had to grind the corn at dawn, so that the village[8] rang with the noise of their mills.

PHERECRATES, The Savages, quoted in
Athenaeus, Deipnosophistae VI, 263 b
(= Kock, Comicorum Atticorum Fragmenta,
fr. 10, I, p. 147)

1 For a passage where work was done at first by the young, cf. no 50C and also the passage of Herodotus. See generally P. Vidal-Naquet, 'Refléxions sur l'historiographie grecque de l'esclavage', *Actes du Colloque 1971 sur l'esclavage* (Paris, 1973), pp. 25–44.
2 The Pelasgians are a more-or-less mythical people, said to have preceded the Greeks in Greece. The Athenians were presented by Herodotus simultaneously as hellenized Pelasgians and as opponents of the Pelasgians.

3 Hecataeus of Miletus, the first Greek historian (sixth century).
4 The most ancient fortification of the Acropolis was known as the *Pelargikon* or *Pelasgikon*.
5 All manuscripts but one bear this mention which most editors have deleted, perhaps wrongly.
6 The *Enneakrounos*: it got this name after the works carried out by the Peisistratids (Thucydides II, 15); it was previously called the 'beautiful stream' (*Kallirhoe*). Note that in the classical Greek world shopping was done by men.
7 Manes is a typically Phrygian name; Sekis is a Greek slave name, which means 'the little slave girl'. See O. Masson, 'Les noms des esclaves dans la Grèce antique', *Actes du Colloque 1971 sur l'esclavage* (Paris, 1973), pp. 9–23.
8 The village: before the emergence of the town and of the city.

16 Myth on the origins of male democracy at Athens

A story in Varro, a Roman scholar contemporary of Cicero, which St Augustine quotes and discusses, explains how at the dawn of time men took away from women the right to vote. The myth links primitive disorder and the vote of women, order and male domination. It can hardly have originated before the citizenship law of Pericles in 451 or 450[1].

> Now this is the reason why, according to Varro, Athens got her name which is obviously derived from Minerva, who is called Athena in Greek. When an olive tree had suddenly appeared there and water gushed forth in another spot, the king was alarmed by these portents and sent to Apollo at Delphi to ask how these should be interpreted and what ought to be done. Apollo answered that the olive tree meant Minerva and the water Neptune[2], and that it was up to the citizens to decide which of the two gods, whose emblem these were, should give its name to the city. Having received this oracle Cecrops[3] summoned all the citizens of both sexes to give their vote (it was the custom in that country at the time that women should take part in public debates). The multitude was therefore consulted and the men voted for Neptune, the women for Minerva; and because there was one more vote on the side of the women, Minerva was victorious. Then Neptune in his

anger devastated the lands of the Athenians with raging waves; it is not difficult for demons to let loose floods of water at their whim. To appease his anger, the Athenians, according to Varro, imposed a threefold punishment on the women: henceforward they would not have the right to vote, none of their children would bear his mother's name[4] and they would not be called Athenian women[5].

VARRO quoted by St Augustine, *The City of God* XVIII, 9

1 For a detailed discussion see the articles of S.G. Pembroke and P. Vidal-Naquet mentioned in Chapter 1, n 45.
2 Athena and Poseidon.
3 The first mythical king of Athens, a culture hero, who invented agriculture and marriage.
4 Greek filiation is strictly patrilinear. Varro's account must be compared with the traditions which present Cecrops as the inventor of marriage. In the 'state of nature' children can only be known by their mothers' names, since they have several 'fathers'. After the 'invention' of marriage, patrilinear filiation becomes the norm.
5 They are not citizen women, but only daughters of citizens.

17 **Nicias versus Alcibiades: the old versus the young? The debate on the Sicilian expedition (415 BC)**

The cleavage between young and adults in a Greek society could take place at quite different levels. One is very far here from the 'rites of passage' which dramatized the young man's entry into the world of adults[1], and very far too from the inhumation rites revealed by the excavators of Eretria: children up to adolescence were inhumated (on the side of nature) while adults were cremated[2]. But even in political assemblies the right to speak was granted first to the older men[3]. The antagonism between Nicias and Alcibiades is therefore doubly significant. Alcibiades ascribes to youth the spirit of innovation which characterizes Athens, but he does not venture beyond a concerted action of young and old (it is the Athenian assembly he has to convince and not a youthful audience). As for Thucydides he knows the sequel of the story, that is to say the disaster in Sicily and Alcibiades' betrayal, and the emphasis is placed on the threat represented by youth.

Nicias   'When I see such persons now sitting here at the side of that same individual⁴ and summoned by him, alarm seizes me; and I, in my turn, summon any of the older men that may have such a person sitting next to him not to let himself be shamed down, for fear of being thought a coward if he did not vote for war, nor to yield, as they themselves might be tempted to do, to the dangerous longing for distant things. Let them remember how rarely success is got by wishing and how often by forecast, and as true lovers of their country, now threatened by the greatest danger in its history, let them vote against the expedition.'

Alcibiades, after recalling among other things the recent successes of his Peloponnesian policy, replies:

'Thus did my youth and so-called monstrous folly find fitting arguments to deal with the power of the Peloponnesians, and by its ardour win their confidence and prevail. And do not be afraid of my youth now, but while I am still in its flower, and Nicias appears fortunate, avail ourselves to the utmost of the services of us both [. . .] And do not let the do-nothing policy which Nicias advocates, or his setting of the young against the old, turn you from your purpose, but in the good old fashion by which our fathers, old and young together, by their united counsels brought our affairs to their present height, do you endeavour still to advance them; understanding that neither youth nor old age can do anything the one without the other, but that the greatest strength comes from uniting the weak, the average and the truly outstanding, and that, by sinking into inaction, the city, like everything else, will wear itself out, and its skill in everything decay; while each fresh struggle will give it fresh experience, and make it more used to defend itself not in word but in deed.'

THUCYDIDES VI, 13, 1; 17, 1; 18, 6
(trans. R. Crawley)

1 Cf. Chapter 1, p. 26 with bibliography in n 47.
2 See Cl. Bérard, *Eretria III. L'Hérôon à la porte de l'Ouest* (Bern, 1970); cf. P. Vidal-Naquet in *Faire de l'histoire* III (Paris, 1974), pp. 147–8.

3 See the study by P. Roussel mentioned in Chapter 1, n 47.
4 Alcibiades.

18 The popular classes as seen by an oligarch

The author of the *Constitution of the Athenians*[1] (commonly
known as 'The Old Oligarch') is one of the oldest witnesses of the
antagonism between rich and poor in the Athenian democracy,
the logic of which he understood perfectly well. This is also a
valuable testimony on the variety of the terminology used to
designate antagonist social groups.

In every country the élite (*to beltiston*) is opposed to democracy. For among the members of the élite there is least wanton-
ness and injustice, and the greatest exactness as regards the
things which befit a gentleman (*ta chresta*), whereas among
the people (*demos*) there is most ignorance, disorder and vice
(*poneria*). For more than others they are driven to shameful
deeds by poverty, lack of education and ignorance, which for
some men is the consequence of lack of means.
Some might say that one should not allow all these people
to speak on an equal footing[2] or to serve in the council, but to
reserve these rights to the cleverest (*dexiotatoi*) and best men
(*aristoi*). But the Athenians in this matter follow the best course
and allow the vulgar people (*poneroi*) to speak. For if the good
men (*chrestoi*) spoke and served in the council, it would be
good for those like them but bad for the members of the people.
But now, since all may speak, any wretch can get up and find
what is good for him and his peers.
Someone might ask, what good can such a man propose for
himself or for the people? But the Athenians realize that the
ignorance, vice and goodwill of such a man is of greater
advantage to them than the good man's excellence, wisdom
and ill-will. It is possible that habits such as these cannot
produce the best kind of city, but they are the best way to
preserve the democracy. For the people does not want to see
the city well governed and fall itself into slavery, but to be free
and rule, and is little concerned about bad government; for
what you call bad government is the source of strength and
freedom for the people. If you are seeking to establish good
government (*eunomia*), you will first of all see the straightest

kind of men establishing the laws for their own good. Then the good men (*chrestoi*) will punish the wretches (*poneroi*); they will determine the policy of the city and prevent madmen (*mainomenoi*) from deliberating, speaking or meeting in assembly. As a consequence of these good measures the people would very quickly fall into slavery[3].

[XENOPHON], *Constitution of the Athenians* I, 5–9

1 See below nos 74 and 85.
2 In the popular assembly.
3 For the sequel, which deals in fact with the slaves, see no 74 below.

19 Social organs, social functions and social classes: Aristotle's terminology

The greatest political theorist of antiquity, Aristotle, describes Greek societies in his time with a threefold terminology. The first is expressly borrowed from biology, of which he was one of the founders: societies have organs without which they cannot live, as for example farmers and artisans. The second modelled on the analysis of the soul is properly functional: a city cannot exist if the deliberative function, the judicial function, and the military function are not provided for. These first two terminologies are actually constantly overlapping, just as the body and the soul, and matter and form overlap. But a third terminology interferes, which corresponds much better to what we call class analysis. The permanent couple of rich and poor cannot be interpreted either in terms of organs or in terms of function, and political regimes are classified according to it. But having made this fundamental distinction Aristotle still endeavours to make within these two groups the organic classifications he believes to be necessary.

States too, as we have repeatedly noticed, are composed not of one but of many parts. One of these parts is the mass of people (*plethos*)[1] concerned with the production of food, or, as it is called, the farming class (*georgoi*). A second, which is called the mechanical class (*banauson*), is the group of persons occupied in the various arts and crafts without which a city cannot be inhabited – some of them being necessities, and others contributing to luxury or the living of a good life. A third part is what may be termed the marketing class (*agoraioi*); it includes all those who are occupied in buying and selling, either as merchants or as retailers[2]; a fourth part is the class of thetes[3]; and a fifth element is the defence force, which is no less necessary than the other four[4], if a state is not to become the slave of invaders. How is it possible, with any propriety, to call by the name of state a society which is naturally servile? It is the essence of a state to be independent and self-sufficing; and it is the absence of independence which is the mark of a slave[5]. [. . .]

Whether these functions [. . .] belong to separate groups, or to a single group, is a matter which makes no difference to the argument. It often falls to the same persons both to serve in the army as hoplites and to till the fields. The general conclusion which we thus reach is that if those who discharge these functions are equally parts of the state with those who supply its bodily needs, they, or at least the hoplites, are necessary parts. The seventh part[6] is the group composed of the rich, who serve the state with their property by means of liturgies. The eighth part is the public servants[7], who serve the state in its offices. No state can exist without a government; and there must therefore be persons capable of discharging the duties of office and rendering the state that service, permanently or in rotation. There only remain the two parts which have just been mentioned in passing the deliberative part, and the part which decides on the rights of litigants. These are parts which ought to exist in all states, and to exist on a good and just basis; and this demands persons of good quality on matters political[8]. The different capacities belonging to the other parts may, it is generally held, be shown by one and the same group of persons. The same persons, for example, may serve as soldiers, farmers and craftsmen; the same persons, again, may act both as a liberative council and a judicial court[9]. Political ability, too, is a quality to which all men pretend; and everybody thinks himself capable of filling most offices[10]. There is one thing which is impossible: the same persons cannot be both rich and poor. This will explain why these two classes – the rich and the poor – are regarded as parts of the state in a special and peculiar sense. Nor is this all. One of these classes being small, and the other large, they also appear to be opposite parts. This is why they both form constitutions to suit their own interest. It is also the reason why men think that there are only two con- stitutions – democracy and oligarchy.

The fact that there are a number of constitutions, and the causes of that fact, have already been established[11]. We may now go on to say that there are also a number of varieties of two of these constitutions – democracy and oligarchy. This is already clear from what has previously been said. These constitutions vary because the people (*demos*) and the class called the notables (*gnorimoi*) vary. So far as the people are concerned, one sort is engaged in farming[12]; a second is engaged in the arts and crafts; a third is the marketing sort, which is engaged in buying and selling; a fourth is the mari- time sort, which in turn is partly naval, partly mercantile (*chrematistikon*), partly employed on ferries, and partly engaged in fisheries. (We may note that there are many places where one of these subdivisions forms a considerable body; as the fishermen do at Tarentum and Byzantium, the naval crews at Athens, the merchant seamen in Aegina and Chios, and the ferrymen at Tenedos.) A fifth sort is composed of unskilled labourers and persons whose means are too small to enable them to enjoy any leisure, a sixth consists of those who are not of free birth by two citizen parents[13]; and there may also be other sorts of a similar character. The notables fall into differ- ent sorts according to wealth, birth, merit, culture, and other qualities of the same order.

Aristotle, *Politics* IV, 1290 b 39–1291 b 30
(trans. E. Barker)

1 A traditional word to refer to the popular classes.
2 It was common to distinguish or even to contrast *emporoi* and *kapeloi* (see for example no 84). See generally M.I. Finkelstein, *CP* 30 (1935), pp. 320–36.
3 Free men but who were dependent on those who gave them work.
4 It is this criterion of necessity which enables Aristotle to make these distinctions for the time being.
5 A paragraph of polemic against Plato's *Republic* is omitted here.
6 Aristotle has not named the sixth which seems to be that of professional judges.

7 *Demiourgikon*, cf. below no 28 and Chapter 1, p. 12.
8 Aristotle is leading one imperceptibly to a quasi-professional conception of the statesman, a conception which arose in the fourth century but remained controversial, as the sequel of the passage shows.
9 In practice Aristotle means that an Athenian, for example, can be simultaneously a member of the council (*Boule*) and of the law-courts (*Heliaea*).
10 That is the very foundation of the democratic idea which is expressed to perfection in the myth told by Protagoras in the platonic dialogue which bears his name (320 c–323 a).
11 *Politics* III, 1278 b 5ff.
12 Aristotle takes up again and develops the distinctions laid down by him for the whole of the city; in the background he identifies popular activities with those belonging to the body of the city, whereas the deliberative and judicial functions belong to its soul.
13 In Athens they were excluded from citizenship since 451–450, but could obtain it in certain circumstances elsewhere, cf. for example no 91.

20   Redistribution of the wealth of the city among the citizens

Siphnos uses the revenue from its mines partly to celebrate collectively its own glory and that of the gods, partly to make distributions among the citizens (though the city cannot be distinguished from the whole body of the citizens). In Athens by contrast the sharing out of the silver between the city and the citizens takes on the form of a choice: either the ten drachmae or the triremes. Therein lies the Athenian innovation, but though it shifted the solution of the problem it did not modify its terms.

A   The gold and silver mines of Siphnos
The Siphnians[1] at that time[2] were at the height of their prosperity. They were the wealthiest among the islanders, as there were mines of gold and silver in their country, and of so rich a yield, that from a tithe of the ores the Siphnians furnished out a treasury at Delphi which was on a par with the grandest there. Every year they would divide out among themselves the yields of the mines.

HERODOTUS III, 57

B   *Themistocles' choice*

The Athenians, having a large sum of silver in their treasury, the produce of the mines at Laurion, were about to share it among the full-grown citizens, who would have received ten drachmae apiece, when Themistocles persuaded them to cancel the distribution and build with the silver 200 triremes for the war (he meant the war against the Aeginetans)[3]. It was the outbreak of this war at that time[4] which was the saving of Greece, as it forced the Athenians to become a maritime people. The new ships were not used for the purpose for which they had been built, but became a help to Greece in her hour of need.

HERODOTUS VII, 144

1   Siphnos is one of the Cyclades, well-known notably through the 'treasure' built by its inhabitants at Delphi.
2   The last two-thirds of the sixth century.
3   Themistocles' naval law was voted in 483–482 (see J. Labarbe, *La loi navale de Thémistocle* (Paris, 1957)).
4   In 480, on the eve of Salamis.

2 The Homeric World

21 The honour of kings

For the ideal king described by Odysseus 'the black earth bears wheat and barley, and the trees are laden with fruit, the sheep bring forth unfailingly and the sea provides an abundance of fish, all out of his good guidance, and the people prospers under him' (*Odyssey* XIX, 111–14). This image which links the fertility of nature and of men with the perfection of the monarch is uncommon in Homer and has, as has been said, an archaic flavour[1]. The king's excellence is martial and his 'economic' privileges are justified by his bravery in battle.

Sarpedon, king of the Lycians, addresses his companion Glaukos to encourage him in the fight:

> Glaukos, why are the two of us so greatly honoured among the Lycians with seats of honour, meat and numerous cups? Why do all men regard us as gods? Why do we hold a vast estate[2] on the banks of the Xanthos, suitable both for orchards and for the tilling of wheat-bearing earth? We must therefore stand among the front line of the Lycians and take part in the raging battle, so that the Lycians who wear strong corslets may say: 'Our kings who rule Lycia are not inglorious men; they eat fat sheep and drink the choicest honey-sweet wine. They also have surely the strength of brave men, since they fight in the front rank of the Lycians.'
>
> *Iliad* XII, 310–21

1 M.I. Finley, *The World of Odysseus* (1967 ed.), pp. 112–13.
2 In Greek: a *temenos*.

22   Homeric values

Nothing is more difficult in the Homeric world than to distinguish
– if indeed one must distinguish – between premonetary instruments which serve as a standard of value for exchange purposes,
objects for hoarding and ostentation[1], goods that were indispensable for the daily life of warriors (such as metal in raw or
worked form), and landed estates pure and simple. Are these
premonetary signs? The ox was the standard of measure: Laertes
purchased Eurycleia for the price of 20 oxen (*Odyssey* I, 430–1),
which does not mean that oxen were a means of exchange. The
list of presents which Agamemnon proposes to give to Achilles to
restore their friendship includes objects which continued to be
used for a long time as 'premonetary'[2] instruments and which as
late as the fourth century in the treasures of temples served
simultaneously as symbolic wealth and as money[3], but it also
includes captive women and cities.

> In the midst of you all I will name the excellent gifts: seven
> tripods which have not been touched by fire, ten talents of
> gold, 20 shining cauldrons, 12 strong prize-winning horses,
> whose feet have already won in the race. [. . .] And I will give
> him seven women skilled in handiwork. [. . .] These I will give
> him, and among them will be the daughter of Briseus I once
> took from him; moreover I will swear a great oath that I never
> went up to her bed to make love to her, as is the custom among
> human beings, between men and women. All this is at his
> disposal here and now. But if the gods should grant us to sack
> one day the great city of Priam, let him come when we the
> Achaeans are dividing the booty[4], and load his ship full of gold
> and bronze, and let him choose himself 20 Trojan women, the
> most beautiful after Helen of Argos. And if one day we come
> to Argos in Achaea, the most fertile of lands, let him become
> my son-in-law. [. . .] I have three daughters in my well-built
> palace, Chrysothemis, Laodike and Iphianassa, let him take
> any of them he wishes to the palace of Peleus, without giving
> me any wedding presents[5]; I shall be the one to offer many
> soothing gifts, such as a man never gave to his daughter. And
> I will give him also seven well-inhabited cities. [. . .] Men live
> there, rich in sheep and cattle, who will honour him with
> offerings like a god, and under his sceptre will bring him rich
> dues.
>
> *Iliad* IX, 121–56

1 See the admirable study by L. Gernet, 'La notion mythique de la valeur en Grèce', *Journal de Psychologie* 41 (1948), pp. 415–62, reproduced in *Anthropologie de la Grèce ancienne*, pp. 93–137, and M.I. Finley, *The World of Odysseus*, pp. 70ff.

2 Thus in Crete where a payment 'in cauldrons' is still specified in an inscription from Cnossos of the fourth or third century and where the Gortyn inscriptions regularly provide for payments in tripods or cauldrons till the end of the sixth century; see G. le Rider, *Monnaies crétoises* (Paris, 1966), p. 167.

3 See for example the inventory of a temple at Thespiae (beginning of the fourth century) republished by P. Roesch and J. Taillardat, in *Revue de Philologie* 40 (1956), pp. 70–87; one finds there side by side cauldrons, 'spit-drachmae' similar to the Spartan iron currency (below, no 56), tripods, domestic utensils, weapons, etc.

4 The division of booty follows precise rules (cf. M. Detienne, *Les maîtres de vérite dans la Grèce archaïque* (Paris, 1967), pp. 81–105), the violation of which is in fact the cause of Achilles' anger. Agamemnon is now proposing to violate them in his (Achilles') favour through an inversion of the rules.

5 Gift and counter-gift were also the rule for Homeric marriage; cf. M.I. Finley, 'Marriage, Sale and Gift in the Homeric World', *Revue internationale des druits de l'Antiquité* 3 (1955), pp. 167–94.

23   The store room of the 'oikos'

The store room (*thalamos*) was, in the house which is the centre of the *oikos*, the secret room, at once a reserve and a treasury. Telemachus goes down to it before sailing off in search of Odysseus.

He went down to the store room of his father, a spacious room with a high ceiling, where gold and bronze lay piled up, and clothes in coffers, and plenty of fragrant olive oil. Jars of old sweet wine stood there, full of the unmixed divine drink, arranged in a row against the wall, for the time when Odysseus would return home after his many sufferings. The doors, well-fitted and double-folding, were locked and day and night a woman housekeeper was there, keeping a close watch over everything, her mind always alert, Eurycleia the daughter of Ops, son of Pisenor.

Odyssey II, 337–47

24　Eumaeus describes the flocks of Odysseus

This description of the rather modest resources of the master of an *oikos* is but a pale reflection of the vast herds listed in the accounts of Mycenaean palaces[1].

For surely his wealth was great past telling: no other hero, whether on Ithaca or on the dark mainland, had as much; not even 20 men put together have so great wealth. I will enumerate it to you: 12 herds of cows on the mainland, as many flocks of sheep, as many herds of swine and as many wide-roaming herds of goats, which are pastured by shepherds or by strangers[2]. Here on Ithaca altogether 11 vast herds of goats grazing in the distance[3], looked after by valiant men.

Odyssey XIV, 96–104

1　Compare for example the facts assembled by J.T. Killen, 'Some Adjuncts to the Sheep Ideogram in Knossos-Tablets', *Eranos* 61 (1964), pp. 69–93; 'The Wool Industry of Crete in the Late Bronze Age', *BSA* 59 (1964), pp. 1–15.
2　In the first instance this may refer to servants directly attached to the *oikos* of Odysseus, in the second to men (the Greek word is *xeinoi*: strangers, guests) bound to him through ties of hospitality.
3　Literally 'at the limit' (*eschatia*), on the frontier zone of the estate.

25　Raiding of flocks

Cattle-raiding is not the normal occupation of the grown-up warrior as he is portrayed in Homer: it is characteristic of the youthful warrior, who does not yet face other warriors in battle, as in the reminiscences of the aged Nestor in the following passage where his opponents are rustics, not warriors. Otherwise it is found in the simile of the lion to which Homeric warriors are likened, and who is normally depicted as attacking flocks and fighting against countrymen and dogs (e.g. *Iliad* XVII, 62ff.).

Would that I were young again and that my strength was as
steadfast as it used to be, as when a quarrel broke out between
the Eleians[1] and us because of cattle-raiding, and I killed
Itymoneus, the brave son of Hypeirochos, who dwelt in Elis.
I was carrying out reprisals, and he, while fighting for his
cattle, was struck in the front rank by a spear from my hand,
and fell, and his men, who were countryfolk[2], fled on all sides.
We brought back much booty from the plain, driving it in
front of us: 50 herds of cattle, as many flocks of sheep, as many
herds of swine[3], as many wide-roaming herds of goats, 150 bay
horses, all mares, and many with their foals under them. These
we all drove to Pylos, the country of Neleus[4], going by night
towards the city, and Neleus rejoiced in his heart at the great
success I had, despite my youth, when going off to war.

Iliad XI, 670–84

1 East of Pylos (*Epano Engliano*), Nestor's capital.
2 Homer juxtaposes the word meaning the group of warriors
   (*laoi*) and the country folk (*agroiôtai*).
3 Compare the enumeration with no 24.
4 Nestor's father.

26 Hospitality: gift and counter-gift

Hospitality follows precise rules which everybody in the Homeric
world is supposed to know very well. 'Gift' and 'counter-gift' are
perhaps less the 'primitive form of exchange' than the sign of the
recognition of equality within the aristocracy, as in the following
dialogue between Athena, disguised as Mentes, and Telemachus.

I am Mentes; I boast of being son of wise Anchialos, and I rule
over the Taphians, lovers of the oar[1]. Now I have landed here
with my ship and my companions, while sailing over the wine-
dark sea to men of foreign speech, travelling to Temesa[2] in
search of copper and bringing shining iron in exchange. My
ship is lying there towards the country, far from the city, in the
harbour of Rheithron, under wooded Neion. We boast of
being hereditary guest-friends of each other from of old: go
and ask the old man, the hero Laertes[3]. [. . .]
Telemachus Stranger, you say these things out of a friendly
heart, like a father to his son, and I shall never forget them.

But come now and stay on, although you are anxious to be on your way: after bathing and enjoying yourself, you will return to your ship with a gift, rejoicing in your heart, a very fine and precious gift, which shall be an heirloom from me, such as dear friends give to friends.

Athena, the grey-eyed goddess, answered: 'Do not detain me, as I am eager to be on my way. The gift, which your heart bids you give me, you will offer it to me on my return to take home. Choose a very beautiful one, and you will get an adequate one in return.'

Odyssey I, 180–9, 306–18

1 A mythical people comparable to the Phaeacians, specialized like them in maritime life, but who admit they practise trade.
2 The identity of this city was much discussed in antiquity; the problem is insoluble.
3 Father of Odysseus and grandfather of Telemachus.

27 Division of tasks and maritime specialization among the Phaeacians

The Phaeacians, a mythical people, are neither traders nor even pilots, since their ships can do without them (*Odyssey* VIII, 555–69), but contrary to the 'real' peoples described in the *Odyssey*, they unite the technical skill of women with the maritime primacy of men.

Of the 50 women servants who live in the palace of Alkinoos, some grind the yellow grain on the millstone, others weave the web and turn the spindle as they sit down, restless as the leaves of the tall poplar[1]; and the oil drips down from the fine-woven linen. For just as the Phaeacian men are skilled more than all other men at driving a swift ship on the sea, so too are the women most skilled at weaving, for Athena[2] has given them the art of beautiful handiwork and good understanding.

Odyssey VII, 103–11

1 The comparison bears on the movement of the women's hands as they weave.
2 It is not clear whether Athena's protection extends both to the sailors and the weavers or only to the latter (cf. M. Detienne, in *Revue de l'histoire des religions*, 1970, no 4, p. 165, who opts for the second alternative).

28 Homeric 'demioergoi'

Those known to the *Odyssey* as *demioergoi*, that is to say 'those who work for the community, the *demos*', constitute a category – if indeed they do – which is as paradoxical as the word itself, which, as has been seen[1], could in Greek refer on the one hand to high-ranking magistrates in parts of the Peloponnese and of north-western Greece, and on the other to artisans proper. The palace of Nestor, king of Pylos, has its professions: a smith gilds for the benefit of the king the horns of a sacrificial animal (*Odyssey* III, 425–35), but the word *demioergos* is not used in connection with him. On the other hand heralds (*kerykes*), who belong to the closest following of the nobles, are described as *demioergoi* (*Odyssey* XIX, 135). In the world of Odysseus the few words spoken about them by Eumaeus show them to be men who are at once indispensable and mobile.

> For who ever invites a stranger from afar, unless he happens to be one of those who serve the community (*demioergoi*), a prophet or a healer of diseases or a builder in wood, or even a divinely inspired minstrel who can delight all with his song? For these are the men who are invited from the ends of the earth.
>
> *Odyssey* XVII, 382–6

1 See above Chapter 1, p. 12 and the article by K. Murakawa, 'Demiurgos', *Historia* 6 (1957), pp. 385–415.

29 The thetes

It is not easy to know whether there really existed in the Homeric world a category which can be referred to as that of the thetes. Poseidon and Apollo were 'thetes' of Laomedon, king of Troy, when they built the walls of that city, and this condition implied a 'salary' (*misthos*) (*Iliad* XXI, 444–57). Achilles prefers to kingship over the dead the condition of 'thete' in the service of a poor man, and it may be the condition of the employer which is important here, while Eurymachus offers to Odysseus disguised as a beggar to enter his service as a thete on the *eschatia* (the furthest parts) of his estate[1].

A Achilles' choice[2]

Do not speak consolingly of death to me, noble Odysseus! I

would rather live on the earth[3] and serve (*theteuemen*) another man, who had no land of his own and little livelihood, than to rule over all these dead men who have passed away.

Odyssey XI, 487–91

B *The offer of the pretender Eurymachus*
Stranger, would you like to enter my service (*theteuemen*)? I would send you far away in the country, and you would get an adequate salary for picking up stones[4] and planting tall trees. I would provide you with food all the year round, I would clothe you and give you shoes for your feet. But since you have only learnt bad ways, you will refuse to apply yourself to your work and will prefer to go begging among the people in order to fill your insatiable belly[5].

Odyssey XVIII, 357–64

1 On the status of the thete see A. Mele, *Società e lavoro nei poemi omerici* (Naples, 1968), challenging the traditional interpretation (cf. above pp. 44–5) already found in Grote.
2 Odysseus has just expressed admiration for Achilles, whose power continues to be exercised among the dead.
3 The adjective *eparouros* is ambiguous and could mean either 'living on the soil' (as a peasant) or 'living on earth' (as opposed to the underworld).
4 A Mediterranean technique of removing stones from fields.
5 Odysseus shows in his answer that he is fully conversant with agricultural work.

30 Barbarians of the golden age: the Cyclopes

The descriptions of the barbarians, in this case of shepherds who only know those products of the earth which nature gives to them with the generosity of the golden age, enable one to understand better by contrast how far the world of Homer and Hesiod linked the condition of man to the cultivation of the soil. But in Odysseus' narrative of his trip to the land of the Cyclopes another theme enters, that of colonization.

With grief in our heart we sailed on and reached the land of the Cyclopes, a brutal and lawless folk, who trusting in the immortal gods neither plant with their hands nor plough. Everything grows for them without sowing or ploughing: wheat, barley and vines, which bear great clusters of the juice of the grape, and the rain of Zeus makes them grow. They have neither assemblies where counsels are discussed nor laws[1]. They live on the top of high mountains in hollow caves, and each without concerning himself for the others lays down the law for his children and his wives[2]. In front of their harbour lies a fertile island covered with woods, neither too near nor too far from the land of the Cyclopes, where wild goats multiply without number. For the steps of men do not scare them away, nor do hunters enter there, who toil as they climb the top of mountains. The island is not occupied by flocks or by ploughed land, but all the year round lies unsown and untilled, empty of men, and feeds the bleating goats. For the Cyclopes do not have with them ships with vermilion cheeks nor carpenters to build well-benched ships; if they had some and could go from one city to another among men, in search of the many goods which men exchange as they sail across the seas, they might have turned their island into a good settlement. For it is not an infertile island, and all fruits would grow there. It has meadows along the shore of the white sea, well-watered and soft; vines would grow there and never die, ploughing would be easy, and because of the richness of the soil, crops would always be deep to reap from year to year. The harbour is well sheltered, there is no need for ropes, for casting anchors or fastening stern cables. It is enough to draw up the ships on the beach until the sailors wish to depart or the winds begin to blow. At the head of the harbour there is a spring of clear water, issuing from a cave, and poplars grow all around.

Odyssey IX, 105–41

1 In Greek *themistes*, the meaning of which is difficult to define.
2 One can recognize here the starting point of representations of the 'patriarchal' age.

31 Good neighbours and self-sufficiency

Are there in the Homeric world any traits which recall village solidarity? When the Phaeacian King Alkinoos tells the other kings that they can get a refund for the presents made to Odysseus by levying contributions 'from the people' (*Odyssey* XIII, 14), one may wonder whether the village is not going to serve as an intermediary, but in general the *Odyssey* sees the work of the peasants only through the framework of the *oikos*, which of course does not mean that the village did not exist in Homer's time. In the *Works and Days*, a poem which comes only shortly after the *Odyssey*, the poet seems to waver between the ideal of good neighbourliness – superior even to family solidarity – and the invitation to self-sufficiency.

Call your friend to a feast[1]; but leave your enemy alone; and especially call him who lives near you: for if any mischief happen in the place, neighbours come ungirt[2], but kinsmen[3] stay to gird themselves. A bad neighbour is as great a plague as a good one is a great blessing; he who enjoys a good neighbour has a precious possession. Your ox would not die but for a bad neighbour. Take fair measure from your neighbour and pay him back fairly with the same measure, or better, if you can; so that if you are in need afterwards, you may find him sure. Do not get base gain: base gain is as bad as ruin. Be friends with the friendly, and visit him who visits you. Give to one who gives, but do not give to one who does not give. A man gives to the free-handed, but no one gives to the close-fisted[4]. Give is a good girl, but Take is bad and gives death. For the man who gives willingly, even though he gives a great thing, rejoices in his gift and is glad in heart; but whoever gives way to shamelessness and takes something himself, even though it be a small thing, it freezes his heart. If you add only a little to a little and do this often, soon that little will become great. He who adds to what he has will keep off bright-eyed hunger. What a man has by him at home does not trouble him: it is better to have your stuff at home, for whatever is abroad is ruinous. It is a good thing to draw on what you have; but it grieves your heart to need something and not to have it, and I bid you mark this.

HESIOD, *Works and Days*, 342–67
(trans. H.G. Evelyn-White)

1 Hesiod is speaking to his brother Perses.
2 That is to say without getting equipped for travel.
3 Kinsmen by marriage (*peoi*).
4 The rules of gift and counter-gift are also valid in the world of the peasants.

3 The Archaic Period (Eighth–Sixth Centuries)

32 The justice of kings: the peasants and the city

On the shield which Hephaistos makes for Achilles one finds the theme of war and peace, a theme which goes back at least to Sumer (*Iliad* XVIII, 490–540). The peaceful city is also the city where justice is rendered in the *agora*, and two talents of gold are set aside for whoever gives 'the straightest sentence'. For Hesiod's peasant justice appears in the shape of the 'bribe-devouring kings'. The city is a luxury which is not meant for the peasant, but it can also be, and that is the whole significance of Hesiod's poem, an appeal to another kind of justice.

A   *Far from the city*

Little concern has he with quarrels and courts who has not abundant provisions laid up in good time, the fruit of the earth, Demeter's grain. When you have got plenty of that, you can raise disputes and strive to get another's goods. But you shall have no second chance to deal so again[1]: rather, let us settle our dispute here with true judgment which is of Zeus and is perfect. For we had already divided our inheritance[2], but you seized the greater share and carried it off, by paying court to the bribe-devouring kings[3] who love to judge such a cause as this.

HESIOD, *Works and Days*, 30–9
(trans. H.G. Evelyn-White)

B   *The common people and the leading men*

And now I will tell a fable for princes, wise as they may be. Thus said the hawk to the nightingale with speckled neck, while he carried her high up among the clouds, gripped fast in

205

his talons, and she, pierced by his crooked talons, cried piti-
fully. To her he spoke disdainfully: 'Miserable thing, why do
you cry out? One far stronger than you holds you fast, and you
must go wherever I take you, songstress as you are. And if I
please I will make my meal of you, or let you go. He is a fool
who tries to withstand the stronger, for he does not get the
mastery and suffers pain besides his shame.' So said the
swiftly flying hawk, the long-winged bird. But you, Perses,
listen to right and do not foster violence (*hybris*); for violence
is bad for a poor man. Even the prosperous cannot easily bear
its burden, but is weighed down under it when he meets
disaster. The better path is to go by on the other side towards
justice; for justice in the end beats violence. But only when he
has suffered does the fool learn this.

HESIOD, Works and Days, 202–18
(trans. H.G. Evelyn-White)

1 Perses, Hesiod's brother, has deprived him of his share of his
   inheritance.
2 This kind of succession practice may have played an important
   role in the crisis revealed by the beginnings of colonization;
   cf. the article by Ernest Will mentioned above in *REG* 78
   (1965), pp. 542–56.
3 The judges, probably the highest magistrates in the budding
   cities.

33 Peasants in the city

More than a century after Hesiod, the poet Theognis of Megara[1],
writing about the middle of the sixth century, complains in the
advice he gives to his young lover Kyrnos, at seeing peasants,
formerly outsiders, becoming the aristocracy of today.

Kyrnos, our city is in travail, and I fear that she may give birth
to a man who will redress our wicked insolence[2]. For although
the men of our city still show restraint, the leaders are advanc-
ing on the path to ruin. Never yet, Kyrnos, have good men
caused the destruction of any city; but when it pleases the bad
men to resort to violence, they corrupt the people and render
justice for the unjust for the sake of personal profit and power,
and you cannot expect such a city to remain quiet for long,

even if at the moment it lies in deep peace, when it becomes dear to the bad men to pursue gains that are accompanied by public disaster[3]. For they only result in seditions, massacres of citizens and monarchies[4]; may such things never please this city. Kyrnos, this city is still a city, but its people have changed[5]. Those who previously did not know justice or laws, but wore out goatskins on their sides, and had their pasture outside this city like deer, they have now become good men; those who formerly were of high estate have now fallen low. Who can bear such a spectacle?

THEOGNIS, 39–58

1 He is so little known, although (or because) his moralizing verses were imitated right through Greek history, and the imitations then assimilated in his work, and what he says is of such a generalized kind, that modern commentators hesitate whether to refer to the city to which he belongs as Megara in Greece or Megara in Sicily (*Megara Hyblaia*).
2 That is to say a tyrant.
3 Theognis' words are very general in scope and one should not interpret this attack on profit as a protest against traders.
4 Theognis' words are retrospective rather than prospective; Theagenes became tyrant of Megara around 630.
5 Non-citizens have become citizens. See in general A. Dovatur, 'Theognis von Megara und sein soziales Ideal', *Klio* 54 (1972), pp. 77–89, who refrains from speculating about the social and economic background of Theognis' Megara.

34 The hoplites' republic

Modern discussions on the role of the 'hoplite reform' in the rise of the Greek city[1] have their starting point in a famous passage in Aristotle. The philosopher has just been discussing the value of some Greek constitutions which recruit their citizen body only from those who, by their wealth, are able to serve as hoplites.

The first form of constitution[2] which succeeded to monarchy in ancient Greece was one in which the soldiery formed the citizen body. At first it consisted only of cavalry. Military strength and superiority were then the prerogative of that arm; infantry is useless without a system of tactics[3]; and as the experience and the rules required for such a system did not exist in early times, the strength of armies lay in their cavalry. When, however, states began to increase in size[4], and infantry forces acquired a greater degree of strength, more persons were admitted to the enjoyment of political rights. For this reason the name 'democracy'[5] was given at that time to constitutions which we now call 'polities'[6]. Yet strictly speaking the ancient 'polities' were oligarchical and monarchical. With their populations still small, states had no large 'middle class'[7]; and the body of the people, still few in number, and because of the military organization of the times, were more ready to tolerate government from above.

ARISTOTLE, *Politics* IV, 1297 b 15–28
(trans. E. Barker)

1 See above Chapter 3, n 5. The fullest commentary on this passage is the book by Henri Jeanmaire, *Couroi et Courètes* (Lille and Paris, 1939).

2 There is a difficult problem here: is Aristotle using the word *politeia* (republic, constitution) in its wide sense, as we believe to be the case, or in the specific sense he frequently gives to the word, that of moderate – one might say 'constitutional' – democracy? If the first alternative is the correct one, the order of succession which Aristotle is implicitly referring to would be the following: republic of the cavalry, republic of the hoplites, republic of the sailors.

3 That is to say, for as long as 'Homeric fighting' prevailed, which actually did not consist of cavalry fights even though the participants were driven to the battlefield on chariots. On the question of cavalry warfare see P. Vanderwaeren, *Historia* 22 (1973), pp. 177–90; P.A.L. Greenhalgh, *Early Greek Warfare: Horsemen and Chariots in the Homeric and Archaic Ages* (Cambridge, 1973).

4 The 'Homeric' state is for Aristotle a city just like the forms which followed it; the 'hoplite reform' lies behind the origins of democracy, not of the city.

5 In so far as the *demos* of hoplites participated, as at Sparta, in the working of institutions, these archaic cities may indeed be regarded as the first democracies.

6 Aristotle is using here the word *politeia* in the technical sense which is peculiar to him.

7 Literally the 'middle' (*meson*), which for Aristotle is the heart of what he calls a 'republic'.

35   Greece exports her hoplites: mercenaries in Egypt (591)
Greek hoplites appear very early as the best soldiers in the Mediterranean world. The permanent difficulties of the archaic age account for the fact that many hoplites went to try their luck elsewhere. The following inscription is one of a series of 32 graffiti scratched by soldiers who occupied the post of Abu Simbel, north of the second cataract, on the frontier with Sudan. Of these inscriptions eight are archaic and date from the campaign of Psammetichos II to Nubia (591). The longest, translated here, is scratched in the Dorian dialect on the left leg of a colossal statue of the temple of Rameses II. The mercenaries whose names are preserved are probably Dorians from Rhodes.

> When King Psammetichos[1] came to Elephantine, this was written by those who sailed with Psammetichos[2] son of Theokles, and they came above Kerkis[3] as far as the river allowed. Potasimto[4] commanded the troops of foreign speech, and Amasis[5] the Egyptians. Those who wrote us were Archon son of Amoibichos and Pelekos[6] son of Eudamos[7].
>
> MEIGGS–LEWIS, no 7 a

1 King Psammetichos II (595–589), Psammis in Herodotus II, 161, who tells of his expedition to 'Ethiopia' (the Sudan), which is also known from Egyptian sources.
2 This Greek officer has taken an Egyptian name, possibly chosen by Theokles in honour of the pharaoh Psammetichos I (664–610).
3 Possibly the Gebel Koulkei, near the fourth cataract. The inscription draws a careful distinction between those who, with the king, did not go beyond Elephantine (first cataract) and those who ventured much further.
4 An Egyptian.
5 It is unlikely that this refers to the future pharaoh of that name who reigned from 568 to 526.
6 i.e. the 'axe-man'.
7 On the Greek and non-Greek mercenaries in Egypt in the archaic age see M.M. Austin, *Greece and Egypt* (Cambridge, 1970), pp. 15–22.

36   Solon: the liberation of the land· and of the men (594)

Athens in the time of Solon saw two fundamental problems arising dramatically: the problem of the land, which was concentrated in a few hands, and the problem of men, some of whom,
the hectemoroi, were by statute in a position of dependence, while
others – to some extent possibly the same people – were tied by
the loans they were unable to repay and were reduced to servitude
with wives and children, on the spot or abroad. The struggle
lasted a long time, according to Aristotle (*Constitution of
Athens* II, 2). The archonship of Solon did not actually solve it
completely, since the ancient Greek tradition is unanimous in
asserting that Solon solved the problem of men, but only solved
metaphorically, or partially, the problem of land by pulling out
the pillars which advertised the debts[1] contracted by men. The
latter, relieved by the cancellation of debts, were also liberated by
the twofold abolition which was Solon's essential social reform:
the suppression of the social and legal condition of the peasant
'sixth-parter' ('hectemoros'), and the suppression of the 'seizure'
of men[2], or more exactly of Athenians[3].

For once the tradition starts with Solon himself, though only
through quotations of his writings, albeit substantial ones, in
Aristotle and Plutarch. Solon's poems do not make clear to us
how the peasants of Attica suddenly found sufficient strength to
threaten with ruin the aristocratic *polis*, nor how Solon, a noble,
succeeded in convincing enough nobles to impose his arbitration.
But at least they are highly revealing of the ideology of a *polis*, the
supreme arbiter of the conflicts between citizens; the consequences of this ideology may still be perceived to this day. Two
passages are included here: the first shows Solon's rejection of the
peasants' radical demand for the redistribution of land, the
second summarizes the abolition of Athenian rural 'slavery'.

A   *The rejection of land redistribution*

They came for plunder and had immense hopes, and expected
that they would each find vast wealth and that in spite of my
smooth and cajoling words I would show an inflexible heart.
Vain were their thoughts, and now they are all irritated against
me and look at me askance like an enemy – wrongly, for what
I promised I have achieved with the help of the gods, and for
the rest I did not act lightly, nor do I wish to do anything with
tyrannical violence[4], nor to give an equal share[5] of the fertile

fatherland to good and bad men alike.

SOLON fr. 23 Diehl = fr. 34 West, quoted by
Aristotle, *Constitution of Athens* XII, 3
and in part by Plutarch, *Solon,* XVI, 3
and Aelius Aristides II, p. 536 (Dindorf)

B   *The cancellation of debts and the abolition of rural
dependency*

But as for me, did I stop before achieving any of the goals for
which I brought the people together[6]? She can best bear witness
for me in the court of Time, the venerable mother of the
Olympian gods[7], Black Earth, from whom I then pulled out
the pillars which were planted in many places; formerly she
was enslaved, now she is free. I brought back[8] to Athens, their
god-founded fatherland, many who had been sold, some
unjustly, some justly, some exiled through the compulsion of
debt, no longer speaking the Attic language, so widely had
they been wandering; others here, who were enduring shameful slavery and trembled before the whims of their masters, I
made free. This I achieved through the force of law, joining
violence and justice, and I carried through to the end what I
had promised. I wrote laws for the good and bad alike, fixing
a straight justice for everyone. But had another than I taken the
goad in hand, a wicked and avid man, he would not have been
able to keep the people in check. For if I had wanted what those
who were in revolt[9] were wanting then, or again what their
opponents would have wished for them, the city would have
been bereft of many men. That is why deploying all my
strength[10] I turned on all sides like a wolf among many hounds.

SOLON, fr. 24 Diehl = fr. 36 West, quoted by
Aristotle, *Constitution of Athens* XII, 4
and in part by Plutarch, *Solon* XV, 6; XVI, 3
and Aelius Aristides II, pp. 536–8 (Dindorf)

1   At least that is the most widespread interpretation – though it
is by no means proven – of the role of the pillars. The normal
consequence of this liberation is to guarantee to the debtor the
possession of land which is threatened with recovery or
seizure, and this is also a consequence of the abolition of the
dependent status of men; for a recent summary of discussions
of this passage see D. Asheri, *Leggi greche sul problema dei
debiti* (Pisa, 1969), pp. 9–14.

2 Though according to Plutarch, *Solon* XXIII, 2, a man preserved the right to sell his unmarried sisters or daughters when
they had slept with a man.

3 Or, to be even more exact, of those whom it will henceforward
be possible, after the evolution which runs from Solon to
Cleisthenes, to call 'the Athenians'.

4 The redistribution of land is one of the possible weapons of
tyrants, but rejection of land redistribution was in fact to bring
Peisistratus to power.

5 Solon draws up laws that are 'the same for good and bad
alike' (cf. the following passage), but he rejects *isomoiria*,
equality before the land, which was the slogan of the peasants.

6 Solon's action marks the beginning in Athens of the organization of the *demos* as a genuinely political force.

7 Gaia is the ancestor of the Olympian family, grandmother of
Zeus and of his brothers.

8 The Greek suggests more precisely that Solon cancelled the
seizure of which the debtors had been victim.

9 The Greek word literally means 'the opponents'.

10 Or 'all my power', according to the text quoted by Aelius
Aristides.

37   Solon and the artisans

Solon's attitude to the problem of the land is attested by direct
evidence, even though it is not as precise as one would wish. The
situation is different with the legislation, or rather the initiative
which is attributed to him, which aimed at turning the Athenians
away from the exclusive pursuit of agriculture and towards the
crafts and commerce[1]; it is found neither in Solon's poems nor
even in Aristotle's account. To be sure, the latter does state that
a few years after Solon a division of power was instituted between
five Eupatrid archons, three countrymen (*agroikoi*) and two
artisans (*demiourgoi*), but this evidence is rightly considered to
be rather suspect[2]. There is no doubt that in practice Solon's
reforms did open up the avenue of craftsmanship to the peasantry
which, though liberated, remained threatened with falling again
into the same difficulties because of the limited extent and the
poor quality of its lands; what is more doubtful, it must be repeated, is the political intention which Plutarch, and Plutarch
alone, attributes here to Solon.

Seeing that the city was getting full of people who were continuously streaming into Attica from everywhere to enjoy security, but that the largest part of the land was infertile and of poor quality, and that maritime traders do not as a rule import anything to those who have nothing to give in return, he turned the attention of citizens towards the crafts (*technai*) and drew up a law that a son who had not been taught a trade (*techne*) by his father was under no obligation to support him. For Lycurgus, who lived in a city which was free from crowds of foreigners and whose territory was, as Euripides put it, 'large for a vast population and more than adequate for twice as many people'[3], and which especially had a large crowd of Helots spread about it[4], whom it was better not to leave idle but to humble with perpetual toil and hardship, for Lycurgus it was fine to free the citizens from the laborious occupations of artisans and keep them constantly under arms, making the military profession (*techne*) the sole object of their education and training. But Solon, who adapted the laws to reality rather than reality to the laws, and who saw that the poverty of the soil barely afforded a living to farmers and could not sustain a large and idle crowd, brought the various trades (*technai*) into credit, and ordered the Council of the Areiopagus to examine how every man got his living and to punish the idle[5].

PLUTARCH, *Solon* XXII

1 For Plutarch, Solon himself is a trader, or at least he says that that is the conclusion to be drawn indirectly from his poems, because of their vulgarity (*Solon* III, 1), and Solon is alleged to have deliberately encouraged the export of oil and hence the cultivation of the olive tree (ibid., XXIV, 1).

2 See L. Gernet, 'Les dix archontes de 581', *Revue de Philologie* 12 (1938), pp. 216–27 and Ed. Will in *Revue historique*, 1967, p. 395. *Contra*, e.g. V. Ehrenberg, *From Solon to Socrates* (London, 2nd ed., 1973), pp. 77–8, 407, n 4.

3 From an unknown tragedy.

4 That is obviously the fundamental difference between a city where the peasants are dependents and a city where they have just gained their freedom. But of course the comparison does not go back to Solon's time.

5 Plutarch returns again to this subject (XXIV, 4) and specifies that Solon granted citizen rights to those who were banished

for life and settled in Athens with their family to practise a
trade.

38   Solon's (alleged) reform of weights, measures and coins

Greek tradition, that is to say the tradition of the fourth century,
attributed to Solon, besides his great reform of personal status
and the status of the land, a reform of the system of weights,
measures and coins. Aristotle and Androtion give two radically
different interpretations of it: the former presents it as a purely
technical measure for which he does not suggest any social and
economic interpretation, while the latter, a 'moderate' in his
political stance if not an oligarch[1], identifies the reform with the
seisachtheia (shaking-off the burden). Few passages have been
discussed so much as the brief paragraph in Aristotle. Only a few
recent interpretations can be mentioned here. According to K.
Kraft[2], Aristotle's information does indeed go back to very
ancient sources, and one may suppose that Solon's choice was
between an ancient system used in the Chalcidian colonies in the
west, and therefore in Euboea, and a system related to that used
by the Achaean colonies in the west. As for the earliest Athenian
coins, the standard of which according to this interpretation was
different from the weight standard, they simply followed the
Corinthian system. But in fact the problem is all the more complex in that nowadays it seems most unlikely that Athenian
coinage appeared in Solon's time[3] and that it is extremely difficult
to visualize how Aristotle obtained technical information from
such a remote period. More convincing is the interpretation of
C.M. Kraay[4], who shows up and accounts for the anachronisms
in Aristotle. The most sceptical view is that of M.H. Crawford[5],
who dismisses (probably rightly) the whole chapter in Aristotle
as a construct of fourth-century historiography, of no value as
evidence for Solon's time. As for Androtion, his thesis is easily
explained as a reaction against any mention of radical reform. He
is less interested in the monetary manipulation attributed to
Solon than in being able to assert that Solon did not cancel debts.

A   Aristotle

These seem, then, to have been the democratic features of his
laws[6]. Before the legislation he carried out the cancellation of
debts, and after it he increased the size of measures and

weights as well as that of the currency[7]. For it was under Solon that measures were made larger than those of Pheidon[8], and the mina which used to contain 70 drachmae was raised to 100[9]. Now the ancient type of coin was the double drachma (didrachm)[10]. Solon also established weights for the currency: 63 minae weighed a talent and the 3 minae were distributed among the staters and the other subdivisions[11].

ARISTOTLE, *Constitution of Athens*, X

B Androtion

Some authorities, and Androtion is one of them, have written that it was not through a cancellation of debts that the poor were relieved and made content, but through a reduction in the interest rate, and they called *seisachtheia* this act of humanity as well as the simultaneous increase in measures and in the value of the currency[12]. For he fixed the mina at 100 drachmae, whereas before it was worth 70[13], so that debtors made a substantial saving by paying back a sum which was numerically equivalent though actually worth less, while creditors were in no way worse off[14].

ANDROTION, *FGrHist* 324 F 34
(quoted by Plutarch, *Solon* XV, 3–4)

1 See F. Jacoby, *Atthis, the Local Chronicles of Ancient Athens* (Oxford, 1949), pp. 75ff., but see P. Harding, *Phoenix* 28 (1974), pp. 282–9; *Historia* 25, 2 (1976), pp. 186–200.

2 K. Kraft, 'Zur Übersetzung und Interpretation von Ar. *A.P.* X (Solonische Münzereform)', *Jahrbuch f. Numismatik und Geldgeschichte* 10 (1959–60), pp. 21–46.

3 See above Chapter 3, p. 56.

4 C.M. Kraay, 'An Interpretation of *Ath.Pol.* Chap. 10', *Studies S. Robinson* (Oxford, 1968), pp. 1–10; see also M. Chambers, 'Aristotle on Solon's Reform of Coinage and Weights', *California Studies in Classical Antiquity* 6 (1974), pp. 1–16.

5 M.H. Crawford, 'Solon's Alleged Reform of Weights and Measures', *Eirene* 10 (1972), pp. 5–8; see further on the controversy Ed. Will, *Revue historique*, July–Sept. 1971, pp. 109–10; ibid., Jan.–March 1974, pp. 162–3, n 5.

6 Aristotle has just summarized the political and judicial reforms.

7 The writer thus distinguishes three stages: (a) the cancellation

of debts, (b) the legislation, (c) the reform of weights and measures, followed itself by the monetary reform.

8 Larger, in the material sense of the word, referring to an enlargement in the measures of capacity. Pheidon, tyrant of Argos, is a little-known figure (end of the seventh century?), but the system of weights which bore his name was still used in the fourth century, as shown by a Delphic inscription (Tod, *GHI* II, no 140), and so may well have been familiar to Aristotle.

9 This refers to the mina as a weight and not as a monetary unit. The passage in Aristotle could be taken to mean that the new mina contained 100 drachmae instead of 70, with the drachma remaining constant; on the other hand Androtion (cf. the following passage) states that the (monetary) mina remained constant, with the drachma being reduced in weight; cf. Crawford, op. cit., p. 7f.

10 The 'ancient type of coin' is for Aristotle the pre-Solonian coin. Aristotle knew, like everyone else, that Athens struck tetradrachms and not didrachms, and therefore implicitly attributes to Solon the creation of the most current Athenian coin. In fact the earliest Attic tetradrachms, the 'owls', which follow the archaic didrachms, do not appear before the last quarter of the sixth century (see most recently E.J.P. Raven, 'Problems of the Earlier Owls of Athens', *Studies S. Robinson*, pp. 40–58).

11 This mysterious passage has a very simple meaning: for the city to cover its costs in striking coins it is necessary for a talent of coined silver to weigh slightly less than a talent of uncoined silver. The difference is here 5 per cent. Sixty minae (a talent in weight) are worth 63 minae. These three minae are distributed among all the subdivisions.

12 Androtion lumps together the measures which Aristotle separates.

13 The manuscripts give the figure as 73 drachmae. We follow F. Jacoby in accepting an obvious correction proposed by Th. Reinach. Androtion's tradition is then the same as Aristotle's with the obvious difference that Androtion is referring to coins where Aristotle refers to weights.

14 The debtor who owes 100 'heavy' drachmae pays 100 'light' drachmae, and the creditor is satisfied since he gets 100 drachmae for the 100 he lent. All this is absurd, particularly the statement about creditors, not because monetary manipulations, which could actually ease debts (by harming the

creditors), were unknown to the Greek world, but because even if one makes the very improbable hypothesis that coinage appeared in Solon's time, the debts of peasants were certainly not expressed in monetary terms.

39 The tyrants, the aristocracy and the lower classes

Archaic tyranny of the seventh and sixth centuries, which is all the more difficult to grasp as the 'sources' and interpretations of it are never contemporary but conflate the old and the new tyranny (in particular that of Dionysius of Syracuse), makes its appearance amidst violent struggles which opposed the rich to the poor. The tyrant, brought to power most of the time by the *demos*, then has to face the political power of the nobles and of the rich and provides a partial solution to the social and economic difficulties which caused his appearance in the first place. But the political problem remains untouched, since the *demos* is used for its physical strength but is then kept away from all specifically political activity. This double aspect of tyranny is recalled in the saga which grew around certain tyrants, and it is expressed on the one hand in the 'parable of the ears of corn'[1], a symbol of the struggle pursued by the tyrant (in this case Periander of Corinth)[2] against the only men who could at the time contest his power, and on the other in the narrative in Aristotle on the relations between Peisistratus[3] and the peasantry of Attica.

A The parable of the ears of corn

Periander had sent a herald to Thrasybulus[4] to ask him what mode of government it was safest to set up in order best to keep the city under his control. Thrasybulus led the envoy of Periander outside the city, and took him into a field of corn, through which he began to walk, while he asked him again and again about his coming from Corinth. And he would cut off all the ears of corn which over-topped the rest, and as he cut them he would throw them to the ground, until he had destroyed in this way all the best and tallest part of the crop. In this way he went through the whole field, and without giving a word of advice he dismissed the herald. When the man returned to Corinth, Periander was eager to know what Thrasybulus had counselled, but the messenger reported that he had said nothing; and he wondered that Periander had sent him to so strange a man, who seemed to have lost his senses, since he did nothing but destroy his own property. And he went on to tell how Thrasybulus had behaved at the interview. Periander, perceiving what the action meant, and having grasped that Thrasybulus was advising him to destroy all the leading men, treated the citizens from this time on with the greatest cruelty. Where Cypselus[5] had spared any from death or banishment, Periander completed what had been left unfinished.

HERODOTUS V, 92

B   *Peisistratus and the peasantry*

Peisistratus governed the city, as I have said before, with moderation, behaving as a citizen rather than a tyrant. In general he was humane and gentle, ready to forgive offenders, and in particular he would lend money to the needy to help them with their work[6], so that they were able to make a living from agriculture. This he did with a twofold purpose in mind, to make sure that they would not spend their time in the city but would be dispersed about the countryside; and so that being moderately well-off and occupied with their private affairs they would have neither the inclination nor the time to concern themselves with public matters. At the same time his revenues increased as the land was put to cultivation, for he imposed a tithe on agricultural produce[7]. For the same reason he instituted the judges of the demes[8], and he himself often visited the countryside to inspect it and reconcile those who had a dispute, thus making sure that they would not come to the city and neglect their lands. [. . .] Hence the tyranny of Peisistratus was frequently celebrated as being a return to life under Kronos[9].

ARISTOTLE, Constitution of Athens XVI, 2–5, 7

1   The phrase is borrowed from Ed. Will, *Korinthiaka* (1955), p. 505.
2   His rule corresponds roughly to the first half of the sixth century, but the exact chronology is very controversial (see J. Servais, *Antiquité Classique* 38 (1969), pp. 28–81; R. Drews, *Historia* 21 (1972), 129–44; S. Oost, *CP* 67 (1972), pp. 10–30).
3   He was tyrant in Athens on three occasions between 561 and 528.

4 Thrasybulus was tyrant of Miletus. The anecdote is related, after Herodotus, sometimes in one direction sometimes in the other. In Rome it was adapted for the benefit of Tarquin the Proud (Dionysius Halicarnassus, *Roman Antiquities* IV, 56, 3).

5 Periander's father.

6 The nature of these loans is not known; they must have reduced the peasants' indebtedness to the nobles and provided the tyrant with a following. The repetition of the Solonian crisis was thus avoided.

7 One-twentieth, according to Thucydides VI, 54, 5.

8 i.e. the villages of Attica. Initially itinerant then resident, there were 40 of these judges in the fourth century, who were drawn by lot and acted as justices of the peace (*Constitution of Athens* LIII, 1–2).

9 i.e. the golden age.

40 A commercial adventure (*c*. 638)

Herodotus has just related how the citizens of Thera (modern Santorini), wishing to found a colony on the Libyan coast (which resulted a few years later, in the second half of the seventh century, in the foundation of Cyrene, cf. no 45), made use of the knowledge of the African coast possessed by one Korobios, a citizen of Itanos in Crete. The narrative which follows about the discovery of Tartessus in the south of Spain, famous for its silver mines (the question of whether it is to be identified or not with the biblical Tarsis has been much discussed[1]), is that of an individual adventure which has sometimes been rather hastily interpreted as a systematic exploration, in the wake of the Phoenicians, of the western Mediterranean. Kolaios and his Samians were the heroes of it, but according to Greek tradition the regular beneficiaries were to be the Phocaeans[2].

A few persons then sailed from Thera to reconnoitre. Guided by Korobios to the island I have mentioned, namely Plataea[3], they left him there with provisions for several months, and returned home with all speed to give the Theraeans an account of the island. During their absence, which was prolonged beyond the time that had been agreed upon, Korobios' provisions failed him completely. Thereupon a Samian vessel, under the command of a man named Kolaios, was diverted to

Plataea while on its journey to Egypt. The Samians, informed by Korobios of all the circumstances, left him sufficient food for a year. They themselves left the island; and, anxious to reach Egypt, made sail in that direction, but were carried out of their course by a gale of wind from the east. The storm not abating, they were driven past the Pillars of Heracles, and at last, by some guiding providence, reached Tartessos. This trading town (*emporion*) was in those days a virgin port, and so the Samians, when they returned home, made from their cargo the greatest profit ever realized by any Greek known to us. [. . .] From the tenth part of their gains, amounting to six talents, the Samians made a brazen vessel, in shape like an Argive krater, adorned all around with the heads of griffins standing out in high relief. This bowl, supported by three kneeling figures (*kolossoi*) in bronze, was dedicated by them in the sanctuary of Hera at Samos[4].

HERODOTUS IV, 151–2

1   See e.g. S. Moscati, *The World of the Phoenicians* (Eng. tr., 1968), pp. 231–2; J.P. Morel, *Parola del Passato* 130–3 (1970), pp. 285–9; K. Galling, 'Der Weg der Phöniker nach Tarsis in literarischer und archäologischer Sicht', *Zeitschrift des deutschen Palästina-Vereins* 88 (1972), pp. 1–18, 140–81. The exact site of Tartessos has not been identified; cf. C.R. Whittaker, art. cit. in no 47, n 1, p. 62; J.P. Morel, *BCH*, xcix, 2 (1975), pp. 889–92.

2   Cf. above pp. 67–8; on the Phocaeans in Spain see, however, J.P. Morel, op. cit., pp. 885–92.

3   Nowadays Bomba, west of Tobruk.

4   Bronzes of this kind, which may be influenced by Urartian art, have been found in large numbers at Samos; see e.g. E. Akurgal, *Die Kunst Anatoliens* (Berlin, 1961), pp. 67ff. More have been discovered since.

41   A business letter from the Black Sea (*c.* 500 BC)

For all its tantalizing obscurity, this remarkable document deserves inclusion as the earliest preserved business letter in Greek history. The inscription, which is written on a lead tablet and well preserved, was found in 1970 on the island of Berezan (ancient name unknown), near Olbia, a Milesian colony on the Black Sea; it is written in the Ionic dialect. On the basis of letter forms, and in the absence of other more precise criteria, the date of the letter would appear to be *c.* 500 BC. *Editio Princeps* by Y.G. Vinogradov, *Vestnik Drevnei Istorii* fasc. 4, 1971, pp. 74–100, but see above all the extensive commentary by B. Bravo, *Dialogues d'histoire ancienne* 1 (1974), pp. 111 87, who has also most generously communicated to us further comments and suggestions; see also briefly J. Chadwick, *Proceedings of the Cambridge Philological Society* 199 (1973), pp. 35–7; A.P. Miller, *ZPE* 17, 2 (1975), pp. 157–60; R. Merkelbach, ib., pp. 161–2.

The letter is inevitably allusive in manner and any interpretation must be conjectural. The following reconstruction, based on the article by B. Bravo, is a possible one. Achillodoros (possibly a citizen of Olbia) is travelling on a business trip on behalf of another man, Anaxagores, in what capacity we do not know for sure (possibly as his dependent – see Chapter 3, n 11), when a third man, Matasys, confiscates his cargo and attempts to reduce Achillodoros to slavery, presumably through due process of law. A probable explanation of the behaviour of Matasys is that he is attempting to exercise, on what grounds and with what justification we cannot say, a right of personal reprisal against the property of Anaxagores. This is a type of reprisal whereby a member (citizen or metic) of a given city enjoyed a right of reprisal against a specific member (citizen or metic) of another city (for other forms of reprisal cf. nos 8, 54, 67). Matasys claims that Anaxagores has deprived him of his own, that Achillodoros is a slave of Anaxagores and therefore liable to seizure by Matasys in compensation for the wrong suffered at the hands of Anaxagores. Achillodoros writes to his son Protagores to inform him of what is happening and to tell him to inform Anaxagores; he protests that he has nothing to do with Matasys, that he is a free man and not a slave of Anaxagores, and therefore not liable to seizure. But he disclaims knowledge of the relations between Anaxagores and Matasys, and thus does not actually deny that Matasys may have a right of personal reprisal against Anaxagores. The end of the letter is difficult to interpret, but this does not affect the main situation referred to in the rest of the text.

Back
This lead belongs to Achillodoros; addressed to his son and to Anaxagores.

Front
O Protagores, your father sends you this message: he is the

victim of an injustice on the part of Matasys[1], for he (Matasys) is reducing him to slavery and has deprived him of his cargo. Go to Anaxagores and say to him: he (Matasys) says that he (your father) is the slave of Anaxagores and says 'My property is in the hands of Anaxagores, male slaves, female slaves and houses.' But he (your father) loudly complains and says that Matasys has nothing to do with him (your father), and he says that he is free and that Matasys has nothing to do with him, but as to whether he (Matasys) has anything to do with Anaxagores they know that between them. Say this to Anaxagores and his wife. He (your father) sends you another message: if you are among the Arbinatai[2], take your mother and your brothers to the city[3], and (in that case) the keeper of the ship[4] will go himself to him (Anaxagores) and then go down to Thyora (?)[5].

Lead letter from Berezan, first published by
Y.G. Vinogradov, *Vestnik Drevnei Istorii* 1971, 4,
pp. 74–100. The text here follows that of
B. Bravo, *Dialogues d'histoire ancienne* 1 (1974),
pp. 111–87, at p. 123

1 A non-Greek name, though if Matasys had indeed owned property in the same city as Anaxagores, as his claim implies, he will presumably have been at one time a citizen of that city. One possibility is that Matasys is a hellenized barbarian with a double status, comparable to Skyles mentioned by Herodotus IV, 78, possessing both rights within the city and an independent position outside it. The name is spelt Matatasys (in the dative) in line 9 which may be an error; Chadwick suggests in fact haplography rather than dittography, Matatasys being a conflation of the name which should have been written twice, at the end of one sentence and the beginning of the next.

2 Possibly a non-Greek people.

3 B. Bravo suggests this refers to the city on the island of Berezan.

4 Thus B. Bravo, who takes the 'keeper of the ship' to be a member of the crew whose function it was to keep the peace on board ship and in particular to keep a register of the cargoes. But the reading is uncertain and others read here a personal name.

5 Thus B. Bravo originally, taking this to be the (otherwise

unknown) name of the city on the island of Berezan, but the word may be a misspelling of the adverb 'straight', as suggested by Chadwick, a suggestion which B. Bravo is now inclined to accept.

42 The wealth of Corinth

'Wealthy' is the adjective used in Homer (*Iliad* II, 570) to describe Corinth and also many other cities or peoples whose commercial 'vocation' was far less 'obvious'. It was a 'wealthy' port which the geographer Strabo visited in the time of Augustus and he may have been tempted to project this commercial wealth back to the time (end of the eighth–beginning of the seventh century) when the city was governed by the oligarchy of the Bacchiads[1].

Corinth is said to be 'wealthy' because of its port of trade. It lies on the Isthmus and controls two harbours, one of which faces towards Asia, the other towards Italy. The exchange of cargoes sailing in both directions is thus made easy for those who live at such a distance from each other. And just as in former times the straits of Sicily used to be dangerous for sailors, so were the high seas, especially beyond Cape Malea[2] because of contrary winds. Hence the proverb: 'When you double Cape Malea, forget about the way home.' It was therefore welcome to traders both from Italy and from Asia to be able to avoid the sea journey round Malea and unload their cargoes on the spot. Similarly the tolls on goods exported by land from the Peloponnese and imported to it were in the hands of those who held the keys of the Isthmus. This state of affairs has persisted ever since, but the advantages derived by the Corinthians in later times increased even further. For the Isthmic competition celebrated there attracted large crowds, and the Bacchiads, having established their tyranny[3], and being wealthy, numerous and of illustrious birth, remained in power for nearly 200 years[4] and exploited the port of trade without stint[5].

STRABO VIII, 6, 20 (378)

1 For a critical discussion of this passage and of the one in Thucydides (no 43), cf. Ed. Will, *Korinthiaka* (1955), pp. 306–19.

2 At the extreme south of the Peloponnese; this is where the wanderings of Odysseus begin.

3 Strabo uses this word improperly to refer to the oligarchy of the Bacchiads.

4 The statement is almost certainly wrong, cf. Ed. Will, op. cit., p. 279.

5 In other words, without being traders themselves, they levied tolls on goods traded.

43   The naval power and revenues of Corinth

Thucydides' aim in writing that part of Book I of his history, which is known as the *Archaeology*, is to find precedents for the most striking historical phenomenon of his time, the maritime domination of Athens. The most obvious example was Corinth, and her position on the Isthmus made it an attractive idea that she had always been a great commercial centre. For Thucydides, the commercial supremacy of Corinth is based on military supremacy. The Corinthians are alleged by him to have been the inventors of the trireme in the eighth century. Some modern scholars accept this statement, but others point out with good reason that innovations in the military sphere tend to spread more rapidly than elsewhere. Now it is around 525 that one sees the fleet of the tyrant Polycrates of Samos made of triremes, whereas previously it consisted of pentaconters. At the battle of Lade in 494 the Greek fleet comprised only triremes[1].

It is said that the Corinthians were the first to approach the modern style of naval architecture, and that Corinth was the first place in Greece where triremes were built; and it seems that it was for the Samians that the Corinthian shipwright Ameinocles built four ships. Dating from the end of this war[2], it is nearly 300 years ago that Ameinocles went to Samos. Again, the earliest sea fight that we know of was between the Corinthians and Corcyraeans; this was about 260 years ago, dating from the same time. Planted on an isthmus, Corinth had from time immemorial been a commercial emporium; as formerly almost all communication between Greeks within and without the Peloponnese was carried on overland rather than by sea, and the Corinthian territory was the highway through which it travelled, Corinth had consequently great money resources, as is shown by the epithet 'wealthy' bestowed by the old poets on the place. When traffic by sea became more common among the Greeks, the Corinthians procured a navy and put down piracy, and opening a mart on both sides of the isthmus, they acquired for their city all the power which a large revenue affords.

THUCYDIDES I, 13, 2–5
(trans. R. Crawley)

1 Cf. Herodotus III, 39 and 44, and the summary by J. Taillardat, 'La trière athénienne et la guerre sur mer aux Ve et IVe siècles', in J.P. Vernant (ed.), *Problèmes de la guerre en Grèce ancienne*, pp. 183–4. The first use of the word dates from the sixth century (Hipponax, fr. 28 Masson); see also J.S. Morrison and R.T. Williams, *Greek Oared Ships, 900–322 BC* (Cambridge, 1968). They 'solve' the chronological difficulty by arguing that Thucydides does not call Ameinokles a builder of triremes, but only a builder of ships (pp. 157–9); on his side L. Casson in *Ships and Seamanship in the Ancient World* (Princeton, 1971), p. 81, favours the seventh century for the invention of the trireme; for another defence of a high chronology see A.B. Lloyd, *Journal of Egyptian Archaeology* 58 (1972), pp. 276–9 and *JHS* 95 (1975), pp. 52–4.
2 421 or 404, depending on whether Thucydides is writing (or altering his text) shortly after the end of the ten-year war or after the defeat of Athens.

44 Aristotle and the 'origins' of coinage

Coinage appeared in Asia Minor at the end of the seventh century, a date which is established by the excavations of the Artemisium in Ephesus[1]. The literary evidence on this event, which nowadays appears to us of immense significance, is virtually restricted to a brief note in Herodotus (I, 94). After saying that about the only difference between the Lydians and the Greeks is that the former prostitute their daughters, Herodotus adds: 'They are the first to our knowledge to have struck and used gold and silver coins; they are also the first to have practised retail trade[2].' But he goes on to add that during a famine the Lydians also invented the games of dice, knuckle-bones and ball. Three centuries after the 'invention' of coinage Aristotle is not in a good position to obtain more accurate information, and in any case the strictly historical problem does not interest him in the least. What he contributes, in a chapter of the *Nicomachaean Ethics*, in which he discusses the establishment of relations of reciprocity within human communities and within the city in the first place, is a profound reflection on coinage, not as an instrument of gain, but as an instrument of measure and equity[3].

In relations of exchange which take place within the framework of the community[4] this sort of justice does hold men together – reciprocity in accordance with a proportion and not on the basis of precisely equal return[5]. For it is by proportionate requital that the city holds together. Men seek to return either evil for evil – and if they cannot do so, think their position mere slavery[6] – or good for good – and if they cannot do so there is no exchange[7], but it is by exchange that they hold together.

This is why they give a prominent place to the temple of the Graces (*Charites*) – to promote the requital of services; for this is characteristic of grace – we should serve in return one who has shown grace to us, and should another time take the initiative in showing it[8].

Now proportionate return is secured by cross-conjunction. Let A be a builder, B a shoemaker, C a house, D a shoe. The builder, then, must get from the shoemaker the latter's work, and must himself give him in return his own[9]. If, then, first there is proportionate equality of goods, and then reciprocal action takes place, the result we mention will be effected. If not, the bargain is not equal, and the community will not hold together; for there is nothing to prevent the work of the one being better than that of the other; they must therefore be equated[10].

And this is true of the other arts also; for they would have been destroyed if what the patient suffered had not been just what the agent did, and of the same amount and kind. For it is not two doctors who constitute a community, but a doctor and a farmer, or in general people who are different and unequal; but these must be equated.

This is why all things that are exchanged must be somehow comparable. It is for this end that money has been introduced, and it becomes in a sense an intermediate (*meson*), for it measures all things, and therefore the excess and the defect –

how many shoes are equal to a house or to a given amount of food. The number of shoes exchanged for a house (or for a given amount of food) must therefore correspond to the ratio of builder to shoemaker. For if this be not so, there will be no exchange and no community. And this proportion will not be effected unless the goods are somehow equal. All goods must therefore be measured by some one thing, as we said before. Now this unit is in truth demand[11], which holds all things together (for if men did not need one another's goods at all, or did not need them equally, there would either be no exchange or not the same exchange); but money has become by convention a sort of representative of demand[12]; and this is why it has the name 'money' (*nomisma*) – because it exists not by nature but by convention (*nomos*) and it is in our power to change it and make it useless[13]. There will, then, be reciprocity when the terms have been equated so that as farmer is to shoemaker, the amount of the shoemaker's work is to that of the farmer's work for which it exchanges. [. . .] That demand holds things together as a single unit is shown by the fact that when men do not need one another, i.e. when neither needs the other or one does not need the other, they do not exchange, as we do when someone wants what one has oneself, e.g. when people permit the exportation of corn in exchange for wine[14]. This equation must therefore be established. And for the future exchange – that if we do not need a thing now we shall have it if ever we do need it – money is as it were our surety[15]; for it must be possible for us to get what we want by bringing the money. Now the same thing happens to money itself as to goods – it is not always worth the same; yet it tends to be steadier[16]. This is why all goods must have a price set on them; for then there will always be exchange, and if so, association of man with man. Now in truth it is impossible that things differing so much should become commensurate, but with reference to demand they may become so sufficiently. There must, then, be a unit, and that fixed by agreement (for which reason it is called money); for it is this that makes all things commensurate, since all things are measured by money. Money, then, acting as a measure, makes goods commensurate and equates them; for neither would there have been association if there were not exchange, nor exchange if there were not equality, nor equality if there were not commensurability. Let A be a house, B ten minae, C a bed. A is half of B, if the house is worth five minae or equal to them; the bed, C, is a tenth of B[17]; it is plain, then, how many beds are equal to a house, namely five. That exchange took place thus before there was money is plain; for it makes no difference whether it is five beds that exchange for a house, or the money value of five beds.

ARISTOTLE, *Nicomachaean Ethics* V, 8, 1132 b 31–1133 b 28
(trans. W.D. Ross)

The diagram below, reproduced from the article by Ed. Will (*Revue historique*, 1954, p. 220), shows clearly Aristotle's interpretation of the phenomenon of money, bearing in mind, of course, no 2.

SOCIETY

General aspect: Social ethics	General stages in the reasoning	Particular aspect: Economy
	I	
Need for social relations	Factor of cohesion	Need
Exchange of services	II Reciprocity	Commercial transactions
Evaluation of services	III Proportionate equality	Evaluation of goods
	IV Conventional standard: MONEY	

1 See above p. 56.
2 The two facts are not necessarily connected, cf. above pp. 56ff.
3 The passage must be compared with no 2, where Aristotle discusses coinage as an instrument of unlimited gain; see also and especially the articles by Ed. Will, mentioned in Chapter 3, n 15.
4 That is the essential word, as clearly seen by Ed. Will from whom the translation of the whole phrase is borrowed.

5 On the concept of proportionate equality see no 114.

6 A slave is someone who when struck cannot hit back.

7 In Greek *metadosis*, communication through giving.

8 On these values, which were deep-rooted in Greek thought, see nos 26, 31.

9 Not his work as an abstract category, in the Marxist sense of labour value, but his work as a concrete subject. A house is the work of the architect.

10 The aim here is not to justify differences in salaries, which as will be seen were relatively small at Athens as between an architect and a workman engaged in channelling a column (no 73), but more simply to prevent one comparing a house and a pair of shoes.

11 This whole analysis of need as the elementary foundation of the community must be read with Plato's analysis of the 'first' city in the background (*Republic* II, 369 c ff.): 'A man then takes another man with him for one particular need, then another for another need, and the multiplicity of needs brings together in the same place several men who constitute a community of mutual help, and it is this cohabitation which we call by the name of city.'

12 Of demand or need, and not of desire, which is aimed at the indefinite (cf. no 2).

13 The first operation is a monetary change: it is decided that a coin which is worth two drachmae shall be worth four or one. The second consists in demonetizing; the words 'to make useless' only acquire their full sense with coins made of metal which has no intrinsic value, such as bronze.

14 Text and translation conjectural.

15 Placing money in reserve is not a case of hoarding, but of anticipation on future purchases.

16 Alexander's conquests were marked by an enormous influx of new coins and a considerable rise in prices, but the *Nicomachaean Ethics* seem to date from just before these events.

17 What Aristotle does not of course mention here is the formation of price within the market.

45 Growth of the Theraean colony of Cyrene (*c.* 570 BC)

The slogan of redistribution of land was a revolutionary one on the mainland of Greece, but in the colonial world it could of course assume quite a different meaning: the 'victims' of the redistribution were not (or, more precisely, not always) the wealthy Greeks but native peoples. In the case of Cyrene, it seems in fact from the passage in Herodotus that a new division of land has not been carried out within the limits of the colony, but that the colony has been enlarged to make room for newcomers whose civic status is actually going to cause problems[1].

The wealth of Cyrene was based on the sale of the crop of *silphion*, a plant which has not been securely identified (*Assa foetida*[2]?), but which had many virtues, both medicinal and as fodder. A well-known 'Laconian' cup in the Bibliothèque Nationale in Paris shows King Arkesilas supervising the weighing of silphion[3].

> During the lifetime of Battos, the founder (*oikistes*) of the colony, who ruled 40 years, and during that of his son Arkesilas, who ruled 16, the Cyrenaeans remained the same in number as they had originally been when the colony was sent out. But under the third king, who was called Battos the Happy[4], the Pythia gave an oracle which urged all the Greeks to sail for Libya to settle the land together with the Cyrenaeans. The Cyrenaeans had offered to all who came a distribution of land; and the oracle had spoken as follows:
> He that comes to delightful Libya after the land has been distributed, I say that he will later regret it.
> Thus a great multitude gathered together to Cyrene, and the Libyans of the neighbourhood found themselves stripped of large portions of their land. So they, and their king Adicran, feeling they were being robbed of their territory and insulted by the Cyrenaeans, sent messengers to Egypt, and put themselves under the rule of Apries[5], the Egyptian monarch. He thereupon levied a vast army of Egyptians, and sent them against Cyrene. The Cyrenaeans marched out in force to the district of Irasa, where, near the spring called Theste, they engaged the Egyptians and defeated them. The Egyptians, who had never before made trial of Greek fighters and so thought little of them, were routed with such slaughter that only a very few of them ever got back home.
>
> HERODOTUS IV, 159

1　See D. Asheri, *Distribuzioni di terre nell' antica Grecia* (Turin,

1966), pp. 28–9; some 30 years after these events one comes across the presence in Cyrene of *perioikoi* (Herodotus IV, 161). These have been interpreted either as natives, or as men from the perioecic territories of Thera (cf. P. Lévêque and P. Vidal-Naquet, *Clisthène l'Athénien* (Paris, 2nd ed., 1973), p. 67); one may wonder whether these *perioikoi* are not simply the descendents of colonists settled in Libyan territory by Battos the Happy (cf. D. Asheri, op. cit., p. 28).

2 See the discussion in F. Chamoux, *Cyrène sous la monarchie des Battiades* (Paris, 1953), pp. 246ff.; *Archaeological Reports for 1971–1972*, p. 32.

3 See J. Boardman, *The Greeks Overseas*, pl. 10 b.

4 For the chronology of these events and the identification of the places, cf. Chamoux, op. cit., pp. 120ff.

5 A pharaoh of the 'Saite' dynasty (589–570 BC).

46 An archaic agrarian law from Locris (late sixth century?)

The following archaic law inscribed on two sides of a bronze plaque from western Locris (the exact find spot is uncertain) has been much discussed since its original publication in 1924 (for a bibliography see E. Lepore in *Problèmes de la terre en Grèce ancienne*, ed. M.I. Finley (1973), p. 28, n 1), yet much of it remains obscure and controversial. The circumstances surrounding this law would seem to be the recent acquisition and partition of fresh territory by an already established Locrian community; the law lays down rules to define, protect and perpetuate the rights of the new settlers, including the right of pasturage (or, according to a different interpretation, the right of inheritance of the lots of land, cf. below); in particular drastic safeguards, of a type known from other agrarian laws[1], are laid down against any future re-distribution of the land, except in case of manpower needs arising out of war, in which case fresh settlers may be invited to share the land with the original settlers.

Obverse

Let this law concerning the land be in force according to the partition of the plain of Hylia and Liskaria, both the separate lots (?) and the public ones. Let the right of pasturage (? or 'the right of inheritance'?[2]) be enjoyed by the parents and the son; if there is no son, by the daughter; if there is no daughter, by the brother; if there is no brother, let the right of pasturage (? or 'the right of inheritance'?) be given to the next of kin according to what is right [. . . ? . . . he shall have the right to give his lot to whoever he wishes³]. Whatever is planted, let it be inviolate. Unless the One Hundred and One Men chosen from the best are compelled by war to resolve in a majority to introduce at least 200 new colonists capable of bearing arms, whoever proposes or votes for a redistribution of land in the council or in the assembly or in the committee, or causes civil strife over the redistribution of land, let him and his family be outlawed for all time, let his property be confiscated and his house destroyed just as under the law for murder. Let this law be consecrated to Pythian Apollo and the gods who share his temple. Let whoever transgresses these rules be vowed to utter destruction, himself, his family and his property, and let whoever respects them be blessed. Let half of the land

Reverse
belong to the original settlers and half to the new settlers⁴. Let one distribute the lots in the valley. Let exchange (of lots) be valid, but let the exchange take place before the magistrate⁵. [. . .]

Text based on the transcription by L.H. Jeffery,
The Local Scripts of Archaic Greece (1961), p. 403
(from pl. 14) and cf. p. 105f.
See also Meiggs–Lewis no 13;
Inscriptiones Graecae XI, 1² fasc. 3, no 609

1 See for example the law of Issa, Dittenberger, *Sylloge*³, 141.
2 The interpretation of the word *epinomia* here and of words related to it later in the text is controversial; the normal meaning of it is 'right of pasturage', and that is how the word has been generally translated. But Cl. Vatin has suggested (*BCH* 87 (1963), pp. 7–8) that the meaning ought to be 'right of inheritance' on the analogy of the word *epinomos* = 'heir' in Delphic inscriptions.
3 The scribe seems to have left here a sentence unfinished, and to have subsequently finished it at the top of the reverse of the plaque. The sentence as a whole is in any case obscure.
4 This presumably refers to the body of new settlers envisaged earlier in the law.

5   The reverse of the bronze plaque carries here a further law on
    illicit profits by magistrates, unrelated to the main body of the
    text and in a different hand.

47   Emporion, a colony of the Phocaeans in Catalonia, as seen by a geographer of the time of Augustus

The passage in Strabo translated here only gives one a very
imperfect picture of the Greek settlement of Emporion. According to a parallel passage in Livy, Emporion seems to have been
founded at the same time as Massilia (*c.* 600 BC), or shortly after,
by the Phocaeans, then taken over in the second half of the sixth
century by the people of Massilia[1]. But the whole history of the
Greek settlements in Spain remains very obscure and it is likely
that Phoenician settlements often preceded the arrival of the
Greeks. The excavations carried out on the most ancient site, the
Palaiapolis of Strabo (St Martin of Ampurias) have produced
relatively few results and do not provide any confirmation of a
Rhodian settlement prior to the colonization by Phocaea. The
name of the city, its dual character, at once Greek and native,
without there having been initially a fusion of the two, do however suggest that originally Emporion was less of a *polis* than a
typical *port of trade* (cf. above Chapter 3, p. 66f) in contact with
another civilization: in the sixth century the people of Emporion
had no coinage of their own but used that of Massilia. Nor is it
easy to understand what purpose exactly was served by the wall:
was it meant to protect both communities, the Greek and the
native, against the threat of other barbarians, or to separate
Greeks and natives at the latter's request, which would correspond
to the normal position of an *emporion* comparable to that at
Naukratis, or on the other hand to preserve the identity of the
Greek settlement at the request of the Greeks? It may well be that
the situation evolved in the course of time: the initial *emporion*
will have been followed by the double city mentioned by Strabo,
then by the mixed city to which was added in the time of Caesar
a Roman colony.

Emporion[2] is a foundation of the people of Massilia, some 40
stades[3] away from the Pyrenees and the frontiers of Iberia and
Gaul. This city too is beautiful and has a fine harbour. In the
same region there is also the little fort of Rhodos[4], founded by

the people of Emporion, though some say by the Rhodians. At Rhodos as at Emporion they worship Artemis of Ephesus. [. . .] The people of Emporion used to live on a small island off the coast, which is now called *Palaiopolis* (the Old City)[5]; now they have settled on the mainland[6]. The city is a double one and its two parts are divided by a wall[7]. This is because in former times it had as neighbours some of the Indicetans[8], who although they wanted to preserve their own institutions nevertheless wished, for security reasons, to have a common wall with the Greeks; hence the double city with the dividing wall in the middle. Later on they joined together to form a single political entity, which had mixed barbarian and Greek customs, as has often happened. Nearby there flows a river[9] which has its source in the Pyrenees, and its outlet serves as a port for the people of Emporion. The people of Emporion are skilled in working flax. The inland plain belongs to them; part of it is of fertile land, the other part, known as the 'Rush Plain', produces rush of a very inferior quality such as grows in marshes. Some of them even occupy the extremities of the Pyrenees as far as the Trophies of Pompey[10], on the way from Italy to what is known as Further Iberia and in particular to Baetica.

Strabo, III, 4, 8–9 (159–60)

1 For a bibliography and a summary of recent discussions see F. Villard, *La Céramique grecque de Marseille* (Paris, 1960), pp. 114–18; F. Benoît, *Recherches sur l'hellénisation du Midi de la Gaule* (Gap, 1965), p. 30; J.P. Morel, in *Parola del Passato* 108–10 (1966), p. 392 and ibid., 130–3 (1970), p. 286; E. Lepore, ibid., pp. 35–6; J.P. Morel, *BCH*, xcix, 2 (1975), pp. 866f, 876f. On the Phoenicians see the survey by C.R. Whittaker, 'The western Phoenicians: colonisation and assimilation', *Proceedings of the Cambridge Philological Society* 200 (1974), pp. 58–79.

2 Ampurias, near La Escala, on the gulf of Rosas, in the province of Gerona; see the sketch map by J. Hind in *Rivista Storica dell' Antichità* 2 (1972), p. 49.

3 7·4 km; this figure is a modern conjecture. The manuscripts of Strabo give the obviously absurd figure of 4,000 stades.

4 Rosas.

5 Because of silting the island has become a peninsula; nowadays it is the site of St Martin of Ampurias.

6 The move seems to have been carried out as early as the fifth century.

7 What Livy says (XXXIV, 9) does not correspond exactly to the passage in Strabo; he states that the Greek city is turned towards the sea, unlike the native settlement, and that it is completely surrounded by a wall of fewer than 400 paces (55 cm); he also mentions a wall which separates the Greek settlement from the Spanish one. One cannot rule out that he may have conflated facts belonging to different periods.

8 Did the natives cultivate the land for the benefit of the Greeks, like the Mariandynians at Heraclea Pontica? The character of the city suggests rather relations of a less unequal type.

9 The Fluvia.

10 Set up in 72 BC at the pass of Perthus.

48 Naukratis

Enough has been said above on the special case of Naukratis (Chapter 3, p. 66) for it to be unnecessary to return to it at length. The rules ascribed by Herodotus to Amasis for the control of Greek trade, which is restricted to Naukratis alone under the Saite dynasty, are characteristic of the *port of trade* as defined by Polanyi, and recall to some extent the position of the Europeans at Canton before the opening up of China. The settlement is a double one: there is on the one hand the city, and on the other the sanctuary and the *emporion* run by the representatives of ten cities in Asia Minor, while other cities keep to themselves. Herodotus does not mention the Egyptian quarter of the town, which has been revealed by excavation.

Amasis[1] was friendly to the Greeks, and granted favours to some of them. Among other favours, he gave to those who came to settle in Egypt the city of Naukratis for their residence. But to those who did not wish to settle there but only sailed to Egypt (for trade) he granted certain lands where they might set up altars and sanctuaries to their gods. Of these temples the grandest and most famous, which is also the most frequented, is that called the Hellenion, which was founded jointly by the following cities: among the Ionians, Chios, Teos, Phocaea and Clazomenae, among the Dorians Rhodes[2], Cnidos, Halicarnassus and Phaselis, and among the Aeolians only Mytilene. The sanctuary belongs to these cities, and they provide the governors (*prostatai*) of the commercial port (*emporion*). All the other cities which lay claim to these prerogatives have no right to do so. But independently of these the Aeginetans have founded on their own a sanctuary of Zeus, and similarly the Samians for Hera and the Milesians for Apollo. In former times, Naukratis alone was a port of trade and there was no other in Egypt apart from it. If anyone entered one of the other mouths of the Nile, he was obliged to swear that he had not come there of his own free will. Having sworn, he had to sail in his ship to the Canopic mouth, or if he was unable to sail against contrary winds, he had to convey his cargo on barges all round the Delta until he reached Naukratis.

HERODOTUS II, 178–9

1　Pharaoh from 570 to 526 BC.
2　i.e. the Rhodian cities of Ialysos, Camiros and Lindos.

49　A communist adventure in the Lipari Islands (*c.* 580)
The following passage from Diodorus (probably derived from Timaeus) is admittedly of direct interest in itself: colonization is a laboratory of social experiments, and the adventure of a group of Greeks, Dorians from Cnidos and Rhodes, who when confronted with Etruscan piracy, adopted for military reasons a complete communist system, followed by a modified form of collectivism and a periodic redistribution of lands, is fairly instructive (assuming it is not the construction of one of the many apologists produced by the Hellenistic age). But its main interest is historiographical; both the advocates and the opponents of the disastrous theory of 'primitive communism' have used it, quite wrongly, as a war horse[1], the former in order to demonstrate that at the beginning of the sixth century some Greeks still practised the said communism, the latter in the name of sacrosanct and eternal private property. The truth, as will be seen, is more modest.

Many years after these events[2], when the islands[3] were becoming steadily more deserted of inhabitants, some men of Cnidos and Rhodes who felt oppressed at the hands of the kings in

Asia decided to send out a colony. They therefore chose as their leader Pentathlos of Cnidos[4], who traced his ancestry back to Hippotes who was descended from Heracles. This was in the 50th Olympiad[5], in which the Laconian Epitelidas won the stadium. These men, then, with Pentathlos at their head, sailed to Sicily to the region around Lilybaeum and found there the people of Egesta and Selinus at war with each other[6]. Having been persuaded to join the side of the Selinuntines they lost many men in the battle and among these Pentathlos himself. Consequently the survivors, since the people of Selinus had been defeated in the war, decided to return back home; they chose as their leaders Gorgos, Thestor and Epithersides, who were kinsmen of Pentathlos, and sailed back across the Tyrrhenian Sea. But having touched at Lipara and received a friendly welcome[7], they were persuaded to settle Lipara jointly with the inhabitants, who were the remnants of the colony founded by Aeolus to the number of only about 500 men. Later on, when they were being harassed by Etruscan pirates[8], they built a fleet and divided themselves into two groups; the first cultivated the islands which they had made the common property of all[9], the second fought against the pirates; they made all their possessions common property, lived according to a system of public messes (*syssitia*) and continued for a while living in this communistic way. At a later stage they divided up among themselves the island of Lipara, where they also had their city, but cultivated the other islands in common[10]. Finally they divided up among themselves all the islands for a period of 20 years, and drew lots for them again once this period had expired[11]. After this they defeated the Etruscans in many sea battles, and from the spoils they frequently set up remarkable tithes which they consecrated at Delphi.

Diodorus V, 9

1 For a summary of the debate at the end of the nineteenth century see Th. Reinach, 'Le collectivisme des Grecs de Lipari', *REG* 4 (1890), pp. 86–96, and in modern times, R.J. Buck, 'Communism in the Lipari Islands', *CP* 54 (1959), pp. 34–9.
2 Diodorus has just mentioned the legendary colonization of the Lipari islands by Aeolus and his descendents.

3 The Lipari islands, north west of Messina.

4 His name recalls the *pentathlon*, a series of five events contested by athletes.

5 580–576.

6 Two cities in the west. of Sicily, one Elymian (cf. no 9), the other Greek, which were traditionally hostile to each other.

7 The presence of natives at Lipara around 580 is highly doubtful, since archaeologists have noted in the main necropolis of the island a gap of more than two centuries between the last 'Ausonian' settlement and the first Greek one. Greek material of the sixth century is in any case extremely scanty; see L. Bernarbò Brea and M. Cavalier, *Meligunis-Lipara* I (Palermo, 1960), p. xxvii.

8 Etruscan piracy is indeed powerful in the middle of the sixth century. The men of Lipara were to acquire for themselves in the fourth century a fine reputation as pirates (cf. Livy V, 28), which made Th. Reinach say (art. cit., p. 96): 'It is not as travellers or nomads that the Cnidians of the Lipara islands practised a communist, then a collectivist, regime, but as brigands. Their socialism was a highway socialism, and naturally vanished when the helmet of the Roman policeman appeared on the horizon.'

9 The first stage, that of complete communism. As a champion of 'primitive communism' G. Thomson translates: 'Some of them continued the collective tillage of the soil' (*The Prehistoric Aegean* (London, 1954), pp. 320–2). This translation is indefensible.

10 The second stage, that of communism limited to the neighbouring islands.

11 The third stage, that of a periodic division of land, a practice attested in many cultures. This evolution may have been facilitated by the decline of Etruscan maritime power. After defeating the Phocaeans at Alalia in 535, the Etruscans were crushed at Cumae in 474. As a stout champion of private property, Fustel de Coulanges was unable to accept even the idea of a periodic distribution of land, and so through a definite mistranslation he understood that after 20 years, weary of the experiment, the colonists decided to share out the land once and for all (quoted by Th. Reinach, art cit.).

50   **The two types of slavery as seen by a philosopher and two historians**

The appearance of chattel-slavery was surely not a precise event. The process must have required a whole series of changes of detail which we cannot grasp clearly; it developed side by side with the assertion of the citizen and the simplification of social hierarchies. At Athens, even after Solon's great reform, there persisted archaic criteria of distinction between free man and slave (no 51). This means that the phenomenon one is studying has not left any traces in the literature of the time. It was when the old type of slavery, that of Sparta, Crete and Thessaly, was shaken by the crises of the fourth century and of the Hellenistic period, and especially by the major event constituted by the resurrection of Messenia and the creation of the city of Messene, that men began to reflect on this phenomenon which suddenly appeared different: a slave who is purchased and who is generally a barbarian is not the same as a 'slave' who is capable of demanding his political freedom and who constitutes a group with his compatriots. Indeed, Greek historiography differs radically in its approach to the two types of slavery[1]. Illustrations of this are provided by a passage in Plato which recommends that slaves ought to be socially pulverized, a passage in Theopompus which credits his native island Chios with the 'invention' of chattel-slavery, and a passage in Timaeus according to which in ancient Greece, before slaves, domestic work was carried out by that other fringe group, the young.

A   Plato (c. 350)
The Athenian[2]   Most Greeks, Megillos, argue and disagree about the helotage of the Lacedaimonians; some are for, others against. There seems to be less disagreement about the type of slavery practised by the people of Heraclea who have reduced the Mariandynians[3] to servitude, and similarly with the Penestae who are enslaved to the Thessalians. In the light of these and similar cases, what ought we to do about the ownership of slaves? [. . .] It is clear that, since the animal 'man' is bad-tempered, and does not lend himself easily, whether at present or in future, to the necessary distinction we are drawing between slaves, free men and masters, the slave will be no easy chattel. Experience has shown this many times

in the form of the frequent and repeated revolts of the Messenians[4] and of all the evils which befall cities which have acquired numerous slaves who speak the same language. [. . .] With all this in mind one may well wonder what to do about all these problems. There are in fact only two expedients left: if one wishes men to accept more easily their servitude, they should not be chosen from the same country nor, as far as possible, should they speak the same language; they should also be properly treated, not only for their own sake, but more so in the master's own interest.

PLATO, *Laws* VI, 776 c–777 d

B   *Theopompus (c. 330)*

The people of Chios were the first Greeks after the Thessalians and the Lacedaimonians to make use of slaves, but they did not acquire them in the same way as these. For it will be seen that the Lacedaimonians and Thessalians recruited their servile class (*douleia*) from the Greeks who inhabited previously the land they now occupy, the former from the Achaeans, the Thessalians from the Perrhaebi and Magnetes. The Lacedaimonians called the people they had reduced to slavery Helots and the Thessalians Penestae. As for the people of Chios they have acquired barbarians as their servants and have done so by purchasing them for a price.

THEOPOMPUS, *Philippika* XVII, in Athenaeus,
Deipnosophistai VI, 265 b–c = *FGrHist* 115 F 122

C   *Timaeus (c. 300)*

It was not the ancestral custom of the Greeks in former times to be served by slaves purchased for money, and they accuse Aristotle of having been completely mistaken as to the customs of the Locrians. For it was not the custom of the Locrians, nor of the Phocians until quite recently, to have male or female servants. On the contrary, the wife of Philomelos, the man who captured Delphi[5], was the first to be attended by two women servants. Similarly Mnason, the friend of Aristotle, acquired a thousand slaves and became very unpopular with the Phocians for having deprived so many of his fellow-citizens of their necessary sustenance[6]. For it was the custom that in domestic service the young should serve their elders[7].

TIMAEUS, *Histories* VIII, in Athenaeus,
Deipnosophistae VI, 264 c–d = *FGrHist* 566 F 11

1 See P. Vidal-Naquet, 'Réflexions sur l'historiographie grecque de l'esclavage', *Actes du Colloque 1971 sur l'esclavage* (Paris, 1973), pp. 25–44.
2 Plato's spokesman in the *Laws*; he is talking to the Spartan Megillos and the Cretan Klcinias.
3 Heraclea Pontica (Eregli), a city on the south coast of the Black Sea; the Mariandynians were a native people reduced to dependence by the Greek colonists.
4 The people of Messenia had recovered their freedom in 369, shortly before the writing of the *Laws*.
5 In 356, during the 'third sacred war'.
6 Phocis is a poor country and the supplying of a thousand slaves, assuming the information is correct, would have meant drawing heavily on the resources available to the citizens.
7 According to other traditions (cf., e.g., no 15), the work of women preceded the work of slaves.

51 Archaic criteria of distinction between free men and slaves

Where the antithesis between free man and slave is not sharply drawn as will be the case in classical Athens, it is the style of life which is imposed or forbidden which enables one to make the distinction. For Aristotle, the military style of living is the only thing which in Crete distinguishes free men from 'slaves' (cf. also no 63). It is very striking that in a law attributed to Solon a prohibition similar to that existing in Crete should be imposed on slaves[1].

A Crete

The first alternative is that all things should belong to them all (the farmers) in common[2]. In that case, what will be the difference between them and the guardians? What advantage will they gain by accepting the government of the guardians? What is to make them actually accept it? – unless it be some shift of policy such as is used in Crete, where the slaves are allowed to enjoy the same general privileges as their masters[3], and are excluded only from gymnastic exercises and the possession of arms.

ARISTOTLE, *Politics* II, 1264 a 17–22
(trans. E. Barker)

B   *A law of Solon*[4]

1   Our fathers[5], when they were legislating on our way of life and what nature compels us to do, forbade slaves to do things they thought ought to be done by free men. 'A slave,' says the law, 'must not exercise in the gymnasium nor anoint himself with oil in the palaistras.' [. . .] Again, the same legislator said: 'A slave shall not be the lover of a free boy, nor follow after him, on pain of being beaten publicly with 50 blows of the whip.'

AESCHINES, *Against Timarchus*, 138–9
(= E. Ruschenbusch, *Solonos Nomoi, Historia Einzelschriften* 9 (1966), F 74 e)

2   Solon in his laws fixed publicly the distance in cubits there must be between the lover and the loved one, and preserved this way of living for free men, by forbidding the slave to be the lover (of a free man) or to anoint himself with oil, and placing the same ban on those guilty of evasion of military service, desertion, failure to maintain their parents and give them a burial, and betraying a fort[6].

HERMIAS OF ALEXANDRIA, *On Plaeto's Phaedrus*
231 c (= Ruschenbusch, op. cit., F 74 a)

1   In the classical period, by contrast, an oligarch complains that there is nothing in their appearance to distinguish free men from slaves (cf. no 74): a criterion such as clothing had become useless.

2   Aristotle is here criticizing Plato's *Republic* and questioning it on the limits of the community of wives and children.

3   It hardly needs to be said that this statement should not be taken literally.

4   This law is quoted in five different passages, of which only two are translated here; the others are: Plutarch, *Solon* I, 6; *Banquet of the Seven Sages* 152 d; *On Love*, 751 b.

5   The author is a fourth-century orator, who is arguing against a debauchee and likes to refer to archaic laws now obsolete.

6   It will be noted that the slave is here in the company of free men who have been downgraded, like the Spartan 'tremblers'.

52   **The living and posthumous glory of the nobles**

A spokesman of the aristocracy, including the new aristocracy created by the tyrants (for whom it was always possible to construct a heroic genealogy), Pindar addresses the *Second Olympian* in 476 to Theron of Acragas, an alleged descendent of Oedipus. According to the myth which is developed there, the souls of the wise who are at the same time the wealthy and powerful enjoy in this world the glory symbolized by gold, an anticipation of the golden age which a few of them will know for ever, in the next world, beside Kronos[1]. Although later than the archaic period the passage in Pindar shows the persistence of aristocratic values.

Opulence adorned with virtues brings many an opportunity and keeps crude care in subjection beneath it; a dazzling star, the truest light of man, if only it falls to someone who knows the future: that among the dead, lawless souls pay the penalty here and at once[2], that there is someone under earth to judge crimes committed in the world ruled over by Zeus[3], and that he renders his verdicts according to an implacable rule; but to light up nights always equal to the days, noble souls have their sun, they have as their share a life free from toil; they do not need to torment the earth with the strength of their arms, nor the waters of the sea, in search of an empty life[4]; among men protected by the gods, among all those who took pleasure in honouring their oaths, they lead a life without tears, while the others endure a drudgery without future; those who, in three sojourns on one side and the other, have had the strength to keep their soul pure from injustice, follow the path of Zeus towards the fortress of Kronos[5]; there the breezes, daughters of Ocean, blow around the isles of the blessed; golden flowers blaze, some on land on resplendent trees, others fostered by the waters; with these branches, they adorn their arms and weave themselves crowns, subject to the just rule of Rhadamanthos[6], whom the almighty father keeps in readiness by his side, the husband of Rhea[7] who occupies the highest throne of all. Peleus and Kadmos[8] live among them; Achilles was brought there by his mother, when by her supplications she had moved the heart of Zeus.

PINDAR, *Second Olympian*, 59–88
(translation based on the
French version by J. Bollack)

1 Cf. J. Bollack, 'L'or des rois. Le mythe de la Deuxième Olympique', *Revue de Philologie* 37 (1963), pp. 234–54; for an

unsound critique of this interpretation, cf. J. Defradas, in *REG* 84 (1971), pp. 131–43.

2 i.e. on earth.

3 Our world, as opposed to that of Kronos.

4 This evocation still refers to our world. Note the two kinds of work that are rejected: agriculture and maritime trade.

5 The description of the golden age begins here; but it must be noted that the 'shining mountain of Kronos' (*First Olympian*, 112–13) is also the hill which overlooks the sacred enclosure of Olympia, the *Altis*.

6 Brother of Minos, one of the three infernal judges.

7 Kronos.

8 The father of Achilles and the legendary founder of Thebes.

4 The Archaic States and Sparta

53 'Ethnos' and 'polis'. The barbarian Aetolians (426)

With his description of the Aetolians, Thucydides takes one back from the present to the past which he had recalled in the Archaeology (cf. no 7). One notes the characteristic details: the absence of fortifications, the unintelligible character of the language (in fact one of the north-western dialects) and of course the eating of raw flesh, which is an almost universal characteristic of the savage world. Yet it has been suggested that the political structure of the Aetolians may not have been as loose as stated here by Thucydides, or rather the Messenians of Naupactus in their successful attempt to entice the Athenian general Demosthenes to Naupactus, for against one of the best hoplite armies of the Greek world the Aetolians displayed skill and decision, and this presupposes a minimum of collective organization which was very soon going to lead to federalism[1].

Demosthenes[2] however had in the meantime been persuaded by the Messenians[3] that it was a fine opportunity for him, having so large an army assembled, to attack the Aetolians, who were not only the enemies of Naupactus, but whose reduction would further make it easy to gain the rest of that part of the continent for the Athenians. The Aetolian nation, although numerous and warlike, yet dwelt in unwalled villages scattered far apart[4], and had nothing but light armour, and might, according to the Messenians, be subdued without much difficulty before they came together to give themselves mutual support. The plan which they recommended was to attack first the Apodotians, next the Ophionians, and after these the Eurytanians, who are the largest tribe in Aetolia, and speak, as is said, a language exceedingly difficult to understand, and eat their flesh raw. These once subdued, the rest would easily come in[5].

THUCYDIDES III, 94, 3–5
(trans. R. Crawley)

1   See J.A.O. Larsen, *Greek Federal States* (Oxford, 1968), pp. 78–80.
2   An Athenian general.
3   i.e. the citizens of Naupactus.
4   Compare nos 7 and 55.
5   In fact Demosthenes was to suffer a terrible disaster.

54   Convention between Oianthea and Chaleion

Although the Ozolian Locrians were considered by Thucydides (cf. no 7) to belong to the barbarian world rather than to Greek civilization, two tiny cities of western Locris concluded all the same, around the middle of the fifth century or a little later, a convention[1] which gave reciprocal guarantees to the citizens of both states when on each other's territory[2]. The text is preserved on a bronze tablet found at Galaxidi (Chaleion).

(Decision) not to seize the stranger: neither the Oianthean on the territory of Chaleion, nor the Chalean on the territory of Oianthea[3], neither his person nor his property, even if (someone) has a right of reprisal. Anyone may with impunity seize him who is making a seizure. If (however) the property of the stranger has been seized at sea, let it not then be subject to seizure, except if the seizure took place in the harbour of the city[4]. In the case of an unjust seizure, the penalty is a fine of four drachmae. Anyone who keeps what he has seized for more than ten days shall owe one and a half times the value of what he has seized. If anyone resides for more than a month, either a Chalean at Oianthea or an Oianthean at Chaleion[5], he shall have access to the legal procedure in force in the place where he resides.

The witness[6], if he bears false witness, shall pay a double fine. If the judges in matters concerning strangers[7] are divided in their verdict, the stranger who brings the suit[8] shall choose jurors among the best men[9], excluding witnesses and guest-friends[10], 15 in suits involving a mina or more, nine in suits involving a smaller sum. If a citizen brings a suit against another citizen according to the convention[11], the *demiourgoi*[12] shall select jurors among the best men after swearing the fivefold oath[13]; the jurors shall swear the same oath, and the majority shall prevail[14].

TOD, *GHI* I, no 34

1 The interpretation and commentary of this inscription are derived for the most part from Philippe Gauthier, *Symbola. Les étrangers et la justice dans les cités grecques* (Nancy, 1972), pp. 222–4 and 242–4; a somewhat modified view will be put forward by B. Bravo in his (unpublished) *Recherches sur le droit de représailles en Grèce ancienne*. See also *Inscriptiones Graecae* IX, I² fasc. 3, no 717.

2 These guarantees are similar to those granted in decrees of personal *asylia*: the right to enter and leave without risk the territory of a foreign city, and especially without being the object of a seizure based on the right of reprisals (cf. no 8).

3 The Oianthean will not be seized by a Chalean and the Chalean will not be seized by an Oianthean.

4 In other words the right of reprisals at sea is free, whereas the harbour is a maritime space integrated in the civic space protected by the convention. Similarly an Athenian advocate in the fourth century speaking to the jurors says: 'As for what happens on sea, you are not in my opinion responsible [. . .] but as to what happens at Peiraieus you are, for you have control of all this' (Demosthenes, *Against Theocrines*, 55).

5 The stranger ceases then to be a temporary resident and becomes a metic.

6 The Greek word is *proxenos*; this probably does not refer to the representative of a foreign city, but to the witness in a trial conducted according to the convention. However B. Bravo, op. cit., interprets *proxenos* in the former sense, his role being here to bear witness that the Chalean who brings a lawsuit at Oianthea (or the Oianthean at Chaleion) has in fact the right to do so through having been resident there for at least a month.

7 This phrase translates a single Greek word.

8 For example, to protest against an illegal seizure.

9 The ruling class in the city.

10 A witness cannot be a juror in a trial, and the private host of a stranger is suspect of partiality in his favour.

11 For example if the host of an Oianthean at Chaleion prosecutes one of his fellow-citizens for unjust treatment of his guest.

12 These are high-ranking magistrates in part of the Peloponnese and north-western Greece, cf. p. 12.

13 According to an unknown local formula.

14 Unanimity is required in the previous cases.

55 Urban contrast between Athens and Sparta

What constitutes 'modernity' for a Greek in the fifth century? Above all the existence of buildings as lavish as possible. The lack of such buildings in Sparta (the treasures discovered by British archaeologists in the sanctuary of Artemis Orthia were probably already buried) is for Thucydides the sign of Sparta's archaism.

> For I suppose that if the city of the Lacedaimonians were to become desolate, and the temples and the foundations of the public buildings were left, that as time went on there would be a strong disposition with posterity to refuse to accept her fame as a true reflection of her power. And yet they occupy two-fifths of the Peloponnese and are leaders of the whole, not to speak of their numerous allies without. Still, as their city has not been brought together in a single town and is not adorned with magnificent temples and public edifices, but composed of villages after the old fashion of Greece[1], there would be an impression of inadequacy. Whereas if Athens were to suffer the same misfortune, I suppose that any inference from the appearance presented to the eye would make her power to have been twice as great as it is.
>
> THUCYDIDES I, 10, 2
> (trans. R. Crawley)

1 Cf. nos 7, 53.

56 The Spartan rejection of economic activity

At the time when Xenophon was publishing the *Constitution of the Lacedaimonians*, the Spartan rejection of economic activity, or more exactly the establishment of the body of the Peers as a society alien to the economy, seemed an anomaly in Greece (cf. also no 37). In fact it had become an anomaly in Sparta (cf. nos 104, 106), but it was still capable of making a deep impression on Xenophon, a soldier of fortune and an Athenian moderate who was himself to seek other ways of ensuring in his native city the radical separation of economics and politics (cf. no 122).

The following customs established by Lycurgus also distinguish Sparta from the other Greeks. In other cities, as we know, all seek to make as much money as possible. One man is a farmer, another a ship-owner, another a long-distance trader, while some make a living from different crafts. But in Sparta Lycurgus has forbidden free men to touch anything that has to do with money-making, but laid it down that they should regard as peculiarly their own the activities that bring freedom to the cities. Why, indeed, should one seek to gain wealth in a country where he prescribed that one should make equal contributions of food and enjoy a common life style, in order to eliminate the urge for wealth and a life of pleasure? Nor is it necessary to make money in order to have fine clothes, for it is physical beauty and not expensive clothing which is their adornment. It is not necessary either for them to amass money to spend on their messmates, since Lycurgus made it more creditable to help one's comrades through one's own physical exertions than through lavish spending, pointing out that the former was the work of the soul and the latter the work of wealth. This is how he prevented unjust acquisition of wealth. First of all he instituted a currency of such a kind that a sum of even ten minae could not be brought into the house without the masters and servants noticing the fact[1]; this would require much space and a wagon to carry it. Moreover, searches are conducted for gold and silver, and if any is found, its possessor is punished. Why then should one attempt to make money when its possession creates more worries than its use brings pleasure?

XENOPHON, *Constitution of the Lacedaimonians*
(*c*. 378), VII

1 The famous iron currency of the Spartans and of archaic Greece. On its material form (spits), cf. P. Courbin, in *Annales* 14 (1957), pp. 209–33; cf. also no 22.

57 The public messes in Sparta

The public messes (*syssitia* or *phiditia*) are one of the archaizing elements in Spartan institutions which exercised the greatest fascination on intellectuals from other cities. Plato takes them as models right from the beginning of the *Laws* and Aristotle adopts the principle in his own ideal city, in Book VII of the *Politics*. The institution is an ancient one, but, in Athens in particular, it had assumed a more symbolically political significance: it is in the Prytaneum, the common hearth of the city, that are entertained the Athenians who receive special honours (such as the descendents of Harmodios and Aristogeiton) and the special guests of the city[1]. In Sparta and Crete it is an institution characteristic of a society of manly and warlike companions.

> The public messes (*syssitia*) are called *andreia*[2] by the Cretans and *phiditia*[3] by the Lacedaimonians. [. . .] They would meet together in groups of about 15, a few more or a few less. Each of the mess-mates would contribute every month a medimnus of barley meal, eight measures of wine, five minae of cheese, two and a half minae of figs[4], and also a little money to make up for extras. Besides, when someone had been sacrificing or hunting, he would send to the public mess the first-fruits of the sacrifice or a portion of the game[5]. For it was allowed to dine at home if one had been sacrificing or hunting till a late hour, but the other members of the mess had to be present[6]. For a long time the institution of the public messes was strictly observed. Thus King Agis[7], when returning from a victorious campaign against the Athenians, wanted to dine with his wife and sent for his portions[8], but the polemarchs[9] would not send them to him. The next day, when anger made him neglect the customary sacrifice, they fined him. The children would also come to the public messes, and were taken there as though to schools of modesty. They would listen to political discussions and would see amusements worthy of free men. They themselves would learn how to play and joke without rudeness, and not to get angry when being joked at[10]. For it was thought to be a specifically Laconian virtue to put up with jokes; but if one found this intolerable, one could simply ask the jester to stop and he would comply. As each one came in, the eldest would point to the door and say 'no word spoken here passes that door'. This is how they would examine candidates for

admission to the public messes. Each member of the company would take in his hand a ball of soft bread, and without saying a word would cast it like a ballot into a vessel which a servant carried on his head. If his vote was favourable he would cast it as it was, if unfavourable he would flatten it hard in his hand; the ball thus flattened had the same force as a perforated ballot[11]. And if only one of these balls is found, they turn down the candidate because they want everyone to take pleasure in the company of each other.

PLUTARCH, *Lycurgus* XII, 1–10

1 Cf. L. Gernet, 'Sur le symbolisme politique: le Foyer commun', *Cahiers internationaux de sociologie*, 1952, pp. 22–43 and *Anthropologie de la Grèce ancienne*, pp. 382–402.
2 i.e. 'which concern men'.
3 The etymology is uncertain, and that given by Plutarch in a paragraph omitted here is fanciful.
4 One Spartan medimnus = 74 litres; one liquid measure here = 4·62 litres; one mina = 618 grams.
5 Spartan hunting was conceived in the image of war. Xenophon specifies (*Constitution of the Lacedaimonians* VI, 3–4) that hunting dogs are common property and that huntsmen leave on their way, for the benefit of their comrades, the surplus of their provisions.
6 They are present symbolically by eating game and sacrificial meat.
7 Son of Archidamus, king from 427 to 400.
8 The kings had a double portion (Xenophon, op. cit., XV, 4).
9 They commanded a detachment of 400 men.
10 All this is pure philosophy and Xenophon is probably nearer the truth in saying that children attended the common meals in silence (op. cit., III, 5).
11 The perforated ballot was, in the Athenian law courts, the vote of condemnation.

58   The Helots of Messenia

Tyrtaeus, a Spartan (?) poet of the seventh century, of whom a few fragments have come down to us either through papyri, or especially through quotations in much later writers (Pausanias, Strabo, the scholia on Plato), is virtually the only written source we possess on the reduction of the Messenians to the status of Helots. The 'Messenian Wars', the first (last third of the eighth century) and the second (middle of the seventh century), are episodes which are all the more obscure as after the rebirth of Messenia in the shape of the city of Messene in 369 the Messenian poets provided their compatriots with a history as precise as it was legendary and which is recalled at length by Pausanias in Book V of his *Description of Greece* (*Periegesis*). But at least Tyrtaeus, the first poet of the hoplites, recalls in a few lines the economic condition of the Helots.

A   The Messenian War

To our king, Theopompus[1] dear to the gods, through whom we conquered spacious Messenia, Messenia good to plough and good to plant. For 19 years they fought unceasingly over it, keeping a stout heart, the spearmen fathers of our fathers[2]. In the 20th year[3], abandoning their rich lands, the enemy fled from the high mountains of Ithome[4].

TYRTAEUS, fr. 4 Diehl = fr. 5 West

B   The Helots

Like donkeys worn out with huge burdens, compelled by a terrible necessity, they bring to their masters[5] a half of all the fruits of the earth[6]. [. . .] They and their wives must make lamentation for their masters, whenever the grievous fate of death strikes them[7].

TYRTAEUS, fr. 5 Diehl = frs. 6–7 West

1   A king of the Eurypontid line (eighth century?) to whom tradition attributed various constitutional innovations.
2   This can hardly be taken to show that the 'first Messenian war' took place two generations before the second, of which Tyrtaeus was contemporary.
3   The detail is highly suspect: the first Messenian war would have lasted exactly twice as long as the Trojan War.
4   A mountain in the centre of Messenia, where the revolted Messenians took refuge in 464 and at the foot of which the city of Messene was to be established.
5   Probably not to individual Spartiates but to the city on which they depend as public 'slaves' (Strabo VIII, 365).
6   Their position is harsher than that of the Athenian *hectemoroi*

who, in the time before Solon, paid only one-sixth of their crop; see above pp. 59–60. Unfortunately the dependants mentioned here are not specified to be Messenians.

7 This probably refers to the funeral of the kings, which according to Herodotus (VI, 58) was a particularly solemn ceremony which the Perioikoi and Helots were compelled to attend. It is possible that this enforced attendance was first imposed on the Helots as a token of allegiance and humiliation.

59 Suppression of Helots in Sparta (424)

The relations of the body of Spartiates with the Helots were defined by an insoluble contradiction which is in sharp contrast with the situation in Athens. On the one hand Sparta could not do without Helots to wage war (at any rate from the Archidamian War onwards), but on the other even lightly armed Helots were a permanent risk for her. Yet Sparta found a solution: the collective murder of those Helots who had singled themselves out as the bravest and most deserving of freedom[1]. The mysterious character of their death is of course part of the ceremony.

The Athenians at the time were threatening the Peloponnese, and especially the territory of the Lacedaimonians; it was hoped that their attacks might be diverted most effectively by annoying them in return through the sending of an army to their allies, especially as they were willing to maintain it and asked for it to aid them in revolting[2]. The Lacedaimonians were also glad to have an excuse for sending some of the Helots out of the country, for fear that the present aspect of affairs and the occupation of Pylos might encourage them to move. Indeed fear of their number and obstinacy even persuaded the Lacedaimonians to the action which I shall now relate, their policy at all times having been governed by the necessity of taking precautions against them. Those Helots who believed they had most distinguished themselves against the enemy were invited by a proclamation to submit their claims, in order that they might receive their freedom; their object being to test them, as it was thought that the first to claim their freedom would be the most high spirited and the most apt to revolt. As many as 2,000 were selected accordingly, who crowned themselves and went round the temples, rejoic-

ing in their new freedom. The Spartans, however, soon afterwards did away with them, and no one knew how each of them
perished.

THUCYDIDES IV, 80, 1–4
(trans. R. Crawley)

1 G. Devereux, 'Psychanalyse et histoire: une application à
   l'histoire de Sparte', *Annales* 20 (1965), pp. 18–44, gives an
   unconvincing Freudian interpretation of this passage.
2 The allies of Athens, who were appealing in this way to the
   Spartiates to be able to revolt under the protection of an
   expeditionary force, were the cities of the Chalcidian peninsula
   in the north east of Greece.

60 Promotions and degradations in Sparta (421)

Here is the counterpart to the fate of the Helots. A Spartan Peer
only remains a Peer in so far as he remains faithful to the rules of
conduct which he was taught in his childhood. The bravest of the
Helots had been put to death; here one sees others, who had
served with Brasidas, being promoted and sent to a frontier area
which was particularly disturbed, while some of the Peers who
had committed the crime of surrendering to the troops of Cleon
at Sphacteria are demoted, without admittedly being put to death,
and only provisionally. In a way, nothing could be further from
the truth than the famous formula quoted by Plutarch (*Lycurgus*,
XXVIII): 'In Sparta the free man is free to the highest degree, and
the slave is slave to the highest degree.'

The same summer the soldiers from Thrace who had gone out
with Brasidas came back [. . .]; and the Lacedaimonians
decreed that the Helots who had fought with Brasidas should
be free and allowed to live where they liked, and not long
afterwards settled them with the Neodamodeis[1] at Lepreon,
which is situated on the Laconian and Elean border; they were
at this time at enmity with Elis. Those however of the Lacedaimonians who had been taken prisoners on the island and
had surrendered their arms[2] might, it was feared, suppose that
they were to be subjected to some degradation in consequence
of their misfortune, and so make some attempt at revolution,
if left in possession of their franchise. These were therefore

disfranchised, although some of them were in office at the time, and thus placed under a disability to take office, or buy and sell anything[3]. After some time, however, the franchise was restored to them.

THUCYDIDES V, 34
(trans. R. Crawley)

1 That is the word generally used to refer to the liberated Helots.
2 292 Lacedaimonian hoplites including 120 Spartiates (*Homoioi*) had been captured on the island of Sphacteria in 425.
3 This status is certainly that of the *Tresantes* (tremblers) known from Herodotus (VII, 231).

61   Subversion in Sparta: the conspiracy of Kinadon (*c.* 397)
Xenophon's narrative of the conspiracy of Kinadon is one of the most remarkable documents of social history handed down to us in Greek literature. Admittedly the date of the events mentioned suggests to place this passage under the heading of 'the crisis and decline of Sparta'. The decline begins in fact for the Lacedaimonians from the moment of their victory in 404, but Xenophon's narrative is one of the very few pieces of evidence which enable one to set in motion the different social categories of Lacedaimonian society.

Agesilaos had been on the throne for less than a year, and one day he was offering one of the regular sacrifices on behalf of the city when the soothsayer said that the gods were revealing to him a most terrible conspiracy. When he offered sacrifice a second time, he said that the sacred signs appeared yet more terrible. He sacrificed a third time and said: 'Agesilaos, the signs appear to me as though we were in the midst of the enemies[1].' Thereupon they sacrificed to the Protecting Gods and to the Saviours[2], and stopped only when after much trouble they had obtained favourable omens. And within five days of the end of the sacrifice someone came to the ephors to denounce a conspiracy and its leader, a man called Kinadon: he combined the physical strength of a young man with mental toughness, but was not one of the Peers (*Homoioi*)[3]. The ephors asked the informer how, in his view, the plan was to be carried out, and he replied that Kinadon had taken him to the end of the *agora* and had told him to count the number of Spartiates present there. 'And I,' he said, 'after counting the King, the ephors, the members of the *Gerousia* and others, making a total of forty[4], then asked him: Why do you tell me to count these men, Kinadon? He replied: Consider all these men to be your enemies, and all the rest your allies, and there are more than 4,000 of them on the *agora* alone[5].' And he said Kinadon pointed out in the streets, as they met them, an enemy here, two enemies there, and all the rest were allies. As far as all the Spartiates who happened to be in the villages, there was one enemy, the master[6], and many allies in each. The ephors then asked him how many people he believed were involved in the plot, and he replied that according to Kinadon the ringleaders had communicated with few men only, but men whom they could rely on, but they claimed that the mass of the Helots, the Neodamodeis, the Inferiors and the Perioikoi[7] were of one mind with them. Whenever there was mention of Spartiates among them, none of them could conceal the fact that he would be glad to eat them up raw if necessary[8]. When the ephors asked again: 'Where did they say that they would find weapons?' he replied that Kinadon had told him: 'Those of us who have to perform military service[9] have as many weapons as we need.' As for the mass of the people, he said that Kinadon had taken him to the iron market and had shown him quantities of daggers, swords, spits, axes, hatchets and sickles. 'And here are weapons', he said, 'for all those who work the land and timber and stone; as for the other industries, the majority had their own tools which would be adequate as weapons, especially when fighting unarmed men.' When being asked again when the plan was to be put into action, he replied he had been told to stay in the city. The ephors on hearing this realized that he was speaking of a well-thought-out plan and were very alarmed; without even summoning the so-called Small Assembly[10] but merely gathering at random a few of the members of the *Gerousia*, they decided to send Kinadon to Aulon[11] with other young men[12], with instructions to arrest and bring back some of the inhabitants of Aulon[13] and a few Helots whose names were written on the staff (*skytale*)[14]. And they also told him to bring back a certain woman, said to be the most beautiful woman in that place, and who had the reputation of corrupting all the Lacedaimonians who came there, old and young. Kinadon had already carried out missions of this kind for the ephors. So then they gave him the staff (*skytale*) with the names of those to be arrested written on it. And when he asked which of the young men he should take with him, they said: 'Go and find the eldest of the commanders of the guard (*hippagretai*)[15] and tell him to give you an escort of six or seven men, those who happen to be around.' They had taken steps to make sure that the commander would know who to send, and that those sent on escort would know that they were to arrest Kinadon. The ephors also said this to Kinadon, that they would send three wagons, hence they would not have to bring their prisoners back on foot; their intention was to disguise as much as possible the fact that the expedition was directed against him alone. They did not want to arrest him in the city, because they did not know how serious the whole matter was, and they wanted to find out first from Kinadon who his accomplices were, before they could realize that they had been betrayed and take to flight. Those who had been sent to arrest him were to keep him under guard, find out from him the names of his fellow-conspirators, and send a list as quickly as possible to the ephors. The latter were so concerned about the matter that they also sent a detachment of cavalry[16] to reinforce those sent to Aulon. Once the man had been arrested a horseman came with the names of those listed by Kinadon; they at once arrested the seer Teisamenos and the most important of the other conspirators. Kinadon was brought back, and convicted of his crime; he made a full confession and named his accomplices; finally they asked him what his aim was in acting as he did, and he replied: 'I wanted to be inferior to no one in Lacedaimon.' Thereupon his hands and neck were tied in a collar, he was scourged and stabbed and led around the city with his accomplices. Such was the punishment they received[17].

XENOPHON, *Hellenica* III, 3, 4–11

1 An excellent definition of the position of the Spartiates.
2 The Protecting Gods are those who keep off evil (*apotropaioi*); the Saviours are the Dioskouroi.
3 Xenophon does not specify his social attachments; he may have belonged to the 'Inferiors' (*hypomeiones*), who may have

been a category of Spartiates who had not inherited a plot of civic land (*kleros*). The sequel of the passage shows that he was employed on secret-police duties.

4 There are two kings, 28 members of the *Gerousia* and five ephors, which leaves few Spartiates proper in the reckoning.

5 An excellent lesson in revolutionary tactics which aim at limiting as much as possible the numbers of the enemy.

6 The owner of each plot of civic land.

7 In other words almost everyone who did not belong to the body of the Peers. No distinction is made between the Helots of Messenia whose demands were nationalistic in character and the Helots of Laconia. It seems likely that the conspiracy was essentially Laconian in character and that its aim was the establishment of a Lacedaimonian democracy, cf. below n 11. If there already were, as is likely, chattel-slaves in Sparta, they were not involved in the conspiracy.

8 This phrase is a colloquialism of Xenophon's. During the last battle which preceded the arrival at the sea, at the end of the *Anabasis*, he urges his men 'to swallow the enemy raw, if possible' (*Anabasis* IV, 8, 14).

9 A large part of the Lacedaimonian population, including frequently the Helots, had the opportunity to fight in the Spartan army.

10 An institution known only from this passage, which may have been an assembly with reduced membership.

11 Aulon is a town in Messenia. The fact that Kinadon is sent there to arrest Helots tends to confirm that the Messenians were not involved in the conspiracy; but it is also conceivable that the ephors were trying to divide their enemies' front.

12 It is unclear what must be understood by these men; possibly 'cavalry' as suggested by the sequel of the passage.

13 Xenophon does not specify their status.

14 The *skytale* is a stick around which is wound a strip of papyrus. The letters written on the strip make sense only when it is rolled around another stick in the possession of the recipient of the message (Plutarch, *Lysander* XIX).

15 The *hippagretai* were three young men who appointed and commanded a corps of 300 'cavalry'. Despite these names of aristocratic origin, they were an élite corps of infantry; they also had policing functions (Xenophon, *Constitution of the Lacedaimonians* IV, 3).

16 Are these real cavalry? That is not absolutely certain, and the reference may also be to a whole group of young men who belonged to the same corps as the companions of Kinadon. But the distance to be covered supports rather the first alternative.

17 Xenophon does not specify what is however likely, namely that Kinadon and his accomplices were executed.

62 Extracts from the Gortyn law code (*c.* 450)

The great inscription from Gortyn, engraved in 12 columns on the inside of a circular wall, is not so much a 'law code' in the modern sense of the word as the result of a more or less systematic revision of ancient laws which are characteristic of an aristocratic society. Two extracts are reproduced here: the first illustrates, in connection with monetary compensations paid in the case of rape or adultery, the diversity in the legal condition of the inhabitants of Gortyn – one is dealing here with a society as little integrated as that of Sparta – the second shows the ambiguity of the status of slavery[1].

A Rape and adultery

If a person commits rape on the free man or the free woman, he shall pay 100 staters[2]; if on account of an *apetairos*[3], ten, and if the slave (*dôlos*)[4] on the free man or the free woman, he shall pay double[5]; and if a free man on a male serf (*woikeus*) or female serf, five drachmae; and if a male serf (*woikeus*) on a male serf (*woikeus*) or female serf, five staters[6]. If a person should forcibly seduce a slave (*dôla*) belonging to the home, he shall pay two staters[7]; but if she has already been seduced, one obol by day, but if in the night, two obols; and the slave shall have preference in the oath[8]. If someone attempts to have intercourse with a free woman who is under the guardianship of a relative, he shall pay ten staters if a witness should testify[9]. If someone be taken in adultery with a free woman in a father's, brother's or the husband's house[10], he shall pay 100 staters; but if in another's, 50; and if with the wife of an *apetairos*, ten; but if a slave with a free woman, he shall pay double[11]; and if a slave with a slave, five[12].

Column II, lines 2–28

B *The fate of children in unequal marriages*
(If the slave) goes to a free woman and marries her[13], their children shall be free[14]; but if the free woman goes to the slave (*dôlos*), their children shall be slaves. And if free and slave children should be born of the same mother, in a case where the mother dies, if there is property, the free children are to have it; but if there should be no free children born of her, the heirs[15] are to take it over[16].

Column VI, line 56–Column VII, line 9

1 The translation used is that in the edition by R.F. Willetts, *The Law Code of Gortyn* (Kadmos, Supplement I, Berlin, 1967), to which the reader is referred for all further details.
2 This does not refer to a fine imposed by the city, but to compensation. 100 staters represent about 1,100 grams of silver.
3 The *apetairos* is apparently a 'free' man but who does not belong to the *hetairiai*, groups of companions (*hetairoi*) which included the adult citizens with full rights.
4 The laws of Gortyn use almost indifferently the words *woikeus* and *dôlos* to describe the 'slave' (comparable to the Spartan Helot); whether there is any significant difference between the two has been much discussed; see P. Vidal-Naquet in *Recherches sur les structures sociales dans l'Antiquité classique* (Paris, 1970), p. 75, n 2.
5 i.e. 200 staters. It will be noted that, although the compensation is very heavy, the possibility is not ruled out. The responsibility of the 'slave' is a personal one, that of his master is not involved, at least here.
6 In these last two cases the importance of the compensation depends not on the legal status of the culprit, but on that of the victim.
7 It is not easy to understand what distinguishes rape from forcible seduction, especially since the terminology is peculiar to Gortyn. Rape concerns both men and women while seduction concerns only women, and also seems to imply that regular relations are instituted. A similar distinction was made in Solon's laws (Plutarch, *Solon* XXIII).
8 In other words in case of dispute, it is the oath of the woman slave which has probative value, a remarkable rule which would have been inconceivable in a state based on chattel-slavery.

9 This refers to a simple attempt (at rape or seduction). Every unmarried or widowed woman is in principle under the guardianship of her father or of a parent.

10 Adultery in the family home is an aggravating circumstance.

11 200 staters.

12 The financial compensation in these last cases is probably paid to the person who exercises guardianship over the woman guilty of adultery. It will be noted that no compensation is foreseen for adultery between a free man and the wife of a slave.

13 This refers therefore to a perfectly legal possibility.

14 The status of the child depends therefore on the residence of the free mother.

15 The members of the family of the free woman, excluding her children.

16 It will be noted that the possibility of a marriage between a free man and a woman 'slave' is not raised. One may either suppose that this kind of legal union was inconceivable (which is not very likely) or on the other hand that the status of these children was clear, that is to say that they were free. By contrast, Hammurabi's Code foresees all possible cases of unions between 'free' and 'slave'. The children are 'free' except when the father who enjoys a status of 'freedom' refuses to acknowledge them.

63   A Cretan aristocrat

In Aristotle's view Crete is characterized by the fact that, as in Egypt, farmers and warriors form two social categories which are radically distinct (*Politics* VII, 1329 b 2). That is exactly the ideology of a brief poem preserved by Athenaeus in a collection of songs, the 'skolion' (drinking song) of Hybreas. Its exact date is unknown; it is sometimes dated as early as the sixth century[1].

My great wealth is in my spear, my sword and my fine shield which protects my skin. With this I plough, with this I reap, with this I tread the sweet wine from the grapes[2], with this I am hailed master of the servile folk[3]. Those who do not dare to have a spear, a sword and a fine shield to protect their skin, all bow before me and fall at my knees, calling me master and great king.

ATHENAEUS, *Deipnosophistae* XV, 695 f–696 a

1 For discussions see R.F. Willetts, *Cretan Cults and Festivals* (London, 1962), pp. 223–37; H. van Effenterre, 'Y a-t-il une "noblesse" crétoise?', *Recherches sur les structures sociales dans l'Antiquité classique* (Paris, 1970), pp. 19–28 (esp. pp. 19–23); for a different view see D.L. Page, 'The Song of Hybrias the Cretan', *Proceedings of the Cambridge Philological Society* 191 (1965), pp. 62–5.

2 A parallel is drawn between the warrior's weapons and the tools of the peasant, but it is a deceptive one, for the warrior does not need to work the land and he is in fact the master of the peasants.

3 This translates the word *mnoia* which seems to have been one of the names of the category of dependent peasants in Crete.

5   Classical Athens

64   What a citizen is not

When Aristotle attempts to define what a citizen is 'in the absolute sense', that is to say someone who participates in judicial and political functions, he begins by enumerating a number of negative traits, as it were, of the function of the citizen. Most of these counter-definitions apply to Athens[1], but it will be seen that at the same time Aristotle is foreshadowing a new world.

A state (*polis*) is a compound made up of citizens; and this compels us to consider who should properly be called a citizen and what a citizen really is. The nature of citizenship, like that of the state, is a question which is often disputed; there is no general agreement on a single definition: the man who is a citizen in a democracy is often not one in an oligarchy. We may leave out of consideration those who enjoy the name and title of citizen in some other than the strict sense – for example, naturalized citizens. A citizen proper is not one by virtue of residence in a given place: metics and slaves share a common place of residence (with citizens). Nor can the name of citizen be given to those who share in civic rights only to the extent of being entitled to sue and be sued in the courts. This is a right which belongs also to aliens who share its enjoyment by virtue of judicial conventions (*symbola*)[2], though it is to be noted that there are many places where metics do not enjoy even this limited right to the full – being obliged to choose a legal protector (*prostates*) so that they share only to a limited extent in the common enjoyment (*koinonia*) of the right[3]. These men[4] may be said to be citizens in the same way as children who are still too young to be entered on the roll of citizens[5], or men who are old enough to have been excused from civic duties[6]. There is a sense in which the young and the old may both be called citizens, but it is not altogether an unqualified sense: we must add the reservation that the young are undeveloped, and the old superannuated citizens, or we must use some other qualification; the exact term we apply does not matter, for the meaning is clear. What we have to define is the citizen in the strict and unqualified sense, who has no defect that has to be made good before he can bear the name – no defect such as youth or age, or such as those attaching to disfranchised[7] or exiled citizens. The citizen in this strict sense is best defined by the one criterion, 'a man who shares in the administration of justice and in the holding of office'.

ARISTOTLE, *Politics* III, 1275 a 1–25
(trans. E. Barker)

1 See Cl. Mossé, 'La conception du citoyen dans la *Politique* d'Aristote', *Eirene* 6 (1967), pp. 17–21, with additional remarks by J. Pečírka, ibid., pp. 23–6.

2 In the fourth century these conventions were treaties which organized the legal protection of aliens and their direct participation in lawsuits as defendants or plaintiffs.

3 The fact that in the law courts a number of people whose status is otherwise distinct enjoy the same rights creates between them a kind of community (*koinonia*). This community could be extended to slaves in the case of 'commercial suits' (cf. L. Gernet, 'Sur les actions commerciales en droit athénien', *REG* 51 (1938), pp. 1–44 and *Droit et société dans la Grèce ancienne* (Paris, 1955), pp. 173–200). It will be noted that Aristotle, as well as reproducing the classical criteria of citizenship as they were used in Athens, also shows that these are in fact being undermined by the development of interstate relations which is characteristic of the fourth century.

4 The beneficiaries of judicial conventions.

5 The roll of the phratries and demes. Aristotle's statement here is a particularly bold one, since he assimilates to imperfect citizens aliens who benefited from *symbola*. One is moving towards a world where *isopoliteia* (the right of reciprocal citizenship granted by treaty between cities) will make it possible to some extent to cross the barrier of reciprocal exclusiveness.

6 Those who are no longer performing military service, but Aristotle may be thinking of cities which after a certain age took away political rights from old men, which they could no longer defend with arms, cf. the study by P. Roussel mentioned above, Chapter 1, n 47.

7 Men punished with *atimia* which deprived them of their political rights.

65 Rural habits of the Athenians (after the decision of Pericles to evacuate Attica)

It is by no means certain that Attica was ever divided, as its tradition would have it, among different cities the unification of which (*synoikismos*) gave birth to Athens, but the strength of local patriotism which caused an inhabitant of Thoricus or Marathon to feel that when he was leaving his deme he was leaving his city is a well-attested fact, illustrated for example by numerous inscriptions in the country demes about important cult-places with their written rules, about which extant literary sources are silent. The old style of warfare implied the defence of this territory. The strategy of Themistocles and Pericles marks a break in this respect. In 431 Attica was not defended, and the imbalance between city and countryside became – in spite of the efforts of theorists – irreversible[1].

The Athenians listened to his advice and began to carry in their wives and children from the country, and all their household furniture, even to the woodwork of their houses[2] which they took down. Their sheep and cattle they sent over to Euboea and the adjacent islands. But they found it hard to move, as most of them had always been used to live in the country. From very early times this had been more the case with the Athenians than with others. Under Cecrops and the first kings, down to the reign of Theseus, Attica had always consisted of a number of independent townships, each with its own prytaneum[3] and magistrates. [. . .]

The Athenians thus long lived scattered over Attica in independent townships. Even after the centralization of Theseus, old habits still prevailed; and from the early times down to the present war most Athenians still lived in the country with their families and households, and were consequently not at all inclined to move now, especially as they had just restored their establishments after the Persian Wars. Deep was their trouble and discontent at abandoning the houses and sanctuaries which had belonged to their fathers ever since the ancient state of affairs, and at having to change their habits of life and to bid farewell to what each regarded as nothing less than his native city. When they arrived at Athens few had houses of their own to go to, or could find an asylum with friends or relatives.

THUCYDIDES II, 14–15, 1; 16–17, 1
(trans. R. Crawley)

1 See nos 125 and 126 and S.C. Humphreys, 'Town and country in Ancient Greece', in *Man, Settlement and Urbanism*, ed. P.J. Ucko, R. Tringham, G.W. Dimbleby (London, 1972), pp. 763–8.
2 i.e. notably doors and windows.
3 The 'common hearth' of the city, cf. no 57, n 1.

66   A peasants' republic?

The link between the citizens and the land mentioned in the previous passage is characteristic not only of Athens but of the Greek city in general[1]. During the Peloponnesian War and at its end a pressure group to which Euripides belonged exalted the peasant-owner as the very strength of the city[2]. This propaganda took a concrete form in 403, during the period of confusion which accompanied the return of the democrats, through the proposal of a certain Phormisios which is reported by a historian of the time of Augustus. One may deduce from it that some 20 to 25 per cent of Athenians at the time were completely without land[3]. On reflection the importance of this proportion is perhaps at least as significant as the existence of a substantial majority of peasants with holdings.

When the people had returned from Peiraieus, although they had passed a decree which brought about a reconciliation with the men of the city and established a general amnesty, there was a fear that the common people, having recovered their former power, would again harass the rich. Many speeches were made on this subject. Phormisios, one of those who had returned with the people, introduced a proposal to the effect that once the exiles had come back citizen rights should not be given to all, but should be restricted to those who owned (the) land[4]; this is also what the Lacedaimonians wanted. Had this decree been voted some 5,000 Athenians would have been deprived of their civic rights[5].

DIONYSIUS OF HALICARNASSUS, *On Lysias*, 34

1 See J. Pečirka, 'Land Tenure and the Development of the Athenian *Polis*', *Studies G. Thomson* (Prague, 1963), pp. 183–201.
2 See R. Goossens, 'République des paysans', *Mélanges F. de Visscher* (Brussels, 1950), 3, pp. 551ff.; *Euripide et Athènes* (Brussels, 1962), pp. 556–8 and 645–6; Cl. Mossé, *La fin de la démocratie athénienne* (Paris, 1962), pp. 251–3.
3 Cf. M.I. Finley, *Studies in Land and Credit*, pp. 56–8.
4 The article is omitted by some editors.
5 An unknown democrat, for whom Lysias wrote the speech 'Against a proposal to destroy the ancestral constitution in Athens', caused the proposal to fail.

67 Mythical aspects of the status of metics in Athens

The fifth-century tragic poets liked to represent and dramatize the welcome given by Athens to strangers. In the *Suppliant Women* (c. 460), Aeschylus imagines a decree of the popular assembly at Argos which grants asylum and the status of metics to the daughters of Danaos who are fleeing from their cousins, the sons of Aegyptios to whom they are betrothed. Similarly Euripides in his tragedy of the same name (422) portrays one of the Seven against Thebes, Parthenopaios, son of Atalante, in the guise of an Argive metic[1]. Passages like these give a semblance of proof to the theory of Wilamowitz who saw in the fifth-century metics 'quasi-citizens'.

A Decree in favour of the Danaids

Danaos Take courage, my children; all is well on the side of the inhabitants of this country. The people has passed a decree which resolves everything[2].
Chorus leader[3] Hail, old man, you who bring such welcome news to me. Tell us how the matter was decided, on what side

the sovereign hand of the people[4] has come down in a majority.
Danaos It has been resolved by the people of Argos[5], without
any contrary vote, and the result has given fresh life to my aged
heart. The air quivered as the whole people, stretching out its
right hands[6], ratified these words: 'We shall enjoy the status
of metics in this land, we shall be free and inviolate[7], protected
against all human reprisals[8]; no one, be he an inhabitant or a
foreigner, shall be allowed to seize us. Should violence be used
against us any inhabitant of this country who fails to give us
help shall be punished with loss of civic rights[9], and exiled
from the country by popular vote.'

AESCHYLUS, *Supplices*, 600–14

B *Parthenopaios, an Argive metic*
The son of the huntress Atalante, Parthenopaios, a most
beautiful child, was an Arcadian. He came to the river Inachos[10]
and was educated at Argos. Being brought up there, first of all,
as is fitting for foreigners who enjoy the status of metics, he
did not cause any distress or odium to his city, nor was he
argumentative, a source of annoyance both with a demesman[11]
and a foreigner. He joined our battalions, like an Argive by
birth, and defended the country, rejoicing in the successes of
the city and being distressed at its reverses.

EURIPIDES, *Supplices*, 888–98

1 The latter example we owe to Philippe Gauthier, *Symbola.*
  Les étrangers et la justice dans les cités grecques, p. 113.
2 The terminology of Aeschylus is systematically legalistic and
  political.
3 Spokesman of the Danaids.
4 The Greek words are those which form the compound
  Demokratia.
5 The formula of decision in decrees.
6 One voted by raising the right hand.
7 No one shall be able to seize them under any pretext to reduce
  them to slavery.
8 On the right of reprisals cf. the notes to nos 8, 41 and 54.
9 *Atimia*, i.e. civic death.
10 At Argos.
11 That is to say, in Athens, a citizen.

68 A call to the metics

In a famous simile Aristophanes shows that for him the citizens are the flour of the Athenian corn, of which the aliens are the husk, easily discarded, and the metics the bran 'which cannot be separated from the unground corn and which thus far is an integral part of it'[1]. Speaking to the metics who served in the Athenian navy in dramatic circumstances, on the eve of the Sicilian disaster (413), the Athenian general Nicias obviously uses less blunt language.

> Bear in mind how well worth preserving is the pleasure felt by those of you who through your knowledge of our language and imitation of our manners were always considered Athenians, even though not so in reality, and as such were honoured throughout Greece, and had your full share of the advantages of our empire in the respect of our subjects, and more than your share in protection from ill treatment. You, therefore, with whom alone we freely share our empire, we now justly require you not to betray that empire.
>
> THUCYDIDES VII, 63, 3–4
> (trans. R. Crawley)

1 J. Taillardat, *Les images d'Aristophane* (Paris, 2nd ed., 1965), p. 393.

69 Biography of a wealthy metic

The biography of Lysias, written by an anonymous author of the imperial period, cannot be considered representative of all the metics; but at least it enables one to understand the process of assimilation which turned a Syracusan by birth into the most 'Attic' of the orators and the son of the great trader Kephalos into the friend and ally of the democrats.

> Lysias was son of Kephalos[1], grandson of Lysanias, and great grandson of Kephalos. Kephalos, a Syracusan by birth, had migrated to Athens through love of the city and at the invitation of Pericles son of Xanthippos, to whom he was linked by ties of friendship and hospitality. He was extremely wealthy, and according to some had been banished from Syracuse at the time of the tyranny of Gelon[2]. Lysias was born in Athens in the

archonship of Philocles, successor of Phrasicles[3], in the second year of the 80th Olympiad, and was educated with the most distinguished Athenians. But when Athens sent off to Sybaris the colony which later changed its name to Thourioi, he went there with his eldest brother Polemarchos (he had two others, Euthydemos and Brachyllos). His father was already dead, and the intention was that he should share in the land allotment[4]. This was in the archonship of Praxiteles, and he was 15 years old; he remained there and completed his education with the Syracusans Teisias and Nicias[5]. He acquired a house and got a plot of land, and enjoyed citizen rights there until the archonship of Kleokritos in Athens[6], altogether 33 years. The next year, in the 92nd Olympiad, after the Athenian disaster in Sicily, when there was unrest among the other allies and in particular in Italy, he was accused of being an Athenian partisan and was exiled with 300 others. He arrived in Athens in the archonship of Kallias, successor of Kleokritos, at a time when the Four Hundred were already ruling the city[7], and he stayed there. After the sea battle of Aigospotamoi, when the Thirty took over the city[8], he was exiled after a stay of seven years, and lost his property and his brother Polemarchos[9]. He himself managed to escape from the house in which he was under guard before being led away for execution (for it had two doors), and spent his time in Megara. When the men of Phyle[10] attempted the return to Athens, he was seen to be a most useful ally, and gave them 2,000 drachmae and 200 shields[11]. He was sent with Hermon[12] to recruit mercenaries, and enrolled 300; he also persuaded his guest-friend Thrasydaios of Elea[13] to make a contribution of two talents. For these services, Thrasybulus proposed a decree granting him citizen rights, after the return to Athens and during the 'anarchy' which preceded the archonship of Eucleides[14]. The people ratified the grant, but when Archinos brought in a suit for illegality on the ground that the proposal had not been previously passed by the Council[15], the decree was quashed. He was thus deprived of citizen rights and lived in Athens for the rest of his life as a metic *isoteles*; he died there at the age of 83, or according to some, 76, or according to others, more than 80, having lived to see Demosthenes as a youth.

[PLUTARCH], *Lives of the Ten Orators, Lysias*, 1–43

1 It is in the house of Kephalos in Peiraieus that Plato's dialogue
   The Republic takes place, which rises from the cave (Peiraieus)
   to the idea of the good.
2 Gelon died in 478 and these two statements cannot of course
   be reconciled.
3 In 459; the date seems too early and modern scholarship
   places the birth of Lysias around 440.
4 This involves an obvious compression, for Thourioi was
   founded in 444 or 443 (archonship of Praxiteles). But at least
   the writer is consistent with himself.
5 Teisias was a famous rhetor, a disciple of Korax. Nicias is
   otherwise unknown.
6 413.
7 During the first oligarchic revolution.
8 404.
9 The episode is related in detail in the speech *Against Eratos-
   thenes*.
10 Thrasybulus and the democrats who had seized this stronghold with him.
11 He was a weapons manufacturer.
12 An Athenian who in particular held a command at Pylos during
   the Peloponnesian War.
13 In Italy.
14 The restoration of Athenian institutions dates from the
   archonship of Eucleides (403).
15 Cf. no 70.

70 **The metic liberators (401–400)**
Having defeated the Thirty Tyrants in 403, Thrasybulus proposed that citizenship should be granted to all those who had
collaborated with the democrats in their battles from Phyle to
Mounichia and then at Athens. The 'moderate' democrat
Archinos imposed more limited rewards[1]. Unfortunately the next
of the inscription which provides this information is seriously
mutilated and it is not even absolutely certain that the recipients
of citizenship were solely metics. The often modest profession of
the honorands is indicated.

Front
[Lysiades] was secretary, [Xenainetos] archon; [it was resolved

by the council and the people; the tribe Hippothontis held the prytany], Lysiades was secretary, Demophilos was *epistates* (president)[2], [Archinos moved: so that adequate recompense should be given to the metics] who took part in the return from Phyle[3] or [who joined in the march down to Peiraieus], let the Athenians decree [concerning them] that they and their descendants [shall enjoy the rights of citizens, and one shall immediately distribute them among the ten tribes], and the authorities shall apply the same laws to them [as to the other Athenians; but as to those who did not take part in the march] but joined in the battle at Mounichia, [helped to save Peiraieus for the Athenians and were present in the city[4]] when the convention[5] was concluded and carried out the instructions given to them, [to these should be granted *isoteleia*[6] when they live in Athens and the right to conclude legally valid] marriages just like the Athenians[7], and as to those . . .

Back[8]

Chairedemos, a farmer; Leptines, a cook; Demetrios, a carpenter; Euphorion, a muleteer; Kephisodoros, a builder; Hegesias, a gardener; Epameinon, an ass driver; [. . .]opos, an oil merchant; Glaukias (?), a farmer; [. . .]on, a nut seller; Dionysios (?), a farmer; Bendiphanes[9], a bath maker (?); Emporion, a farmer; Paidikos, a baker; Sosias, a fuller; Psammis[10], a farmer; Egersis (*no trade indicated*); [. . .]; Eukolion, a hired servant; Kallias, a statuette maker. In the tribe Aigeis: Athenogeiton . . . Phrynichos . . . Zoilos . . . Timaios . . .

Tod, GHI II, no 100

1 Aristotle, *Constitution of Athens* XL, 2; Aeschines, *Against Ctesiphon*, 187; cf. no 69.
2 President of the tribe which held the prytany.
3 A stronghold to the north west of Athens, the starting point of the recapture of Peiraieus then of the city by the democrats.
4 In the democratic camp.
5 The conventions between the democrats and the provisional regime which succeeded in Athens the Thirty Tyrants (*Constitution of Athens* XXXIX).
6 A metic *isoteles* was from the fiscal point of view the equal of an Athenian.

7 They will have the right to marry Athenian women through the rite of *engyesis*, which does not mean that their children will be citizens.

8 The names of the honorands were arranged by tribes; only 34 have been preserved of which only the less mutilated are reproduced here.

9 The name is that of a devotee of the Thracian goddess Bendis whose cult was introduced in Athens during the Peloponnesian War.

10 An Egyptian name.

71 Honours granted by Athens to Strato, king of Sidon (*c.* 367?)

The stele set up in honour of Strato, king of Sidon[1] falls into two parts: (a) a decree of Kephisodotos which grants to the king[2] personally the privilege of proxeny, which makes him and his descendants into the hosts of the Athenians at Sidon and would earn him exceptional honours if he came to Athens, as his representative is invited to the prytaneum. Strato and Athens agree on the exchange of *symbola*, i.e. conventionally defined tokens, which enable their holders (whether private individuals or the representatives of states) to make themselves identified; (b) an amendment to this decree is introduced which concerns this time the traders from Sidon staying in Athens. Instead of being treated as separate individuals, as was the case with the metics in the fifth century who did not in any way represent their city of origin, they are implicitly placed under the protection of their king. The latter, the benefactor (*euergetes*) of the Athenians, is therefore at the same time the guarantor of the commercial interests of his subjects. Better still, the traders from Sidon are exempted from those obligations which were inherent in the status of metics, a status which any foreigner who had stayed for a certain lapse of time in Athens was compelled to assume. The Sidonian traders will be Sidonians when in Athens, and not second-class Athenians.

[. . .] Since Strato took care that the ambassadors sent by the people to see the Great King should make the journey in the best possible conditions; let one give answer to the envoy of the king of the Sidonians that in future, since he is devoted to the people of Athens, there is no request from the Athenians which he shall not obtain; and let Strato, king of Sidon, be proxenos of the Athenians, himself and his descendants. Let the secretary of the council inscribe this decree on a stone stele within ten days and place it on the acropolis; and for the inscription of the stele let the treasures give to the secretary of the council 30 drachmae from the ten talents[3]. And let the council make *symbola* (tokens) with the king of the Sidonians, so that the people of Athens may know·when the king of the Sidonians is sending a message to Athens to make a request from the city and that the king of the Sidonians may know when the people of Athens is sending an envoy to him. And let the envoy of the king of the Sidonians be invited tomorrow to receive hospitality at the prytaneum[4].

Menexenos moved: for the rest as proposed by Kephisodotos[5]; let all the Sidonians who reside in Sidon and enjoy rights there, and who come to stay in Athens for trade, be exempted from the payment of the metic tax and the obligation of being choregos, and let no tax (*eisphora*) be levied on them.

TOD, *GHI* II, no 139

1 A hellenized Phoenician and vassal of the Great King; he had done a service to an Athenian embassy at a date which cannot be securely established because of the loss of the top part of the stele (dates have been suggested ranging from 378 to 360).
2 Sometimes described as king of Sidon and sometimes as king of the Sidonians, an illustration of the difficulty felt by Greeks in describing foreign political institutions (see also no 72).
3 A special fund, known from other inscriptions, cf. Tod, op. cit., pp. 65, 118.
4 i.e. he will be given a meal.
5 A formula for amendments.

72 Permission given to merchants from Kition (Cyprus) to found a sanctuary to Aphrodite (333)

The following stele, found in Peiraieus, contains first a decree of the council which leaves it to the people to decide, without any prior motion, what answer to give to the request of the traders from Kition¹ who wanted to found a sanctuary to Aphrodite, the great goddess of Cyprus, and second the decree of the assembly which grants the permission. The mover of this latter decree is the famous orator Lycurgus.

> Gods. In the archonship of Nikokrates, when the tribe Aigeis was holding the first prytany; of the presidents Theophilos of the deme of Phegous put the question to the vote; it was resolved by the council; Antidotos son of Apollodoros of the deme of Sypalettos moved: concerning the request put forward by the men of Kition² about the foundation of a sanctuary to Aphrodite, let the council decree that the president drawn by lot to preside over the next meeting of the assembly should introduce them before the people and lay the matter open for debate, and communicate to the people the decision of the council, namely that the council resolved that the people should hear the request of the men of Kition about the foundation of the sanctuary as well as any other Athenian who wishes to speak, and decide whatever seems best to it. In the archonship of Nikokrates, when the tribe Pandionis was holding the second prytany; of the presidents Phanostratos of the deme of Philaidai put the question to the vote; it was resolved by the people; Lycurgus son of Lycophron of the deme of Boutades moved: concerning the demand of the men of Kition which seemed within the bounds of the law, namely the request they make from the people to be allowed to acquire a plot of land on which to found a sanctuary to Aphrodite, let the people resolve to give to the merchants of Kition the right to acquire a plot of land on which to found a sanctuary of Aphrodite, just as the Egyptians built a sanctuary to Isis.

> TOD, *GHI* II, no 189

1 Kition is one of the main Phoenician cities of Cyprus. The presence of many non-Greeks among foreigners resident in Athens is characteristic of the fourth century, though by no means unknown in the previous century; cf. no 70, n 10.
2 The request is put forward by the traders (*emporoi*) of Kition, not apparently as metics, but in the name of the *demos* of Kition which is thus assimilated to a Greek city.

73   Frieze and columns of the Erechtheion: citizens, slaves and metics at work (408–407)

The inscriptions found at Athens on the Acropolis and which relate to the construction, or rather to the completion, of the Ionic temple dedicated to Athena and Poseidon, constitute an invaluable source of information[1]. Not only did the construction of temples represent in the budget of a city an important item, and in certain years an essential one[2] – can one imagine for example what the construction of ten temples at Acragas in the fifth century alone can have represented[3]? – but the documents of the Erechtheion have something more to contribute. Admittedly one only apprehends the work at its point of completion; the workmen mentioned in the accounts are mostly highly skilled men; furthermore, the years from 409 to 407 are a time of acute military and political crisis, and it is likely that this crisis will have had an impact on the composition of the working population. But at least one has a unique opportunity to see how the three categories of the Athenian population, citizens, metics and slaves, were associated in a single enterprise[4].

An extract from the accounts of the year 408–407 is translated here; it refers to payments for sculptures on the frieze and the channelling of the east columns of the temple. In this specific case payments are made per item. The rest of the inscriptions show that part at least of the personnel was paid at a rate of a drachma a day, this applying equally to the architect and to the workmen[5]. Others are paid by measure. No difference in salary is made between slaves and their masters when they work on the site, but it is likely, though not certain, that the salary of slaves was collected directly by the master. The slaves whose names are mentioned are all qualified artisans, but the inscriptions also mention, without naming them, other categories of artisans, for example sawyers, who are probably also slaves[6].

A   The Sculptures

. . . the man holding the spear: 60 drachmae[7]. Phyromachos of the deme of Kephisia[8] – the youth beside the breast-plate: 60 drachmae. Praxias who lives in the deme of Melite – the horse and the man appearing behind it and striking it in the flank: 120 drachmae. Antiphanes of the deme of Kerameis – the chariot and the youth and the two horses being harnessed: 240 drachmae. Phyromachos of the deme of Kephisia – the man leading the horse: 60 drachmae.

Mynnion who lives in the deme of Agryle – the horse and the man striking it – and he subsequently added the stele[9]: 127 drachmae. Soklos who lives in the deme of Alopeke – the man holding the bridle: 60 drachmae. Phyromachos of the deme of Kephisia – the man leaning on a staff near the altar: 60 drachmae. Iasos of the deme of Kollytos – the woman and the little girl leaning against her: 80 drachmae.

Total of the payments for sculpture[10]: 3,315 drachmae.
Receipts[11]: 4,302 drachmae 1 obol.
Expenditure: the same sum.

BREAKDOWN OF TRADES BY CIVIC STATUS

	Citizens	Metics	Slaves	Unknown	Totals
Architects	2	—	—	—	2
Under-secretary	1	—	—	—	1
Guard	—	—	—	1	1
Masons	9	12	16	7	44
Sculptors	3	5	—	1	9
Wax modellers	—	(2)	—	—	(2)
Woodcarvers	1	5	—	1	7
Carpenters	5	7	4	3	19
Sawyers	—	1	—	1	2
Joiner		1			1
Lathe worker	—	—	—	1	1
Painters	—	2	—	1	3
Gilder	—	1	—	—	1
Labourers	1	5	—	3	9
Unknown trade	2	3	—	2	7
Totals	24	42	20	21	107

The table emphasizes both the relative complexity of the division of trades and the relative predominance of slaves in the less specialized trades. Citizens and metics are found in the principal branches. The number of the metic wax modellers is uncertain. The table is reproduced from R.H. Randall, 'The Erechtheum Workmen', *AJA* 57, 3 (1953), p. 201 (Table 1).

B   *The channellings of the columns*

In the 8th prytany of the tribe Pandionis.

Received from the treasurers of the goddess, Aresaichmos of the deme of Agryle and his colleagues in office[12]: 1,239 drachmae 1 obol.

Expenditure

(a) Purchases: two boards on which we inscribe the accounts[13], at a drachma each: 2 drachmae. Total of purchases: 2 drachmae.

(b) Stonework: for channelling the columns at the east end opposite the altar. The third column from the altar of Dione, Ameiniades who lives in the deme of Koile: 18 drachmae; Aischines[14]: 18 drachmae; Lysanias: 18 drachmae; Somenes (slave) of Ameiniades: 18 drachmae; Timokrates[15]: 18 drachmae.

– The next column – Simias who lives in the deme of Alopeke: 13 drachmae; Kerdon[16]: 12 drachmae 5 obols; Sindron[17] (slave) of Simias, 12 drachmae 5 obols; Sokles (slave) of Axiopeithes[18]: 12 drachmae 5 obols; Sannion (slave) of Simias: 12 drachmae 5 obols; Epiekes (slave) of Simias: 12 drachmae 5 obols; Sosandros (slave) of Simias: 12 drachmae 5 obols[19].

– The next column – Onesimos (slave) of Nikostratos[20]: 16 drachmae 4 obols; Eudoxos who lives in the deme of Alopeke: 16 drachmae 4 obols; Kleon[21]: 16 drachmae 4 obols; Simon who lives in the deme of Agryle: 16 drachmae 4 obols; Antidotos (slave) of Glaukos: 16 drachmae 4 obols; Eudikos[21] (?): 16 drachmae 4 obols.

– The next column – Theugenes of the deme of Peiraieus: 15 drachmae; Kephisogenes of the deme of Peiraieus: 15 drachmae; Teukros who lives in the deme of Kydathenaion: 15 drachmae; Kephisodoros who lives in the deme of Skambonidai: 15 drachmae; Nikostratos: 15 drachmae; Theugeiton of the deme of Peiraieus: 15 drachmae. For smoothing the orthostates, the two near the altar of Thyechoos[22] – Polykles of the deme of Lakiadai: 35 drachmae.

For channelling the columns at the east end, opposite the altar, the column next to the altar of Dione – Laossos of the deme of Alopeke: 20 drachmae; Philon of the deme of Erchia: 20 drachmae; Parmenon (slave) of Laossos: 20 drachmae; Karion[23] (slave) of Laossos: 20 drachmae; Ikaros[24]: 20 drachmae.

– The next column – Phalakros of the deme of Paiania: 20 drachmae; Philostratos of the deme of Paiania: 20 drachmae; Thargelios (slave) of Phalakros: 20 drachmae; Philourgos (slave) of Phalakros: 20 drachmae; Gerys[25] (slave) of Phalakros: 20 drachmae.

– The next column – Ameiniades who lives in the deme of Koile: 20 drachmae; Aischines: 20 drachmae; Lysanias: 20 drachmae; Somenes (slave) of Ameiniades: 20 drachmae; Timokrates: 20 drachmae[26].

– The next column – Simias who lives in the deme of Alopeke: 14 drachmae 2 obols; Kerdon: 14 drachmae 2 obols; Sindron (slave) of Simias: 14 drachmae 2 obols; Sokles (slave) of Axiopeithes: 14 drachmae 2 obols; Sannion (slave) of Simias: 14 drachmae 2 obols; Epieikes (slave) of Simias: 14 drachmae 1 obol; Sosandros[27]: 14 drachmae 1 obol.

– The next column – Onesimos (slave) of Nikostratos: 18 drachmae $3\frac{1}{2}$ obols; Eudoxos who lives in the deme of Alopeke: 18 drachmae 2 obols ? [. . .]

IG I², 374; L.D. Caskey in *The Erechtheum* XVII, col. I (pp. 388–93)

METHODS OF PAY

By day	By measure	By piece	By salary
			Architects
Carpenters Joiners Labourers		Carpenters Joiners	
	Masons (finishing stone)	Masons (fluting columns)	
		Masons (laying stone)	
Sawyers	Painters (encaustic)	Painters (wood) Sawyers Sculptors	
			Under-secretary
		Wax modellers Woodcarvers	

Only the people who depend directly on the city are paid by prytany, i.e. the architects and the under-secretary. The less specialized trades are paid by the day, the more sophisticated by the piece. There remain certain activities which, for reasons which generally escape us, are paid by measure according to a rate fixed for the material used. The table is reproduced from R.H. Randall, art. cit., p. 208 (Table 6).

1 The inscriptions fall into four groups: (1) the report of the commission entrusted by the city with verifying the progress of work (409–408); (2) the accounts for the year 409–408; (3) the accounts for the year 408–407; (4) fragments of the accounts of the following years. They are fully published by L.D. Caskey in the collective volume edited by G.P. Stevens, *The Erechtheum* (Cambridge, Mass., 1927), pp. 277–422.

2 See in general A. Burford, 'The Economics of Greek Temple Building', *Proceedings of the Cambridge Philological Society*, 1965, pp. 21–34.

3 Cf. M.I. Finley, *Daedalus*, Winter 1971, p. 186 (=*The Use and Abuse of History* (London, 1975), p. 101).

4 The inscriptions have been carefully studied from this point of view by R.H. Randall Jr, 'The Erechtheum Workmen', *AJA* 57 (1953), pp. 199–210. Citizens are normally referred to by the mention of their deme of origin, metics by the deme in which they are resident, slaves by the name of their owner, who is usually working on the site.

5 The difference, which is very real, is that the architect has a guaranteed salary for the whole of the prytany year. His secretary has a guaranteed salary of 5 obols a day (1 drachma = 6 obols).

6 The restoration of missing letters being virtually all certain no attempt has been made to point these out in the typography of the translation.

7 The inscription gives, in an order which varies, the name of the sculptor, a brief description of the piece, the price paid; 60 drachmae may correspond to 60 days' work. The sculptures of the frieze, contrary to normal practice, were made of inserted pieces of white marble fastened by means of iron dowels and blocks of dark limestone from Eleusis. The preserved fragments are very mutilated.

8 All the demes mentioned for citizens as well as for metics are

urban demes or demes from the near vicinity.

9 The block of Eleusinian limestone placed behind the relief? The element of improvization in the decoration is visible here.

10 It will be noted that the sculptors are all citizens or metics and this is true of the whole set of inscriptions; see the table, p. 277.

11 From the treasures of the goddess. This sum covers work other than the sculptures.

12 There are ten of these, drawn by lot, originally from the wealthiest Athenians (Aristotle, *Constitution of Athens* XLVII). They are the main treasurers of the city.

13 This refers to wooden boards (*sanides*) and not to stelai or stone slabs, the price of which was much higher. The accounts we have are therefore copied from these boards.

14 Status unknown: this person and the next are again subsequently mentioned together with Ameiniades.

15 The name of the slave is followed by that of his owner in the genitive, which led the editors of *The Erechtheum* to believe that it referred to filiation; the theory is to be rejected completely, cf. R.H. Randall, art. cit., pp. 199–200. The status of Timokrates is unknown.

16 A name generally borne by a slave, which means 'he who earns money'; here this refers most probably to a slave of Axiopeithes. Cf. L.D. Caskey, in *Erechtheum* XIII, 1–18, where he reappears in that capacity, unless this is a case of identity of name.

17 A name which means 'slave, son of a slave' (Seleukos in Athenaeus, *Deipnosophistae* VI, 267 c).

18 This metic, who lives in the deme of Melite, does not work on this site, but another inscription (L.D. Caskey, in *Erechtheum* X, 2, 16) shows him as a mason.

19 If the genitives are taken as showing a filiation, then Simias has at least four sons working with him on the same site, two of whom bear 'slave names'!

20 Although this person reappears in the inscriptions, cf. below, it is not known whether he was a metic or a citizen.

21 Status unknown.

22 The account of the columns is suddenly interrupted here and resumes immediately afterwards. The word *Thyechoos* means 'who pours the offering'; this refers to the priest, *Boutes*, who officiated at the festival of the Bouphonia, according to G.W.

Elderkin, in *Hesperia* 10 (1941), pp. 114–15.

23 A typical slave name: the Carian.

24 Status unknown.

25 A Persian name.

26 This is the team already met above (cf. n 14). Does this refer to a master, his slave and his companions? or to a master accompanied by his slaves? Teams of this kind reappear in the accounts; cf. below.

27 This time one may be sure (cf. above n 19) that Sosandros is a slave of Simias; the presence of slaves who are not expressly mentioned as such is therefore not unlikely in the previously mentioned teams.

74   Metics and slaves at Athens

The *Constitution of the Athenians* is a shrewd pamphlet which has come down to us among the works of Xenophon. Nowadays no one seriously defends this attribution any longer, and the writer is commonly referred to as the 'Old Oligarch'. It seems in fact very likely that he is an opponent of democracy writing about 430. His main concern is to try to show that the Athenian system forms a logical and coherent whole and ultimately that the integration and participation of the *demos* in sovereignty carry with them a certain form of integration for metics and even for slaves. One should not take him too literally: the 'liberalism' he describes is a liberalism born of prosperity, and it did not prevent distinctions between legal categories from being deeply felt.

As far as slaves and metics are concerned, it is in Athens that you see them behaving with the greatest insolence; you may not strike them there[1] and the slave will not stand out of your way. The reason for this local custom is this: if there was a law allowing the free man to strike the slave, the metic or the freedman, he would often have struck an Athenian thinking he was a slave. For the common people (*demos*) there are no better dressed than the slaves and the metics, nor any better in appearance[2].

Should anyone be surprised at the fact that they allow the slaves in Athens to live in luxury, and some of them to lead a life of great splendour[3], this too is done deliberately by them. In a country which bases its power on its navy, it is necessary for financial reasons for us to be slaves of our human live-stock[4]. We must get from them the money they owe us[5], and therefore allow them to be free. Where there are wealthy slaves there is no advantage in my slave being afraid of you, but in Sparta my slave fears you[6]. For if your slave was afraid of me, there is a possibility that he would hand over his own money to free himself from personal danger.

This is why we have granted to slaves the right of equal speech (*isegoria*) towards free men, and similarly to metics towards citizens, because the city needs the metics on account of the multiplicity of trades and because of the fleet. Accordingly it is with good reason that we have given the right of equal speech to metics as well.

[XENOPHON], *Constitution of the Athenians* I, 10–12

1 i.e. any free man may not strike a slave who does not belong to him.
2 What the Old Oligarch finds most striking is ultimately less the insolence of slaves and metics than the massive presence of the common people.
3 This refers to slaves 'living apart' who carried on a business.
4 *Andrapoda*, a word coined from *tetrapoda* (four-footed animals).
5 The text is conjectural; this may refer to slave overseers or managers, who collect the revenue from the work of other slaves. All these activities are related, directly or indirectly, to trade and maritime life.
6 In Athens a slave is my slave or your slave, in Sparta a Helot depends on the community of Spartiates.

75 The slaves of the metic Kephisodoros

In 414 the property and chattels of men accused of having mutilated the stone pillars of Hermes (the Hermocopids) were confiscated and auctioned. Fragments of the stele summarizing these sales have been found in Athens. Forty-five slaves are found among the items mentioned and sold; among these the most important lot is the (incomplete) one of the 16 slaves of the metic Kephisodoros[1]. The first column, on the left, shows the tax (about 1 per cent) paid by the buyer. The second shows the purchase price, the third the ethnic origin and sex of the slaves sold. Except for the case of the little Carian child there is no way of explaining the variation in prices. The expensive women are probably young.

PROPERTY OF KEPHISODOROS, A METIC LIVING AT PEIRAIEUS

2 drachmae	165 dr.	A Thracian woman
1 dr. 3 obols	135 dr.	A Thracian woman
[2 dr.]	170 dr.	A Thracian
2 dr. 3 ob.	240 dr.	A Syrian
[1 dr.] 3 ob.	105 dr.	A Carian
2 dr.	161 dr.	An Illyrian
2 dr. 3 ob.	220 dr.	A Thracian woman
1 dr. 3 ob.	115 dr.	A Thracian
1 dr. 3 ob.	144 dr.	A Scythian
1 dr. 3 ob.	121 dr.	An Illyrian
2 dr.	153 dr.	A man from Colchis
2 dr.	174 dr.	A Carian child[2]
1 dr.	72 dr.	A little Carian child[2]
[3 dr.] 1 ob.	301 dr.	A Syrian
[2 dr.]	151 dr.	A (man or woman) from Melitene[3]
1 dr.	85–89 dr.	A Lydian woman
	(figure incomplete)	

MEIGGS–LEWIS no 79, A 33–49

1 This man, one of the informers in the affair, is known from Andocides, *On the Mysteries* XV. He should not of course be confused with his namesake in no 73 who lives in another deme nor with his other namesake in no 70.
2 Others believe that the words *pais* (child) and *paidion* (little child) have here simply their frequent meaning of 'slave', which seems unlikely in view of all the other names which do not have the mention *pais*.
3 A region in Cappadocia; some have also suggested Malta or the island of Melite in Illyria.

76 **Material losses and flight of slaves after the occupation of Deceleia (summer 413)**

Alcibiades had advised the Spartiates to occupy Deceleia, a stronghold in the Parnes range north of Attica, and had foreseen among other consequences a fall in the revenues from Laurion (Thucydides VI, 91, 7). Laurion is a long way from Deceleia, but thanks to the insecurity engendered by the campaign, more than 20,000 artisans ran away, according to Thucydides – obviously only a rough estimate; it was not their business to start off a revolution, but they were fated to fall into the hands of the Boeotians who sold them for a good price[1]. There is no doubt that many of these 'artisans' must have been miners[2], but one cannot deduce from this figure of 20,000 any statistical data on the number of slave miners. Besides, it does not look as though the production of silver came to a sudden halt[3].

Indeed since Deceleia had been occupied, first by the whole Peloponnesian army which fortified it during this summer, then by garrisons from the cities relieving each other at stated intervals, it became a base of operations against the territory of Athens and was doing great mischief to the Athenians; in fact this occupation, by the destruction of property and loss of men which resulted from it, was one of the principal causes of their ruin. Previously the invasions were short, and did not prevent their enjoying the land during the rest of the time: the enemy was now permanently fixed in Attica; at one time it was an attack in force, at another it was the regular garrison overrunning the country and making forays for its subsistence, and the Lacedaimonian king, Agis, was in the field and diligently prosecuting the war; great mischief was therefore done to the Athenians. They were deprived of their whole country: more than 20,000 slaves had deserted, a great part of them artisans, and all their sheep and beasts of burden were lost; and as for the cavalry [. . .] their horses were either lamed by being constantly worked upon rocky ground, or wounded by the enemy.

THUCYDIDES VII, 27, 3–5
(trans. R. Crawley)

1 *Hellenica Oxyrhynchia* XII, 4.
2 The fact is vouched for by Xenophon, *Ways and Means* IV, 25.
3 Cf. S. Lauffer, *Die Bergwerkssklaven von Laureion* (Wiesbaden, 1955–6), pp. 140ff.

77   The revenue from one slave (415)

This is a good example of a short and seemingly straightforward passage, but which is in fact ambiguous. Diocleides has a slave who works at Laurion, and he rises at dawn to collect the payment (*apophora*) which the latter owes to him. But who is this slave? He may be an ordinary miner[1], but it has also been suggested that he was a slave overseer who supervised the work of other slaves[2].

> He[3] said he had a slave working at Laurion and he had to go and collect the payment (he owed to him). He got up early to start on his way but got the time wrong. It was full moon.
>
> ANDOCIDES, *On the Mysteries*, 38

1   See Cl. Mossé, *La fin de la démocratie athénienne* (1962), p. 91, n 2; P. Vidal-Naquet, in *Archives européenes de sociologie* 6 (1965), p. 134.
2   S. Lauffer, *Die Bergwerkssklaven von Laureion*, op. cit., pp. 107–8.
3   A certain Diocleides, an informer in the affair of the Hermocopids (those who had mutilated the statues of Hermes) in 415; cf. no 75.

78   Shepherds on the borders

In the Greek world of the classical and Hellenistic periods, it is rare for shepherds to be mentioned, except when their flocks are being kept away from cultivated lands, both sacred and profane, or when their testimony is invoked in the case of frontier disputes. It is most unusual to find an Athenian who died at the beginning of the fourth century and who had come from 'divine Lemnos', i.e. who was a former cleruch, describing himself as the friend of the flocks[1]. 'Those people live far from the city, on the pasture land, the moors and the woods which usually form the boundary of the territory of the city, isolated and silent' (Louis Robert). There is a sharp contrast with 'Homeric' times, so greatly has the citizen-farmer taken precedence of the shepherd. In a famous scene in Sophocles' *Oedipus Rex* (*c.* 420), Oedipus calls two shepherds to witness, one of them a salaried Corinthian, the other a slave of the king of Thebes, both of whom pastured their flocks on Mt Kithairon in the summer season[2].

Oedipus You there, old man, look at me straight and answer my questions. You were once in the service of Laios?

Herdsman I was a slave, not purchased, but reared in his house.

Oedipus What task were you employed in? What kind of life did you live?

Herdsman Most of my life I tended flocks.

Oedipus What regions did you mostly frequent?

Herdsman Sometimes it was Kithairon, sometimes the neighbouring country.

Oedipus (pointing to the Corinthian shepherd) And there, do you think that you saw this man?

Herdsman What was he doing there? What man are you referring to?

Oedipus This man here. Have you met him before?

Herdsman Not enough to enable me to speak at once from memory.

The Corinthian No wonder, master, but since he does not recognize me, I will revive his memory. For I know well that he remembers the time when we were neighbours in the region of Kithairon, he with two flocks and I with one; we did this three times for six months from the beginning of spring to the rise of Arcturus[3]. When winter came[4], we would drive back our flocks, I to my own fold and he to those of Laios. Is there any truth in what I say or not?

Herdsman You speak the truth, but it was a long time ago.

SOPHOCLES, *Oedipus Rex*, 1121–41

1 *IG* II², 7180; see L. Robert, 'Bergers grecs', *Hellenica* VII (Paris, 1949), pp. 152–60, to which add *Hellenica* X (1955), pp. 28–33 and *Antiquité Classique* 35 (1966), pp. 383–4. For some archaic bronze statuettes of shepherds, cf. M. Jost, *BCH* 99, 1 (1975), pp. 339–45.

2 See now the valuable study by Stella Georgoudi, 'Problèmes de transhumance dans la Grèce ancienne', *REG* 87. (1974), pp. 155–85 (pp. 167–9 on the passage in Sophocles).

3 The heliacal rising of Arcturus marked for the Greeks the beginning of autumn.

4 The winter months.

79   The navy is a profession

In the speech which he gives to Pericles in 431 to encourage the
Athenians to go to war, Thucydides emphasizes the notion –
which one meets frequently in Greek literature – that maritime
power, by contrast with landed power, presupposes a special
training which is linked to urban life[1].

> For our naval skill is of more use to us for service on land, than
> their military skill[2] for service at sea. Familiarity with the sea
> they will not find an easy acquisition. If you, who have been
> practising at it ever since the Persian Wars, have not yet
> brought it to perfection, is there a chance of anything consider-
> able being effected by an agricultural, unseafaring population,
> who will besides be prevented from practising by the constant
> presence of strong squadrons of observation from Athens?
> [. . .]
> It must be kept in mind that seamanship, as much as any-
> thing else, is a matter of professionalism (*techne*), and will not
> admit of being taken up occasionally as an occupation for
> times of leisure; on the contrary, it is so exacting as to leave
> leisure for nothing else.

THUCYDIDES I, 142, 5–9
(trans. R. Crawley)

1 For other aspects of Greek thought on maritime power see
   A. Momigliano, 'Sea Power in Greek Thought', *Classical
   Review* 58 (1944), pp. 1–7 = *Secondo Contributo alla storia
   degli studi classici* (Rome, 1960), pp. 57–68.
2 That of the Peloponnesians, especially the Spartans.

6 The Greek Cities and Economic Problems

80 The corn from the Black Sea

Evidence for the grain trade from the Black Sea is mainly Athenian in origin and dates mostly from the fourth century, but we learn casually from a digression in Herodotus that this trade was much older and concerned many cities other than Athens[1].

Xerxes was at Abydos[2] when he saw some corn ships, which were passing through the Hellespont from the Euxine on their way to Aegina and the Peloponnese. His attendants, hearing that they were the enemy's, were ready to capture them, and looked to see when Xerxes would give the signal. Xerxes asked whither the ships were bound. They answered: 'To your enemies, Master, with corn on board.' He rejoined: 'We too are bound thither, laden, among other things, with corn. What harm is it, if they carry our provisions for us?'

HERODOTUS VII, 147

1 Note, however, T.S. Noonan, 'The Grain Trade of the Northern Black Sea in Antiquity', *AJP* XCIV (1973), pp. 231–42, who doubts any regular trade in corn from the northern Black Sea to the Greek world before the late sixth century.

2 On the Asiatic side of the strait of the Dardanelles (Hellespont). Xerxes is on his way to Greece, at the beginning of the second Persian War (480).

81 Leukon, king of the Bosphorus, supplier of Athens in corn

A certain Leptines had secured the passing of a law in 356 which cancelled the privileges of exemption from taxes and liturgies which Athens granted to some of her citizens, and by assimilation to specially favoured foreigners, who were 'representatives' (*proxenoi*) and 'benefactors' (*euergetai*) of the Athenian people[1]. The descendants of Harmodios and Aristogeiton were the only ones to be exempted from this measure. The aims of the law were strictly internal and financial; but Demosthenes, speaking against the law in 355–354, points out that it could also be applied to Leukon, king of the Cimmerian Bosphorus[2] (the Crimea) and Athens' main supplier in corn. The argument was a clever one, for these very important people were above the arguments of rival politicians. Ten years after the law of Leptines, a superb inscription, which was found in Peiraieus, honours the sons of Leukon 'for undertaking before the Athenian people to look after the sending of corn as their father did' (Tod, *GHI* II, no 167). The movers of this decree are two personal rivals of Demosthenes[3].

You are of course aware that we consume more foreign corn than any people in the world. Now the corn which comes in from the Black Sea equals the whole quantity that comes in from other markets. And no wonder; not only because that district has an abundance of corn, but because Leukon, who rules there, has granted exemption from duty to those who export to Athens, and his heralds proclaim that merchants bound for our port shall load their ships first. Although he enjoys exemption for himself and his children only, he has given exemption to everyone of you. Now see what this amounts to. He levies a tax of one-thirtieth on those who export corn from his country. Now about 400,000 medimni of corn are imported from the Bosphorus[4], as one can see from the records of the commissioners of the corn trade (*sitophylakes*)[5]. Therefore, for the 300,000 medimni he gives us a rebate of 10,000, and for the 100,000 about 3,000. And so far is he from depriving out city of this gift, that when he opened a new place of trade (*emporion*) at Theodosia[6], which sailors say is in no way inferior to that at Bosphorus, he gave us exemption there too. I could recall many benefits which you have received from him or from his ancestors, but I will mention only one: two years ago, when there was a shortage of corn in the whole world, he not only sent you enough corn for your needs, but you were even left with a surplus worth 15 talents, the management of which was placed in the hands of Kallisthenes[7].

DEMOSTHENES, *Against Leptines*, 31–3

1 On the changing role of benefactors (*euergetai*) from classical to Hellenistic, then Roman, times, see now P. Veyne, *Le Pain et le cirque* (Paris, 1977). The evolution may be summarized as follows. Inscriptions of the fifth century and of most of the fourth century show the benefactor (*euergetes*) to be an outsider who is also usually granted the title of *proxenos*; he may be seen as an agent of the city, and is proud to serve it, even when he is a non-Greek ruler. In Hellenistic times the *euergetes-proxenos* has become a man on whom the city depends. Concurrently with this external evolution another one takes place internally in the city, whereby the wealthy citizen who undertakes 'liturgies' (see Chapter 6) becomes himself a *euergetes*. Veyne's book emphasizes the latter aspect at the expense of the former.

2 The kingdom of Bosphorus has a Greek capital (Pantikapaion = Kertch) and a barbarian hinterland; it is a good example of a 'prehellenistic' political structure.

3 See further J.B. Brashinsky, 'Epigraphical Evidence on Athens' Relations with North Pontic Greek States', *Acta of the Fifth International Congress of Greek and Latin Epigraphy, Cambridge 1967* (1971), pp. 119–23.

4 1 medimnus = 51.84 litres. These figures are probably exaggerated; cf. L. Gernet, 'L'approvisionnement d'Athènes en blé', *Mélanges d'histoire ancienne de la Faculté des Lettres de Paris* 25 (1909), pp. 301ff.

5 They were drawn by lot, five for Athens and five for Peiraieus, and supervised the selling of grain at a just price and at just weights (cf. below nos 89, 102).

6 See the map p. 62.

7 An orator and politician of the time.

82 Text of a law forbidding loans on ships commissioned to transport corn elsewhere than to Athens (*c.* 350)

Maritime loans based on a written contract are, as will be seen (cf. below no 121), one of the innovations of fourth-century Athens, but they must not serve ends other than those fixed by the city for trade, namely to ensure the supplying of the people;

hence the law forbidding loans on ships not bound for Athens. The fact that the law was necessitated probably proves that the rule was transgressed.

> ### The Law
> It shall be unlawful for any Athenian, or any of the metics residing in Athens, or any person under their control[1], to lend out money on a ship which is not commissioned to bring corn to Athens or any other goods mentioned above[2]. And if anyone lends out money contrary to this enactment, the prosecution will be introduced and the confiscation of the money carried out before the inspectors of the commercial port (*epimeletai emporiou*)[3] in the same way as is laid down for the ship and the corn[4]. There shall be no right of action for the money lent out to any other place than Athens, and no magistrate shall bring any suit thereupon to trial.
>
> [DEMOSTHENES], *Against Lakritos*, 51

1 Women, minors, slaves.
2 In a part of the law which has not been preserved. This is one of the several possible interpretations of this difficult passage.
3 Cf. nos 89 (end), 102.
4 i.e. according to the procedure laid down by the law forbidding the transport of corn elsewhere than to Athens.

83 The Peiraieus, an invention of Athens

For Isocrates who, in the *Panegyricus* of 380, takes up and develops for the benefit of Athens the old theme of the 'first inventor', the market of Peiraieus is itself a deliberate invention of the city for the good of mankind.

> As each people does not possess a country that is self-sufficing, but has sometimes less and sometimes more than it needs, and as there was much uncertainty as to where one should dispose of some goods and whence one should import others, once again Athens remedied these problems. For she set up Peiraieus as a market in the middle of Greece, where there is such an abundance of goods that things which one finds elsewhere only with difficulty and one at a time are all easy to procure here[1].
>
> ISOCRATES, *Panegyricus*, 42

1 See also [Xenophon], *Constitution of the Athenians* II, 7; Thucydides II, 38, 2; Hermippos, fr. 43 Kock.

84 For the importers of corn, against the retail dealers

Athens depended closely, for the supplying of a population which was enormous by Greek standards, on the import of foreign corn. The corn was imported by traders (*emporoi*) and sold by retail dealers (*sitopolai*); they were both metics, but their relations with the city did not have the same basis. The retail dealers were subjected to strict supervision and in particular to legislation which prohibited them from buying more than a limited quantity of corn at a time. Control over their activities was relatively easy. It was much less easy to control the importers, who were themselves dependent on sources of import which, at the time when Lysias was writing the speech *Against the Corn Dealers* (386)[1], were far from being all under the control of Athens. The amount of corn imported and its bulk price were therefore largely outside the control of Athens. Between the two groups of traders the speaker chooses, logically but cynically, to side with the importers[2].

You must be quite clear that it is impossible for you to acquit these men[3]: for if you spare them when they admit themselves that they combined against the merchants, you will be thought to be conspiring against the importers. Were they to follow another line of defence, no one could criticize you for acquitting them; it is up to you to decide which of the two sides you want to believe[4]. But how can you avoid appearing to behave in an outrageous way, if you let go scot-free men who admit they have broken the law? Remember, gentlemen of the jury, that in the past many have been accused of this offence and have denied the charge and produced witnesses, but you condemned them to death and placed more trust in the words of the accusers. Would it not be amazing that in judging the same offences you showed greater eagerness to punish those who denied the charge? Furthermore, gentlemen of the jury, I think it is clear to all that trials of this kind are in the highest degree a matter of concern to all the members of the city; they will enquire about your verdict, in the belief that if you condemn these men to death, the rest will henceforward be better behaved. But if you let them go unpunished, you will have voted to give them full licence to do whatever they wish. Gentlemen of the jury, one must punish these men not only for the past, but also to set an example for the future; for it is by doing so that they will become bearable, and only just. Bear in mind that many in this business have had to face capital charges; yet so great are the profits they make from it that they still prefer to risk death every day than to stop making unjust gains at your expense. They may implore and beseech you: this will not justify your feeling pity for them; you must rather pity those citizens who have died through their wickedness, and the merchants against whom they combined⁵. You will gratify the merchants and make them more zealous if you condemn these men. If not, what opinion do you think they will have when they learn that you have acquitted the retailers who admitted to having conspired against the importers?

I do not see that I need say any more. In other trials it is up to the accusers to tell you about the charges against the accused, but you all know about the wickedness of these men. If therefore you condemn them you will do justice and corn will be cheaper to buy; if not, it will be more expensive.

LYSIAS, *Against the Corn Dealers*, 17–22

1 The speech written by Lysias is delivered by a member of the Council, the accuser in the trial.
2 For a detailed discussion, cf. R. Seager, 'Lysias against the Corn-Dealers', *Historia* 15 (1966), pp. 172–84.
3 The retail dealers who are accused of having tried to push prices up by buying at once more corn than the permitted amount of 50 'measures' (it is not known what these 'measures' corresponded to). The retail dealers defended themselves by saying that they had been invited by Anytos, a commissioner of the corn trade (*sitophylax*, cf. nos 81, 89, 102), to agree among themselves to avoid a competition which would have resulted precisely in pushing prices up. The whole speech revolves around the ambiguity of a Greek verb which can mean at once *to buy in common, to buy in bulk,* and *to buy for hoarding.*
4 The tactics of the speaker consist in presenting condemnation as an obligation for the jurors: you do not have to choose between different arguments, but to apply a law which has

been openly violated.
5 The jurors are citizens and it is necessary to make them think
that the interest of the city is at stake, but the city depends on
the importers, hence the efforts of the speaker to associate the
two categories of interests.

85 Athens and strategic materials

The pamphlet of the 'Old Oligarch' (cf. above no 75) gives a good
account of the advantages derived by Athens from her naval
power. It will be borne in mind that the ships mentioned here are
warships.

Alone, the Athenians are capable of possessing the wealth of
Greeks and barbarians. For if a city is rich in timber for ship-
building, where will it export it, if it does not reach an understanding with the rulers of the sea? Again, if a city is rich in
iron, or copper, or linen[1], where will it export these, if it does
not reach an understanding with the rulers of the sea? Now
these are the materials from which I build my ships. From one
country comes timber, from another iron, from another
copper, from another linen, from yet another wax. In addition,
if our rivals wish to export these materials elsewhere than to
Athens, they will be prevented by us from doing so or will have
to avoid going by sea. And I, without doing anything, get all
the produce of the land via the sea. Yet no other city possesses
two of these at once; the same city does not have timber and
linen, but where linen is most abundant, the land is flat and
without woods. Copper and iron do not come from the same
city; in general, one does not find two or three products in a
single city, but one product here and another there.

    [XENOPHON], *Constitution of the Athenians* II, 11–12

1 For sails.

86 Athens restores her monopoly of Kean ruddle (before 350)

Keos, a tiny island in the Cyclades, was divided into four cities:
Ioulis, Karthaia, Koresos and Poessa. Keos was known in the
Greek world for the excellence of her ruddle (*miltos*), a product
which was useful notably for painting the hulls of triremes, but

which also had pharmaceutical uses. At an unknown date Athens had secured a monopoly of ruddle from Keos. Since the cities of the island had rejoined the Athenian alliance after various incidents in 362[1], it is tempting to date from about the same time the renewal of the Athenian monopoly. The stone from which the following passage is taken was found on the Acropolis; it comprised an Athenian decree (now lost), three similar decrees of Karthaia, Koresos and Ioulis, and a list of the Athenian ambassadors. Only the last inscriptions are preserved in part, though very unequally; the decree of Koresos, the least mutilated of the group, has alone been translated here. The decree, which is supposed to emanate from an independent city, follows faithfully the formulae of Athenian inscriptions and it is most likely that it was drawn up at Athens.

> Theogenes moved: be it resolved by the council [and the people of Koresos, concerning the request put by the Athenian] envoys, that the ex[port] of ruddle [to Athens should take place] as in the past. So that the decrees [formerly passed by the Athenians] and the Koresians about the ruddle should be enforced, let it be exported on the ship [designated by the Athenians and on] no other ship; and let the producers pay [to the ship-owners] a *naullos* (transport charge) of one obol per [talent][2]. If anyone exports on another ship [let him be liable to . . . ?]. And let this decree be inscribed on a stone stele and [placed in the sanctuary of] Apollo[3] and let the law be [enforced] as previously. [Let information] be lodged with the astynomoi[4], and let the astynomoi submit the matter to a law court [for adjudication within 30] days[5]; let whoever denounces (a fraud) or gives information [receive half? . . .]; if the informer is a slave, if he belongs to the exporters [let him be free and receive three-]quarters[6], and if he belongs to someone else, let him be free [and receive . . . ?]. Let there be transfer of law suits to Athens for whoever denounces (a fraud) or gives information[7]. If the Athenians [pass any other decrees] on the safeguard of the ruddle, let [the decrees] come into force from the moment of their arrival. Let the [producers] pay the tax of one-fiftieth to the collectors of the tax[8]. Let the Athenians[9] [be invited] to receive hospitality at the prytaneum tomorrow.
>
> TOD, *GHI* II, no 162, lines 9–24

1 See the inscription Tod, *GHI* II, no 142 (= H. Bengtson, *Die Staatsverträge des Altertums* II, no 289).

2 Whether this is a measure of weight or a monetary value is unknown, but the word is in any case restored in the text.

3 The Ioulis decree provides for the exhibition of the decree 'in the harbour'; this detail is to be explained precisely by the fact that Ioulis was the only 'urban' centre of Keos which was not on the coast. In these circumstances the decree must be displayed in the immediate vicinity of the place of shipment.

4 Doubtless the astynomoi of Koresos; it is only as a second instance that the trial will be conducted in Athens. In the preserved fragment of the Ioulis decree, a procedure for lodging information at Athens is provided for.

5 A particularly speedy procedure, similar to that which came to exist in Athens for commercial actions.

6 Of the value of the illegally exported cargo.

7 The transfer before another instance (which is not quite the same thing as what we call an appeal) is in theory reserved only for the plaintiff; see U.E. Paoli, *Mélanges F. de Visscher* IV (Brussels, 1950), pp. 325–37. Athens protects the interests of the informers by specifying that a decision by the tribunal in Koresos can be examined in second instance by an Athenian tribunal.

8 This probably does not refer to a local tax but to the tax paid at Peiraieus (cf. no 93).

9 The ambassadors who conveyed the instructions of Athens to Keos.

87 The financial resources of Athens in 431

The treasure of Athens (which had recently been concentrated on the Acropolis) is the expressive and practical manifestation of the power of the city. One should compare the figures given here[1] with the 'pottering' which characterizes the Spartan war effort as revealed by the next passage. This wealth does not rest only on the contributions of the 'allies' but on the gold of the statues and other offerings, which can be put to use. At this time Athens does not rely, for the financing of her war and her projects, on direct taxation in the form of the *eisphora*. The principle of the *eisphora* exists already and seems to be attested in the Kallias decree (Meiggs–Lewis no 58) in 433, and possibly even earlier, though the size of the sums raised is not known, but it was only in 428 that an *eisphora* was raised to finance the Peloponnesian War (Thucydides III, 19, 1). One talent, it will be recalled, represents about 6,000 days' work.

Here they had no reason to despond[2]. Apart from other sources of income, an average revenue of 600 talents was drawn from the tribute of the allies; and there were still 6,000 talents of coined silver in the Acropolis, out of 9,700 that had once been taken there, from which the money had been taken for the Propylaia of the Acropolis, the other public buildings and the Potidaea expedition[3]. This did not include the uncoined gold and silver in private and public offerings, the sacred vessels for the processions and competitions, the spoils taken from the Persians, and similar resources to the amount of 500 talents[4]. To this he added the treasures of the other temples; these were by no means inconsiderable and might fairly be used. Indeed, if they were absolutely driven to it, they might even take the gold ornaments of Athena herself[5]; for the statue contained 40 talents of pure gold[6] and it was all removable. This might be used for self-preservation, but would have to be completely restored subsequently.

THUCYDIDES II, 13, 3–5
(trans. R. Crawley)

1 They have been much discussed; see Gomme's commentary vol. II, pp. 26–33; vol. III, p. 723 (Addenda) and H.T. Wade-Gery and B.D. Meritt, 'Athenian Resources in 449 and 431', *Hesperia* 26 (1957), pp. 163–97.
2 Pericles is speaking to the Athenians.
3 The siege of Potidaea in 432, one of the events which were the prelude to the Peloponnesian War.
4 It will be noted that these exceptional resources add up to a figure which is well below that of the coined treasure proper, and this again is peculiar to Athens.
5 The chryselephantine statue of Pheidias.
6 To get the monetary value which corresponds to this weight the figure must be multiplied by about 13.

88 Individual and collective contributions to the Spartan war effort (426 or 396–395)

This stone, found near Sparta, is seriously mutilated. The readings, restorations and hence the translation are highly conjectural, but the weakness of Sparta's monetary resources and the way in which she is compelled to resort to every expedient are readily apparent. It should be added that few texts were inscribed in Sparta; the exceptional character of this document makes it all the more significant.

Front

[So-and-so] or [the citizens of?] [has] or [have] given to the Lacedaimonians [so many] darics. [So-and-so] or [the citizens of?] [has] or [have] given to the Lacedaimonians [for the war] nine minae and ten staters². [So-and-so] son of Lykeidas, from Olenos (?)³, [has given to the Lac]edaimonians for the war 32 minae of [silver, being the pay for the rowers of so many] triremes. The friends of the [Lacedaimonians] at Chios [have given so many] Aeginetan staters. [The citizens of?] [have given] to the Lacedaimonians for the [war] 4,000 [medimni]⁴ and another 4,000 [medimni] and [so many] talents⁵ of grapes. [So-and-so] son of [so-and-so] has given to [the Lacedaimonians] much [. . .], 800 darics and three talents of [silver]⁶. [The citizens of . . .] have given for the war one talent and 30 minae [of silver], and 3,000 medimni [of . . .] and [also] [ ]ty medimni and 60 [minae] of silver. The Ephesians [have given] to the Lacedaimonians [for] the war 1,000 darics.

Side

The Melians⁷ have given to the Lacedaimonians 20 minae of silver. Molon (?) of Locri has given to the Lacedaimonians one talent (or so many talents?) of silver. The Melians have given to the Lacedaimonians . . .

MEIGGS–LEWIS no 67

1 R. Meiggs argues for the first date and D.M. Lewis for the second in their joint work, *A Selection of Greek Historical Inscriptions*, p. 184.
2 The monetary standard is not specified, but in any case this is a fairly modest sum.
3 In Achaea.

4   A medimnus in Sparta = 74 litres.

5   There is a switch from a measure of capacity to one of weight.

6   A very large 'individual' contribution which can only come from a wealthy inhabitant of a city in Asia Minor or an official or dynast in the Persian Empire.

7   The inhabitants of Melos in the Cyclades, an island captured by the Athenians in 416.

89   Athenian magistrates entrusted with the supervision of economic activity

Between the enumeration of the officials concerned with street cleaning (in particular those who pick up the bodies of people who die in the street) and on the other hand the designation of magistrates entrusted with police duties and the execution of capital sentences, Aristotle enumerates the magistrates who were concerned with the smooth functioning of trade, not of course for the benefit of traders but for that of the citizen consumers. An unusual fact[1], but one which is easily explained, is that some of these magistrates are designated not for Athens but for Peiraieus.

They appoint by lot ten inspectors of the markets (*agoranomoi*), five for Peiraieus and five for the city. Their duty, as prescribed by law, is to make sure that all goods for sale are pure and unadulterated. They also appoint by lot ten inspectors of measures (*metronomoi*), five for the city and five for Peiraieus. They inspect all weights and measures to make sure that sellers use just ones. There used to be ten commissioners of the corn trade (*sitophylakes*)[2], appointed by lot, five for Peiraieus and five for the city, but now there are 20 for the city and 15 for Peiraieus. Their task is first to ensure that the unground corn is sold in the market at a just price, and second that the millers sell barley meal at a price related to that of barley and bakers sell the loaves at a price related to that of wheat and of a weight determined by them; for the law instructs them to fix the weight. They also appoint by lot ten inspectors of the commercial port (*epimeletai emporiou*), whose function it is to supervise the markets (*emporia*) and to compel the merchants to bring to the city two-thirds of the corn which is imported by sea to the corn market.

ARISTOTLE, *Constitution of Athens* LI

1 Aristotle gives only one other example (LIV, 8): 'A demarch of Peiraieus, whose function is to celebrate the Dionysia there, is drawn by lot according to the general procedure.'

2 For these and the *epimeletai emporiou* below see also nos 81, 82, 102.

90 An Athenian policy of large-scale public works?

The funeral oration which Thucydides attributes to Pericles (II, 35-43) is remarkably discreet on questions which we describe as 'social and economic'. The speaker merely points out that poverty is no bar to political activity, that Athens receives 'all the produce of the earth' (but no reference is made to traders), and – an even more significant detail – that wealth is not at Athens a pretext for ostentation but for action. These fairly simple maxims have become in the terminology of some modern historians (especially G. Glotz) a policy of 'state socialism'. But already in the second century AD Plutarch visualized the great public works through which Athens in the fifth century proclaimed her own glory in the guise of the generosities which the benefactors (*euergetai*) of the cities of the Hellenistic and Roman world, including the emperor himself, showered on their native cities whether large or small (*panem et circenses*)[1].

But what provided Athens with the greatest delight and adorned the city most of all, what provoked the greatest amazement among other men, and what is nowadays the sole proof Greece has that her traditional power and ancient prosperity are not mere stories, are the monuments built by Pericles. And yet of all the political acts of Pericles these are the ones that were most attacked and slandered by his enemies in the assembly. They cried out that the people was disgracing itself and acquired a bad reputation by removing the common funds of the Greeks from Delos to Athens[2], and that the most honourable excuse that could be offered to critics, namely that fear of the barbarian had caused them to remove the treasury from there to the safety of Athens, had been invalidated by Pericles. 'Greece is outraged', they cried, 'and feels a victim of blatant tyranny when she sees the contributions she is forced to make for the war being used by us to gild and beautify the city like a vain woman, dressing her up with precious stones and statues and 1,000-talent temples.' Pericles' answer to this was to explain to the people that they did not owe any accounts to their allies, as they fought the wars on their behalf and kept the barbarians at a distance. 'They do not provide any cavalry, ships, or hoplites', he said, 'but only money, and money belongs not to those who give it but to those who receive it, so long as they furnish in return what they get the money for. Now that the city is well equipped with all its needs for war, she must devote her resources to works which, once completed, will win her everlasting fame, and which will provide her with a ready source of prosperity during their construction. Enterprises and needs of every kind will be created, which will stimulate every craft and keep occupied all available hands, and so provide pay to almost the whole of the city, who will at once embellish and maintain herself from her own resources.'

Those who were of the right age and were strong could earn generous pay from the public funds for military service[3], but as regards the crowd of artisans who were not enrolled in the military forces[4], he did not want them to be without share in the city's profits but neither would he let them partake in them while remaining idle and unemployed. So he put forward before the people ambitious building projects and plans for constructions which would provide work for many different crafts. In this way the population which stayed at home would have cause to benefit from and have a share in public funds no less than those who manned the ships, carried out garrison duties or went on campaigns.

The available materials included stone, bronze, ivory, gold, ebony and cypress wood, while the trades needed to work and fashion these included carpenters, modellers, coppersmiths, stoneworkers, workers in gold and ivory[5], painters, embroiderers and engravers; for the transport and supply of all the materials there were traders, sailors and pilots on sea, and on land wagon-makers, keepers of draught animals, drivers, rope-makers[6], weavers, leather-workers, road-builders and miners. Each particular craft, like a general at the head of a private army, had under its command the crowd of thetes and ordinary workers[7] who were subordinated to it like an instrument or a body. In this way the various needs divided and distributed the city's prosperity among men of almost every age and condition.

PLUTARCH, *Pericles* XII

1 On the changing role of benefactors (*euergetai*) from classical to Hellenistic, then Roman, times, see now P. Veyne, *Le Pain et le cirque* (Paris, 1977). The evolution may be summarized as follows. Inscriptions of the fifth century and of most of the fourth century show the benefactor (*euergetes*) to be an outsider who is also usually granted the title of *proxenos*; he may be seen as an agent of the city, and is proud to serve it, even when he is a non-Greek ruler. In Hellenistic times the *euergetes-proxenos* has become a man on whom the city depends. Concurrently with this external evolution another one takes place internally in the city, whereby the wealthy citizen who undertakes 'liturgies' (see Chapter 6) becomes himself a *euergetes*. Veyne's book emphasizes the latter aspect at the expense of the former.

2 Probably in 454.

3 A highly questionable statement; by far the highest rate of pay known to us is that given to the Athenians who besieged Potidaea in 432–428, which was two drachmae a day; it was paid for the complete maintenance of a hoplite and of his camp follower (Thucydides III, 17). This is anyway a special case and other figures vary between one-quarter and one-half of it. See generally W.K. Pritchett, *The Greek State at War*, Part I (Berkeley and Los Angeles, 1971), pp. 3–24.

4 A flagrant error: the common people was enrolled in the fleet.

5 Literally 'dyers in gold, softeners of ivory'.

6 The question of 'transport' no longer applies here and the enumeration becomes almost lyrical in character.

7 Literally privates.

91 Fiscal and monetary stratagems
The second part of Book II of the *Economics* of Ps.-Aristotle is a repertory of fiscal and monetary stratagems[1]. Some concern cities (like Byzantium here) which are almost permanently in financial difficulties (the case of Athens as described in no 87 is altogether exceptional), others men entrusted with a command, as here the Athenian general Timotheus (on whom cf. also no 124). The stratagems attributed to the Byzantines cannot be dated.

A Byzantium
The people of Byzantium being in need of money sold the

sacred enclosures belonging to the state[2]. The productive ones they sold for a limited period of time, the unproductive ones in perpetuity. They did the same with lands belonging to religious associations (*thiasoi*) and to phratries[3] and all those situated on private estates; for the owners of the remaining part of these estates would pay high prices for them. They sold to members of religious associations other lands belonging to the state, which were near the gymnasium, the *agora* or the harbour. They also sold places where markets were held and traders operated, the sea fisheries, the traffic in salt, places reserved to jugglers, soothsayers, drug peddlers and other such professions, and imposed on them a tax amounting to one-third of their earnings. They sold to a single bank the right to change money, and no one else had the right to buy or sell money to or from anyone else under penalty of confiscation[4]. There was a law among them which restricted citizen rights to those descended from both citizen parents[5], but such was their need of money that they decreed that anyone born of one citizen parent could become a citizen on paying a fee of 30 minae[6].

On one occasion being short of food supplies as well as funds, they called in to harbour all the ships from the Black Sea[7]. After a while, when the traders were becoming impatient, they undertook to pay them a supplement of 10 per cent, but also ordered the purchasers to pay this supplement of 10 per cent in addition to the price[8].

Some metics had lent money on the security of landed property, although they did not have the right to hold such property (*enktesis*); they decreed that whoever paid (to the treasury) a sum of money equivalent to one-third of the loan would acquire a title to the property[9].

[ARISTOTLE], *Oeconomica* II, 2, 3

B The Athenian general Timotheus

Timotheus of Athens, while at war against the Olynthians[10] and being short of silver, struck a bronze coinage[11] which he distributed to his soldiers. When they protested, he told them that traders and retailers would be selling to them all their goods in the usual way. He also instructed the traders to use any bronze coinage they received to purchase the commodities of the country which were for sale as well as anything which was brought in from booty. Should there be any bronze coins left to them, they should bring it to him and they would get silver in exchange[12].

While he was waging war in the neighbourhood of Corcyra[13] and was short of funds, his soldiers asked him for their pay[14], became mutinous and talked of going over to the enemy side. He called together an assembly and said that the bad weather was preventing the arrival of the silver he was expecting, but that he had such an abundance of resources in his possession that he would give them as a free gift the three months' food rations which he had advanced to them[15]. Imagining that Timotheus would not have given away so much money to them had he not been really expecting the silver to come, the soldiers kept quiet about their pay and gave him time to settle matters as he wished.

During the siege of Samos[16] he would sell to the Samians their crops and what was still left on their fields, and so had plenty of money for his soldiers' pay. When there was a shortage of provisions in the camp[17] because of the coming of visitors[18], he prohibited the retailing of ground corn; corn was not to be sold in amounts of less than a *medimnus* nor liquids in amounts of less than a *metretes*[19]. Accordingly the commanders of divisions and companies bought up the food in bulk and redistributed it to the soldiers, while visitors had to bring their own provisions, and sold anything that was left over on their departure. In this way the soldiers had an abundance of provisions[20].

[ARISTOTLE], *Oeconomica* II, 2, 23

1 The word stratagem is used in its fullest sense to refer to a type of behaviour modelled on the ruses of war.
2 i.e. lands belonging to the sanctuary of a state cult.
3 *Thiasoi* were religious associations maintained from the revenue of landed property. Phratries grouped together citizens around the cult of a 'common ancestor'.
4 Cf. below no 103 (the monetary law from Olbia).
5 A law identical with the famous one of Pericles at Athens (451–450).
6 The sale of citizenship was to become a characteristic phenomenon of the Hellenistic age; see L. Robert in *Hellenica* I (1940), pp. 37–42.

7 Loaded with corn from Crimea and the Ukrainian coast in particular.

8 The passage is difficult to interpret; we understand it thus: to get the traders, who were bound for places other than Byzantium, to sell their corn to the people of Byzantium, the latter guarantees them a supplementary profit (literally an interest) of 10 per cent in relation to the normal sale price of corn, but as the city has no money, it recovers the amount of this supplement in the form of a tax on the purchases of corn. See also G.E.M. de Ste Croix, *Origins of the Peloponnesian War*, op. cit., pp. 47, 314.

9 To understand this difficult passage one must recall that in ancient Greece, in case of failure to refund a loan on the security of real property, the security becomes the property of the creditors without any sale taking place. In the case of a loan on the security of land from a metic this procedure does not in theory apply since the metic (except in exceptional cases where *enktesis* is granted to him) cannot own land. In other words the people of Byzantium are offering to metics in this position the right of *enktesis* in exchange for a tax equivalent to one-third of the sum lent.

10 In 364. A similar anecdote is told by Polyaenus, *Stratagems* X, 1.

11 Small bronze 'owls' have in fact been found near Olynthus; this series is not represented at Athens and has been very plausibly attributed of Timotheus; cf. E.S.G. Robinson and M.J. Price, 'An Emergency Coinage at Timotheos', *Numismatic Chronicle* 1967, pp. 1–6.

12 In other words Timotheus imposes the use of his emergency coinage under a guarantee of repayment.

13 In 375.

14 These are probably mercenaries.

15 Soldiers' pay included, in theory, on the one hand the pay proper and on the other the maintenance indemnity, all of which was often paid in a lump sum.

16 In 366–365.

17 This is hardly surprising after the measures mentioned in the previous paragraph.

18 e.g. courtesans, traders of various kinds, possibly members of the soldiers' families.

19 One *metretes* = a little. under 39 litres; one *medimnus* = a

little under 52 litres.
20 The same episode in Polyaenus, *Stratagems* III, 10, 10.

92 Indirect taxes at Cyzicus (sixth century)

One of the most ancient documents we possess on the practice of indirect taxes in the cities is an inscription from Cyzicus, a very large city on the south coast of the Propontis (sea of Marmara) which was famous for its tunny fisheries and its electrum coinage[1]. The inscription is a decree granting exemption (*ateleia*) from certain indirect taxes to the children and descendants of two citizens who probably died for their native land[2]. The passage unfortunately gives only the list of the taxes from which the beneficiaries are not exempted.

Side B[3]
In the (Prytany)[4] of Maiandrios
The city has given to the (son) of Medikes and to the sons of Aisepos and to their descendents exemption from taxes and public maintenance in the prytaneum[5], with the exception of the *nautos*[6], the tax paid for the use of public weights and measures, the tax on horses, the tax of one-quarter[7], and the tax on slaves; they shall be exempted from all others; and about these exemptions the people swore an oath over the sacrificed victims[8]. The city gave this stele to Manes son of Medikes.

DITTENBERGER, *Sylloge*[3], no 4

1 See no 103.
2 The inscription was engraved for the first time in the sixth century and reinscribed in the first century BC, either for 'archaeological' reasons, or more likely because the descendants of the original beneficiaries were still alive and were anxious not to let their privilege lapse.
3 Side A, all that survives of the sixth-century document, gives the text of the last line of Side B.
4 The eponymous magistracy of Cyzicus.
5 The highest honour which a city can confer is the privilege which Socrates claims from his judges after his condemnation.
6 An unknown tax. The word may have been incorrectly copied by the first-century engraver; it has been compared with a tax

called *naussos* at Cos, the nature of which is unknown; one
can also think of the *naulon*, a ferry or freight tax.

7 Possibly a tax on production or more likely a tax on certain
consumer goods.

8 A characteristic rite of the sacrifice which accompanies an
oath.

93   Manipulations on the tax of one-fiftieth at Peiraieus (399)

Is it possible to calculate the volume of traffic, both imports and
exports, handled by Peiraieus at the beginning of the fourth
century? On the surface nothing seems simpler: the toll levied
on entering and leaving the harbour was at a flat rate of 2 per cent
ad valorem, and Andocides gives the prices paid by the contractors of the tax: 30 talents, then 36, then the profits realized by
them: six talents, then a profit which is not specified but which
must have been substantial. All this produces an approximate
figure of 2,000 talents, which is about 1,200,000 days' work, a
relatively high figure, but one which can of course hardly be
compared to the traffic of any large modern harbour. Against
these calculations it has been pointed out that we know little
about the functioning of tax farming[1]. This seems, however,
relatively simple, but in any case the revenue which Athens as a
city, and even the Athenians as individuals, derived from the
harbour cannot be compared with the profits drawn from the
empire in the days of its existence. A toll raised on entering and
leaving the harbour cannot of course favour any kind of commercial imperialism.

Agyrrhios[2], that honest man you know well, had been for two
years the chief contractor of the tax of one-fiftieth. He had
farmed it for 30 talents and had as his associates all those men
who meet under the white poplar[3]. You know the kind of
people they are. Why did they meet there? I believe they had
two aims in mind, to get paid for not raising the bidding, and
to have a share in taxes bought cheap. Having made a profit
of six talents and seeing what a profitable business they were
on to, they formed a syndicate, bought off rivals by giving
them a share in the profits and again offered 30 talents for the
taxes. As no one was putting in a rival bid I came forward
before the council and topped their offer, and purchased the

rights for 36 talents. Having thus ousted those men and provided you with sureties, I collected the money and paid it back to the city, without making any loss – my associates and I even made a small profit. Thus thanks to me these men were prevented from sharing out among themselves six talents of your own money.

ANDOCIDES, *On the Mysteries*, 133–4

1 J. Hasebroek, *Trade and Politics in Ancient Greece* (London, 1933), p. 80.
2 An Athenian democrat known only for having created and increased the indemnity paid to members of the *Ecclesia* at the beginning of the fourth century and for (allegedly) having re-established the theoric fund (cf. nos 111, 115) in 395–394.
3 A place name (?), otherwise unknown.

94 The mines of Thasos in the fifth century

The description given by Herodotus of the resources of Thasos recalls the case of Athens: the revenues from the mines enable Thasos to build, before the Persian Wars, warships and fortifications. They also enable her to strike a coinage which was particularly abundant at the end of the sixth century and at the beginning of the fifth. The figures given by Herodotus include both the mining revenues and all the income from the 'peraea', that is to say the zone on the mainland occupied by the Thasians in Thrace. This revenue of 200 talents may be compared with the sum spent by the Thasians when they were obliged to entertain Xerxes and his army: 400 talents (Herodotus VII, 118).

The Thasians [. . .], who enjoyed a very large income, used their wealth to build ships of war, and to surround their city with a stronger wall. Their revenue was derived partly from their possessions on the mainland, partly from their own mines. Among the former the gold mines at *Skapte Hyle*[1] produced an average yield of 80 talents, while the mines of Thasos produced less, but enough yet to enable the Thasians, besides being entirely free from tax on landed produce, to have an income from their mainland possessions and from their mines, in common years of 200, and in the best years of 300 talents. I myself have seen the mines in question: by far the most remarkable of them are those which the Phoenicians discovered at the time when they went with Thasos and colonized the island. [. . .] These Phoenician workings are in Thasos itself, between places known as Coinyra and Ainyra, over against Samothrace[2]: a huge mountain has been turned upside down in the search for ores.

HERODOTUS VI, 46–7

1 i.e. the 'dug-up forest', on the Thracian coast.
2 On these mines, which have been discovered, cf. École française d'Athènes, *Guide de Thasos* (Paris, 1968), p. 3.

95 The silver mines of Laurion: the leases of 367–366

The mines of silver-bearing lead at Laurion, at the southern end of Attica, were exploited since the Bronze Age[1]. The role they played in the fifth century in the expansion of Athens appears to be a fundamental one, but if the material organization of production and the condition of the slave miners there are gradually becoming better known thanks to archaeology[2], the scanty allusions in literary sources of the fifth century do not give any information on how the mines were leased, on the role of the city, on the relative importance of mining concessions[3], and on the evolution of an industry which enabled Athens to strike her famous 'owls'. It is mainly for the fourth century that there is evidence in any detail. Aristotle in the *Constitution of Athens* (XLVII, 2) specifies that the ten Sellers (*poletai*) of the city, who carry out public auctions, put up for sale the exploitation of the mines and ratify the concessions granted by the Council, which are of two kinds: for three years in the case of mines already under exploitation, and for seven (?) years in the case of mines already leased[4].

Several dozen inscriptions which reproduce the acts of the *poletai*[5] have been found in the *agora* in Athens. These documents enable one to form a picture of an industry which was never unified in the form of a large modern enterprise and where lessees working on a small scale existed side by side with others working on a large scale. Indeed mining was carried out 'as an activity sometimes on a large scale and very profitable, sometimes on a small scale and risky, at all times amateurish, at one period actively pursued, at another neglected'[6].

The passage translated below includes the portion which concerns mines in the only inscription which has been found intact, the list of 367–366. It was not the first register to have been set up since reference is made to a pre-existing stele, but it is the oldest one to have come down to us, and the institution certainly cannot have been very ancient since one finds in subsequent documents a series of formulae in administrative style which do not exist in this document.

Mining concessions are given out at each prytany (the sixth, eighth and tenth are not represented in this particular document). The leases bear the following indications: name of the mine, site determined by the adjoining lands and the name of their owners, name of the lessee, price of the concession. The same prices are repeated too often for one to be able to talk of a real market, while mines must have had very diverse characteristics. The considerable number of new concessions leased at a uniform price of 20 drachmae will be noted; the price rose to 150 drachmae at the end of the century. All the lessees and, in this document, all the owners are citizens. The first rule apparently knows of no exception in those documents that have been published so far. Other leases seem to indicate that metics from the mining island of Siphnos (cf. no 20A) had been granted the right of *enktesis ges* and owned land in the mining region (Margaret Crosby in *Hesperia* 19 (1950), pp. 205–65). The only document where a Siphnian appears as a lessee (*Hesperia* 19 (1950), no 5, p. 212) is too mutilated for any reliance to be placed on it.

Words enclosed in parentheses are found in the text only in elliptical form.

Poletai (sellers) in the archonship of Polyzelos.

Polyeuktos of the deme of Lamptrai, Deinias of the deme of Erchia, Theaios of the deme of Paiania, Theotimos of the deme of Phrearrhoi, Aristogenes of the deme of Iphistiadai, Glaukos of the deme of Lakiadai, Kephisokles of the deme of Peiraieus, Nikokles of the deme of Anaphlystos[7], with as secretary Exekestos of the deme of Kothokidai, sold the following having received them from the Eleven[8], Phaiax from the deme of Aphidna and his colleagues in office. [. . .]

In the first prytany of the tribe Hippothontis (the following) mines were leased: Dexiakon[9] in the Glen at the Look-Out[10], of which the boundaries are on all sides (the property of)

Nikias of the deme of Kydantidai[11], lessee Kallias of the deme of Sphettos: 20 drachmae. Diakon at Laurion[12], of which the boundaries are to the east the lands of Exopios, to the west the mountain, lessee Epiteles of the deme of Kerameis: 20 drachmae. At Sounion in the (lands) of the sons of Charmylos[13], of which the boundaries are, to the north (the property of) Kleokritos of the deme of Aigilia, to the south (the property of) Leukios of the deme of Sounion, lessee Pheidippos of the deme of Pithos: 20 drachmae. Poseidoniakon in the Glen, one of those inscribed on the stele[14] in the (lands) of Alypetos, of which the boundaries are the (property) of Kallias of the deme of Sphettos and Diokles of the deme of Pithos, lessee Thrasylochos of the deme of Anagyrous: 1,550 drachmae[15]. Hagnosiakon, one of those inscribed on the stele, lessee Telesarchos of the deme of Aixone: 1,550 drachmae. Artemisiakon, one of those inscribed on the stele, lessee Thrasylochos of the deme of Anagyrous: 150 drachmae.

In the second prytany of the tribe Antiochis, at Laurion the same (Artemisiakon) and the cuttings[16], of which the boundaries are, to the north (the property of) Diopeithes of the deme of Euonymon and the furnace[17] of Demostratos of the deme of Kytheros, to the south the workshop of Diopeithes, the carriage road and the ravine of the men of Thorikos, lessee Kephisodotos of the deme of Aithalidai: 20 drachmae. Demetriakon in the (lands) of Timesios, in the Glen, of which the boundaries are (the property of) Nikias of the deme of Kydantidai, to the south (the property of) Diokles of the deme of Pithos, lessee Philinos of the deme of Sounion: 20 drachmae. At Maroneia, Hermaikon, of which the boundaries are (the property of) Diophanes of the deme of Sounion, lessee Philinos of the deme of Sounion: 20 drachmae.

In the third prytany of the tribe Oineis, at Laurion, Theognideion, (one of these inscribed) on the stele, of which the boundaries are the field of Exopios, lessee Kallias of the deme of Lamptrai: 50 drachmae.

In the fourth prytany of the tribe Kekropis, at Sounion, in the Glen[18], Pyrrhieion, of which the boundaries are, to the east (the property of) Kallias of the deme of Alopeke, to the west (the property of) Nikias of the deme of Kydantidai, lessee Kallias of the deme of Sphettos: 20 drachmae. At Thorikos, Archegeteion in the (lands) of Demophilos, of which the boundaries to the north and south are (the property of) Demophilos, lessee Kephisophon of the deme of Sybridai: 20 drachmae. In the Glen, in the lands of the wife of Charmylos[19], of which the boundaries are the field of the wife of Alypetos, to the north (the property of) Teleson of the deme of Sounion, to the east the field of Teleson of the deme of Sounion, to the west (the property of) Epikrates of the deme of Pallene[20], lessee Epikles of the deme of Sphettos: 20 drachmae.

In the fifth prytany of the tribe Aigeis, Archegeteion and the cuttings, which do not have a stele[21], at Besa in the (lands) of Kephisodotos and Kallias, of which the boundaries are, to the east (the property) of Kallias of the deme of Lamptrai, a tower[22] and a house, to the north the workshop of Kephisodotos, to the south the Archegeteion[23], lessee Kephisodotos of the deme of Aithalidai[24]: 20 drachmae.

In the seventh prytany of the tribe Leontis, at Sounion, at Thrasymos, Kerameikon, of which the boundaries are (the property of) Diopeithes of the deme of Euonymon, lessee Aleximachos of the deme of Pelekes: 20 drachmae. At Sounion, in the Glen, in the (lands) of the sons of Charmylos, of which the boundaries are, to the north (the property of) Pyrrhakos of the deme of Aigilia, to the south (the property of) Leukios of the deme of Sounion, lessee Pheidippos of the deme of Pithos: 20 drachmae.

In the ninth prytany of the tribe Erechtheis, at Sounion, one of those inscribed on the stele: Leukippeion at Besa, lessee Chairedemos of the deme of Hagnous: 150 drachmae.

Stele of pentelic marble found in the Agora in
Athens; published by Margaret Crosby, in
Hesperia 10 (1941), pp. 14–27

1 *BCH* 91 (1967), p. 628; see also, on the Belgian excavations which have established this fact, the collective volume *Thorikos 1964* (Brussels, 1967).

2 Thus the Belgian excavations have brought to light a washing place for the silver ore, together with the workshop and quarters of the slaves. On these see the somewhat idyllic book by S. Lauffer, *Die Bergwerkssklaven von Laureion* (Wiesbaden, 1955, 1956 and 1975, 2nd edition). For a full bibliography on Laurion see R. J. Hopper, 'The Laurion Mines: a Reconsidera-

tion', *BSA* 63 (1968), pp. 293–326 and his earlier study, ibid., 48 (1953), pp. 200–54.

3 Besides the passage in Herodotus quoted above (no 20), there is also the allusion in Aeschylus to the 'spring of silver', a treasure 'which the earth preserves for them' and which makes the fortune of the Athenians (*Persians*, 238); Thucydides VI, 91, 7 (the interest of the Peloponnesians in depriving the Athenians of their mines) and the jokes of Aristophanes (*Knights*, 362; *Birds*, 593, 1106) which show that the mines were a source of wealth both for individuals and for the state.

4 The papyrus is illegible here and the preserved traces have been the subject of heated debate (cf. M. Chambers, *TAPA* 96 (1965), pp. 31ff.). The figure seven is deduced from epigraphic evidence.

5 Thirty-eight of these documents are restored and provided with a commentary by M. Crosby, 'The Leases of the Laureion Mines', *Hesperia* 19 (1950), pp. 189–312. The dates range from 367 to the very end of the century or the beginning of the next one.

6 R.J. Hopper, art. cit., p. 301.

7 The *poletai* are only eight here, belonging to eight of the ten tribes.

8 The Eleven are the executors of judicial decisions and they hand over to the *poletai* property confiscated by the city (Aristotle, *Constitution of Athens* LII, 1).

9 The mines are named after a god or hero, here Dexios.

10 *Nape:* the Glen; *Skopia:* the Look-Out; these places have not been identified.

11 A grandson of the Athenian general Nicias, whose wealth was based to a great extent on the leasing of slaves for the mines (Xenophon, *Ways and Means* IV, cf. no 96). Generally speaking, both owners and lessees belong to wealthy families, all of them citizen families, whose members held at least the trierarchy (see M. Crosby in *Hesperia* 10 (1941), pp. 26–7 and for a general prosopography R.J. Hopper, *BSA* 48 (1953), pp. 242–5).

12 This village did not become a deme at the time of Cleisthenes' reform, as for example Sounion did.

13 This inscription enables one to distinguish the ownership of the land which is private property and that of the subsoil

which belongs to the city, but it is not known how the surface installations were marked out for the concessions.

14 A mine clearly already under exploitation and which figured on the stele of the previous year.

15 That together with the following mine is by far the highest sum paid in this document. Demosthenes in the speech *Against Pantainetos*, 22, mentions a mine 'bought' for 9,000 drachmae. The inscriptions do not specify whether payments are made for three years, for one year, or for a prytany (as believed by Hopper, art. cit., n 11, p. 239). The payments of 20 drachmae certainly correspond to new mines. Thrasylochos of Anagyrous is himself the member of an extremely wealthy family and the brother of Meidias who was attacked by Demosthenes as one of the wealthiest men of his time. Here he is the lessee of two mines.

16 It is not known what exactly is meant by the word *katatome* used here; possibly additional shafts of which it is specified that they are included with the mines (M. Crosby, *Hesperia* 19 (1950), p. 199).

17 Certainly a foundry.

18 This mention does not enable one to identify the Glen (*Nape*) as being in the deme of Sounion. As may be seen from the mention of the last mine leased, a mine said to be 'at Sounion' is in fact in the deme of Besa. Sounion was perhaps here the place where the mines were registered.

19 An unknown person, but whose children, as has been seen, owned land in the region. See also below.

20 A man of the same name was accused about 330 of having illegally extended his mine (Hypereides, *For Euxenippos*, 35). This refers to the same man, or his grandson.

21 M. Crosby translates 'having no boundary stone', but more likely the drafter of the inscription simply noted that this concession did not figure on the stele of the previous year, which is confirmed by the price paid.

22 Probably the tower of an estate. A tower of this kind has been found at Thorikos, cf. *BCH* 91 (1967), p. 628.

23 The sanctuary of the hero founder (*archegetes*), possibly the patron of the deme, who gave his name to the mine.

24 Kephisodotos is therefore both owner and lessee, a by no means unique case (cf. R.J. Hopper, art. cit., pp. 243–5). Similarly Diopeithes owns both land and a workshop.

96   For an unlimited development of mining activity

It is worth placing beside a practical document like the previous passage the project, which is essentially ideological in nature, of Xenophon in his *Ways and Means* (*c.* 355)[1]. This short treatise, like *The Art of Siegecraft* of his contemporary Aeneas Tacticus, represents the reaction of a 'man with ideas' who applies to the practical sphere the 'clever' teaching of the sophists. At first sight the work seems to be something altogether exceptional; it is one of the very few works of antiquity which gives the impression that the notion of economic development was not completely foreign to ancient thought. But one must be careful: in the aftermath of the failure of the second imperial adventure of Athens, Xenophon is suggesting to his fellow-citizens that they should divert towards 'economic' activities the spirit of enterprise and audacity which had characterized their political adventures. Alcibiades said to them in 415: 'We cannot fix like a manager the extent of our domination[2].' By making use, if necessary, of an economic paradox to explain that silver mines can be indefinitely profitable, Xenophon is simply making these sentiments his own, though he transposes them to another register.

As for the silver mines, if they were to be exploited properly, they would, I believe, produce considerable wealth independently from the other sources of revenue. I therefore wish to draw attention to the possibilities of the mines for those who do not know; knowing these you will be in a better position to decide about their use. Now it is clear to everyone that they have been worked from a remote past[3], and indeed no one tries to say when they were first opened. And yet although the silver ore has been dug up and extracted for so long, bear in mind how small are the mounds which have been excavated in comparison with the natural hills which have silver. And it is obvious that the silver-producing area, far from shrinking in size, is constantly expanding even further. At the time when there was the highest number of men employed there, no one was ever short of work, and in fact there was always more work to do than workmen available. Even today those who own slaves in the mines never reduce the size of their labour force but on the contrary constantly seek to increase their number as far as possible. The fact is, I believe, that when there are few men digging and searching for ore, then the amount of silver that is found must be small, but when there are many, the amount of silver ore that is discovered is greatly increased. Hence of all activities known to me this is the only one where expansion does not lead to jealousy. Farmers can all tell you how many teams of oxen and how many workmen they need to cultivate their land; and if someone puts to work more than is necessary, they reckon he is making a loss. But in silver mining they will all tell you that they are short of labour. The case is different from what it is with, for example, coppersmiths: when coppersmiths are plentiful, the price of copper work falls, and they go out of business; similarly with smiths. Similarly too, when there is a glut of corn and wine, the price of crops is cheap, farming becomes an unprofitable business and many men give up working the land and turn to commerce, retail trade and moneylending. But with silver ore, the greater the amount extracted and the larger the quantity of silver produced, the greater the number of people who take up this activity. Silver is not like furniture: when you have got enough for your house, you do not buy any more, but no one has ever had so much silver that he did not want more of it. If anyone acquires a great quantity he takes just as much pleasure in burying away the surplus as he does in using it[4].

One may add that when the cities enjoy prosperity the demand for silver is very high. Men are keen to spend on fine weapons and good horses and houses and lavish establishments, and women on expensive clothes and gold jewellery. But when the cities are ailing, whether from the failure of crops or from war, then land goes out of cultivation and the demand for silver to purchase food supplies or to pay for mercenary troops is even greater[5].

But someone may say that gold is no less useful than silver. I would not dispute this, but I know that when there is an abundance of gold, it loses itself its value while the value of silver increases[6].

I have pointed out all these facts so that we need not hesitate to attract as many men as possible to the silver mines and put them to work there, in the certain expectation that the silver ore will never fail and that the value of silver will never fall. I believe in fact that the city has reached this conclusion before me, for it grants the status of *isoteleis* to any foreigners who wish to work in the mines[7].

To make myself clearer on the subject of the means of sustenance, I shall now explain how the silver mines can be exploited with the greatest advantage to the city. I do not expect that what I have to say will cause surprise as though I had discovered something difficult to find. Some of the things I shall mention are visible to all up to this day, while as for past conditions we hold it from our fathers that they were similar. But what can cause surprise is that the city, although she is aware that private individuals are making a fortune at her expense, nevertheless does not imitate them[8]. Those of us who are interested in the subject have heard long ago that Nicias son of Niceratus owned a thousand slaves in the silver mines, which he let out to Sosias the Thracian on condition that he would pay him an obol a day net per man and that he would always keep the number constant[9]. [. . .]

After mentioning other cases similar to that of Nicias, Xenophon continues:

But why talk about the past? There are still many men in the silver mines nowadays who are let out on the same conditions. If my suggestions were to be carried out, the only innovation would be that, just as private individuals who have acquired slaves have provided themselves with a permanent source of revenue, so the city would acquire public slaves up to a ratio of three slaves for each citizen.[10]

XENOPHON, *Ways and Means* IV, 1–17

1 The normal rendering of the Greek *Poroi*, though the real meaning is more exactly *Resources*. But see the excellent commentary by Ph. Gauthier (Paris and Geneva, 1976), which corrects and amplifies on a number of points some of the views expressed in this book.
2 Thucydides VI, 18, 3 (cf. no 17).
3 That is correct, cf. the introduction to the previous passage in this book (p. 310).
4 Xenophon is quite familiar with the law of supply and demand, and he even knows (cf. the sequel) that it can apply to precious metals, but he makes allowance for a fundamental 'extra-economic' factor, the taste for hoarding. It is strange however that he should not mention explicitly the argument which is at the back of his reasoning: silver is struck in the form of coinage

by the city of Athens, and Athenian silver does indeed enjoy considerable international prestige thanks to its purity, hence the silver of Laurion cannot in fact be a commodity like any other.

5 The paradox is flagrant here. Xenophon can allow himself to risk it as he is moving from the private sphere (men need silver when the city is prosperous) to the public one (the city needs silver when things are going wrong). This dichotomy between public and private is in itself characteristic of the fourth century.

6 Here again one must remember that Athens coined in silver and only very exceptionally in gold. But the success of the gold coins struck by Philip of Macedon was soon going to deprive him of his illusions.

7 It is not easy to know what Xenophon means here by 'work' (*ergazesthai*). S Lauffer argues from the fact that in the inscriptional evidence the word has the meaning 'to open a shaft' to conclude that Athens was offering *isoteleia* to those metics who leased a mine (op. cit., p. 209); that is quite unbelievable, since foreigners do not seem to have had access to mines any more than to the land. It is better to confess ignorance.

8 Xenophon's 'modernism' (cf. especially no 122 below) is always put at the service of the city and not of individuals, even though, as in the present case, private activities serve as a model.

9 On the mining activities of the general Nicias see also Plutarch, *Nicias* IV. The lease of livestock whereby the lessee of cattle or of human beings (prostitutes, for example) undertakes to replace any animal or human being dead or lost, so that the herd or flock is said to be 'immortal' is frequently attested in the Hellenistic period; cf. Cl. Préaux, 'Les troupeaux immortels et les esclaves de Nicias', *Chronique d'Egypte* 41 (1966), pp. 161–4. The exact role in the mines of Sosias is not easy to define. He may have been himself a slave used as a foreman (S. Lauffer, op. cit., p. 11), possibly also a metic.

10 Xenophon is not suggesting here to Athens to exploit directly her mines, but to buy a few tens of thousands of slaves to be let out to claim-holders. He does however suggest subsequently that the city could offer slaves to each of the ten tribes, and the produce of the new seams discovered on the initiative of each tribe would be shared out among the whole city.

97 Liturgies: the obligations of a wealthy Athenian

Socrates in Xenophon's *Oeconomicus* (*c.* 361) reminds Critobulus of his obligations to the gods of the city and to his friends.

In the first place I see you are compelled to offer many lavish sacrifices, otherwise you would be on bad terms with gods and men. Then it is your duty to entertain many strangers[1], and to do this in grand style. Then you must invite your fellow-citizens to dinner and shower benefits on them, or you would be destitute of allies[2]. Furthermore I notice that the city is already laying heavy expenses on you, for keeping horses[3], acting as choregos[4], gymnasiarch[5] or undertaking some important function[6], and should war break out, I know that they will impose on you the trierarchy[7], the soldiers' pay and contributions[8] so great that you will not find it easy to bear them. And if ever you are thought to have fallen short in the performance of these duties, I know that the Athenians will punish you just as much as if they had caught you stealing their own property[9]. In addition I can see you fancy you are wealthy, you are not interested in devices to raise money, and you devote your attention to young boys, as though you were in a position to do this. For these reasons I feel sorry for you and I fear that some irreparable disaster may overtake you and plunge you in deep poverty. In my case, should I be in need of anything, I know (and this you admit yourself) that there are people who will help me, and they need provide only very little to flood me with wealth. But your friends, who have more than enough for their life style than you have for yours, only look to you in the expectation of some advantage[10].

XENOPHON, *Oeconomicus* II, 5–8

1 Probably as *proxenos* of their cities.
2 As candidate for an elective magistracy, for example, or in case of trouble in the law courts.
3 This does not refer to private breeding but to a liturgy imposed on Athenians wealthy enough to serve in the cavalry.
4 A *choregos* paid for tragic or comic performances and in particular for the training of the chorus.
5 Gymnasiarchs assumed on behalf of their tribe the costs of equipping the gymnasium and the expenses of the athletes who trained there.

6 The Greek word *prostateia* probably has here a very general meaning.

7 One of the best known of liturgies: a trierarch equipped a trireme, commanded it and occasionally paid the crew.

8 The *eisphora*, an extraordinary direct contribution.

9 That is the very essence of the liturgy. Personal wealth is owned only through delegation by the city.

10 A phenomenon of clientship such as was going to develop in the Hellenistic and Roman periods.

98 The Athenian domination, the treasury and the poor: a polemic

The justification for the domination of Athens over the cities of the 'empire' was, in the eyes of Athenian democrats, that only this domination, and the resources, direct and indirect, that it provided made possible the maintenance of the 'people-king'. It is this widespread notion which Aristophanes challenges in the dialogue in which the judge Philocleon (the 'Cleon-lover') and his son Bdelycleon (the 'Cleon-hater') confront each other in the *Wasps* (422).

Bdelycleon Now listen to me, daddy dear, and don't frown so much. First of all make a rough calculation, not with stones but using your fingers, of the tribute which comes to us from all the cities together. Then, in addition and separately, calculate the taxes, the many 1 per cent dues[1], the deposits[2], mines[3], markets, harbours, rents and confiscations[4]. Altogether that comes to about 2,000 talents in revenue. Now subtract from that a year's pay (*misthos*) for the jurors, 6,000 in all – there are never more than that residing in the country – that would seem to make 150 talents[5].

Philocleon The pay we get is then not even one-tenth of our revenue?

Bdelycleon Certainly not, by Zeus.

Philocleon Where then does the rest of the money go?

Bdelycleon To those who say 'I will not betray the Athenian rabble, but I will always fight for the mob[6]'. You yourself, dad, allow yourself to be cajoled by these pretty little words and choose them as your masters. And they meanwhile extort bribes from the cities, 50 talents at a time, terrifying them with threats of this kind: 'You will give the tribute, or I will thunder against your city and destroy it.' And you are content to nibble away at the crumbs of your empire. As for the allies, they observe that the rest of the mob scrapes the bottom of the ballot box and has virtually nothing to eat[7], and they think as much of you as of the vote of Konnos[8], but bring as presents to these pickles, wine, rugs, cheese, honey, sesame, cushions, cups, coats, crowns, necklaces, beakers, health and wealth. But as for you, 'after much toil on land, and much toil on the sea'[9], none of those you rule will give you so much as a garlic head for your fish soup.

Philocleon Yes, by Zeus, and even yesterday I sent for three cloves of garlic from Eucharides[10]. But this slavery I am supposed to be enduring, you have not proved it, and this exasperates me.

Bdelycleon Is it not a great slavery to see all these holding office, themselves and their pay-earning flatterers? But you are thankful if you are given your three obols, which you earned with great toil, rowing ships, fighting on land, besieging cities. [. . .]

Philocleon Is that how they treat me? What are you saying? You stir me to the depths of my being and win over my mind more and more. I don't know what you are doing to me.

Bdelycleon Just think: you could be rich like all of them, but somehow you let yourself be cooped up by these perpetual popular leaders. You rule very many cities from the Black Sea to Sardinia, and what profit do you get? Next to nothing. And this they dole you out in dribblets, a little at a time, as oil from wool, just enough to make a living[11]. They want you to be poor, and I will tell you the reason why: it is that you may know who tames and feeds you so that when he wants to let you loose on one of his enemies, you will pounce on them savagely. If they wanted to provide a livelihood to the people, it would be easy. There are a thousand cities which are now paying tribute to us. If one were to tell each to provide maintenance for 20 men, then 20,000 democrats would live amid an abundance of dishes of hare, crowns of all sorts, beestings fresh and curdled, and would enjoy delights worthy of this country and of the trophy of Marathon. But now like olive-pickers[12] you follow behind the paymaster.

ARISTOPHANES, *Wasps*, 655–712

1 Dues paid notably on entering and leaving the harbour.
2 Sums deposited before the opening of a trial.
3 Cf. no 95.
4 All the revenue from property confiscated and sold by the *poletai* (cf. nos 75, 95).
5 The calculation is correct if one imagines that the jurors of the Heliaea got their indemnity of three obols every day of the year. It hardly needs to be said that the city of Athens has other expenses besides the pay for jurors!
6 Parody of a standard oath formula, attributed here to the 'demagogues', i.e. the popular leaders.
7 On this image, cf. J. Taillardat, *Les images d'Aristophane*, pp. 83–4.
8 A music teacher whose electoral weight cannot have been very great.
9 A parody or quotation of tragic verses.
10 A vegetable seller.
11 A large admission.
12 Waiting to be paid by the owner who employs them.

99 Athenian settlement at Brea in Thrace (*c.* 445 ?)

One of the manifestations of the fifth-century Athenian 'empire' was the establishment through most of its history of a number of settlements abroad, partly or wholly of Athenian citizens, which varied greatly in size, character and purpose and are not easily classified; indeed, the precise character and legal status of the various settlements have been much discussed[1]. Apart from settlements outside the immediate sphere of Athenian power, whether on Greek or on non-Greek territory, some were made directly at the expense of 'allied' cities and had obvious strategic and military motives. The following inscription records part of the decree on the sending of an Athenian colony to Brea in Thrace; the earlier part of the inscription is lost (some 30 to 35 lines) and will presumably have contained details e.g. about the establishment of the colony and the numbers of settlers to be sent out. The exact site of Brea is unknown; the settlement may or may not be identical with the one sent among the Bisaltai by Pericles (Plutarch, *Pericles* XI, 5, where a figure of 1,000 settlers is given), but in any case it has no history for us apart from its establishment.

Front

[. . .] Let the colony leaders provide them with the means of offering favourable sacrifices on behalf of the colony, [as much as] they think fit. Let one choose [ten men] to distribute the land, one from each tribe. Let these divide [the land. Let Dem]okleides have full powers to establish the [colony] to the [best] of his ability. [Let the sacred] enclosures already marked out be left as [they are], and [let no fur]ther enclosures be consecrated. Let (the colonists) [des]patch a cow and [a panoply] to the Great Panathenaia and a phallus to the [Dionysia]². If anyone marches [against the territory] of the colonists let the [cities] come to their help [as swiftly] as possible according to the agreements concerning [the cities] in Thrace which was made when [. . . . . .]tos was secretary. Let [this decree] be inscribed on a [stele] and placed on the Acropolis. Let the colonists [provide] the stele [at their own expense]. If anyone puts to the vote a motion contrary to [the stele] or if an orator urges or [tries to] issue a summons to reverse or rescind any part of the decree, let he and his children [lose their citizen rights], let his property be confiscated and a [tithe] be consecrated to the [goddess], except if the colonists themselves [. . .] make the request. Let those soldiers who enrol to share [in the colony] be present at Brea within 30 days of their return to [Athens]. Let the colony be led out within 30 days, and let Aischines go with them to give them the money³.

Side

Phantokles moved: concerning the colony (sent) to Brea, as moved by Demokleides; but let the prytany of the tribe Erechtheis introduce Phantokles to the council at its first session; let the colonists sent to Brea be chosen from the thetes and zeugitai⁴.

MEIGGS–LEWIS no 49

1 For a list see A.H.M. Jones, *Athenian Democracy* (1957), pp. 168–73, and for recent discussions of the character and status of the various settlements see P.A. Brunt, 'Athenian Settlements Abroad in the Vth Century B.C.', in *Ancient Society and Institutions (Studies V. Ehrenberg, 1966)*, pp. 71–92; Ph. Gauthier, 'Les clérouques de Lesbos et la colonisation athénienne au Ve siècle', *REG* 79 (1966), pp. 64–88.

2 A religious obligation which Athens sought to extend to all her allies (and not just her colonies), certainly by 425 and possibly earlier still; cf. generally R. Meiggs, *The Athenian Empire* (Oxford, 1972), Chapter 16.

3 A late writer commenting on a speech of Demosthenes (Argument to Speech VIII) states that 'it was an ancient custom with the Athenians to send out the poor and property-less to cities they controlled abroad; at the start of their journey the settlers received weapons and travelling money at public expense'.

4 i.e. from the two lowest property classes; the settlement of poorer Athenian citizens will have been at times a motive in a number of Athenian foundations (cf. previous note), though not necessarily the only nor indeed the most important one, as it is very likely that a number of cleruchies (military garrisons established on allied territory) were only temporary in character.

100 The 'empire' of Sinope around 400

The huge domination of Athens often conceals the existence of tiny 'empires' based on the same principle of tribute. It is an 'empire' of this kind that the Greek mercenaries who have survived the *Anabasis* come across.

At this point there arrived a deputation from Sinope[1]. They feared for the city of Cotyora (for it belonged to them and paid them tribute) and for the land, which they were told was being ravaged. They entered the camp and made the following speech (their spokesman was Hecatonymus, who was reputed to be a clever orator): 'The city of Sinope sent us, soldiers, to congratulate you on the victory you won, Greeks over barbarians, and to express its delight that after going through many perils, as we are told, you have now arrived safely here. But we, who are Greeks, expect to be well treated by you, who are also Greeks, and to suffer no harm; indeed, we have never taken the initiative in doing you any wrong. The people of Cotyora here are colonists of ours[2], and we gave them this territory which we took away from the barbarians. That is why they pay a fixed tribute to us just like the people of Cerasus and Trapezus. Therefore any harm you do to them the city of

Sinope will consider is done to it as well.'

XENOPHON, *Anabasis* V, 5, 7–10

1 Sinope, Cotyora and Trapezus are Greek cities on the south coast of the Black Sea.

2 Cotyora was founded by men from Sinope but, contrary to what happened frequently in the earliest days of colonization, it kept ties of economic and political dependence towards her metropolis.

101 Athenian decree imposing on the cities of the empire the use of Athenian coins, weights and measures

The Athenian decree imposing on all the cities of the empire the coins, weights and measures of Athens raises many difficult problems: first of all that of the date of a document which has been found in fragments scattered all over the area of Athenian domination; scholars waver between the early 440s and the late 420s[1]. In the *Birds* (414), Aristophanes parodies the decree. A decree-seller proposes a new decree: 'The citizens of Cloud-cuckoo city are to use the same measures, weights and decrees (or coins) as the Olophyxians' (1040–1). The political aspects of the decree are obvious: to forbid the striking of coins is to diminish the sovereignty of the 'allied' cities. The alleged 'economic' motives are far less obvious. Even if one makes allowance for a possible charge on the restriking of allied coins, it is not certain that the operation is in itself a profitable one; as for the strictly commercial interest, it could only exist in so far as Athens was able to impose on her allies the use not only of her own coinage, but of her silver as well, a monopoly she never enjoyed. The unification of weights, measures and coinages could in the end advantage all traders, and not only the Athenians. It is better therefore to see the decree as one further instrument among others of Athens' crushing political domination[2]. It should be added that whatever the date of the decree the evidence of the coinage of the allies clearly suggests that it was in fact never fully enforced by Athens, for what reasons we can only guess.

Let the people choose heralds [to bring to the notice of the cities[3] what has been voted]; let one herald be sent to the Islands, [one to Ionia, one to the Hellespont], and one to

Thrace[4]; [let the generals] help in the sending of the heralds [by providing transport to each of them]; [if they fail to do this let them each be] fined 10,000 [drachmae]; let the magistrates in the cities[5] [transcribe] this decree on a stone stele and place it in the agora of [each] city, and let the masters of the mint set up the decree [in front of] the mint; let the [Athenians][6] carry out these instructions, if the magistrates refuse to; let the herald sent on the spot require them to carry out the orders of the Athenians; let the secretary of the [council] add to the oath of the council[7] the following words [for all future time]: 'If anyone strikes silver coinage in the cities and does not use the coins, weights or measures of the Athenians, but uses [foreign] coins, weights and measures, [I will punish and penalize him according to the] former decree proposed by Klearchos[8]; [let anyone who wishes be free to hand] over any foreign silver [he has and exchange it] whenever he wishes [on these same terms]; let the city [give him in exchange Athenian coins]; let everyone [bring to Athens] in person [and deposit at the] mint any silver he holds; let the mint masters draw up a list [of all the silver deposited by each person with them] and set up [a stone stele in front of the] mint for anyone who wishes to inspect it; [let them list on one side all the] foreign [currency] keeping [the silver and gold separate, and on the other side all the] Athenian silver . . .

MEIGGS–LEWIS no 45, 9–14

1 A summary of the debate is given by Meiggs and Lewis, who opt for the earlier date; see also R. Meiggs, *The Athenian Empire* (1972), pp. 599–601. But the whole question has been exhaustively re-examined by E. Erxleben, 'Das Münzgesetz des delisch-attischen Bundes', *Archiv für Papyrusforschung* 19 (1969), pp. 96–139, 212; 20 (1970), pp. 6–132; 21 (1971), pp. 145–62, who opts for the later date after a detailed study of the coinage of the allies of Athens. But since the effects of the decree on the allies' coinage are not obviously traceable at any given date, as Erxleben's survey shows, the problem of the date of the decree may in fact be insoluble on the available evidence.

2 This summarizes the discussion by M.I. Finley in the report quoted above, Chapter 1, n 1, pp. 28–9.

3 The 'allied' cities.

4 These are the different administrative districts of the Athenian empire.
5 The magistrates and mint officials of the 'allied' cities.
6 The Athenians on the spot.
7 The oath sworn since 501 by every councillor before entering office.
8 Nothing is known of this man and of this decree which may have dealt not with coinage but with the punishment of culprits.

102 An Athenian law on silver coinage (375–374)

This recently discovered (1970) inscription from the Athenian *Agora* provides valuable evidence, among other things, on the activities of a hitherto little-known Athenian official, the 'tester' (*dokimastes*), a public slave, whose function it was to examine coins in Athens for their purity; according to the inscription another tester is to be appointed for Peiraeus. Although the inscription is securely dated to 375–374 nothing specific is known from literary sources of the circumstances which caused traders to distrust both Athenian coins and (according to Stroud's restoration in line 8) foreign imitations of Athenian coins such as were struck at this time in Egypt and the Levant, and which then led to the emergency legislation recorded in this inscription. The crisis must have been an exceptional one, probably connected somehow with Athens' financial difficulties at this time (cf. nos 91B, 124), and otherwise Athenian coins generally enjoyed a reputation for purity and were in high demand (cf. nos 96, 122, n 12). For a detailed commentary see the *editio princeps* by R.S. Stroud, *Hesperia* 43 (1974), pp. 157–88; for a different interpretation see A. Giovannini, 'Athenian Currency in the Late Fifth and Early Fourth Century B.C.', *Greek, Roman and Byzantine Studies* 16, 2 (Summer 1975), pp. 185–95.

It was resolved by the *nomothetai*[1], in the archonship of Hippodamas (375–374); Nikophon moved: let Attic silver currency be accepted when [it is shown to be][2] of silver and bears the official [type]. Let the public tester sitting among the tables[3] test (the coins) according to these regulations every [day except] when payments of money are made[4]; at that time let him test in the [council] chamber. If anyone brings to him

[. . .]⁵ which bear the same type as the Attic [. . .], let (the tester) return it to the one who brought it to him. If it has a core [of copper], or of lead, or is counterfeit, let him cut it across [. . .] and let him consecrate it to the Mother of the Gods⁶ and [deposit] it with the council. If the tester does not hold session or test (coins) according to the law, let the *syllogeis*⁷ of the people strike him with 50 blows of [the whip]. If anyone refuses to accept the silver currency which has been tested by the tester let him be deprived of the value of what he has sold [that] day⁸. Let denunciations for offences in the [corn market] be made before the commissioners of the grain trade (*sitophylakes*)⁹, for offences committed in the *agora* and in the rest of the city before the *syllogeis* of the people, and for those committed in the commercial port and in Peiraeius before the inspectors of the commercial port (*epimeletai tou emporiou*) except for those in the corn market which should be made before the commissioners of the grain trade (*sitophylakes*). For all denunciations which do not exceed ten drachmae, let the magistrates have authority to give a verdict, but for those which exceed ten drachmae let them introduce them to the law court. Let the *thesmothetai* assign them a court drawn by lot whenever they request one or let them be fined [. . .] drachmae. Let the informer receive one-half if [the culprit] is convicted¹⁰. If the seller is a male or female slave let him or her receive 50 blows of the whip from [the magistrates] dealing with each particular case. If any magistrate does not act in accordance with the written rules, let any Athenian who wishes and who is qualified bring him before the council. If he is convicted, let him be deposed from office and in addition let the council impose on him a fine of up to 500 drachmae. So that there should be a tester in Peiraeius for the benefit of the [ship] owners and the merchants and [all] the others, let the council appoint one from among the public slaves [. . .] or let it purchase one, and let the receivers (*apodektai*) [set aside] the required sum. Let the inspectors of the commercial port see to it that he sits near the stele of Poseidon and observes the law in the same way as was specified for the tester in the city. Let this law be inscribed on a stone stele and a copy be placed in the city among the tables, and another copy in Peiraeius in front of the stele of Poseidon. Let the secretary of the council report the price to the sellers (*poletai*). Let the sellers communicate it to the council. Let the salary for the tester in the commercial port be paid to him, in the archonship of Hippodamas (375–374) from the moment of his appointment and let the receivers set aside for him a sum equivalent to that for the tester in the city, and in future let his salary come from the same source as for the workers in the mint. If there is any decree inscribed anywhere on a stele which contravenes this law, let the secretary of the council pull it down.

Marble stele from the Athenian *agora*,
published by R.S. Stroud, *Hesperia* 43
(1974), pp. 157–88

1 A body of legislative officials appointed yearly (in the fourth century) from among the jurors (see D. MacDowell, *JHS* 95 (1975), pp. 62–74); there is no reference in the inscription to ratification of this law by either the council or the assembly, though this need not mean they were in fact 'excluded from the law-making process' (Stroud).

2 The exact words are lost but the sense is clear.

3 The tables of the bankers and money-changers in the *agora*.

4 Payments of public revenue made to the receivers (*apodektai*) on whom cf. Aristotle, *Constitution of Athens* XLVII, 5–XLVIII, 2.

5 Stroud suggests [foreign silver currency]: this would refer to foreign imitations of Athenian coins current in the East and especially Egypt, and would mean that these were legal tender in Athens; for a different view see A. Giovannini, op. cit.

6 Counterfeit coins were frequently removed from circulation by being dedicated to a god or goddess.

7 A little-known body of 30 officials drawn from the council who performed various policing and priestly functions.

8 Compare the provisions in the law from Olbia, no 103.

9 For these and the following officials see no 89, also nos 81, 82.

10 The exact words are lost but the sense is clear.

103 Decree from Olbia on the import of foreign coins (*c.* 350?)
This epigraphical text which sets up at Olbia, a Milesian colony on the Black Sea (cf. the map, p. 62), a monopoly of local silver and bronze coinage (which probably proves that other coinages circulated and were in practice legal tender) should not be inter-

preted any more than no 101 on the lines of mercantile considerations of any kind[1]. The profit which the city can make by exploiting the difference between the value of the coined and the uncoined metal is slight, and there may even be a loss when one has to re-strike foreign coins. The city is therefore imposing the use of her own coins for no other reason than she imposes the use of her laws.

Let anyone who wishes have access to Borysthenes[2] on the following conditions. It was resolved by the council and the people; Kanobos son of Thrasydamas put forward the motion; the import and export of any amount of coined gold and silver are free[3]. Whoever wishes to sell or buy coined gold or silver, let him sell and buy at the stone in the assembly's meeting place[4]. Anyone who sells or buys elsewhere shall be fined a sum equal to the silver sold in the case of a sale or a sum equal to the price paid in the case of a purchase; let all sales and purchases be carried out with the currency of the city, with the bronze and silver of the Olbiopolitans[5]; whoever sells or buys with another currency[6] shall be deprived, in the case of a sale of the value of the sale[7], in the case of a purchase of the price he will have paid; let the payment of fines on those who have transgressed the decree in any way be exacted by the contractors for the collection of fines from transgressors, once they have secured a conviction in court[8]; let gold be sold and bought at the following price[9]: one Cyzicene stater[10] against ten and a half staters[11], neither more nor less, and let all other coined gold and silver be sold and bought by mutual agreement; let no tax be levied on coined gold and silver whether it is being bought or sold[12].

(The end of the inscription is mutilated)

DITTENBERGER, *Sylloge*[3], no 218

1 Cf. M.I. Finley, survey quoted Chapter 1, n 1, pp. 28–9, also *The Ancient Economy* (1973), p. 168. G. Le Rider has kindly provided help with the commentary on this inscription.

2 An ancient name for the city of Olbia, as pointed out to us by B. Bravo; Olbia controlled the whole of the 'liman' (lagoon) which was common to the estuaries of the Hypanis (Bug) and Borysthenes (Dniepr).

3 Literally 'let there be import of all gold bearing a sign and

silver bearing a sign and also export'.

4 A place name where the money-changers must have operated (cf. no 102, n 3).

5 Olbia did not strike at the time any gold coins, which explains why only silver and bronze are mentioned here; cf. below.

6 This no longer refers to the exchange of gold and silver but to trade in general, which is to be conducted solely with local coins. Foreign traders must therefore purchase these. This will be the procedure of Ptolemy Philadelphus in Egypt, cf. Claire Préaux, *L'Économie royale des Lagides* (Brussels, 1939), pp. 271–5.

7 Literally 'of what he will have sold'.

8 The city of Olbia farmed out the collection of fines; in other words, the farmers took charge themselves of the organization and costs of legal proceedings but kept for themselves the sums recovered.

9 There is no difference between the purchase price and the sale price.

10 Cyzicus was a very large city on the south coast of the Propontis (sea of Marmara), cf. no 92. From the sixth to the fourth centuries she struck a coinage that was famous in the Greek world, which was not in fact of gold but of electrum, a natural alloy of gold and silver; the proportion of gold is irregular but averages at about 45 per cent. Since a Cyzicene weighs about 16 grams and the staters of Olbia around 12·50 grams, and since the ratio of gold to silver in the fourth century was 1 to 13·3, a very simple calculation shows that the rate fixed is highly favourable to the coinage of Cyzicus, and this must have political reasons; cf. J.P. Guépin, 'Le cours du cyzicène', *Antiquité Classique* 34 (1965), pp. 199–203 and R. Bogaert, *Banques et banquiers dans les cités grecques* (1968), pp. 121–4 for a detailed discussion. On the circulation of coins in the Black Sea see E. Schönert-Geiss, *Klio* 53 (1971), pp. 105–17, which shows (among other things) the popularity and circulation of Cyzicene staters (pp. 109–11).

11 That is to say, a gold piece from Cyzicus (one stater = two drachmae) will be exchanged for ten and a half drachmae of local silver. The text is mutilated and it has also been suggested that one should understand $11\frac{1}{2}$ drachmae, which would give to the Cyzicene an even more favourable rate.

12 As can be seen the city is not carrying out a commercial

operation. On this inscription see also Ed. Will, in the collective volume *Numismatique Antique, Problèmes et Méthodes* (Nancy-Louvain, 1975), p. 101.

7 The Time of Crises

104 Sparta's decline after her victory

Xenophon's *Constitution of the Lacedaimonians*, a political pamphlet in praise of Sparta, has a double and curious epilogue. After drawing a lively picture of the decline of Sparta, Xenophon ends by emphasizing the permanence of the monarchy, which may be an anticipation of the Hellenistic age[1].

If anyone asked me whether the laws of Lycurgus appear to me to remain undisturbed to this day, by Zeus, I would not have the courage to maintain this still. I know that in former days the Lacedaimonians preferred to remain at home among themselves and live with modest means rather than be harmosts[2] in the cities and be corrupted by flattery. And I know that formerly they were afraid to be found in possession of gold[3]; but now there are some who even take pride in its possession. And further I know that formerly the reason why they expelled strangers and were not allowed to go abroad was to prevent the citizens from being softened by contact with strangers. But now I know that those who are thought to be the leading men in the city are anxious that they should never cease to be harmosts abroad. There was a time when they strove to be worthy of leadership; but now their concern is much rather to exercise rule than to be worthy of it. This is the reason why formerly the Greeks went to Sparta to ask them to exercise leadership[4] against those they felt were doing them wrong; but now there are many who exhort each other to prevent them recovering their rule. One must therefore not be surprised that such criticisms are made against them, when they clearly no longer obey the deity nor the laws of Lycurgus.

XENOPHON, *Constitution of the Lacedaimonians* XIV

1 The exact date of the work is unknown and much discussed. For example, E. Delebecque, in *Essai sur la vie de Xénophon* (Paris, 1957), p. 508, believes that the picture of decline dates from 369, and the rest of the work from 387. Many editors invert Chapter XIV in the manuscripts, reproduced here (the picture of Spartan decline), and Chapter XV on the kings. It is not certain that Xenophon did not want to end with what guaranteed the permanence and future of Sparta.

2 The harmosts were the governors of the cities controlled by Sparta after her victory in 404; the institution originated in the Peloponnesian War.

3 See also no 105.

4 To exercise military hegemony, as during the Peloponnesian War.

105 The clandestine gold of the Spartans (about 375)

The testimony of Plato is not very different from that of Xenophon. Plato draws up a hierarchy of existing cities by reference to the ideal city, the principles of which he has outlined. The Spartan regime is the best of existing regimes and Plato describes it as 'timocratic' because the sense of honour is predominant there. But gold is already finding its way in.. . .

Socrates At the same time men of this kind will resemble the ruling class of an oligarchy in being avaricious, cherishing furtively a passionate regard for gold and silver; for they will now have private homes where they can hoard their treasure in secret and live ensconced in a nest of their own, lavishing their riches on their women or whom they please.

Very true, he said[1].

They will also be miserly, prizing the money they may not openly acquire, though prodigal enough of other people's wealth for the satisfaction of their desires. They will enjoy their pleasures in secret, like truant children, in defiance of the law; because they have been educated not by gentle influence but under compulsion, cultivating the body in preference to the mind and caring nothing for the spirit of genuine culture which seeks truth by the discourse of reason.

PLATO, *Republic* VIII, 548 a–c
(trans. F.M. Cornford)

1 Glaukon, Plato's brother, in conversation with Socrates.

106   The law of the ephor Epitadeus

The final piece of evidence on the subject of the 'decline' of Sparta is the brief narrative with which Plutarch prefaces the life of Agis, the third-century reforming king.

> The beginning of the decline and of the disease in the Lacedaimonian state coincided with the destruction of the Athenian hegemony when they filled themselves with gold and silver. And yet, so long as the number of households remained the same as once fixed by Lycurgus, and the lots of land were passed on from father to son[1], the preservation of this order and equality somehow managed to compensate for the other errors committed by the city. But when a powerful man called Epitadeus, who was headstrong and violent in temper, became ephor, as a result of a quarrel with his son he introduced a law allowing one to bestow on whoever one wished one's patrimony and lot of land, either by gift during one's lifetime or by bequest in one's will[2]. In introducing this law he was indulging his own private resentment, but the other citizens welcomed and ratified it through greed and so destroyed the best of institutions. For from this date onwards powerful men accumulated inheritances without limits, putting aside the claims of the true heirs[3], and in a short time wealth was concentrated into a few hands and the city as a whole became impoverished. The process brought in its wake servility, indifference towards what is honourable as well as envy and resentment against those who owned property. There were only 700 Spartiates left, no more, and of these perhaps a hundred owned land as well as a (hereditary) lot[4]. The remaining mass of people lingered on in the city without resources or political rights, fighting foreign wars without energy or spirit, and always on the lookout for an opportunity for change and revolution[5].
>
> PLUTARCH, *Agis* V

1   Whether this alleged equality of land ever existed is very much open to debate (see F.W. Walbank, *Commentary on Polybius* I (Oxford, 1958), pp. 728–31).
2   Epitadeus is completely unknown otherwise, but the law instituting the freedom of bequest is known to Aristotle, *Politics* II, 1270 a. Plutarch is compressing in this passage the whole evolution of Sparta in the fourth and even in the third

centuries. See further J. Christien, 'La Loi d'Epitadeus: un aspect de l'histoire économique et sociale à Sparte', *Revue historique de droit français et étranger* 52 (1974), pp. 197–221.

3 This refers then not only to the freedom of gift and bequest, but even to the freedom of all transactions on land in general. It is doubtful whether this could have been granted in this way at one stroke.

4 Every Spartiate must by definition have his hereditary lot (*kleros*). The 'hundred' mentioned are probably those who have both this lot and an additional estate.

5 Cf. no 61 (the conspiracy of Kinadon).

107 Ancient and modern warfare

Demosthenes, who is not usually very aware of the changes which characterize his time, is however struck in the following speech, which was delivered in May 341, by the transformations in the art of war, their causes and their social and economic consequences.

> To be sure, there is a foolish argument put forward by those who wish to reassure the city, namely that Philip is not yet as powerful as the Lacedaimonians once were, when they ruled the sea and all the land, had the Great King as their ally, and nothing could resist them; and yet the city faced up to them and was not destroyed. But I myself believe that, although almost everything has progressed and the present bears no relation to the past, nothing has changed and progressed so much as the art of war. First I am told that in former times the Lacedaimonians and all the other Greeks would invade and ravage the enemy's land with hoplites and citizen armies for four or five months only during the campaigning season, and then return home. They were so old-fashioned in outlook, or rather so civic-spirited, that they would not purchase any service from anyone, but war was waged according to rules and openly. But now you see that the greatest damage has been done by traitors, and not as a result of regular pitched battles. You hear of Philip marching where he pleases followed not by a phalanx of hoplites, but by light-armed troops, cavalry, archers and mercenaries – this is the kind of army he has around him. When, further, he falls upon a people torn by

internal strife and no one marches out to defend the land, so suspicious are they of one another, he brings up his engines and lays siege to the city. I pass over the fact that he draws no distinction between summer and winter, and that he has no season set apart for suspending operations.

DEMOSTHENES, *Third Philippic*, 47–50

108 Isocrates and the mercenaries

From the *Panegyricus* (380) to the *Philip* (346) via the pamphlet *On the Peace* (354?), Isocrates develops and specifies the most 'realistic' of his propaganda themes: how to eliminate the scourge of mercenary service through the conquest of the East.

A   It is much more glorious to wage war on the Great King for his kingdom than to be quarrelling among ourselves over hegemony. This expedition must take place during the present generation, so that those who have experienced misfortune should also enjoy prosperity and should not spend all their time in misery. The time that has passed is enough, and it has witnessed every conceivable kind of disaster. Many evils are inherent in human nature, but we have had to invent more than what is inevitable: we have introduced among ourselves wars and civil dissensions, causing some to be killed in their own country in violation of legality, others to wander abroad with wives and children, and many through lack of daily necessities to take up mercenary service under constraint, and be killed while fighting on the enemies' side against their friends. No one has ever protested against this, and men prefer to shed tears over the fictitious disasters related by poets. [. . .]

ISOCRATES, *Panegyricus*, 166–8

B   We[1] seek universal rule, but are unwilling to serve ourselves; we declare war on almost the whole of mankind, but to wage it we do not submit ourselves to training, but call on men who are either stateless, or deserters, or a collection of individuals versed in every kind of misdeed, who will follow anybody against us so long as their pay is increased. [. . .] We have reached such a degree of folly that while we ourselves are lacking in daily necessities, we have undertaken to maintain mercenaries, and we harass and pressurize each of our own allies to provide pay for the common enemies of mankind. We fall far short of our ancestors, not only the illustrious ones, but also those who attracted hatred: if they voted to go to war against anyone, although the Acropolis was full of silver and gold[2], they believed they had to expose themselves to risk to carry out their own decisions, while we who are in such poverty and are so many in number make use of mercenary armies just like the Great King. Formerly when they equipped triremes, they put foreigners and slaves on board as sailors[3] and sent out the citizens as hoplites. But now we use foreigners as hoplites and compel the citizens to row the ships, so that when they land on enemy territory, the self-styled rulers of the Greeks disembark with their rower's cushion, while the others whose character I have described a moment ago, bear arms and expose themselves to danger.

ISOCRATES, *On the Peace*, 44, 46–8

c What opinion you must expect all to have of you[4] if you achieve this project[5], and in particular you try to destroy the entire Persian kingdom, or at least cut off as large a piece of territory as possible, slicing Asia from Cilicia to Sinope, as some say, and then found cities in this area and settle those who at present are wandering about through lack of daily necessities and are a scourge to all those they meet. If we do not prevent them from banding together by giving them sufficient means of livelihood, they will become such a vast force without our realizing it that they will be no less formidable to the Greeks than to the barbarians. We give no thought to this problem, but choose to ignore the growth of a fearful danger which threatens us all.

ISOCRATES, *Philip*, 120–1

1 'We' refers here to the Athenians. Isocrates is supposed to be speaking before the failure of the second Athenian confederacy (end of 355), but in all probability he is writing after it.
2 Through the possession of the federal treasury; see nos 87, 90.
3 The argument is essentially rhetorical since in the fifth century the poorer classes of the citizen population served as rowers.
4 Isocrates after recalling the sensational achievements of the Thessalian Jason now addresses Philip who has just concluded with Athens the provisional 'Peace of Philocrates'.
5 The project of war against the Persians.

109 **After the fall of Spartan power and the loss of Messenia, a Spartan prince describes in his way the social disturbances in the Peloponnese (366)**

The Spartans, as is well known, were not very talkative, but to offset this others made them talk a great deal, as for example Isocrates whose conservative instincts work here in favour of the old enemy of Athens and against the Messenians and the peoples liberated from Spartan domination. Archidamus, son of king Agesilaus and future king of Sparta, speaks:

> I believe that the whole population of the Peloponnese, and even the common people, whom we imagine to be most hostile to us, are now regretting the days of our overlordship. For since their revolt, none of their expectations has been realized: instead of freedom they have found the opposite; they have lost their best citizens and fallen at the mercy of the worst. Instead of autonomy, they have been plunged into lawlessness of many terrible kinds. Previously they were used to march with us against other peoples, but now they see others campaigning against them, and the civil dissensions which formerly they knew of only from hearsay and abroad, are now an almost daily occurrence with them. They have been so levelled by disasters that no one can say who is the worst off among them. None of their cities has remained intact, none is free from enemies on its borders; hence the land has been ravaged, cities sacked, private dwellings destroyed, constitutions subverted and laws abolished, which used to make them the best governed and the happiest of the Greeks. Their mutual relations are based on such distrust and hostility, that they are more afraid of their fellow-citizens than of the enemies. In place of the harmony which prevailed in our time and the abundance they enjoyed among each other, they have reached such a peak of mutual hatred that those who own property would prefer to throw their possessions into the sea than to give help to the needy, while those in poorer circumstances would rather seize by force the wealth of the rich than merely come across it fortuitously[1].

ISOCRATES, *Archidamus*, 64–7

1 On this and the previous passages from Isocrates (no 108) see further the collection of material by A. Fuks, 'Isokrates and

the social-economic situation in Greece', *Ancient Society* 3 (1972), pp. 17–44.

110 Measures to promote concord inside a beleaguered city
Aeneas Tacticus[1], a technician of military matters who published about 357 a short treatise on how to defend properly a stronghold, was well aware that 'military' and 'social' problems cannot be dissociated and that it might be necessary to take 'revolutionary' measures to strengthen resistance to the enemy.

Towards those in the city who are opposed to the existing state of affairs one must behave in the way described above[2]. Concord must be promoted among the mass of citizens for as long as possible; this must be achieved gradually in various ways, including measures for the relief of debt by a reduction in the interest rate or its complete cancellation, and in situations of extreme danger by cancelling part or even, if necessary, the whole of the debts. For the presence of men such as these among the reserve force[3] is the greatest source of danger. One must also provide adequate resources to those who are lacking in them.

AENEAS TACTICUS, *On Siegecraft* XIV, 1

1 For the importance of Aeneas Tacticus' evidence for the social history of Greece in the fourth century see e.g. H. Bengtson, 'Die griechische Polis bei Aineias', *Historia* 11 (1962), pp. 458–68 (=*Kleine Schriften* (Munich, 1974), pp. 178–89) and more briefly in *The Greeks and the Persians* (London, 1969), pp. 263–6; D.M. Pippidi, 'Luttes politiques et troubles sociaux à Héraclée du Pont à l'époque classique', *Studii classice* 11 (1969), pp. 235–8, and especially Y. Garlan, *Recherches de poliorcétique grecque* (Paris, 1974). (There is a good edition and translation in French of Aeneas Tacticus by A.M. Bon and A. Dain in the Budé series.)
2 Chapter XI.
3 The translation of the Greek word *ephedroi* is uncertain.

111 Festivals or war: the arguments of an Athenian speaker (349)
The theoric fund, which was originally a relief fund meant to enable poor citizens to attend dramatic festivals, had become

under the direction of Eubulus in the late 350s the most important fund of the Athenian treasury and the manager of the fund was the most influential statesman in the city[1]. It is besides in 349–348 that there is the earliest mention of a military treasury, the funds from which are used in the struggle against Macedon. In antiquity and even more in modern times the theoric fund has been attacked as being responsible for the defeat of Athens, as though the Athenians had preferred 'butter' to 'guns'. The truth is more complicated. Demosthenes does not by any means challenge the principle of the theoric fund (see no 115), which is not essentially different from the distributions of its revenues which the city makes to the citizens (see no 20). It remains true that Themistocles' choice was not repeated and the cautious proposal of Demosthenes, that money from the theoric fund should be paid in relation to services rendered, was only picked up belatedly. The dramatic festivals did not affect the issue, but they were themselves involved in the decline: tragedy as an original creation is dead and comedy has as its subject private life.

As regards the available money and the other items on the agenda of this assembly, men of Athens, it appears to me that two courses are equally easy. One may either condemn those who distribute and give away the public funds and so gain credit with those who believe that this institution is detrimental to the city, or approve and encourage the right to receive distributions of money, and so win the favour of those who are most in need of them. In fact neither the supporters nor the critics of these distributions have the good of the city at heart, but they are influenced respectively by their own poverty or affluence. As far as I am concerned I propose neither to defend nor to attack this institution. But I advise you to consider and reflect in your minds that while the sum of money which we are talking about may be slight, the habit of mind which it creates is a serious matter. Now if you will lay it down that the right to receive distributions should be related to the performance of duty, not only will you not harm, but you will even do a great deal of good to the city and to yourselves. But if every festival and every pretext becomes an opportunity for getting a distribution, while you refuse to hear a word about what ought to follow after, then beware lest what seems to you right now will appear to you later to have been a serious mistake.

My opinion is – and do not interrupt me before I have spoken, but listen first before making up your minds – that just as we have devoted a meeting of the assembly to the question of the money distributions, so we must devote a meeting to the organization and preparations for war. I ask everyone of you, men of Athens, not only to be prepared to listen to what is said but also to be ready to take concrete action, so that your hopes of success may rest with you yourselves and you should not be asking what this or that person is doing (about it).

DEMOSTHENES, *On Organization*, 1–3

1 See the account in Cl. Mossé, *La Fin de la démocratie athénienne* (1962), pp. 158ff., 308ff. and G. Cawkwell, *JHS* 83 (1963), pp. 47–67.

112 The rich and the poor in Plato's 'Republic' (*c.* 375)
Describing the decadence of the model city of the *Republic*, Plato comes to the transition from oligarchy to democracy.

Socrates Such being the condition of rulers and subjects, what will happen when they are thrown together, perhaps as fellow-travellers by sea or land to some religious festival or on a campaign, and can observe one another's demeanour in a moment of danger? The rich will have no chance to feel superior to the poor. On the contrary, the poor man, lean and sunburnt, may find himself posted in battle beside one who, thanks to his wealth and indoor life, is panting under his burden of fat and showing every mark of distress[1]. 'Such men', he will think, 'are rich because we are cowards'; and when he and his friends meet in private, the word will go round: 'These men are no good: they are at our mercy.'

PLATO, *Republic* VIII, 556 c–e
(trans. F.M. Cornford)

1 See also *Republic* VIII, 551 d–e, where Plato explains that oligarchs are unable to wage war 'since they are forced to give arms to the people and to be even more afraid of it than of the enemy, or, if they do not do this, to show in the battle that they are the smaller number'.

113 Class mentality in fourth-century Athens

More significant still than direct clashes between rich and poor are the appeals made by Attic orators to a common mentality and to a tradition which, much as it may assert that poverty is not a vice, none the less believes that prosperity is a sign of virtue and that destitution is something to be condemned. Demosthenes is a democrat and a patriot. Aeschines is politically a moderate, who followed Eubulus in the policy of caution abroad and financial reform after the fiasco of the second Athenian confederacy (356)[1]. Demosthenes is speaking in 330 as a *synegoros* (private advocate) of Ctesiphon, who had secured the voting of a crown to him, against Aeschines before a popular jury of heliasts. None the less the arguments he develops when comparing the education he received with that of Aeschines are class arguments.

In my boyhood, Aeschines, I had the advantage of going to respectable schools and of having such means as is necessary to avoid doing anything disgraceful through poverty. After my childhood, my career was in accordance with this; I was choregos, trierarch, and paid taxes; no act of generosity, whether of a private or of a public kind was overlooked by me, and I proved myself equally valuable to the state and to my friends. When I decided to turn to public affairs, my policies were such as to earn me many crowns from my native city as well as from many other Greeks, and not even you my enemies would venture to say that my policies were anything but honourable. Such, then, has been the fortune of my life; although there is much more I could say about this, I will leave it aside, for fear that my pride might give offence to someone. But you, the proud man who spit upon others, see what your fortune has been in comparison. As a child you were brought up in great poverty, helping your father in a school, grinding the ink, wiping the benches, sweeping the waiting-room[2], doing the duty of a slave[3] and not a free-born boy. When you reached manhood, while your mother was performing her initiation rites[4], you would read out the books to her[5] and help in all the ceremonies. At night you would hold out the fawn-skin and the crater, you would purify the initiates and spatter them with mud and bran, and you would raise them after the lustration and tell them to say 'I have escaped from evil, I have found the good', priding yourself on yelling more powerfully than anyone else[6] (I can well believe him; do not imagine that with the powerful voice he has he cannot produce some ear-splitting noises). [. . .] When you were enrolled on the list of demesmen (by what means I will not enquire) you immediately chose the noblest of professions, to be secretary and assistant of minor officials[7]. When you gave up this job as well, after doing all the things you accuse others of, your subsequent career did not, by Zeus, disgrace your beginnings. You hired your services to those actors known as 'the bellowers', Simykkas and Socrates, you played the third roles[8], picking up figs, grapes and olives like a vegetable merchant from someone else's estates. [. . .] But leaving aside things which might be attributed to your poverty I want to go on to accusations which concern your own character. [. . .] Consider therefore side by side, calmly and without bitterness, what our respective lives have been, Aeschines. Then ask these gentlemen here whose fate each of them would choose. You taught writing, I went to school; you initiated, I was being initiated; you were a scribe, I took part in the assembly; you played third roles, I was a spectator; you fell down, I booed.

DEMOSTHENES, *On the Crown*, 257–65

1 On the common elements among these 'moderates' (Isocrates, Xenophon, Aeschines), see J. de Romilly, 'Les modérés athéniens vers le milieu du IVe siècle: échos et concordances', *REG* 67 (1954), pp. 327–54.
2 The waiting-room for the 'pedagogues', slaves who accompanied their young masters to school.
3 Demosthenes suggests several times in the *De Corona* that his opponent is in reality the son of a slave and a prostitute, a theme which was to be expected in a speech delivered before a jury of citizens.
4 The mother of Aeschines was priestess in a Thracian mystery cult.
5 The word is again offensive: a free man has the volume, which needs unravelling, read out to him, he does not read it himself. Aeschines is reading here the initiation books.
6 The Greek word refers to the shouts of women at the moment of the sacrifice.

7 Part of the secretarial personnel of the city was composed of slaves.

8 The third actor played the least important roles.

114 Equality and the origin of revolutions

The whole of Book V of Aristotle's *Politics* is a meditation on *stasis*, the internal conflicts of the cities, whatever may be otherwise the direction assumed by these upheavals; this meditation obviously draws on the crises of the fourth century in which the philosopher was, as Plato had tried to be before, a direct agent[1] and it also draws of course on what he knows of previous history. To these crises, which nowadays we would describe as economic and social, but which are all political crises, and to this history, Aristotle does not in any way try to give a 'meaning'. The change from oligarchy to democracy is in no way privileged in his view as compared with the opposite evolution[2]. Aristotle is seeking to describe what lies at the root of sudden changes and finds the answer in the different forms assumed by the aspiration towards equality and inequality.

> We must first assume, as a basis of our argument, that the reason why there is a variety of different constitutions is the fact – already mentioned – that while men are all agreed in doing homage to justice, and to the principle of proportionate equality, they fail to achieve it in practice[3]. Democracy arose on the strength of an opinion that those who were equal in any one respect were equal absolutely, and in all respects. (Men are prone to think that the fact of their all being equally free-born that they are all absolutely equal.) Oligarchy similarly arose from an opinion that those who were unequal in some one respect were altogether unequal. (Those who are superior in point of wealth readily regard themselves as absolutely superior.) Acting on such opinions, the democrats proceed to claim an equal share in everything, on the ground of their equality; the oligarchs proceed to press for more, on the ground that they are unequal – that is to say, more than equal. Both democracy and oligarchy are based on a sort of justice; but they both fall short of absolute justice. This is the reason why either side turns to sedition (*stasis*) if it does not enjoy the share of constitutional rights which accords with the concep-

tion of justice it happens to entertain. Those who are pre-eminent in merit would be the most justified in attempting sedition (though they are the last to make the attempt); for they – and they only – can reasonably be regarded as enjoying an absolute superiority[4]. There are also those who, possessing an advantage of birth, regard themselves as entitled to more than an equal share on the ground of this advantage. Good birth is commonly regarded as the attribute of those whose ancestors had merit as well as wealth. These, in a general sense, are the sources and springs of sedition (*stasis*), and the causes of seditious action. These considerations will also explain the two different ways in which constitutional changes may happen. Sometimes sedition is directed against the existing constitution, and is intended to change its nature – to turn democracy into oligarchy, or oligarchy into democracy; or, again, to turn democracy and oligarchy into 'polity'[5] and aristocracy, or, conversely, the latter into the former. Sometimes, however, it is not directed against the existing constitution. The seditious party may decide to maintain the system of government – an oligarchy, for example, or a monarchy – as it stands; but it will desire to get the administration into the hands of its members. Also, a seditious party may wish to make it more pronounced or more moderate. It may wish, for example, to make an oligarchy more, or less, oligarchical. It may wish to make a democracy more, or less, democratic. It may similarly seek to tighten, or loosen, the strings in any of the other forms of constitution.

ARISTOTLE, Politics V, 1301 a 25–1301 b 18
(trans. E. Barker)

1 Aristotle's role as tutor of Alexander, or the links established by him with a tyrant like Hermeias of Atarneus, are essentially different from the role Plato, an aristocrat whose family was involved in Athenian life, could hope to play in Athens or even in the Sicilian adventures of the disciples of Socrates. The founder of the Lyceum was at Athens a metic; this marginal position had some part in his detachment and lucidity (see further D. Whitehead, 'Aristotle the Metic', *Proceedings of the Cambridge Philological Society* 201 (1975), pp. 94–9).

2 By contrast the great debate on political regimes which Herodotus (III, 80–3) attributes to the three Persian leaders

suggests that in his view the democratic regime represents, for the Greeks at least, a privileged historical outcome.

3 Justice is for Aristotle a proportionate mean between two inequalities (see *Nicomachean Ethics* V, 1131 a ff.); a just sharing between two unequal persons is a proportionate sharing, and therefore an unequal one in the eyes of ancient democrats, and it is this proportionality which Aristotle calls 'equality'. Democracies are right in seeking equality, but wrong in thinking that all must be equal; oligarchies put forward the principle of inequality, but forget that inequality must be reserved for unequals only and that the criterion of distinction must not be wealth alone; see *Politics* III, 1280 a 6ff. and in general F.D. Harvey, 'Two Kinds of Equality', *Classica et Mediaevalia* XXVI (1965), pp. 101–46 and XXVII (1966), pp. 99–100.

4 Contrary to the wealthy and 'well-born'.

5 *Politeia*, the word frequently used by Aristotle in a technical sense to describe a 'mixed constitution'.

115 The theoric fund as an instrument of conflict between rich and poor in Athens? (340)

After witnessing the violence of the struggles between rich and poor one may now return to the theoric fund. On the eve of the decisive confrontation between Philip and Athens Demosthenes approaches it in a traditional way. Since the time of Solon the city acts as arbiter in the struggle between rich and poor (cf. no 36) and it is still in those terms that Demosthenes approaches it: it is normal that the rich should be rich and want to remain so, and it is normal that the poor, who are citizens and who are therefore 'our fathers' (it should be repeated that the city is not the abstract state), should expect the city to provide for their maintenance plus a little extra. Let one therefore ask the rich to perform their civic duty and the poor not to perpetually slander the rich and not drag them too often before the Heliaea. But was that the real issue? The extremely rapid development of the theoric fund comes essentially after 356, the date of the failure of the second Athenian confederacy. It does not in any way look like a democratic conquest but rather like an instrument of the moderates who, in a spirit not unlike that of Xenophon (see nos 96, 122), are offering the poor a substitute for what had always been their policy, namely foreign domination. At a time when no programme of this kind was conceivable any longer for Athens, it was a point of view which Demosthenes could hardly put forward.

There is another matter[1] which does harm to the city; she is subjected to unjust abuse and unseemly slander, and this further gives an excuse to those who are unwilling to perform any of their duties as citizens; indeed you will find that this is the pretext put forward whenever anyone fails to discharge his obligations. I am very wary of touching on this subject, but I shall speak out all the same. For I believe that I can put the case for the poor to the rich, with advantage to the city, and the case for the owners of property to the poor, provided we remove from the discussion[2] both the calumnies which some direct unjustly at the theoric fund and the fear that the fund cannot be maintained without grave risk. Nothing would help our cause more than this, nothing would strengthen more the city as a whole.

Consider the problem. I shall speak first on behalf of those who appear to be in need. There was a time, not long ago, when the revenue of the city did not exceed 130 talents. Yet none of those who qualify for trierarchic service or for the payment of war tax (*eisphora*) thought of evading his obligations on the grounds that there was no surplus of money, and triremes were launched, money was found and we did everything we had to. After this the fates smiled on us and increased the public revenues so that we got 400 talents instead of 100[3]; none of the property owners has been victimized, on the contrary they have done well, for all the rich come to take a share in the surplus, and rightly so. Why then do we reproach one another over this and treat it as a pretext for evading our obligations? Unless we grudge the relief which fortune has brought to the poor. I for one will not reproach them for this, nor do I think it right to do so. In private families I do not see any young man treating his elders in this way, nor showing such lack of feeling and unreasonableness as to pretend that if everybody does not do the same as he does he will refuse to do anything himself. Such a person would certainly come under the laws for ingratitude. For I believe that the maintenance of parents, which is prescribed both by nature and by law, should be provided honestly and willingly. Now, just as each of us has a father, so we must consider all the citizens to be the common fathers of the whole city, and it is therefore right not only that they should not be deprived of anything they receive from the city, but also that one should find other resources elsewhere should these fail, to make sure that they are not left in want of anything. I think that if the rich keep to this principle they will not only do justice but even act in their own interest. To deprive someone of necessaries by a public decision is to cause many to become dissatisfied with the existing state of affairs.

But as for those who are in need, I would advise them to put an end to an abuse which exasperates the property owners and justifies their complaints. In talking on behalf of the wealthy I shall follow the same procedure as before and shall not hesitate to say the truth. I cannot believe that anyone, let alone an Athenian, is so wretched and hard-hearted as to resent the assistance received by the poor and needy. Where then is the pinch of the matter and whence the discontent? It is when they see certain persons transferring a habit established with public funds to private property[4], and prosecutors becoming immediately influential with you and enjoying a guarantee of impunity, and your secret votes contradicting your public clamours. This is what creates distrust and resentment. What is needed, men of Athens, is that within the community all should practise reciprocal justice; the wealthy must feel secure in their livelihoods and should be free from fear over this matter; in times of danger they must place their property at the disposal of the community for its preservation; the others must regard as common property in which all have a share only what is so, but must treat as private property what each individual possesses. It is in this way that a small city becomes a large one and that a large one preserves itself. This is perhaps how one may describe the reciprocal rights and obligations of each side; to bring about their observance through law, some regulation should be made.

DEMOSTHENES, *Fourth Philippic*[5], 35–45

1 The speaker has just been talking about the relations of Athens with, respectively, the Great King and Philip of Macedon.
2 In Greek: remove from the middle (*meson*).

3 It will be noted that to enhance his point the speaker substitutes a round but lower figure for the 130 talents mentioned in the previous sentence. However there may conceivably be an error in the manuscript tradition.

4 It is a duty for the good citizen to denounce those who squander the wealth of the state, but the speaker is also attacking the 'sycophants' who slander the rich to obtain the confiscation of their fortune, partly for their own profit.

5 The attribution to Demosthenes of this speech which does not seem to have been delivered is disputed by some scholars.

116   The wealthy today

Nothing is more commonplace in the fourth century than the following remarks of Demosthenes in a speech in the law courts in 352: the private sphere has taken over from the public one, the wealth of individuals has replaced that of the state. The monuments of the age of Pericles are already 'classical'.

In former times the city was wealthy and magnificent, but in private life no individual was raised above the multitude. Here is the proof: if any of you knows by chance the sort of house that Themistocles, or Miltiades, or one of the great names of that time had, he can see that it is no more impressive than that of the common people, whereas the public buildings and constructions are so grand and of such quality that there is no likelihood that they will ever be surpassed in future – I mean the Propylaea, the shipyards, the stoas, Peiraieus and other constructions which now adorn the city. But nowadays all professional politicians are so wealthy that they have built themselves private houses which are more impressive than many public buildings, and some of them have acquired more land than is owned by all of you in this court. As to the public buildings you put up and whitewash, I am ashamed to say how small and shabby they are. [. . .] In those days Aristeides, who was given full powers to fix the tributes[1], did not get richer by a drachma, and at his death he had to be buried at the city's expense. Any time you needed money, there was more in the public treasury than all the other Greeks had, so that pay was available for the whole duration of any expedition you voted to send out. But now those who manage public affairs have changed from beggars to rich men, and have accumulated enough to live in abundance for a long time; while you do not have enough in the treasury to pay for a single day's campaigning, and if there is need to do anything you do not have the means for it. For in those days the people was master of the politicians, now he is their servant.

DEMOSTHENES, *Against Aristocrates*, 206–9

1 The tributes paid by the members of the 'Delian League' founded by Aristeides.

117 Internal struggles in Sicily (from *c.* 466)

Social and political struggles in Sicily are liable to be complicated (1) by the frequent presence of the Carthaginian enemy, which encouraged military tyranny; (2) by the action of a native population which occasionally makes demands for land and may even adopt Greek modes of organization for the purpose; (3) by the existence, itself a consequence of the first two points, of many groups of mercenaries who sometimes mean to establish themselves as Greek cities. That is why the 'democratic interlude'[1] in Sicily was to be short-lived.

In Sicily the Syracusans, who were at war with the mercenaries who had revolted[2], kept launching regular attacks on Achradina and the island. They defeated the rebels in a sea fight, but on land were unable to expel them from the city because of the strength of these two positions. But later on a battle took place on open land; both sides fought with spirit and took risks, both sides suffered heavy casualties, but victory lay with the Syracusans. After the battle they crowned the élite troops, 600 in number, who were responsible for the victory, and gave them as prize for valour a mina of silver each[3].

While this was happening Ducetius the leader of the Sicels, who resented the way in which the settlers of Catana had seized the land of the Sicels, made an expedition against them. And since the Syracusans had also sent an army against Catana, they jointly shared out the land among themselves and waged war on the settlers who had been established by the dynast Hieron[4]. The inhabitants of Catana resisted but were defeated in many battles, and so they were expelled from

Catana and took possession of the place now called Aitna, but formerly known as Inessa[5]; as for the original inhabitants of Catana, they returned to their native city after a considerable lapse of time[6].

After these events the peoples who had been expelled from their own cities under the tyranny of Hieron, now that they had allies on their side, returned to their native cities and expelled from them those who had wrongfully seized the cities of others; among these were the people of Gela, Acragas and Himera. Similarly the people of Rhegium with the help of those of Zancle[7] expelled the children of Anaxilas[8] who were ruling over them and freed their native cities. Later on the people of Gela, who were the original settlers of Camarina, divided up its territory in lots. Virtually all the cities, being anxious to have finished with the wars, came to a common decision and made terms with the mercenary colonists; they received back the exiles and restored the cities to their former inhabitants, but to the mercenaries who because of the tyrannies were in possession of the cities of others they gave permission to take with them their own chattels and go and settle *en masse* in Messenia[9]. In this way, then, the civil wars and disturbances in Sicily were brought to a conclusion[10], and the cities abolished the constitutions imposed on them by outsiders, and almost without exception divided their own territory in lots among all their citizens.

DIODORUS XI, 76

1 The title used by M.I. Finley (*Ancient Sicily*, pp. 58–73) to summarize the events of the years 466–405.

2 Democracy had been set up in Syracuse in 466 after the expulsion of the tyrant Thrasyboulos, brother of Hieron and the last representative of the Deinomenids, but the first gesture of the victorious democrats was allegedly to refuse to the mercenaries introduced by the tyrant Gelon the full status of citizens. The mercenaries revolted and occupied the island of Ortygia and the quarter of Achradina (cf. Diodorus XI, 72–3).

3 This involved running the risk of seeing a new military aristocracy establish itself.

4 In 476 Hieron had expelled the population of Catana, renamed Etna, and had settled there 5,000 (?) Peloponnesians and as many Syracusans. The inhabitants of Catana were themselves

settled at Leontinoi (Diodorus XI, 49).

5 At the foot of Mt Etna, between Paterno and Santa Maria di Licadia.

6 Diodorus does not tell us how the former inhabitants of Catana came to an understanding with the Sicilians of Ducetius, but the latter was soon to assume the position of leader of the natives against the Greek settlers.

7 Reggio di Calabria and Messina. On these events, cf. G. Vallet, *Rhégion et Zancle* (Paris, 1958), pp. 337ff.

8 Anaxilas of Rhegium had seized Zancle in 490, settled there his Messenian compatriots and renamed the city Messina. He died in 476.

9 One must recall that at the time it was occupied by the Spartans.

10 Diodorus is not being sarcastic here.

118 Alcibiades and the social and political disturbances in Sicily (415)

Alcibiades justifies the Athenian expedition to Sicily by alleging the social instability of the Greek cities of the island (cf. also no 17). Similar arguments are developed (according to Thucydides VI, 38–9) by the Syracusan democrat Athenagoras who refuses however to believe in the possibility of an Athenian expedition.

And do not rescind your resolution to attack Sicily, on the ground that you would be going to attack a great power. The cities in Sicily are peopled by motley rabbles; the body of citizens is frequently unstable in composition and open to newcomers[1]. And consequently the inhabitants, being without any feeling of patriotism, are not provided with arms for their persons, and have not established themselves regularly on the land; every man thinks that either by fair words or by party strife he can obtain something at the public expense, and then in the event of failure settle in some other country, and makes his preparations accordingly. From a mob like this you need not look for either unanimity in counsel or concert in action; but they will probably one by one come in as they get a fair offer, especially if they are torn by civil strife, as we are told.

THUCYDIDES VI, 17, 2–4
(trans. R. Crawley)

1 Thucydides has notably recalled (V, 4) how the ruling class of Leontinoi was recently absorbed in the citizen body of Syracuse.

119 Timoleon resettles Sicily (*c.* 338–337)

When the Corinthian Timoleon captured Syracuse and defeated both the tyrants and the Carthaginians, his aim was in theory to 'restore democracy on the ruins of tyranny'. In fact Timoleon transplanted populations as had been done in Sicily for the last century and a half, resettled Greek Sicily as a single large unit (and the results of his action are visible in archaeology), and placed his seal on the failure of the city in Sicily, perhaps even more deeply than his contemporary the victor of Chaeronea. For it was indeed in Sicily that for the first time the transition from the city as a social form to the state was made[1]. Plutarch's *Timoleon* from which the famous description which follows is taken derives for the most part from the history of Timaeus of Tauromenium (Taormina), son of the tyrant Andromachus, who was the friend and ally of the Corinthian condottiere and reformer.

> Once he had captured the city[2], he found it deserted of citizens, some having been killed in wars or internal struggles, others exiled by the tyrannies. Because of the decline in population the *agora* of Syracuse had been covered with such a thick overgrowth that horses could pasture there while their grooms lay down in the grass. All the other cities with very few exceptions were full of deer and wild boars, while in the suburbs and around the walls those who had leisure would often go hunting. Nobody who lived in a stronghold or fort would agree to return to the city, and all were seized with horror and loathing of the *agora*, politics and the tribune, which had produced the majority of their tyrants. Timoleon and the Syracusans therefore decided to write to the Corinthians to ask them to send settlers from Greece to Syracuse. Otherwise the country would remain deserted, and they were expecting a major war from Libya. [. . .] When this letter of Timoleon was delivered, accompanied by Syracusan ambassadors who urged them to take care of the city and become its founders for the second time[3], the Corinthians did not seize the opportunity for their own aggrandizement by appropriating Syracuse. On the con-

trary, they started by visiting the sacred competitions in Greece[4] and the greatest of the festivals, and issued a proclamation through heralds that the Corinthians, after overthrowing the tyranny and expelling the tyrant, now invited the Syracusans and any other of the Sicilian Greeks[5] who were willing to come and live in the city, enjoying freedom and autonomy and dividing up the land on just and equal terms[6]. Subsequently they sent messengers to Asia and the islands where they had heard the majority of exiles were living scattered about, and invited them to assemble all at Corinth; they promised to provide at their own expense a safe escort, ships and generals to take them back to Syracuse. Through these proclamations the city of Corinth earned the justest praise and the noblest fame, for freeing the island from her tyrants and saving her from the barbarians, and restoring the country to its citizens. However, the men who assembled at Corinth not being sufficient in number, they asked to receive additional settlers from Corinth and the rest of Greece. Then when the settlers had reached the number of 10,000, they sailed to Syracuse. Many had already joined Timoleon from Italy and Sicily, 60,000 in number[7] according to Athanis[8]; Timoleon divided up the land, but he sold the houses for a total sum of 1,000 talents. He granted the original Syracusans the possibility of buying back their own property, and in this way provided an abundance of funds to the people, so short of money for the war and for all other purposes that they had to offer the statues for sale[9]. A vote was taken on each in turn and an accusation lodged, as though they were magistrates submitting their accounts. It was on this occasion, it is said, that the Syracusans preserved the statue of Gelon the former tyrant, whereas all the others were condemned, because they admired and honoured the man for the victory he had won at Himera[10] against the Carthaginians.

As the city was reviving in this way and receiving an influx of citizens from every quarter, Timoleon, intent on freeing the other cities and eradicating completely tyranny from Sicily, marched against their territory. [. . .] He was determined that his mercenaries should live off the enemy's territory and not remain idle. [. . .] He therefore sent them under the leadership of Deinarchus and Demaretus[11] to the Carthaginian enclave (in the west of the island). They induced many cities to revolt from the barbarians, and not only did they themselves enjoy abundance, but they also provided funds for the war from the booty captured.

PLUTARCH, Timoleon XXII, 4–XXIV

1 On Timoleon see the special issue of the Sicilian periodical *Kokalos* (4, 1958), the somewhat conflicting accounts by M.I. Finley, *Ancient Sicily*, pp. 94–100 and P. Lévêque, 'De Timoleon à Pyrrhos', *Kokalos* 14–15 (1968–9), pp. 135–51, and most recently R.J.A. Talbert, *Timoleon and the Revival of Greek Sicily 344–317 B.C.* (Cambridge, 1974)

2 Syracuse. Plutarch places the repopulating of Syracuse after the capture of the city (343–342); it is better to follow Diodorus XVI, 82–3, who places it later, about 339–338 after the defeat of the Carthaginians. In any case it must have been a long-term undertaking.

3 Second foundations of cities, whether by their former metropolis or by another city, will be characteristic of the Hellenistic and Roman periods.

4 In the fourth century they are the Olympic, Pythian, Nemean and Isthmic Games.

5 Before being addressed to all the Greeks the call is made to all the Sicilians, which shows that through force of circumstances there did not exist an exclusive Syracusan loyalty. This is in sharp contrast with Greece proper.

6 The Corinthian appeal must have attracted all the more notice as it was made at the same time as the 'League of Corinth' was founded, which prohibited, among other subversive measures, redistribution of land.

7 A Syracusan historian of the third century.

8 Diodorus (XVI, 82) gives the following figures: 40,000 settlers for the territory of Syracuse, and 10,000 for that of Agyrrhium (west of Mt Etna).

9 The statues of tyrants, which must have been plentiful.

10 In 480.

11 Probably identical with mercenary captains known to have served with Philip of Macedon (H.W. Parke, *Greek Mercenary Soldiers* (1933), p. 173), and therefore unconnected with their namesakes in Syracusan history at the end of the fourth century.

120   The fortune of Demosthenes' father (*c.* 380)

The fortune of Demosthenes' father, as described by him, though not without some inaccuracies, is made up solely – with the one exception of a house – of movable property: skilled slaves, some of whom (like the makers of beds) have been handed over to him as security for a loan, maritime loans and bank deposits. Fortunes of recent origin are numerous in Athens, but when Demosthenes attacks the *nouveaux riches* he says: 'Some of them have acquired more land than is owned by all the members of the court together'[1] and certainly, although one hears of various fortunes in which loans and movables played a very important role[2], the fortune of Demosthenes' father is the only one on this scale known to us which did not include a rural estate. The value of the slaves, those at least whose price is specified, is well in excess of the prices listed in no 75, which admittedly resulted from a public auction; the technical competence of the slaves may also be another explanation[3].

My father, men of the jury, left two factories, in each of which a substantial trade was carried on. One was a knife factory consisting of 32 or 33 workmen, some worth five or six minae, others at least 3 minae; from them my father got a clear annual income of 30 minae. The other was a bed factory consisting of 20 workmen, which were given to him as security for a debt of 40 minae[4]. Further there was a talent of silver which had been loaned at an interest of one drachma per mina[5]; the annual interest amounted to more than seven minae. So much for the productive capital left by my father, as my opponents[6] will admit: in all a capital of four talents, 5,000 drachmae, which produced 50 minae every year. In addition, there was ivory and iron for use in the factory, and wood for the beds worth about 80 minae, and gall[7] and bronze bought for 70 minae. Also a house worth 3,000 minae, furniture, cups, golden objects, clothes, my mother's jewellery, all worth about 10,000 drachmae, and in the house 80 minae in silver. So much for what was left at home. Besides there were 70 minae in maritime loans to Xuthus, 2,400 drachmae deposited at Pasion's bank, 600 at Pylades', 1,600 drachmae in the hands of Demomeles son of Demon, and loans of 200 or 300 drachmae at a time which amounted to a talent. All this added up to a total of more than eight talents and 30 minae[8].

The grand total of all this you will find amounts to 14 talents.
DEMOSTHENES, *Against Aphobos* I, 9–11

1 *Against Aristocrates* 23, 208 (see no 116).
2 For example that of the opponent of Phainippos in the speech *Against Phainippos* of Ps.-Demosthenes (XX). The speaker actually emphasizes that the property of Phainippos does not run the risks his does.
3 See Cl. Mossé, *La fin de la démocratie athénienne*, pp. 192–3.
4 One must therefore distinguish (1) the price of the slaves who make knives, which is a market price, (2) the total sum of the loan for which the 20 slaves who make beds have been handed over to the father of Demosthenes as a security. It is clear that the deposit was worth much more than the loan; cf. M.I. Finley, *Studies in Land and Credit*, p. 116.
5 From the context one must understand a drachma per mina and per month, which corresponds to a monthly interest of 1 per cent and an annual interest of 12 per cent.
6 The uncles and tutors of Demosthenes, whom he is accusing of having squandered his inheritance.
7 Used for dyeing.
8 That is the figure in the manuscripts, and editors have sought to correct it, since the addition gives in fact eight talents and 50 minae; but one need not suppose that Demosthenes' arithmetic was flawless and in any case it is impossible to reach exactly the total of 14 talents given in the text.

121 **A written contract for a bottomry loan** (*c.* 340)
The contract for a bottomry loan in the speech *Against Lakritos* is the one surviving example for the fourth century of this type of contract, the first novelty of which was to exist in a written form. In this kind of operation the ship and its cargo serve as security for the loan. There is a clause covering the possible inadequacy of the security, in which case the creditor has the option of seizing other property belonging to the debtors, but in conformity with the fundamental rule of security in ancient Greece, there is no clause to cover the possibility of the security producing a sum higher than the debt. The security once seized belongs to the creditor. As in all these types of contract the rate of interest is fairly high (and it varies according to the distance

and the season of the year); this is sufficiently accounted for by
the risks run. It has been seen (no 120) that Demosthenes' father,
a fairly wealthy manufacturer, bequeathed at his death a sum of
money deposited in a bank. Bank deposits and bottomry loans
share with certain forms of loans on the security of real estate
(see nos 123, 124) the common characteristic of being based on
written documents, but this does not imply any form of link
between these three forms of setting money free. M.I. Finley has
shown that the world of the *Horoi*, that of wealthy landowners
getting into debt in order to preserve their social status, had nothing in common with the world of bottomry loans[1], and similarly
R. Bogaert has shown on his side that there is no known example
of a banker taking part in a bottomry loan[2]. The innovators
remain outsiders, and this was to be the case throughout Hellenistic history.

> Androcles of the deme of Sphettus and Nausikrates of Carys-
> tus[3] have lent to Artemon and Apollodorus, both of Phaselis[4],
> 3,000 drachmae for a voyage from Athens to Mende or
> Skione[5], and thence to Bosphorus, or if they wish, on the left
> coast[6] as far as Borysthenes[7], and back to Athens. The interest
> is at the rate of 225 for 1,000, and if they set sail from Pontus
> to Hieron[8] after the rise of Arcturus[9], 300 for 1,000. The loan
> is made on the security of 3,000 jars of wine from Mende, to be
> uplifted at Mende or Skione in the 20-oared ship commanded
> by Hyblesios, the security to be free from all loans present or
> future[10]. The goods purchased in Pontus in exchange for this
> cargo[11] shall be brought back to Athens in the same ship. Once
> they have been brought safely back to Athens, the borrowers
> shall repay to the lenders the capital and the interest within 20
> days according to the agreement, in full except for jettison[12]
> carried out by a common decision of the passengers or ransom
> paid to the enemy, and no reduction to be granted for any
> other loss. The security shall be made available to the creditors,
> to remain under their full control until the payment of the
> capital and interest in accordance with the agreement. If pay-
> ment is not made within the stipulated period, the creditors
> shall be allowed to pledge the security or sell it at current
> prices. And if the sum raised falls short of the sum owed to the
> creditors according to the agreement, the creditors shall have
> the right, whether singly or jointly, to levy the amount by

execution against Artemon and Apollodorus and all their property, whether on land or sea, wherever they happen to be, as if judgment had been given against them and they were in default of payment. If they do not complete their voyage, they should remain in the Hellespont for ten days after the rising of the dog star and unload their goods in a port where no reprisals may be exercised against the Athenians[13], and then sail back to Athens and pay the interest written into the agreement the year before. And if the ship in which the goods are conveyed should meet with any irretrievable disaster, and if any of the goods serving as security are saved[14], what is saved shall belong jointly to the creditors. On all these matters the present agreement is to have final authority. Witnesses: Phormio of the deme of Peiraieus, Cephisodotus of Boeotia, Heliodorus of the deme of Pithos.

[DEMOSTHENES], *Against Lakritos*, 10–13

1 *Studies in Land and Credit*, p. 27.
2 'Banquiers, courtiers et prêts maritimes à Athènes et à Alexandrie', *Chronique d'Egypte* 40 (1965), pp. 140–56. See generally G.E.M. de Ste Croix, 'Ancient Greek and Roman Maritime Loans', in *Debits, Credits, Finance and Profits. Essays in Honour of W.T. Baxter*, ed. Harold Edey and B.S. Yamey (London, 1974), pp. 41–59, esp. pp. 44–6.
3 A city in Euboea.
4 A Dorian city in Asia Minor. It will be noted that lenders and borrowers belong to three different cities.
5 In Chalcidice.
6 i.e. following the west coast of the Black Sea.
7 As pointed out to us by B. Bravo, this refers to the city of Borysthenes (Olbia), not to the river (Dniepr) nor to the 'liman' (lagoon) of the Dniepr and Bug.
8 At the outlet of the Bosphorus into the Black Sea.
9 At the beginning of autumn.
10 The cargo which serves as security cannot guarantee another loan, for example.
11 The merchants will sell in a port on the Black Sea the wine taken on board at Skione or Mende; goods purchased with the proceeds of that sale will constitute the lenders' security.
12 Rules on 'jettison', that is to say on the obligation which might arise in rough weather to throw overboard part or whole of

the cargo, are one of the foundations of maritime law from
antiquity to the present time. See G.E.M. de Ste Croix, op. cit.,
pp. 57–8.

13 Either in a city in which no citizen can show a debt against an
Athenian which gives him the option of seizing Athenian
goods or in a city which has ratified with Athens a convention
forbidding reprisals (cf. above no 54). B. Bravo, however,
would interpret the passage differently, rendering 'in a place
where the Athenians do not find themselves in a state of
reprisals'; this would refer to a situation arising where the
authorities of a given state proclaim that any member of that
state (citizen or metic) may seize the goods of any member
(citizen or metic) of another (specified) state, in this case
Athens, an ambiguous situation intermediary between the
state of war and the state of peace; see his forthcoming
Recherches sur le droit de représailles en Grèce ancienne.

14 In case of total loss of the cargo, the creditors will not get
anything.

122   Xenophon: foreigners and traders in the city

The proposals put forward by Xenophon to increase the number
of metics and encourage the settlement of traders at Athens and
Peiraieus remain, like those of Plato (nos 126, 127), within the
traditional framework of the city. Xenophon, around 355, wants
the Athenians to perform their military obligations (whereas the
army is in fact dominated by mercenaries) and would like to
entrust the economic sector to outsiders. He is drawing the
conclusion from one major fact: as seen, whereas metics in the
fifth century were, in Athens, Greeks and even 'quasi-Athenians',
by the mid-fourth century they are fundamentally non-Greeks
(many of whom must admittedly become rapidly hellenized). But
Xenophon is probably not well aware of the profoundly subversive aspects of some of his proposals, notably the proposal to
extend for the benefit of the metics the right to own land in the
city. '(The) proposal is to be taken as . . . a very enlightened
attempt to change, though very partially, the legal situation of
the metic population according to their real economic role in
fourth-century Athens[1].' The proposal was not of course adopted,
but it is a fact that the majority of decrees granting to foreigners
the right to own land date from the fourth century[2], and that

some of them are in favour of traders, while others reward wealthy 'benefactors' (*euergetai*) who contribute through their generosities to the enriching of Athens[3]. From this point of view, as from many others, Xenophon is already a man of the Hellenistic age.

All the advantages I have mentioned are, I believe, due to the country itself[4]. But to our indigenous advantages it would be worth adding concern for the metics; they seem to me to be among the finest sources of revenue, since they are self-supporting, confer many advantages on the cities, yet do not get any salary but pay the *metoikion*[5]. Concern for the metics would be adequately shown, in my view, by the lifting of restrictions on them[6] which do no good to the city, and by relieving them of the obligation to serve as hoplites together with the citizens. It represents a great risk for them, and it is a serious matter for them to have to leave their occupations or their houses. The city itself would gain if the citizens were to serve in the ranks together instead of being mixed up, as is the case at present, with Lydians and Phrygians and Syrians and other barbarians from all over the world; for there are many metics of this kind. In addition to the advantage they would gain in being exempted from military service, it would be an honour for the city that the Athenians should be thought to rely in battle on themselves rather than on foreigners. I believe further that if we were to grant to the metics admission to various honorific functions, including serving in the cavalry[7], we would make them even better disposed to us and would increase the greatness and strength of the city. Further, since there are within the walls[8] many empty spaces without houses, if the city were to confer on worthy candidates the right to own land on which to build houses, I believe that there would be many more foreigners and of greater distinction who would be keen to live in Athens. Finally, if we were to institute a body of guardians of the metics similar to the existing guardians of the orphans[9], and some kind of distinction were to be conferred on those who could show the longest list of metics, this would also make them better disposed and it would be reasonable to expect all stateless individuals to be anxious to become metics in Athens and thus to increase our revenues.

I shall now talk about the exceptional amenities and advantages of our city for commerce[10]. In the first place she has the finest and safest harbourings for ships; one can anchor there and rest secure from bad weather. Moreover in the majority of cities traders must bring a return cargo with them as the currency they use is not valid abroad[11]; but at Athens the majority of goods that are of use to anyone can be taken as return cargoes, and if one does not want to do this, one can export silver, an excellent commodity, since wherever one sells it one makes a profit on the original investment[12]. And if one were to give prizes to the magistrates of the markets for the just and speedy settlement of disputes[13], so that one would not be detained from sailing off when one wished, then traders would come in much greater numbers and with greater readiness. It would also be an excellent idea to assign seats of honour to traders and shipowners and on occasion even to offer public hospitality to those who appear to be useful to the city through the size of their ships and of their cargoes[14]. Thanks to these honours they would be eager to visit us as friends for the sake of honour[15] as well as for profit. The increase in the number of residents and visitors would obviously result in an increase in the volume of imports and exports[16], of sales, rents and custom dues.

To bring about such an increase in our revenues would not cost us anything beyond the passing of decrees of welcome[17] and measures of control[18]. [. . .]

I know too that heavy expenditure has often been incurred to send out triremes without anyone being at all clear whether this would do harm or good, and the only certain thing was that the subscribers[19] would never recover their original outlay and would not even get a share of their contribution. But there is no better investment than one in which one recovers one's initial capital outlay: for anyone who paid a contribution[20] of ten minae, bringing three obols a day, would get a return of nearly 20 per cent[21], as much as from a maritime loan[22], and anyone who subscribed five minae would get more than a third. The majority of Athenians would get an annual return higher than their original investment, for those who advanced one mina would get a revenue of nearly two, which would be guaranteed by the city, the most secure and long-lasting of human institutions[23]. I believe also that if their names were to be inscribed for all time with the title of benefactors[24], then many foreigners would be prepared to contribute, and perhaps some cities would also be keen to have their names inscribed in this way. I hope too that some kings and tyrants and satraps would want to share in this favour[25]. Once the capital was available it would be an excellent idea to build for the ship-owners lodging houses in the vicinity of the harbours in addition to the existing ones, and it would be good also to build for the traders places organized for buying and selling, and public lodging houses for visitors. And if one were to build houses and shops in Peiraieus and in the city even for retail traders, it would both be a distinction to the city and a major source of revenue.

It also seems to me to be worth trying to see whether it was possible for the city, just as she owned public triremes, similarly to acquire public merchant ships and to lease them under security as she does with other public property[26].

XENOPHON, *Ways and Means* II–III

1 J. Pečirka, 'A note on Aristotle's conception of citizenship and the role of foreigners in fourth century Athens', *Eirene* 6 (1967), pp. 23–7, at p. 25.

2 See J. Pečirka, *The Formula for the Grant of Enktesis in Attic Inscriptions* (Prague, 1966). One of these decrees is translated above, no 72.

3 For example the decree of 329, moved by the reformer Lycurgus, a traditionalist if ever there was one, granting *enktesis* to Eudemos of Plataea who had 'promised to give to the people for the war, if necessary, 4,000 drachmae and who actually gave for the construction of the stadium and of the Panathenaic theatre the work of a thousand team of oxen' (Tod, *GHI* II, no 198). On the changing role of benefactors (*euergetai*) from classical to Hellenistic, then Roman, times, see now P. Veyne, *Le Pain et le cirque* (Paris, 1977) and c.f. no 81, n 1. The evolution may be summarized as follows. Inscriptions of the fifth century and of most of the fourth century show the benefactor (*euergetes*) to be an outsider who is also usually granted the title of *proxenos*; he may be seen as an agent of the city, and is proud to serve it, even when he is a non-Greek ruler. In Hellenistic times the *euergetes-proxenos* has become a man on whom the city depends. Concurrently with this external evolution another one takes place internally in the city, whereby the

wealthy citizen who undertakes 'liturgies' (see Chapter 6) becomes himself a *euergetes*. Veyne's book emphasizes the latter aspect at the expense of the former. On the whole passage of Xenophon see now the commentary of the *Ways and Means*, by Ph. Gauthier (Paris and Geneva, 1976).

4 Xenophon has just drawn an idyllic picture of the advantages of the climate and position of Athens.

5 The moderate tax paid by metics (12 drachmae a year for men, 6 for women).

6 This renders the Greek *atimia* which refers specifically to the position of the citizen punished with 'civic death'; the terminology is characteristic. Xenophon is probably thinking especially of the obligation of metics to have a personal patron (*prostates*).

7 This is a considerable paradox, for Xenophon, who did so much to transform the military role of cavalry, removes the metics from the infantry but admits them to the cavalry. One must recall here that what is in Xenophon's eyes an élite corps is also a parading squadron in which the wealthiest Athenians served and took part in processions; the second Athenian property class was in fact called the 'knights' (*hippeis*).

8 The Long Walls which protected Athens and Peiraieus.

9 The patrons of metics were private individuals, and the polemarch exercised general authority over them. In a way which is not very clear and even contradictory (since there is to be a competition between the *metoikophylakes* to find out who had most dependents), Xenophon would like to turn this patronage into an official institution of the city. One will note the assimilation of metics and orphans whose education was provided by the city (cf. R.S. Stroud, 'Theozotides and the Athenian Orphans', *Hesperia* 40 (1971), pp. 280–301, on a recently discovered inscription). On the provisions in this passage for rewarding the 'guardians of the metics' compare Xenophon, *Hiero* IX.

10 Xenophon moves in this paragraph from metics proper, whom he will not mention again, to traders, but the transition is a natural one.

11 On the control exercised by the cities over the exchange of coins see nos 102, 103.

12 Athenian silver circulated almost everywhere because of the reputation for excellence of the 'owls'. Besides, many hoards

in the East, in countries which did not have a coinage, were made of Athenian coins, whether melted down or not. Silver was therefore an exceptionally valuable commodity. See the collection of evidence in E. Schönert-Geiss, 'Die Geldzirkulation Atticas', *Klio* 56, 2 (1974), pp. 377–414.

13 The *dikai emporikai* (commercial actions), which must be decided within a month, would to some extent answer (from *c.* 350 onwards) Xenophon's wish. See the previously mentioned article by L. Gernet, 'Sur les actions commerciales en droit athénien', *Droit et société dans la Grèce ancienne* (Paris, 2nd ed., 1964), pp. 173–200, though cf. too p. 154, n 19.

14 These proposals are again deeply subversive: honorific seats in the theatre were normally reserved for magistrates and for the highest priests. Xenophon is in fact suggesting that one should invite the traders to the prytaneum – an exceptional honour – simply in relation to the importance of their cargo. A quarter of a century after the publication of Xenophon's pamphlet Athens passed a fourfold decree in honour of Heracleides, a merchant from Salamis in Cyprus, who in difficult circumstances during the famine of 330–331, had provided Athens with cheap corn. This inscription (Dittenberger, *Sylloge*[3], no 304) grants a series of honours to this man (a crown, presentation to the people, etc.), but not explicitly hospitality in the prytaneum. Xenophon's proposal goes further as it is based on strictly commercial criteria.

15 By contrast one must emphasize here the importance of non-commercial motivations.

16 There is therefore no question of encouraging exports at the expense of imports. There is no trace of mercantilism in this work.

17 This renders the Greek *philanthropa*.

18 Omitted here is a paragraph in which Xenophon explains that the actual expenditure he is thinking of should not appear heavy for a people who has spent so much for the war.

19 Those who shared in the trierarchy. What Xenophon is suggesting here, in a somewhat allusive way, is that one should replace triremes by merchantmen, and the trierarchical liturgy by a commercial liturgy which would have the advantage of bringing in money instead of costing money. The modernity of the proposal should not be exaggerated. At Phocaea, or at Massilia, trade was a state concern; what is

new is the openly proclaimed theme of individual profit.
20 The Greek word is *eisphora* (tax).
21 One mina = 100 drachmae = 600 obols. This works out at an annual rate of interest of 18 per cent.
22 See no 121.
23 Xenophon's plan which takes into account the traditional policy of the city is to pay a higher rate of interest to small contributors than to large ones. One can see how the city remains at the heart of the plan for commercial development.
24 If the city passed a fine decree which would be inscribed 'on a stone stele'.
25 Xenophon might be thinking of men like Strato of Sidon (cf. no 71). The favour of kings had always been one of the elements of economic acquisition for the cities, but there again Xenophon is innovating when he links the benefactions of kings, satraps and tyrants to an enterprise of merchantmen.
26 The whole of the previous paragraph presupposes the realization of a plan of that kind.

123   Horoi

The existence of these pillars (*horoi*) which, in Athens and in a few other cities in the fourth and third centuries, warned passers-by that a mansion, a house or an estate, or even in some exceptional cases a workshop with the slaves working in it, was encumbered, is to be explained first by a very simple fact: at Athens legislation on the land is virtually non-existent, there is no land register and nothing remotely comparable to a register of mortgages. In case of imposition one is believed on the evidence of one's own statement, though an Athenian might volunteer to demonstrate that he is less wealthy than another Athenian who ought to take over the liturgy which is being imposed on him. The fourth-century pillars have nothing to do with those Solon pulled out (see no 36) and are not evidence for a crisis affecting small peasants. The debtors are men of substance who want to provide a dowry for their daughters, for example, at least when the purpose of the operation is known. In the first inscription one notes a reference to a written contract, and it has been suggested that the rudimentary kind of publicity provided for the debts by the pillars might reflect the diffuse and indirect influence of 'commercial law'. It is difficult to decide.

A   Marble stele at Athens (end of the fourth century)
Pillar of the land and the house hypothecated for 800 drachmae: on condition that the creditor have power[1] according to the agreement deposited[2] with Deinias of the deme of Euonymeia.

M.I. Finley, *Studies in Land and Credit*, no 1 (p. 119)

B   Stele of blue marble, Vari (Attica) (315–314)
In the archonship of Praxiboulos, pillar of the house and of the land and of the house in town sold on condition of release[3], 3,000 (drachmae) to Mneson of the deme of Halai, Mnesiboulos of the deme of Halai, Charinos of the deme of Halai[4].

ibid., no 14 (p. 124)

C   Stele found near Thorikos, in an ancient mine
Gods. Pillar of a workshop and of slaves sold on condition of release to Pheidon of the deme of Aixone. One talent[5].

ibid., no 88 (p. 142)

D   Marble stele, Acharnai (Attica) (302–301)
In the archonship of Nikokles, pillar of the lands, of the house and of the watercourse attached to the lands forming two lots put up as security with evaluation (*apotimema*)[6], for the benefit of Chairippos and Charia, orphans of the (metic) *isoteles* Charias.

ibid., no 116 (p. 151)

E   Marble stone found at Sochoria (Attica)
Pillar of land (put up as security) for the dowry of Hippokleia daughter of Demochares of the deme of Leukonoe: one talent; by whatever it is worth in excess it is hypothecated to the members of the tribe Kekrops, to the members of the *genos* of the Lykomidai, to the members of the deme of Phlya[7].

ibid., no 146 (p. 160)

1   An exceptional clause: the land and the house which are hypothecated are actually handed over as security to the creditor; for the phrase cf. M.I. Finley, *Studies in Land and Credit*, p. 12 with n 11, p. 204.
2   A written act, an innovation characteristic of the fourth century.

3 The owner who has contracted the debt has the option of buying back his property, within a period of time which is never specified, by repaying the lender.

4 There are three lenders, which seems to confirm that the debtor remained in possession of the property which was 'sold' and for which he was paying interest. It should be noted that in this act which is not public the name of the same deme is spelt in three different ways (cf. M.I. Finley, op. cit., p. 199).

5 The workshop is 'sold' at the same time as the slaves whose number is not specified.

6 The hypothecated property is that of the farmer of a pupillary inheritance and not that of the minors themselves. The guarantee affects a portion of the hypothecated property which is estimated to be equal to the sum of the minors' fortune. The latter are in this document (and therein lies its originality) the children of a metic *isoteles*, who had probably been granted the right to own land in Attica, though this is not certain as the minors' fortune may not have consisted in land.

7 The land serves as security for the dowry of Hippokleia up to the value of one talent. It is hard to visualize the operations for which the rest of the land was put up as security; cf. M.I. Finley, op. cit., esp. pp. 98–100, 107–8.

124 Financial difficulties of the Athenian general Timotheus (373–372)

We have already met the Athenian general Timotheus in an earlier passage (no 91) where he was compelled to improvise an emergency coinage to enable his soldiers to purchase supplies. His opponent in the speech which figures among the writings of Demosthenes is Apollodorus son of Pasion, the one-time slave banker who became a citizen and a landowner. This family is unfortunately the only one known to us which provides a semblance of justification to the theory according to which there grew up in the fourth century a 'bourgeoisie', or at least a civilian society which gradually eliminated the former antagonisms between different orders in society. Timotheus is a statesman and it is because of this that he runs into debt since the city is no longer fulfilling its obligations. Perhaps the most striking detail in the passage is the insistence with which the banker Apollodorus emphasizes that the bank keeps written evidence of an oral understanding[1]. Visibly there is an innovation here: the use of written documents has passed from the political to the private sphere.

> Timotheus obtained from my father everything he wanted; he got money from the bank at a time when he was in grave difficulties and in great risk for his life; but not only did he not thank me but he even means to deprive me of what was given to him. Yet if anything had happened to him the obligation[2] incurred with my father would have lapsed, since it was contracted without security and without witnesses. But if he got off safely[3], it was left to him to repay us in his own time, when he had the means. And yet, gentlemen of the jury, my father thought less of his financial advantage than of doing a service to Timotheus in his hour of need. He believed that should Timotheus escape from his present dangers and return home from the Great King's country, he would be in better circumstances than he was then. Not only would my father get his money back from Timotheus, but he would be able to expect services from him. But matters turned out differently from my father's expectations: Timotheus, after the favour done to him when my father gave him from his bank the loan he was requesting, now believes that after my father's death he will have to repay the debt only if convicted in court after hostile legal procedure, and that if he can deceive you into believing that he does not owe anything he will deprive us of our money. I therefore believe I must tell you the whole story from the beginning, about the loans, the use each of them was put to and the date at which the obligations were contracted. And let none of you be surprised that we should know all this in detail: for it is the practice with bankers to keep a record of the money they lend, and for what purpose, and of deposits made with them, so that they should have the facts about debits and credits available for accounting purposes. [. . .]

The speaker goes on to relate, among other things, how Timotheus was relieved of his duties after a military setback.

> These were the charges against him and he was desperately short of money. For all his property had been pledged, pillars (*horoi*) were set up on it, and he no longer owned it[4]. His estate

in the plain was made over as security with estimation⁵ to the
son of Eumelidas, the rest of his estate was pledged to each of
the 60 trierarchs who had sailed with him for seven minae, the
sum he as general had compelled them to pay to the crews for
maintenance. After being deposed by popular vote, he entered
in his accounts this sum of seven minae per ship as having been
given him out of the military treasury, but being afraid the
trierarchs might testify against him and convict him of false-
hood, he contracted a loan of seven minae with each of them
and gave them his property as security. Now he has cheated
them of this money and pulled up the pillars.

[DEMOSTHENES]⁶, *Against Timotheus*, 2–5, 11–12

1 See Cl. Préaux, 'De la Grèce classique à l'Egypte hellénistique.
   La banque-témoin', *Chronique d'Egypte* 33 (1958), pp. 243–55.
2 *Symbolaion* means, in fourth-century terminology, an obligation in general, as opposed to a *syngraphe* (a written contract).
   The contract concluded with Timotheus is purely oral, but
   Pasion's bank keeps a written record of it.
3 Timotheus has borrowed money twice from Pasion's bank: in
   373, on the eve of a military expedition which failed (he had to
   provide the sailors' pay); a second time, in 372, when he
   entered the service of the Great King at war with the Egyptian
   rebels. In the opening of his speech the speaker confuses the
   two events.
4 This does not mean that the creditors were actually occupying
   the estates of Timotheus.
5 Cf. the previous passage (D).
6 The author of the speech may be Apollodorus himself.

125 From the peasant-citizen to the boor

At a century's distance the literary profile of the Athenian peasant
changes. In Aristophanes' *Peace* (421), the peasant admittedly
complains that his turn to go off to war comes back too often and
he curses his commander, but the poet idealizes his way of life
and portrays him as the ideal citizen *par excellence*. By contrast
the 'boor' in Theophrastus' *Characters* (319) is, like the peasants
in New Comedy, a worthless citizen, who is closer to his slaves
than to his fellow-citizens from the town, and an object of
ridicule for them¹.

A   *The Chorus of* The Peace

Chorus   When the cicada sings her sweet note, it is a delight to inspect my Lemnian vines to see they are getting ripe, for it is a precocious plant, and I watch the fig swelling; when it is ripe I eat it avidly, singing at the same time 'Friendly seasons'[2] and I grind the thyme soup; I grow fat at that time in summer.

Chorus leader   That is better than to look at a hated captain[3] with his triple crest and bright purple coat. He says it is dyed in purple from Sardis[4], but if he has to go and fight with that coat on, then his colour changes to a Cyzicene dye[5]. Then he is the first to run away like a tawny cockhorse[6], shaking his crest, while I stand there like a hunter watching the nets[7]. When they get home, it's intolerable what they do to us, inscribing some on the roster, striking others off, all haphazardly and two or three times over. 'Tomorrow we're off on a campaign.' Someone hasn't bought provisions for the campaign; he didn't know he was due to go off. Then standing in front of the statue of Pandion[8] he saw his name on the list, and perplexed by this calamity off he goes with tears in his eyes. That is how we, the peasants, are treated by them, but they treat the townfolk better, these deserters of gods and men. One day, god willing, they will account[9] to me for all this. They have done me many wrongs, these lions in the house, these foxes in the battle!

ARISTOPHANES, *Peace*, 1159–90

B   *The boor*

Boorishness, it would appear, is a disgraceful ignorance. The boor is the kind of man who drinks his thyme soup[10] before going to the assembly and says that nothing smells better than thyme. He wears shoes that are too large for his feet and talks in a loud voice. He distrusts his friends and relatives, but reveals all his most important concerns to his slaves, and back from the assembly tells the labourers he employs on his farm everything that was said there. When he sits down he draws his coat up over his knee so that one can see his nakedness. In the streets nothing causes him surprise or astonishment, but if he sees an ox, a donkey or a goat, he stands there in amazement. Occasionally he takes something from his larder and eats like a glutton, and drinks his wine undiluted. He tries to make love secretly to the baker girl then helps her to grind enough corn for himself and all the members of his household[11]. While having his lunch he goes to give fodder to the draught animals. When someone knocks at the door he answers himself, he takes his dog with him, holds him by the snout and says: 'Here is the guardian of the farm and of the house.' If someone gives him money he tests and refuses it, saying the coins are too light[12] and asks for others instead. If he has lent a plough, a basket, a sickle or a bag, he cannot sleep at night. When he goes to town he asks the first person he meets the price of hides and salted fish [. . .] then he says, he wants to go for a haircut and that on his way he will get salted fish from Archias[13]. At the public bath he sings. He puts nails on his shoes.

THEOPHRASTUS, *Characters* IV

1 See generally O. Ribbeck, 'Agroikos, Eine ethologische Studie', *Abhandlungen der sächsischen Gesellschaft der Wissenschaften*, Philologisch-Historische Klasse, 10, 1 (1888).

2 A popular song.

3 The taxiarch, one of the ten commanders of the hoplite regiments.

4 Purple-dyed material was made there.

5 There is an untranslatable pun here on the name of the city of Cyzicus where a pitch-coloured balm was produced (Pausanias IV, 35, 8) and the verb meaning 'to shit'.

6 A fantastic animal supposed to be swift, mentioned by Aeschylus as a figurehead on ships and represented on vases in the guise of a horse with red wings, whose hind legs and tail are those of a cock; cf. J. Taillardat, *Les Images d'Aristophane*, op. cit., p. 136.

7 Like a hunter entrusted with watching the nets and left abandoned.

8 Mobilization orders were posted on the monument of the ten eponymous heroes of the tribes in the middle of the *agora*. The peasant mentioned hère belongs to the tribe Pandionis.

9 In the political sense of the word. Every magistrate had to submit his accounts.

10 'White thyme' or savory. Savory was, and still is, a very common plant in Attica; mixed with wine, flour and honey it produced a soup (*kykeon*) much liked by peasants, though townsmen apparently disliked its smell.

11 The text is very conjectural.

12 Either because they are worn out, or because they do seem to him too light (Greek coins can vary a good deal in weight, while still retaining the same theoretical value).

13 Presumably a salt-provision merchant.

126 Plato: against the separation of city and countryside (*c*. 350)

The following proposals which aim at making every citizen both a townsman and a countryman are formulated, and that is one of the most significant things about them, at a time when in real life the antithesis between the city and the countryside is growing deeper[1].

> (After this) the legislator must establish the city as far as possible in the centre[2] of the country, after choosing a spot which has all the other requisite advantages; these are not difficult to imagine and enumerate. Next he must divide the space in 12 parts, but he must begin by setting aside a sacred area for Hestia, Zeus and Athena[3] which he will call acropolis and surround with a circular enclosure; then he will divide into 12 parts both the town itself[4] and all the country. The 12 parts must be equal in the sense that parts made up of good land should be smaller and those made up of inferior land should be larger. Five thousand and forty lots must then be marked off, but each of these must be divided in two so that each lot is made up of two parts, one from near the centre and the other from the periphery. One lot will be made up of a part near the city and one near the frontier area, the second next to the city and the second next to the frontier area will constitute another, and so on. And with each half section one must also make sure that the relative quality of the soil is equalized, in the way I have mentioned, by varying the size of each portion of land.

> PLATO, *Laws* V, 745 b–d

1 Cf. J.P. Vernant, *Mythe et pensée chez les Grecs* (Paris, 1965), p. 181.

2 On the values attached to the *centre* in Greek political thought, cf. M. Detienne, *Les maîtres de vérité dans la Grèce archaïque* (Paris, 1967), pp. 83–98.

3 Zeus, god of sovereignty, Hestia, goddess of the 'common-hearth' (prytaneum), Athena goddess of the *Metis* of artisans and of the intellect (see M. Detienne and J.P. Vernant, *Les Ruses de l'intelligence, la Métis des Grecs* (Paris, 1974)).
4 *Polis* here clearly means town.

127 Plato: one must receive foreign traders outside the city and have the fewest possible relations with strangers (*c.* 350)

Like Xenophon (no 122) and in conformity with the Spartan tradition (nos 37, 56), Plato accepts the principle whereby part of economic activity (maritime commerce) must be left to outsiders. However, contrary to Sparta, and contrary to the *Republic*, the city of the *Laws* has its territory cultivated by citizens with full rights. Yet Xenophon had seen that the coming of foreign traders implied some rather substantial concessions. As for Plato he preserves from the Athenian experience the idea of correct justice towards foreign traders, but he keeps them on the fringes of the city.

> Next we must consider how to receive the visitor from abroad. There are four types of foreigners which call for mention[1]. The first is like a migratory bird who comes back regularly, usually during summer. Like birds many of them fly over the seas, traders avid for profit, and come in the summer season to visit foreign cities. Magistrates appointed to deal with these must receive them in market places, harbours and public buildings, near the city but outside it[2]. They must make sure that none of this kind of foreigners introduces any subversive innovation; they shall administer straight justice to them[3], and will have with them only the bare minimum of relations, what cannot be avoided.
>
> PLATO, *Laws* XII, 952 d–953 e

1 Plato deals successively with the trader, the intellectual tourist, the ambassador and the philosopher. Only the paragraph concerning traders is reproduced here.
2 That is to say, in a frontier zone, as it were.
3 Plato is accepting here the principle of the *dikai emporikai* known to Athenian law (cf. no 122, n 13).

128 Aristotle's city and its territory

Compared with Plato's distrust of the sea, Aristotle, whose 'ideal city' is no larger than that of Plato's *Laws* (5,040 households), adopts radically different solutions, for reasons which are both military and economic.

As for the general lie of the land, it is easy to make the suggestion (though here a number of questions arise on which the advice of military experts ought to be taken) that the territory of a state should be difficult of access to enemies, and easy of egress for its inhabitants[1]. What was said above of the population[2] – that it should be such as to be surveyable – is equally true of the territory. A territory which can be easily surveyed is also a territory which can be easily defended. The ideal position for the central city[3] should be determined by considerations of its being easy of access both by land and by sea. The first, which has already been mentioned[4], is that the city should be a common military centre for the dispatch of aid to all points in the territory. The second is that it should also be a convenient commercial centre, where the transport of food supplies, timber for building, and raw materials for any other similar industry which the territory may possess, can easily be handled[5].

It is a hotly debated question whether connection with the sea is to the advantage, or to the detriment, of a well ordered state. There are some who maintain that the introduction of strangers, who have been born and bred under other laws, and the consequent increase of population, is prejudicial to good order[6]. They argue that such an increase is inevitable when numbers of merchants use the sea for the export and import of commodities; and they regard it as inimical to good government[7]. On the other hand, and if only this increase can be avoided[8], there can be no doubt that it is better, in the interest both of security and of a good supply of material necessities, for the city and the territory of a state to be connected with the sea. In order to enjoy security, and to meet enemy attacks more easily, a state should be capable of being defended by sea as well as by land. It will also be in a better position for taking the offensive, and inflicting losses on its assailants, if it is able to use both elements, and to act on one or the other if not on both simultaneously. Similarly, in order to procure supplies, it is imperative that a state should be able to import commodities which it does not itself produce, and to export, in return, the surplus of its own products. It should act as a merchant for itself – but not as a merchant for others[9]. States which make themselves marts for the world only do it for the sake of revenue; and if a state ought not to indulge in this sort of profit making, it follows that it ought not to be an exchange centre (*emporion*) of that kind[10]. We see from the practice of our own times that territories and cities often have ports and harbours which are conveniently placed in relation to the main city – distinct and separate, but not too remote, and thus in a position to be commanded by connecting walls and other and similar fortifications. Any advantage which can be derived from connection with ports and harbours will obviously be secured by these methods; any disadvantage which may threaten can easily be met by legislation which states and defines the persons who may, or may not, have dealings with one another[11].

ARISTOTLE, *Politics* VII, 1326 b 39–1327 a 40

(trans. E. Barker)

1 Either when one must evacuate it completely, as the Athenians did at the time of Salamis (480), or when one merely removes to a safe spot abroad one's flocks, herds, wives, children and movables.
2 *Politics* VII, 1326 b 24.
3 *Polis*, but the word becomes in the fourth century increasingly synonymous with *asty*.
4 *Politics* VII, 1326 b 40.
5 As for example the transport of all mining products.
6 *Eunomia*, a word which is used from Tyrtaeus onwards to describe a well-governed city.
7 That is what Plato notably believes.
8 Thanks in particular to precautions mentioned by Aristotle (see the next passage).
9 A fundamental point. The whole work of Max Weber and J. Hasebroek is simply a commentary on this formula of Aristotle's.
10 After accepting the necessity of maritime commerce Aristotle goes back and condemns the principle of the *emporion* which goes beyond the strict needs of the political community.

11 The unit made up by a city, a harbour and fortifications is characteristic of trading cities for which the defence of the city and of the harbour are more important than the defence of the territory proper (Yvon Garlan, cf. no 110, n 1). Aristotle does not adopt the radical solution of fifth-century Athens – defending only the space enclosed by the 'Long Walls' – but he has to take this urban model into consideration, and expresses the hope that his ideal city can be a trading city, like Massilia, while avoiding subversion and the dangerous contacts brought about by maritime life.

129   The ideal city must separate the 'commercial agora' from the 'free agora'

On the problem raised by the passage in Plato (no 127) Aristotle takes a somewhat less radical position (though not much). He borrows from the Thessalians the idea of the *free agora*, reserved for citizens with full rights, and keeps the name of *agora* for what the old public 'square' had largely become, namely the commercial centre of the city. The *free agora* is carefully integrated with those institutions which concern adults specifically.

Below this site (reserved for public cults) provision should be made for an *agora*, of the sort which is called in Thessaly the *free agora*[1]. This should be clear of all merchandise; and no mechanic, or farmer[2], or other such person, should be permitted to enter, except on the summons of the magistrates. The place would be all the more pleasant if the gymnasia for the older men[3] were included in its plan. The arrangements for the gymnasia (like those for the common tables)[4] should be different for different age groups; and if this plan be followed some of the magistrates[5] should stay with the younger men, while the older men should remain with the magistrates[6]. To be under the eyes of the magistrates will serve, above anything else, to create a true feeling of modesty and fear[7] which should animate free men. The *agora* for buying and selling should be separate from the *free agora*, and at a distance from it: it should occupy a site which forms a good depot, alike for commodities imported by sea and those which come from the state's own territory.

ARISTOTLE, *Politics* VII, 1331 a 30–1331 b 3
(trans. E. Barker)

1 That is to say the place reserved only for those who are free men in the fullest sense. On this passage see R. Martin, *Recherches sur l'agora grecque* (Paris, 1951), pp. 172ff. Exactly the same concept of the *free agora* is applied by Xenophon to his idealized picture of Persian institutions (*Cyropaedia* I, 2, 3–5).

2 Greek political thought is constantly hesitating between two ways of looking at farmers: as the useful citizens *par excellence* (thus Xenophon, cf. no 4) or as men to be excluded from the political community, in the same way as Helots.

3 Yet another example of the separation of age classes, as important as that of social classes.

4 Aristotle has discussed these earlier on.

5 Those in charge of education.

6 With all the magistrates.

7 Fear (*phobos*) and modesty (*aidos*) constitute a pair of qualities which is characteristic of the good citizen from the archaic age onwards.

130 Xenophon's colonization plan (400)

The *Anabasis* was, in Taine's words, a 'travelling republic'. Was it possible to fix it?

At that time Xenophon, seeing all this crowd of Greek hoplites, peltasts[1], archers, slingers and cavalry, all of them seasoned and well-trained, gathered on the Black Sea, where it would have been difficult to collect such a large force without considerable expense, thought that it would be a glorious achievement to increase the territory and power of Greece through the foundation of a city. It seemed to him that it would grow to a considerable size, when he reckoned the number of his compatriots and those who live around the Black Sea. He was making a sacrifice about this plan, before saying a word to any of the soldiers, with the assistance of Silanos of Ambracia who had been the soothsayer of Cyrus[2]. Silanos was afraid that the project would be realized, and that the army would remain on the spot, so he spread a rumour among the ranks that Xenophon wanted the army to stay there and found himself a city which would bring him fame and power. Silanos was personally anxious to return to Greece as soon as possible; he had

managed to preserve intact the 3,000 darics[3] he had received
from Cyrus for predicting accurately during a sacrifice what
would happen within the next ten days. When the soldiers
heard this, some of them thought it would be best to stay, but
the majority disagreed.

XENOPHON, *Anabasis* V, 6, 15–19

1 A light-armed soldier; the *pelte* is a small round shield of
Thracian origin.
2 The Younger Cyrus, the Achaemenid prince with whom the
'Ten Thousand' had taken service.
3 A huge sum.

131　**Plato on war between Greeks**
The following discussion between Socrates and Glaukon on the
usages of war in the ideal state is one of several passages in
fourth-century writers in which the acceptability of wars between
Greeks is challenged, in response no doubt to the increasing
spread and ineffectiveness of such wars. War as such, however,
remains legitimate when directed against non-Greeks[1].

Socrates　And next, how will our soldiers deal with enemies?
– In what respect?
– First take slavery. Is it right that Greek states should sell
Greeks into slavery? Ought they not rather to do all they can
to stop this practice and substitute the custom of sparing their
own race[2], for fear of falling into bondage to barbarians?
– That would be better, beyond all comparison.
– They must not, then, hold any Greek in slavery themselves,
and they should advise the rest of Greece not to do so.
– Certainly. Then they would be more likely to keep their
hands off one another and turn their energies against barbarians.

After rejecting the custom of stripping the dead in battle and
dedicating trophies, Socrates continues:

– And what of ravaging Greek lands and burning houses?
How will your soldiers deal with their enemies in this matter?
– I would like to hear your own opinion.

– I think they should do neither, but only carry off the year's harvest. Shall I tell you why?

– Please do.

– It seems to me that war (*polemos*) and civil strife (*stasis*) differ in nature as they do in name, according to the two spheres in which disputes may arise: at home or abroad, among men of the same race or with foreigners. War means fighting with a foreign enemy; when the enemy is of the same kindred, we call it civil strife.

– That is a reasonable distinction.

– Is it not also reasonable to assert that Greeks are a single people, all of the same kindred and alien to the outer world of barbarians?

– Yes.

– Then we shall speak of war when Greeks fight with barbarians, whom we may call their natural enemies. But Greeks are by nature friends of Greeks, and when they fight, it means that Hellas is afflicted by dissension which ought to be called civil strife.

PLATO, *Republic* V, 469 b–c, 470 a–c
(trans. F.M. Cornford)

1 See for example no 108 (Isocrates); Aristotle, *Politics* VII, 1324 a 36–1325 a 15; 1333 b 11–1334 a 10 and the following passage; generally, Cl. Mossé, *La fin de la démocratie athénienne* (1962), pp. 426–39.

2 This again echoes a growing feeling in the fourth century; cf. Cl. Mossé, op. cit., p. 190.

132   The peoples of Asia, Europe and Greece

The theme of the comparison between the peoples of Europe, Asia and Greece, with for the latter country a position which is at once measured and central is at least as old as Herodotus[1], and the same applies to the theme of the barbarians of Asia who are doomed to slavery[2], but it was not automatically accompanied by the idea that the Greeks should reduce to slavery all the barbarians. Yet that is what one can read between the lines right through Aristotle's *Politics*, in the time of Alexander, and for example in the following passage (cf. also the passages from Isocrates and Plato, nos 108 and 131).

The peoples of cold countries generally, and particularly those of Europe, are full of spirit, but deficient in intelligence and skill[3]; and this is why they continue to remain comparatively free[4], but attain no political development and show no capacity for governing their neighbours. The peoples of Asia are endowed with skill and intelligence, but are deficient in spirit; and this is why they continue to be peoples of subjects and slaves. The Greek stock, intermediate in geographical position, unites the qualities of both sets of people. It possesses both spirit and intelligence: the one quality makes it continue free; the other enables it to attain to the highest political development, and to show a capacity for governing every other people[5] – if only it could achieve political unity.

ARISTOTLE, *Politics* VII, 1327 b 22–33
(trans. E. Barker)

1 For example I, 142, where it is Ionia which is privileged in this way.
2 On this theme and those that competed against it see H.C. Baldry, *The Unity of Mankind in Greek Thought* (Cambridge, 1965).
3 The importance of *techne* is realized, but Aristotle does not deny it to the barbarians of Asia, though he does to those of Europe.
4 They are not doomed to slavery 'by nature'.
5 The whole passage is a clear example of the link between freedom and the capacity to rule others; cf. above Chapter 6, pp. 125–6.

Index of Ancient Sources

Note: only sources actually quoted are listed here; unless otherwise specified, italic numbers after colons refer to the texts in Part 2; sources quoted by other writers, e.g. Theopompus quoted by Athenaeus, *Deipnosophistae*, are referred to under their own name only.

——, *On Organization* (XIII), 1–3; *111*
——, *On the Crown* (XVIII), 257–65: *113*
——, *Against Leptines* (XX), 31–3: *81*
——, *Against Aristocrates* (XXIII), 206–9: *116*
——, *Against Aphobos* I (XXIX), 9–11: *120*
——, *Against Euboulides* (LVII), 30–6: *12*
[Demosthenes], *Against Lakritos* (XXXV), 10–13: *121*; 51: *82*
——, *Against Timotheus* (XLIX), 2–5, 11–12: *124*
Diodorus V, 9: 49: XI, 76: *117*
Dionysius of Halicarnassus, *On Lysias*, 34: *66*
Euripides, *Supplices*, 888–98: *67* B
Hermias of Alexandria, *On Plato's Phaedrus*, 231 c: *51* B
Herodotus II, 166–7: 3; II, 178–9: 48; III, 57: *20 A*; IV, 151–2: *40*;
  IV, 159: *45*; V, 92: *39 A*; VI, 46–7: *94*; VI, 137: *15 A*; VII, 144:
  20 B; VII, 147: *80*
Hesiod, *Works and Days*, 30–9: *32 A*; 202–18: *32 B*; 298–316:
  10; 342–67: *31*; 376–80, *p. 59*; 493–5: *10, n 1*; 598–608: *p. 59*
Homer, *Iliad* IX, 121–56: *22*; XI, 670–84: *25*; XII, 310–21: *21*
  ——, *Odyssey* I, 180–9, 306–18: *26*; II, 337–47: *23*; VII,
  103–11: *27*; IX, 39–42: *p. 42*; IX, 105–41: *30*; XI, 487–91:
  29 A; XIV, 96 104: *24*; XVII, 382–6: *28*; XVIII, 357–61:
  29 B

Inscriptions
B. Bravo, *Dialogues d'histoire ancienne* 1 (1974), p. 123: *41*
L.D. Caskey, *The Erechtheum* (1927), pp. 388–93: *73*
M. Crosby, *Hesperia* 10 (1941), pp. 14–27: *95*
Dittenberger, *Sylloge³*, 4: 92; 218: *103*
M.I. Finley, *Studies in Land and Credit in Ancient Athens*
  500–200 B.C. (1952), nos 1, 14, 88, 116, 146: *123*
Meiggs-Lewis, 7: *35*; 13: *46*; 42: *8*; 45: *101*; 49: *99*; 67: *88*; 79: *75*
R.S. Stroud, *Hesperia* 43 (1974), pp. 157–88: *102*
Tod, *GHI* I, 34: *54*
  ——, II, 100: *70*; 139: *71*; 162: *86*; 189: *72*
R.F. Willetts, *The Law Code of Gortyn* (1967), col. II, lines 2–28:
  62 A; col. VI, line 56–col. VII, line 9: *62 B*
Isocrates, *Panegyricus* (IV), 42: *83*; 166–8: *108 A*
  ——, *Philip* (V), 120–1: *108 C*
  ——, *Archidamus* (VI), 64–7: *109*
  ——, *On the Peace* (VIII), 44, 46–8: *108 B*

Supplementary Bibliography

Note: books and articles already mentioned in Part 1 are not, in principle, listed here.

Chapter 1

Andrewes, A., *The Greeks* (London, 1967); paperback edition: *Greek Society* (Harmondsworth, 1971)

Aymard, A., *Études d'histoire ancienne* (Paris, 1967)

Beloch, K.J., *Die Bevölkerung der griechisch-römischen Welt* (Leipzig, 1886)

Bolkestein, H., *Economic Life in Greece's Golden Age* (Leyden, 1958)

——, *Wohltätigkeit und Armenpflege im vorchristlichen Altertum* (Utrecht, 1939)

Bourriot, F., *Histoire générale du travail* I: *Préhistoire et Antiquité*, Postface d'A. Aymard (Paris, 1959)

Burford, A.M., 'Heavy Transport in Classical Antiquity', *Economic History Review*, 2nd series, 13 (1960), pp. 1–18

Busolt, G., and Swoboda, H., *Griechische Staatskunde*, 2 vols (3rd ed., Munich, 1920–6)

Ehrenberg, V., *The Greek State* (London, 2nd ed., 1969; the most up-to-date edition is the French version, *L'État grec*, Paris, 1976)

Finley, M.I., *The Ancient Greeks* (London, 1963; paperback edition, Harmondsworth, 1966)

Francotte, H., *L'Industrie dans la Grèce ancienne*, 2 vols (Liège, 1900–1)

Forbes, R.J., *Studies in Ancient Technology*, several vols (Leyden, 1955–)

Glotz, G., *Ancient Greece at Work* (London, 1926)

Hands, A.R., *Charities and Social Aid in Greece and Rome* (London, 1968)

Heichelheim, F.M., *An Ancient Economic History*, 3 vols (Leyden, 1958–70)

Lacey, W.K., *The Family in Classical Greece* (London, 1968)
Mickwitz, G., 'Economic Rationalism in Graeco-Roman Agriculture', *English Historical Review* 52 (1937), pp. 557–89
Mossé, Cl., *The Ancient World at Work* (London, 1969)
de Ste Croix, G.E.M., 'Greek and Roman Accounting', in *Studies in the History of Accounting*, ed. A.C. Littleton and B.S. Yamey (London, 1956), pp. 14–74
Vigneron, P., *Le Cheval dans l'antiquité gréco-romaine* (Nancy, 1968)
Will, Ed., *Le Monde grec et l'Orient* I: *Le Ve siècle (510–403)* (Paris, 1972), II: *Le IVe siècle et l'époque hellénistique* (with Cl. Mossé and P. Goukowsky) (Paris, 1975)
Zimmern, A., *The Greek Commonwealth* (Oxford, 5th ed., 1931)

Chapter 2
Lesky, A., *Thalatta. Der Weg der Griechen zum Meer* (Vienna, 1947)
Martin, R., *Recherches sur l'agora grecque* (Paris, 1951)
Wace, A.J.B., and Stubbings, F.H., *A Companion to Homer* (London, 1962)

Chapter 3
Asheri, D., *Distribuzioni di terre nell'antica Grecia* (Turin, 1966)
—— , 'Supplementi coloniari e condizione giuridica della terra nel mondo greco', *Rivista storica dell' antichità* 1 (1971), pp. 77–91
Chamoux, F., *Cyrène sous la monarchie des Battiades* (Paris, 1953)
Dunbabin, T.J., *The Greeks in the West* (Oxford, 1948)
Ehrenberg, V., *From Solon to Socrates* (London, 2nd ed., 1973)
Kirsten, E., *Die griechische Polis als historisch-geographisches Problem des Mittelmeerraumes* (Bonn, 1956)
Martin, R., *L'Urbanisme dans la Grèce ancienne* (Paris, 1956)
Vallet, G., *Rhégion et Zancle* (Paris, 1958)
Villard, F., *La Céramique grecque de Marseille* (Paris, 1960)
Wycherley, R.E., *How the Greeks Built Cities* (London, 2nd ed., 1962)

Chapter 4
Lerat, L., *Les Locriens de l'Ouest*, 2 vols (Paris, 1952)
Roussel, P., *Sparte* (Paris, 2nd ed., 1960)

Willetts, R.F., *Aristocratic Society in Ancient Crete* (London, 1955)

Chapter 5

Davies, J.K., *Athenian Propertied Families* (Oxford, 1971)

Ehrenberg, V., *The People of Aristophanes* (Oxford, 2nd ed., 1951)

Gomme, A.W., *The Population of Athens in the Fifth and Fourth Centuries* (Oxford, 1933)

Harrison, A.R.W., *The Law of Athens*: I *Family and Property* (Oxford, 1968), II *Procedure* (Oxford, 1971)

Jones, A.H.M., *Athenian Democracy* (Oxford, 1957)

Lauffer, S., *Die Bergwerkssklaven von Laureion*, 2 vols (Wiesbaden, 1955–6 and 1975, 2nd ed.)

Momigliano, A., 'Sea Power in Greek Thought', *Secondo contributo alla storia degli studi classici* (Rome, 1960), pp. 57–68

Chapter 6

Andreades, A.M., *A History of Greek Public Finance* (Cambridge, Mass., 1933)

Boeckh, A., *Die Staatshaushaltung der Athener*, 3rd ed. rev. by M. Fränkel (Berlin, 1886)

Jarde, A., *Les Céreales dans l'Antiquité grecque* (Paris, 1925)

Stroud, R.S., 'Theozotides and the Athenian Orphans', *Hesperia* 40 (1971), pp. 280–301

Thomsen, R., *Eisphora: a Study of Direct Taxation in Ancient Athens* (Copenhagen, 1964)

Veyne, P., 'Panem et circenses: l'évergetisme devant les sciences humaines', *Annales* 24 (1969), pp. 785–825

Chapter 7

Finley, M.I., *Ancient Sicily to the Arab Conquest* (London, 1968)

Momigliano, A., *Filippo il Macedone* (Florence, 1934)

Mossé, Cl., *Athens in Decline 404–86 B.C.* (London, 1973)

Perlman, S., 'Political Leadership in Athens in the Fourth Century', *Parola del Passato* 114 (1967), pp. 161–76

Préaux, Cl., 'Sur les origines des monopoles lagides', *Chronique d'Egypte* 29 (1954), pp. 312–27

Riezler, K., *Über Finanzen und Monopole im alten Griechenland* (Berlin, 1907)

Index

The references are all to page numbers. For ancient authors see also the separate Index of Ancient Sources on page 384.